THE GARDENER'S GUIDE TO
SHRUBS &CLIMBERS

THE GARDENER'S GUIDE TO
SHRUBS
&CLIMBERS

CHOOSING AND GROWING SHRUBS AND CLIMBERS FOR A RANGE
OF SEASONAL AND COLOUR EFFECTS WITH OVER 600 PHOTOGRAPHS

JONATHAN EDWARDS

LORENZ BOOKS

This edition is published by Lorenz Books

Lorenz Books is an imprint of Anness Publishing Ltd
Hermes House, 88–89 Blackfriars Road, London SE1 8HA
tel. 020 7401 2077; fax 020 7633 9499
www.lorenzbooks.com; info@anness.com

© Anness Publishing Ltd 2006

UK agent: The Manning Partnership Ltd, 6 The Old Dairy,
Melcombe Road, Bath BA2 3LR; tel. 01225 478444;
fax 01225 478440; sales@manning-partnership.co.uk

UK distributor: Grantham Book Services Ltd, Isaac Newton Way,
Alma Park Industrial Estate, Grantham, Lincs NG31 9SD;
tel. 01476 541080; fax 01476 541061; orders@gbs.tbs-ltd.co.uk

North American agent/distributor: National Book Network,
4501 Forbes Boulevard, Suite 200, Lanham, MD 20706;
tel. 301 459 3366; fax 301 429 5746; www.nbnbooks.com

Australian agent/distributor: Pan Macmillan Australia, Level 18,
St Martins Tower, 31 Market St, Sydney, NSW 2000;
tel. 1300 135 113; fax 1300 135 103;
customer.service@macmillan.com.au

New Zealand agent/distributor: David Bateman Ltd,
30 Tarndale Grove, Off Bush Road, Albany, Auckland;
tel. (09) 415 7664; fax (09) 415 8892

A CIP catalogue record for this book
is available from the British Library.

Publisher: Joanna Lorenz
Editorial Director: Judith Simons
Project Editor: Clare Hill
Designer: Nigel Partridge
Production Controller: Wendy Lawson

1 3 5 7 9 10 8 6 4 2

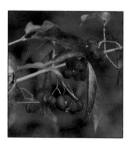

Contents

Introduction

Shrubs and climbers are the mainstay of the garden, providing structure and an ever-changing tapestry of colour throughout every month of the year. Their variety is both a delight and a dilemma – with so many to choose from there's almost certainly one to suit you and your garden, but the choice is so vast it can be totally bewildering.

Enjoying plants

Even if you stick to the basic fare offered by most garden centres, you may have 400 varieties of shrubs and nearly as many climbers to consider. So where do you start?

Well, not with an empty trolley at the garden centre, because impulse buys almost always lead to disappointing results. If you are planting a new border from scratch, buying all the plants in this way at best leads to a border that looks good at one time of year. The safest way to buy the right plant for your garden is to ask yourself the following questions while standing in your garden viewing your plot:

A garden only really comes together with maturity. This means that thought should be given to the eventual size and staying power of the plant when you are setting out your design.

Where is it to be planted?

Consider the amount of direct sun the plot gets; the type of soil and its condition; and the plot's exposure to wind, rain and cold. It is also worth noting the space available.

What will the plant's role in the garden be? Is it to fill a gap, add height and/or colour, extend the period of interest, cover the ground or a fence, hide an eyesore, act as a barrier or backdrop or is it to be used a specimen or focal point?

How quickly must it perform?

Do you want results in a year or two, or are you prepared to wait a little longer? Bear in mind that many fast-growing plants will continue to get bigger and so will either need regular pruning or moving. Others, such as *Lavatera*, are short-lived and will need replacing after a few years.

Any special requests?

In certain circumstances you might want to avoid certain plants. For example, if your gardening time is

very limited or unpredictable, you might want to avoid high-maintenance plants that require a lot of pruning or training. On the other hand, if you have young children or young visitors, you should avoid or remove any poisonous plants that you have in your garden. With this

Climbers can be grown up exterior walls to hide eyesores such as outdoor pipes.

Clematis 'Comtesse de Bouchard' is ideal for growing against a sunny wall.

Rosa 'Queen of Denmark' is one of the finest old-fashioned shrub roses and is ideal for an open, sunny site. It is a vigorous, disease resistant plant.

Learning the ropes

There is no need to worry overly much about gardening techniques. Most gardening is common sense, and if you do make a mistake, you can always put it right the following year. Having said that, there are, of course, a few basic, sensible and effective practices that have been developed over many generations, and all of these are clearly outlined in the book.

Choosing your plants

Plants form the basis of all good gardens, and none more so that the backbone of the garden, the shrubs and climbers. We have therefore produced two directories to introduce you to the best shrubs and climbers available.

However, there are far, far more than can be featured in any one book and there are always many new varieties being introduced. As you develop your garden, you will become more interested in certain plants and will go to greater lengths to seek out more and more of them.

information in mind, you are then in a position to draw up a shortlist of potential plant candidates. You can follow the same procedure when planning a whole border from scratch. The first three questions apply to the border as a whole, then the last can be considered for each individual element.

through for inspiration – and there is nothing more enjoyable for the enthusiastic gardener than being able to wander around other people's gardens, horticultural displays or the grounds of stately homes in search of new ideas and planting styles.

Working with colour

Many beginners are worried about combining colours, but the key is simply to go for plants and effects that you like, without worrying about what other people do.

Remember, we all have some ability where colour is concerned: we choose what goes with what when we get dressed every morning, and we choose colours for decorating and furnishing our home. Planning a garden is really no different. In the same way that there are fashion and style magazines to advise you about these areas of your life, there is no shortage of different types of gardening magazines to browse

Shrubs provide a multitude of different shapes, colours, textures and sizes. Blending them together, as shown by the variety of green backdrop foliage plants and trees above, allows the stunning hues of the *Daboecia cantabrica* 'Atropurpurea' pride of place in the foreground.

How plants are named

Although many garden plants have familiar common names, most are just local names that are not recognized universally. Some plants have many different common names, while other common names are applied to quite different plants.

Confused?

All the different names for the same plant can make life a bit confusing. For this reason, a Swedish naturalist, Carl Linnaeus (1707-1778), suggested that every plant should be given a two-word Latin name that would uniquely identify it. This would allow scientists and growers to talk about and trade in specific plants with the confidence that others would know exactly what they were referring to.

These days a Latin name still has two main parts: genus (first name); and species (second name). The genus refers to the general group of related plants to which an individual belongs, while the species sub-divides this group into collections of plants that share a range of particular major characteristics but differ in one or two minor ones. A third name, either variety or

By convention, plants have their Latin names in italics, with a capital letter for the genus, lower case for the species and their cultivar name in a roman font surrounded by single quote marks – hence the plant above is called *Viburnum opulus* 'Xanthocarpum'.

cultivar, is then applied to the plants to show how they differ from others in their species. Naturally occurring variations are given a variety name and those that are selectively bred are given a cultivar name.

Latin names do actually mean something, too. However, knowing this isn't always that helpful. For example, the Latin genus *Fuchsia* commemorates Leonard Fuchs, a famous 16th-century herbalist.

Species names are generally more informative for the gardener and usually indicate a major identifying feature of that particular group of plants, examples include: 'purpureus' (purple), 'macrophylla' (small leaved), 'nana' (dwarf), and 'glauca' (blue). Variety and cultivar names are extremely variable, often commemorating breeders, their family members and friends or famous people, but some are more helpful because they emphasize a particularly desirable feature of the plant, such as 'Golden Showers' – an excellent description of the flowers.

Hybrid species

When a plant species breeds with another, the result is a hybrid. Rare in the wild, crossing is very common among plant breeders and it is done in order to produce plants with desirable qualities, such as larger or double blooms, variegated foliage and greater weather resistance. An 'x' figure indicates a hybrid, with the name often giving a clear idea of the hybrid's origins.

Viburnum plicatum 'Mariesii' is so named as 'viburnum' is the genus name, 'plicatum' is the species name and 'Mariesii' is the cultivar name. Its common name is Japanese snowball bush.

How to use the directories

With so many thousands of varieties of shrubs and climbers to choose from, selecting the right plants for your garden can be a bewildering exercise. To help with this selection process, this book has been divided into two directory sections:

Plants are arranged alphabetically, by genus. Each main entry features a general introduction to that genus, plus specific useful information such as tips on propagation and which hardiness zone the genus belongs to. This is followed by a selection of

plants from that genus, also arranged alphabetically according to their most widely accepted names. One of these entries might be a species, a hybrid, a variety, form or cultivar. Each has a useful description that includes height and spread.

Caption

The full botanical name of the plant in question is given with each photograph.

Genus name

This is the internationally accepted botanical name for a group of related plants.

Common name

This popular, non-scientific name applies to the whole of the plant genus, but can be different in other countries.

Cultivation

This section gives the level of sun and shade that the plant either requires or tolerates, advice on the best type of soil in which it should be grown and other helpful tips, as appropriate.

Pruning

Pruning details specific to each plant are included. The type of pruning and the correct season in which to prune are given.

Propagation

This section gives essential information on how and when to increase the plant – from seed, cuttings or layering.

Individual plant entry

This starts with the botanical name of the plant in bold. This can refer to the species, subspecies, hybrid, variant or cultivar. If a synonym (syn) is given, this provides alternative names by which the plant is known.

Sarcococca confussa

SARCOCOCCA
Sweet box
A genus of around 15 species, including the dense-growing, evergreen shrubs featured here, grown for their neat habit and sweet vanilla-scented winter flowers. An ideal choice for a dark, shady corner where nothing else will grow. Well suited to urban gardens as it is pollution tolerant.
Cultivation Grow in a moisture-retentive, well-drained garden soil that is reasonably fertile and in dappled or deep shade.
Pruning No routine pruning is necessary. Remove any damaged growth in mid-spring.
Propagation Take hardwood cuttings in mid-autumn.

Sarcococca confusa
A dense, evergreen shrub with glossy dark green leaves that bears clusters of sweetly scented white flowers from early winter to early spring.
H 2m (6ft) S 1m (3ft).
Aspect: semi-shade to deep shade
Hardiness: ❀❀❀ Zones: 7–8

Photograph

Each entry features a full-colour photograph that makes identification easy.

Genus introduction

This provides a general introduction to the genus. Other information featured here may include general advice on usage, preferred conditions and plant care, as well as sub-species, hybrids (indicated by an 'x' symbol in the name), varieties and cultivars (featuring names in single quotes) that are available.

Plant description

This gives a description of the plant's key features, along with any other information that may be helpful.

Size information

The average expected height and spread of a genus or individual plant is given, although growth rates may vary depending on location and conditions. Average heights and spreads are given as H and S.

Plant hardiness and zones

The plant's hardiness and appropriate zones are given at the end of this section (see page 256 for details of hardiness and zones, as well as a zone map).

Choosing shrubs and climbers

To establish quickly, grow well and perform superbly, a new shrub or climber needs to be in the best possible condition when you buy it. However, even a top-quality plant will languish if it does not suit the conditions you have in your garden. For this reason, it is essential that you choose the right plant for the position you have in mind.

It is also worth considering how the plant will fit in with your existing garden residents. Some plants produce a spectacular but brief display, while others give a more restrained performance over a much longer period of time. A few plants are of particular value in the garden because they offer more than one season of interest, with summer flowers, autumn berries and foliage as well as colourful winter stems. It is also worth choosing reliable shrubs and climbers that are not susceptible to pest and disease.

If you are filling a new garden with shrubs and climbers, try to include a proportion of quick-growing plants, such as forsythia and buddleja, to give an instant display while the others are getting established.

The careful choosing, nurturing and siting of shrubs and climbers can produce the most stunning effects in the garden.

Buying shrubs and climbers

How well a new plant performs in your garden will depend largely on the quality and condition of the plant you buy. The following will provide a useful guide to choosing the best possible new candidate for your garden.

Check out the supplier

The most important advice to any would-be planter is to go to a reputable plant supplier. If they are known for offering good quality, well-looked-after and reasonably priced plants, the chances are you will not be disappointed.

However, even reputable garden centres, nurseries and internet suppliers can have their off days, particularly towards the end of a busy spring, when many essential tasks are put off, as well as towards the end of summer, when unsold stock has become pot-bound and running short of nutrients. The best time to visit a garden centre is early in the season, when they are up to date with their maintenance and stock. Ideally, find out which days they get their deliveries so that you will have the best choice possible.

One drawback with most garden centres is that they tend to have a very limited range of the most

Choose the healthiest looking plants. Opt for those with a strong, bushy habit (centre) and avoid those with any signs of leaf yellowing (right). Plants with stunted, straggly growth (left) should be rejected, as should those with premature leaf fall.

Garden centres tend to stock the most popular and commonly available shrubs and climbers and will offer growing advice.

popular and easy-to-propagate varieties, so if you want something a little unusual or are after a particular variety, you would be better off going to a specialist nursery.

If you are trying a new garden centre for the first time, walk around the plant beds and take an overall view. Look at plants you know, to check that the labels are correct and not faded – a tell-tale sign that the plant has been hanging around the outlet for too long.

Inspect the plant

Pots should be weed and moss free, and there should not be excessive roots coming out of the bottom of the pot – a tell-tale indication that the plant has been in the pot too long. On the other hand, a plant with loose compost is likely to have been potted only recently, which means it will need to be grown on in its pot until well established, before it is ready to plant out. If you are

unsure, ask if you can see the rootball to make certain the plant's roots have filled the pot but are not pot-bound.

Check the label before you buy, to see if the plant has any special soil requirements, then check to see if it needs to be planted in sun or shade. Also bear in mind that only fully hardy plants will survive outside all year round in cooler climates. If the information on the label is unclear or ambiguous, don't be afraid to ask for advice, or check out the information for yourself here, or in another reputable plant reference book.

Buying a climber

When bought during the growing season, the ideal climber should have several new stems that are putting on vigorous growth. New shoots should also be coming from near the base. Grafted climbers such as wisteria and budded climbers such as roses

Rootballed plants have a ball of soil around the roots and are protected by a covering of net or hessian.

Bare-rooted plants are usually sold covered with plastic wrapping. Keep the wrap intact until you are ready to plant.

foliage. If you are buying bare-rooted plants, the roots should be moist and well covered.

Getting your plants home

Once you have chosen your top-quality plants, don't destroy all your good work by damaging them on the way home. If you are transporting plants in cold weather, wrapping them in a blanket or bubble wrap not only provides good padding but also protects the plant from getting over-chilled. When buying in hot weather, avoid leaving plants in the car for any length of time, as the inside can turn into a furnace in sunny weather and may destroy the plants. Protect from direct sun by throwing a cover over them and make sure you drive them straight home, giving them a good drink of water when you arrive.

Small shrubs and climbers can be easily transported by car but tall plants need to be transported lying down. Cover them to stop the soil escaping and secure them to stop them from rolling around in the car.

should have a strong, well-healed union with all the stems coming from above it. Check that the shoots of all climbers are in good condition and not broken or damaged.

Another important point is that they should not be showing any signs of pest or disease attack. In particular, watch out for colonies of tiny insects in the growing tips (aphids) and white (mildew) or brown (leaf spots) patches on the leaves. On roses also look out for orange spots (rust) on the undersides of leaves.

Buying a shrub

A well-grown deciduous shrub should be roughly symmetrical, with vigorous, well-branched shoots. Evergreen shrubs should have healthy-looking foliage right down to the compost level.

Do not be seduced by buying big, as a small, vigorous shrub will establish itself more quickly than a larger shrub, and it will soon catch up in size when it is planted in the border. By buying small, you'll save money, too. The only exceptions to this rule are for very slow-growing

shrubs, such as acers, which are worth buying larger, and flowering shrubs that you want for providing an instant display in a prominent container on the patio.

As with climbers, you should check for any signs of pests or disease and watch out for all-green shoots on variegated varieties. Avoid shrubs with withered or yellow

Specialist nurseries carry a wider range of shrubs and climbers. Plants can also be ordered from catalogues or bought via the Internet. This is especially helpful if you are after a plant that is unusual or not carried by your local garden centre.

Right plant, right place

Before you decide which plant to buy for your garden, make sure that it is suited to the growing conditions available. It should be hardy enough to survive the winter and will have particular soil and sun requirements.

Sun or shade?

All plants need sunlight to enable them to photosynthesize. This is a process by which plants use energy from sunlight to produce food. However, some have adapted to thriving on the forest floor, where light levels are low and diffused, while others thrive at the wood's edge or in open country, where they get full sun for at least part of the day.

To make choosing plants easier, labels carry symbols for three levels of light: full sun; partial shade; and full shade. Full sun represents an open site that gets direct sunlight for at least half of the day during the growing season, with little shade from nearby buildings, fences or trees. Most areas in south-facing gardens and parts of east- and west-facing gardens will be in full sun. Partial shade includes areas with reduced light levels, as well as areas that are shaded for much of the day. All gardens have some areas of partial shade. Full shade describes areas that are shaded permanently by trees, hedges or buildings throughout the year. All gardens have at least one shaded corner or north-facing wall or fence, but north-facing plots are the worst affected.

What type of soil?

You need to understand your soil both physically and chemically before you can choose suitable plants. All soils are made up of sand, clay, silt and loam in various proportions, which determine its physical make-up. Sand particles are large and irregularly shaped and so do not pack together tightly. This means that they have lots of air spaces between them. Clay particles are tiny and pack together tightly, leaving very few air spaces between them. This means that a soil with a high proportion of sand will drain freely in winter, warm up quickly in spring and be prone to drought in summer. Conversely, a soil with more clay particles will be poorly drained in winter, cold and difficult to work in spring, and liable to severe shrinkage and cracking in a dry summer. The best soils have a balance of the different-sized particles.

The important chemical considerations are how acid or alkaline a soil is as well as the nutrients it contains. How acid or alkaline your soil is will determine which types of plants you can grow well. The acidity of a soil can be measured on the pH scale, on which the mid-point is 7 (neutral). Anything higher than this is increasingly alkaline and anything lower is increasingly acid. The pH of a soil also can affect the amount and types of nutrients a plant can take up from the soil. So, even if your soil contains a lot of essential plant nutrients, such as potash (K), phosphate (P) and magnesium (Mg), if it is very acid or alkaline the plants will not be able to absorb them. Most plants prefer a neutral (pH7) to slightly acidic soil (pH6). A few plants, including azaleas and rhododendrons, need a slightly acidic soil to thrive, while other plants, such as lilacs, prefer slightly alkaline conditions (*see also*, Know your soil, page 80).

How hardy?

Hardiness indicates the ability of a plant to cope with winter cold. Fully hardy plants can cope with temperatures down to -15°C (5°F), frost hardy plants can withstand frosts down to -5°C (23°F), half-hardy plants can't cope with

This *Rhododendron macabeanum*, like almost all rhododendrons and azaleas, is an acid-loving plant and so will thrive on ericaceous (lime-free) soil when grown in containers.

For shady sites, the variegated evergreen *Euonymus fortunei* 'Emerald Gaiety' (shown in the background) will add colour and depth.

temperatures below 0°C (32°F) and tender plants need a minimum night temperature of 5°C (41°F). However, also bear in mind how exposed the garden is because wind-chill will need to be taken into consideration, so always err on the side of caution when choosing plants for your garden.

Plants for difficult areas

Although it is a worthwhile exercise trying to find a shrub or climber that is recommended for growing in the conditions you have in your garden, there are certain areas that are so demanding that even the toughest of plants would struggle to survive. In these circumstances it is important to choose plants with real survival skills, and although they won't perform to their full potential, they will provide useful cover where it would otherwise be bare.

Shady corners Every garden has a shady corner at the foot of a north-facing wall or fence. Here the soil is often dry so that plants struggle to get established. If the soil is impoverished, replace it with fresh soil. The best way to give dark, shady areas a lift is to use shade-loving plants with shiny or variegated leaves. These will reflect the available light and help lift the display. Shrubs such as *Fatsia japonica*, with huge, glossy, palm-shaped leaves, are particularly useful for these areas or you could try one of the decorative large-leaved ivies, such as *Hedera colchica* 'Dentata Variegata' or 'Sulphur Heart'. Add interest with colourful evergreen shrubs, such as *Euonymus fortunei* 'Emerald 'n' Gold' or 'Emerald Gaiety'.

Deep shade This lighting is usually found under trees and large shrubs. Low light is compounded by dry soil that is found in this area, so you will have to improve the soil environment by clearing fibrous roots from planting areas and adding plenty of moisture-holding organic matter, such as well-rotted farmyard manure or garden compost (soil mix). Take care not to damage the roots of suckering shrubs, such as robinia and rhus, because they will respond by throwing up a thicket of suckers.

It is often tempting to raise the soil level around trees by adding topsoil, but this can have serious implications for the trees – and may kill them. If you want to plant an under-storey of choice, non-vigorous specimens, you may have to create special planting sanctuaries by digging out large planting holes and lining the sides with old, untreated timber that will eventually rot away. In the meantime, the wood will help to prevent tree roots invading the planting holes, giving the new plants extra time to get established. Under trees with a dense canopy, you can try the real survivors, such as periwinkle and variegated ivy.

Wind tunnels Shade and a constant buffeting from winds that are being funnelled between buildings is a common problem in urban and city gardens. Good wind-resistant shrubs and climbers for shade include cotoneaster, *Hydrangea petiolaris*, ivies and periwinkles. In sunny but windy spots, try berberis, *Cistus x corbariensis*, *Helianthemum nummularium*, *Lavandula angustifolia*, *Salvia officinalis* and *Spartium junceum*.

Growing plants in containers

If the conditions are simply too much in your problem area, you can always grow plants in pots and move them in and out of the 'dead' spot so they can recover.

The fragrant and wind-resistant English lavender (*Lavandula angustifolia*) is a good choice for planting in a sunny site by the coast, as the wind will not damage it.

Plant selector: multi-season interest

The following Plant Selector has been structured to make choosing the right plants for your garden as easy as possible. There are Selectors for each season and colour, as well as for scent. However, we must first look at those plants that offer particular garden value, because they provide a range of different ornamental features that enable them to spread their period of interst over two or more seasons.

Location, location

Shrubs and climbers are permanent additions to your garden, so it is important that you not only choose the right plant for a particular spot but also select a good variety that can justify itself. Over the next few pages some of the best garden shrubs and climbers for every season have been outlined, but first we must consider the few highly rated shrubs and climbers that offer two, three or even four seasons of interest.

The impressive coral-bark maple, *Acer palmatum* 'Sango-kaku', provides year-round interest in this way and is an ideal choice for small gardens. The brilliant coral-red young shoots dramatically set off the emerging palm-shaped, orange-yellow leaves in spring. Then the leaves gradually turn green in summer, before taking

Viburnum opulus 'Roseum' produces big, white, snowball-like blooms in May.

Multi-season shrubs and climbers to try

Shrubs

Acer palmatum 'Osakazuki' (leaves, fruits, autumn colour)
Acer palmatum 'Sango-kaku' (leaves, stems, new shoots, autumn colour)
Amelanchier lamarckii (leaves, flowers, autumn colour)
Berberis darwinii (leaves, flowers, berries)
Cornus alba cultivars (leaves, stems, flowers, autumn colour)
Cornus sanguinea 'Midwinter Fire' (leaves, stems, flowers, fruits, autumn colour)
Corylus maxima 'Purpurea' (leaves, flowers, nuts)
Cotinus coggygria 'Royal Purple' (leaves, flowers, autumn colour)
Cotoneaster horizontalis (leaves, flowers, fruit)
Daphne mezereum (leaves, flowers, berries)
Fatsia japonica (leaves, flowers)
Hamamelis mollis 'Pallida' (flowers, leaves, autumn colour)
Hydrangea quercifolia (leaves, flowers, autumn colour)
Mahonia japonica (leaves, flowers, fruits)
Rhamnus alaternus 'Argenteovariegata' (leaves, flowers)
Rhododendron luteum (leaves, flowers, autumn colour)
Rhus typhina 'Dissecta' (leaves, stems, new shoots, autumn colour)
Rosa 'Blanche Double de Coubert' (leaves, flowers, hips, autumn colour)
Rosa rugosa 'Rubra' (leaves, flowers, hips, autumn colour)

Skimmia japonica 'Rubella' (leaves, flower-buds, flowers)
Viburnum opulus 'Roseum' (leaves, flowers, fruit, autumn colour)
Viburnum plicatum 'Mariesii' (leaves, flowers, fruit, autumn colour)

Climbers

Akebia quinata (flowers, foliage)
Aristolochia macrophylla (flowers, foliage, autumn colour)
Clematis alpina cultivars (leaves, flowers, seed-heads)
Clematis 'Bill MacKenzie' (leaves, flowers, seedheads)
Clematis tangutica (leaves, flowers, seed-heads)
Hedera helix 'Green Ripple' (leaves, winter colour)
Hydrangea petiolaris (leaves, flowers, seed-heads, autumn colour)
Parthenocissus henryana (leaves, autumn colour)
Passiflora caerulea (leaves, flowers, fruit)
Rosa filipes 'Kiftsgate' (flowers, hips)
Rosa 'Madame Grégoire Staechelin' (flowers, hips)
Rosa 'Rambling Rector' (flowers, hips)
Sollya heterophylla (flowers, foliage, fruit)
Vitis coignetiae (leaves, autumn colour, fruit)
Vitis vinifera 'Purpurea' (leaves, autumn colour, fruit)
Wisteria floribunda (leaves, flowers, pods, autumn colour)

on fabulous shades of yellow in autumn, falling to reveal the coloured stems through winter.

Another deciduous shrub that provides year-round interest is the dogwood *Cornus sanguinea* 'Midwinter Fire'. This relatively new cultivar bears clusters of tiny, creamy-white flowers during early summer, against green leaves that transform in autumn, when they take on orange-yellow hues and when spherical

bluish fruits are also produced. But it is in winter that it really comes to the fore, revealing spectacular glowing, red-tipped, orange and yellow winter stems that shine out in the winter garden.

In a larger garden, the snowy mespilus, *Amelanchier lamarckii*, provides excellent value. It is a spectacular shrub at both ends of the growing season and is covered in a profusion of star-shaped, white flowers accompanied by bronze-tinted emerging leaves during spring. In autumn, the dark-green foliage transforms into a beacon of orange and red. Sweet and juicy dark red fruits are also produced during early summer.

The purple-leaved smoke bush, *Cotinus coggygria* 'Royal Purple' makes an impressive specimen in any size of garden as it responds particularly well to hard pruning each spring. Airy plumes of pale pink flowers that darken with age are produced from mid-summer. The rich, red-purple leaves offer a colourful point of focus in the summer shrubbery or mixed garden border before turning brilliant scarlet in autumn.

Although the stag's horn sumach, *Rhus typhina*, has developed a troublesome reputation for suckering, the named cultivar 'Dissecta' is less of a problem and has the bonus of more finely cut, decorative foliage. Like the species, it also offers velvet-covered, red winter shoots as well as foliage that turns fiery shades of orange-red in the autumn. Spectacular bristly fruits

The Japanese *Acer palmatum* 'Osakazuki' will brighten up any garden, particularly during the autumn when its leaves turn a rich, vibrant red.

The autumn leaf colours of *Cotinus obovatus* can be yellow, red, orange or reddish-purple.

follow insignificant mustard flowers on conical spikes during the summer. The ornamental buckthorn *Rhamnus alaternus* 'Argenteovariegata' is worth a mention for its year-round white-edged evergreen foliage and red fruits that ripen to black in autumn.

The oak-leaved hydrangea, *Hydrangea quercifolia*, is a good garden shrub, offering attractive oak-leaf-shaped foliage that turns shades of bronze-purple in autumn. But it is the named cultivar 'Snow Queen' that steals the show, with its brilliant white conical flower clusters, produced in summer, that fade to pink as they age.

Another deciduous favourite that provides good colour is the Japanese snowball bush *Viburnum plicatum* 'Mariesii'. This produces tiered branches that carry white, lacecap-like flowers throughout late spring over toothed, prominently veined, dark-green leaves that turn red-purple in autumn.

A few climbers also offer year-round interest. Evergreens, such as ivy, are more or less ubiquitous, but for real garden value you want ever-changing displays like that offered by the climbing hydrangea, *Hydrangea petiolaris,* which bears huge, flat heads of creamy, lacecap flowers that stand out against a backdrop of dark green leaves from late spring. Then in autumn, the leaves turn butter-yellow before falling to reveal attractively flaking brown bark.

Clematis 'Bill MacKenzie' and *C. tangutica* are worth mentioning in this respect, too. The former produces butter-yellow, bell-shaped flowers in succession from mid-summer against ferny, mid-green leaves, followed by large, fluffy seed-heads, while the latter offers small, nodding, yellow, lantern-shaped flowers with waxy-looking lemon peel-like petals from mid-summer, again followed by fluffy seed-heads later on.

Plant selector: early spring

The weather in early spring is very variable, with wide fluctuations in temperature from day to night, from day to day and from year to year.

Keep an eye on the weather

The contrast in the weather is often at its greatest the further north you go and also on higher, more exposed locations. Rain can be heavy and the winds strong, although the sun is increasing in strength as the garden moves out of its winter slumbers.

Early spring is often less wet than the winter and this provides good opportunities to get on with some planting and other winter garden tasks that you have been unable to complete because soil conditions were not suitable. However, be wary of cold north-easterly winds. These can be very damaging at this time of the year, as they can burn vulnerable blossom and scorch the tips of emerging leaves.

Frosty welcome

Frost can also be a problem throughout early spring in most areas. It can be very penetrating if it is accompanied by northerly winds,

Early spring shrubs and climbers to try

[Note: each variety is in season when it starts flowering. Check individual entries for finish flowering times.]

Shrubs

Abeliophyllum distichum
Abeliophyllum distichum Roseum Group
Acer palmatum 'Sango-kaku'
Amelanchier lamarckii
Amelanchier x grandiflora 'Ballerina'
Camellia japonica 'Adolphe Audusson'
Camellia japonica 'Hagoromo'
Camellia japonica 'Lady Vansittart'
Camellia japonica 'Mikenjaku'
Camellia 'Leonard Messel'
Camellia japonica 'Nobilissima'
Camellia x williamsii 'Anticipation'
Camellia x williamsii 'Donation'
Camellia x williamsii 'E.G. Waterhouse'
Camellia x williamsii 'J. C. Williams'
Camellia x williamsii 'Jury's Yellow'
Camellia x williamsii 'Mary Phoebe Taylor'
Chaenomeles speciosa 'Geisha Girl'
Chaenomeles speciosa 'Moerloosei'
Chaenomeles speciosa 'Nivalis'
Chaenomeles x superba 'Crimson and Gold'
Chaenomeles x superba 'Nicoline'
Chaenomeles x superba 'Pink Lady'
Chimonanthus praecox

Chimonanthus praecox 'Grandiflorus'
Chimonanthus praecox 'Luteus'
Coronilla valentina subsp. glauca
Coronilla valentina subsp. glauca 'Citrina'
Corylus avellana 'Contorta'
Corylus maxima 'Purpurea'
Daphne mezereum
Forsythia 'Beatrix Farrand'
Forsythia x intermedia 'Spring Glory'
Forsythia x intermedia 'Week-End'
Kerria japonica 'Golden Guinea'
Kerria japonica 'Picta'
Kerria japonica 'Pleniflora'
Leucothoe 'Scarletta'
Magnolia stellata
Magnolia stellata 'Rosea'
Magnolia stellata 'Royal Star'
Magnolia stellata 'Waterlily'
Mahonia aquifolium 'Apollo'
Pieris japonica 'Valley Valentine'
Prunus tenella 'Fire Hill'
Prunus triloba
Rhododendron 'Cilpinense'
Skimmia japonica 'Rubella'
Skimmia x confusa 'Kew Green'
Spiraea prunifolia

Climbers

Akebia quinata
Clematis armandii 'Apple Blossom'
Clematis armandii 'Snowdrift'

Rhododendrons are good-value shrubs to have in the garden. Their glossy green leaves last all year, with a huge range of different coloured blooms.

so keep tender plants well protected until late spring. Try to take advantage of any spells of good weather during early spring to carry out essential seasonal tasks, such as rose pruning or planting hardy shrubs and climbers.

Although many garden plants will still remain dormant throughout early spring, those that do break through will offer some of the most spectacular flowering displays – all the more welcome after a long, grey winter. Spring-flowering bulbs, such as snowdrops and early daffodils, are traditionally the harbingers of spring, but there are many hardy shrubs and climbers that are even more dramatic. Just take a look around local gardens in your area and you'll find breathtaking displays of both evergreen and deciduous varieties. Who can fail to be impressed by the spectacular magnolias? Star of the show must be *Magnolia stellata* and its varieties, with their silky buds that open on bare branches during early spring to reveal lightly scented, white or pink flushed, star-shaped flowers. For classical goblet-shaped flowers consider 'Heaven Scent' (pale pink), 'Susan' (purple) or, slightly later, the white or pink blooms of the larger *Magnolia x soulangeana*.

Pink, white and red camellias shine out against their leathery evergreen foliage, including the peony-shaped, yellow-centred, white flowers of 'Nobilissima', the large, semi-double, bright red flowers of 'Adolphe Audusson' and the ever-flowering and ever-popular semi-double, sugar-pink 'Donation'. Covering the ground, swathes of winter-flowering heathers are still in bloom: *Erica carnea* 'Myretoun Ruby' offers masses of urn-shaped, large

Ceanothus 'Dark Star' produces small but profuse flowers that appear in spring, which are a vivid dark blue to blue-violet colour.

ruby-red flowers that mature to crimson against dark green foliage, the pure white 'Springwood White' is still going strong, while 'Pink Spangles' adds a splash of shell-pink to the scene. Rose-pink is also offered by highly fragrant daphnes, including *Daphne bholua* 'Jacqueline Postill', *Daphne mezereum* and *Daphne odora* 'Aureomarginata'.

Yellow is an even more eye-catching colour, especially when light levels are low. Mahonias keep the garden glowing well into early spring with their elegant sprays of fragrant, flowers, such as pale yellow 'Bealei', the deeper shade of 'Apollo' and the lemon-yellow 'Charity'. Later, the early spring garden lights up with the ever-popular forsythias, such as the golden-yellow 'Lynwood', pale yellow 'Spring Glory' or the rich yellow flowers of 'Week-End'. For something a little more unusual, try the orange-yellow 'Beatrix Farrand'.

Reluctant climbers

Although there are few climbers putting on a show during early spring, those that do are worth seeking out. The chocolate vine *Akebia quinata* is a real gem, offering pendent clusters of maroon-chocolate flowers that have a sweet and spicy fragrance against lobed, purple-tinged, dark green foliage.

As a complete contrast, the massed pale pink, fragrant flowers of *Clematis* 'Apple Blossom' or C. 'Snowdrift' are a sight to behold in the early spring garden.

Daphne bholua 'Jacqueline Postill' produces clusters of scented, deep purple-pink flowers early in the year, accompanied by lance-shaped, dark green leaves.

Plant selector: late spring

In some years, spring can be delayed for several weeks so keep an eye on local weather forecasts and gauge the temperature. Use these as a guide to your gardening activities, rather than doing things just because it is the season to do them.

Protect your plants

By late spring, the threat of frost recedes and in milder areas it's safe to plant out tender shrubs and climbers, but always keep a sheet of garden fleece to hand to cover vulnerable plants if an unseasonally late frost is forecast after planting has taken place.

Variations in weather conditions are generally less marked as the spring progresses, so there are fewer sharp frosts and the weather generally becomes calmer. In cooler areas, however, you will have to be a good deal more cautious and should wait until early summer to put tender plants outside.

Growth spurts

In the garden, shrubs and climbers are making up for lost time as they break into growth and compete for your attention.

Camellia x *williamsii* 'Jury's Yellow' has creamy-yellow, anemone-flowered blooms.

Late spring shrubs and climbers to try

Shrubs
Berberis darwinii
Berberis linearifolia 'Orange King'
Berberis thunbergii 'Atropurpurea Nana'
Berberis thunbergii 'Aurea'
Berberis x *stenophylla*
Berberis x *stenophylla* 'Crawley Gem'
Berberis x *stenophylla* 'Irwinii'
Calluna vulgaris 'Spring Cream'
Camellia japonica 'Adolphe Audusson'
Camellia japonica 'Elegans'
Camellia japonica 'Lady Vansittart'
Camellia 'Leonard Messel'
Camellia x *williamsii* 'Debbie'
Camellia x *williamsii* 'Donation'
Camellia x *williamsii* 'E.G. Waterhouse'
Camellia x *williamsii* 'J. C. Williams'
Camellia x *williamsii* 'Jury's Yellow'
Ceanothus 'Puget Blue'
Chaenomeles speciosa 'Geisha Girl'
Chaenomeles speciosa 'Moerloosei'
Chaenomeles speciosa 'Nivalis'
Chaenomeles x *superba* 'Crimson and Gold'
Chaenomeles x *superba* 'Nicoline'
Chaenomeles x *superba* 'Pink Lady'
Choisya 'Aztec Pearl'
Choisya 'Goldfingers'
Choisya ternata
Choisya ternata 'Sundance'
Cytisus multiflorus
Cytisus x *praecox* 'Allgold'
Cytisus x *praecox* 'Warminster'
Drimys winteri
Exochorda x *macrantha* 'The Bride'
Forsythia x *intermedia* 'Lynwood'
Fothergilla major
Leucothoe fontanesiana 'Rainbow'
Magnolia 'Heaven Scent'
Magnolia stellata 'Royal Star'
Magnolia x *loebneri* 'Leonard Messel'
Magnolia x *soulangeana*
Osmanthus delavayi
Osmanthus x *burkwoodii*
Paeonia delavayi
Paeonia lutea var. *ludlowii*
Paeonia suffruticosa 'Duchess of Kent'
Paeonia suffruticosa 'Duchess of Marlborough'
Paeonia suffruticosa 'Mrs William Kelway'
Paeonia suffruticosa 'Reine Elisabeth'
Pieris formosa var. *forrestii* 'Wakehurst'

Pieris 'Forest Flame'
Pieris japonica 'Purity'
Pieris japonica 'Variegata'
Prunus laurocerasus 'Otto Luyken'
Prunus laurocerasus 'Rotundifolia'
Prunus laurocerasus 'Zabeliana'
Prunus lusitanica
Rhododendron 'Blue Diamond'
Rhododendron 'Glowing Embers'
Rhododendron 'Grumpy'
Rhododendron 'Koster's Brilliant Red'
Rhododendron 'Persil'
Rhododendron 'Pink Drift'
Rhododendron 'Pink Pearl'
Rhododendron 'Sapphire'
Rhododendron 'Scarlet Wonder'
Ribes sanguineum 'Brocklebankii'
Ribes sanguineum 'King Edward VII'
Ribes sanguineum 'Pulborough Scarlet'
Salix lanata
Skimmia japonica subsp. *reevesiana*
Skimmia japonica subsp. *reevesiana* 'Robert Fortune'
Sophora microphylla
Sophora microphylla 'Sun King'
Spiraea 'Arguta'
Spiraea thunbergii
Viburnum carlesii
Viburnum 'Eskimo'
Viburnum x *burkwoodii*
Viburnum x *carlcephalum*
Viburnum x *juddii*
Vinca major
Vinca minor 'Illumination'

Climbers
Clematis alpina 'Frances Rivis'
Clematis alpina 'Frankie'
Clematis alpina 'Pamela Jackman'
Clematis alpina 'Pink Flamingo'
Clematis 'Early Sensation'
Clematis 'Helsingborg'
Clematis macropetala 'Markham's Pink'
Jasminum polyanthum
Lonicera japonica 'Halliana'
Lonicera japonica 'Hall's Prolific'
Lonicera japonica var. *repens*

Rhododendron 'Pink Pearl' is a delightful plant, bearing huge trusses of beautiful soft pink, funnel-shaped flowers that eventually fade to white as they age.

Many of the early flowering shrubs, including camellias and magnolias, are still going strong, but they are joined by equally impressive displays from popular plants such as peonies and rhododendrons. Perhaps the best peony of all is 'Ludlowii', which looks magnificent when furnished with large bright yellow flowers against bronze-tinted, bright apple-green lush foliage. If you are looking for a red, consider *Paeonia delavayi* instead, for its single, cup-shaped, blood-red flowers. Pale pink peonies are always popular, and the flamboyant 'Duchess of Marlborough', with its double, crinkle-edged flowers, is hard to beat.

Dramatic plants

There's a huge array of dramatic rhododendrons to choose from that will to add flower power to a late spring garden. Evergreen rhododendrons include the unusual violet-blue shade of 'Blue Diamond', which bears masses of funnel-shaped, flowers that age to lavender-blue. 'Grumpy' offers attractive pink-flushed, cream flowers in flat-topped trusses, while the compact 'Pink Drift' blooms are a rose-lavender shade – a good choice for small gardens. Well liked for good reason are the white-edged, soft pink, funnel-shaped flowers of 'Pink Pearl'.

Vivid azaleas

Deciduous azaleas come into bloom during late spring, too. The aptly named 'Glowing Embers' shows off its flaming, reddish-orange, funnel-shaped flowers, while 'Koster's Brilliant Red' offers vivid, orange-red blooms. For large clusters of orange-flushed, white flowers, look no further than the brilliant 'Persil'.

The appeal of flowering quince can be an acquired taste, but they'll never let you down with their startling flowers on a twiggy framework, often followed by aromatic, yellow-tinged green fruit. Good names to look out for at this time of the year are the apricot-pink and yellow, double flowers of 'Geisha Girl', the large white, apple blossom-like blooms of 'Moerloosei', the snow-white 'Nivalis' or the scarlet 'Nicoline'. But, perhaps the pick of the bunch is the compact and easy to grow 'Crimson and Gold'. This offers vivid red flowers with contrasting golden anthers.

Another late spring stalwart if you have an acid soil is the lily-of-the-valley shrub, pieris. It's particularly remarkable because it bears its pendent clusters of fragrant, urn-shaped flowers just when the glossy, brilliant-red young foliage emerges – a startling contrast that works perfectly together. 'Wakehurst', 'Forest Flame' and 'Purity' are all good white cultivars, while 'Valley Valentine' is dark pink.

Spring climbers

Popular climbers that are on display in the late spring garden include the many forms of alpine clematis, which bear small, nodding, bell-shaped flowers, often with contrasting centres. Look out for 'Frances Rivis' (blue), 'Helsingborg' (deep purple) and 'Pink Flamingo' (pink). Other floriferous early clematis that are at their best right now are: 'Early Sensation', which bears a single flush of small, green-centred, white, bowl-shaped flowers, and the semi-double 'Markham's Pink', which offers pink flowers with creamy-yellow centres.

Pieris 'Forest Flame' has glorious red leaves that fade to a pale pink and then dark green.

Plant selector: early summer

By early summer a westerly airflow dominates the weather, but winds are lighter and rain is less frequent. Dull days can be humid, while on sunny days temperatures can soar.

Propagation and pruning

Many shrubs and climbers can be propagated from early summer and it's the right time to start routine spraying of roses to prevent outbreaks of disease through the summer months.

Early flowering shrubs should be pruned to improve displays in subsequent years, while repeat-flowering plants can be enhanced by regular deadheading throughout the summer months.

In the garden, scented shrubs and climbers come to the fore. Lilacs are among the best of the scented shrubs, with their gloriously fragrant flowers. There are many cultivars but few can beat 'Superba' (rose-pink), 'Palibin' (purple-pink), 'Charles Joly' (dark purple), 'Katherine Havemeyer' (lavender-purple), 'Madame Lemoine' (white) or 'Michel Buchner' (rose-mauve).

Rosemarinus officinalis

Other very fragrant shrubs are the mock orange (*Philadelphus*) and *P. coronarius* 'Aureus', which has golden-yellow leaves that turn greenish-yellow in summer. Also enjoyed for their aroma are the single, cup-shaped, white flowers of 'Belle Etoile' or the double white 'Virginal'. In milder gardens, French lavender is worth considering for its tufted

Clematis 'Mrs Cholmondeley'

Arbelia x grandiflora 'Gold Spot'

Buddleja alternifolia

Early summer shrubs to try

Shrubs
Abelia 'Edward Goucher'
Abelia x *grandiflora*
Abutilon 'Kentish Belle'
Azara dentata
Banksia coccinea
Berberis julianae
Berberis thunbergii 'Dart's Red Lady'
Brugmansia suaveolens
Buddleja alternifolia
Buddleja globosa
Callistemon citrinus 'Splendens'
Camellia japonica 'Elegans'
Carpenteria californica
Carpenteria californica 'Ladhams' Variety'
Ceanothus arboreus 'Trewithen Blue'
Ceanothus 'Concha'
Ceanothus 'Italian Skies'
Ceanothus thyrsiflorus var. *repens*
Chaenomeles speciosa 'Geisha Girl'
Chaenomeles speciosa 'Nivalis'
Chaenomeles x *superba* 'Pink Lady'
Choisya 'Aztec Pearl'
Choisya 'Goldfingers'
Choisya ternata
Choisya ternata 'Sundance'
Cistus 'Silver Pink'
Cistus x *aguilarii* 'Maculatus'
Cistus x *corbariensis*
Cistus x *dansereaui* 'Decumbens'
Cistus x *purpureus* 'Alan Fradd'
Cistus x *skanbergii*
Convolvulus cneorum
Cornus florida 'Cherokee Chief'
Cornus florida 'Rainbow'
Cornus florida f. *rubra*
Cornus kousa var. *chinensis*
Cotoneaster conspicuus 'Coral Beauty'
Cotoneaster dammeri
Cotoneaster frigidus 'Cornubia'
Cotoneaster horizontalis
Cotoneaster salicifolius 'Gnom'
Cytisus 'Boskoop Ruby'
Cytisus multiflorus
Cytisus x *praecox* 'Allgold'
Cytisus x *praecox* 'Warminster'
Daboecia cantabrica f. *alba*
Daboecia cantabrica 'Atropurpurea'
Deutzia gracilis
Deutzia x *elegantissima* 'Rosealind'
Diervilla x *splendens*
Enkianthus campanulatus
Enkinathus cernuus f. *rubens*

Erica cinerea 'Pink Ice'
Escallonia 'Apple Blossom'
Escallonia rubra 'Crimson Spire'
Euonymus europaeus 'Red Cascade'
Fremontodendron 'California Glory'
Fuchsia 'Mrs Popple'
Gaultheria mucronata 'Mulberry Wine'
Gaultheria mucronata 'Wintertime'
Gaultheria procumbens
Genista lydia
Genista pilosa 'Vancouver Gold'
Genista tinctoria 'Royal Gold'
Grevillea juniperina f. *sulphurea*
Grevillea 'Robyn Gordon'
Halesia monticola
Halesia tetraptera
Hebe pinguifolia 'Pagei'
Hebe rakaiensis
Hebe 'Red Edge'
Hebe 'Rosie'
Helianthemum 'Chocolate Blotch'
Helianthemum 'Wisley Primrose'
Helianthemum 'Wisley White'
Hypericum calycinum
Hypericum x *moserianum* 'Tricolor'
Indigofera heterantha
Jasminum humile 'Revolutum'
Kalmia angustifolia f. *rubra*
Kalmia latifolia 'Ostbo Red'
Kolkwitzia amabilis 'Pink Cloud'
Lantana camara 'Radiation'
Lantana camara 'Snow White'
Lavandula 'Helmsdale'
Lavatera x *clementii* 'Barnsley'
Leptospermum scoparium 'Red Damask'
Nerium oleander
Olearia ilicifolia
Philadelphus 'Beauclerk'
Philadelphus 'Belle Etoile'
Philadelphus coronarius 'Variegatus'

Syringa x *josiflexa*

Philadelphus x *lemoinei* 'Lemoinei'
Phlomis fruticosa
Phlomis italica
Phygelius x *rectus* 'Moonraker'
Phygelius x *rectus* 'Salmon Leap'
Potentilla fruticosa 'Abbotswood'
Potentilla fruticosa 'Goldfinger'
Potentilla fruticosa 'Primrose Beauty'
Prostanthera cuneata
Rhododendron 'Blue Danube'
Rhododendron 'Blue Peter'
Rhododendron 'Cunningham's White'
Rhododendron 'Debutante'
Rhododendron 'Dopey'
Rhododendron 'Geisha Red'
Rhododendron 'Gibraltar'
Rhododendron 'Homebush'
Rhododendron 'Klondyke'
Rhododendron luteum
Rhododendron 'Marty'
Rhododendron 'Purple Splendour'
Rosmarinus officinalis
Rosmarinus officinalis 'Majorca Pink'
Rosmarinus officinalis 'Miss Jessopp's Upright'
Rubus odoratus
Salvia officinalis 'Icterina'
Salvia officinalis 'Tricolor'
Spartium junceum
Spiraea nipponica 'Snowmound'
Syringa x *josiflexa*
Syringa vulgaris 'Charles Joly'
Syringa vulgaris 'Katherine Havemeyer'
Viburnum davidii
Viburnum opulus 'Roseum'
Viburnum plicatum 'Mariesii'
Weigela florida 'Foliis Purpureis'
Weigela 'Florida Variegata'

Rhododendron 'Marty'

spikes of fragrant flowers. Of the many different varieties, 'Helmsdale' offers dark purple flowers topped by purple wing-like bracts; 'Papillon' bears lavender-purple flowers, with matching bracts; 'Fathead' has broad, almost rounded midnight-purple flowerheads with plum-purple feathers; and 'Snowman' bears slender spikes of white flowers, topped by snow-white flags.

New introductions

Excellent new introductions include 'Kew Red', with plump, fragrant, cerise-pink flower heads topped by pale-pink bracts, and 'Rocky Road' – goblet-shaped purple flower spikes topped by large, pale-violet wings.

The earliest roses start to bloom as spring turns into summer. The first to show include the shrub roses, such as 'Cornelia', with its very fragrant, double, apricot-pink flowers; 'Fantin-Latour', which offers slightly fragrant, double, pale pink blooms; 'Felicia', with its sweetly fragrant, double, apricot-yellow flowers that are flushed with pale pink; and 'William Lobb', which bears wonderfully fragrant, semi-double, purple-magenta flowers that age to lavender. Some plants offer

Hydrangea petiolaris

Early summer climbers to try

Climbers

Actinidia kolomikta	*Eccremocarpus scaber*
Ampelopsis aconitifolia	*Hibbertia scandens*
Aristolochia littoralis	*Hoya carnosa*
Aristolochia macrophylla	*Hydrangea petiolaris*
Berberidopsis corallina	*Jasminum beesianum*
Billardiera longiflora	*Jasminum officinale*
Bougainvillea glabra	*Jasminum x stephanense*
Bougainvillea glabra 'Snow White'	*Lonicera henryi*
Bougainvillea glabra 'Variegata'	*Lonicera periclymenum* 'Belgica'
Bougainvillea 'Miss Manila'	*Lonicera x americana*
Bougainvillea 'Raspberry Ice'	*Lonicera x heckrottii* 'Gold Flame'
Bougainvillea 'Scarlett O'Hara'	*Lonicera x italica* 'Harlequin'
Clematis 'Barbara Jackman'	*Lonicera x tellmanniana*
Clematis 'Bees' Jubilee'	*Plumbago auriculata*
Clematis 'Belle of Woking'	*Rosa* 'Albéric Barbier'
Clematis 'Doctor Ruppel'	*Rosa* 'Albertine'
Clematis 'Duchess of Edinburgh'	*Rosa* 'American Pillar'
Clematis 'Fireworks'	*Rosa* 'Climbing Iceberg'
Clematis florida var. *seiboldiana*	*Rosa* 'Emily Gray'
Clematis 'General Sikorski'	*Rosa* 'Guinée'
Clematis 'Gillian Blades'	*Rosa* 'Madame Grégoire Staechelin'
Clematis 'Lasurstern'	*Rosa* 'Maigold'
Clematis 'Marie Boisselot'	*Rosa* 'Paul's Scarlet Climber'
Clematis 'Miss Bateman'	*Rosa* 'Veilchenblau'
Clematis montana var. *rubens* 'Elizabeth'	*Rosa* 'Zéphirine Drouhin'
Clematis montana var. *rubens* 'Pink Perfection'	*Solanum crispum* 'Glasnevin'
	Solanum jasminoides 'Album'
Clematis montana var. *rubens* 'Tetrarose'	*Sollya heterophylla*
Clematis 'Mrs Cholmondeley'	*Stephanotis floribunda*
Clematis 'Mrs N.Thompson'	*Wisteria floribunda*
Clematis 'Multi Blue'	*Wisteria floribunda* 'Alba'
Clematis 'Nelly Moser'	*Wisteria floribunda* 'Macrobotrys'
Clematis 'The President'	*Wisteria floribunda* 'Royal Purple'
Clematis 'Vyvyan Pennell'	*Wisteria sinensis*
Clerodendrum thomsoniae	*Wisteria sinensis* 'Alba'
Clianthus puniceus	*Wisteria x formosa*
Cobaea scandens	

aromatic foliage too. Rosemary shouldn't be missed for its strongly aromatic evergreen foliage that forms a dense and rounded bush and bears purple-blue flowers.

Early summer bloomers

Many unsung heros of the shrub border start to flower during early summer. If you have got room for only a few, choose from escallonia, hebe, helianthus, kolkwitzia, lavateras, potentilla, salvia, viburnums and weigela. Or opt for the brilliant, if short-lived, display provided by broom: the golden-yellow flowers of *Genista lydia* festoon prickly, arching, grey-green leaves; *G. pilosa* 'Vancouver Gold' is a spreading shrub with masses of golden-yellow flowers; while the extremely long-flowering *Genista tinctonia* 'Royal Gold' bears golden-yellow blooms until late summer.

Quick-growing shrubs

Quick-growing shrubs, such as lavatera, can be used to provide instant colour at this time of the year. 'Barnsley' bears large, white blooms, each with a red eye, which are produced in succession from now onwards. Other cultivars to consider are 'Burgundy Wine' (dark pink flowers), 'Kew Rose' (frilly, dark pink) 'Peppermint Ice' (pure white) and 'Rosea' (dark pink).

If you're looking for something more unusual, consider the crimson bottlebrush, which bears its distinctive flower-spikes at the tips of stiffly arching branches, or flowering dogwood such as 'Eddie's White Wonder', which offers insignificant purplish-green flowers, each surrounded by striking white, petal-like bracts.

Another sought-after dogwood that is well worth seeking out is *Cornus kousa* var. *chinensis*, which bears conspicuous, creamy-white flower bracts that fade to white before turning red-pink.

Climbers to watch

Climbers to look out for at this time of the year include the huge array of clematis. Among the best are 'Barbara Jackman' (pale purple), 'Bees' Jubilee' (dark pink), 'Belle of Woking' (silvery-mauve), 'Doctor Ruppel' (dark pink), 'Duchess of Edinburgh' (white), 'Fireworks' (purple with red bars), var. *seiboldiana* (white with a central boss of deep purple stamens), 'Gillian Blades' (mauve-flushed, white), 'Lasurstern' (cream-centred, purple-blue), 'Elizabeth' (fragrant, pale pink), 'Mrs Cholmondeley' (chocolate-centred, lavender-blue), 'The President' (red-centred, purple) and 'Vyvyan Pennell' (golden-centred, mauve, violet and purple).

Bougainvillea

Clematis 'Bees' Jubilee'

Rosa 'Climbing Iceberg'

Rosa 'Albertine'

Wisteria sinensis

Solanum jasminoides 'Album'

Plant selector: late summer

Calm weather patterns continue through the summer months, although prolonged periods of rain are possible. However, there's still time to take cuttings and it is the ideal time to prune many early summer-flowering shrubs and climbers to keep them flowering well, year after year.

Glorious roses

In the garden, roses are at their best throughout the summer and will produce long-lasting displays if regularly deadheaded. The most impressive large-flowered bushes include: 'Alexander', which has double, slightly fragrant, vermilion-red flowers with scalloped petals; 'Congratulations', which bears double, slightly fragrant, rose-pink flowers on long stems; the unusually coloured 'Just Joey', with fragrant, double, coppery-red flowers with wavy-margined petals; 'Peace', which is covered in double, pink-flushed, deep yellow, slightly fragrant flowers; 'Royal William', which carries double, deep-crimson flowers with a spicy fragrance; and 'Silver Jubilee', which bears fragrant, double, rose-pink flowers, flushed salmon-pink.

If you're looking for a cluster-flowered bush rose that produces masses of flowers throughout the summer, consider the aptly named

Clematis 'Jackmanii Superba'

Rosa 'Ingrid Bergman'

'Amber Queen', with fragrant, double, amber-yellow flowers; 'Arthur Bell', with large, semi-double, very fragrant, golden-yellow flowers that age to cream; 'Mountbatten', which carries large, fragrant, double, golden-yellow flowers; 'Southampton, which is covered in large, double, slightly scented, red-flushed apricot flowers with ruffled petals; and 'Queen Elizabeth', which offers double, slightly fragrant, pale pink flowers.

Patio varieties

Other roses looking their best right now are the celebration patio varieties, which make ideal gifts and can be grown in containers or at the front of the border. Check out 'Golden Anniversary', with large, semi-double, slightly fragrant, apricot-pink flowers; 'Happy Anniversary', which bears sweetly fragrant, deep-pink flowers; 'Happy Birthday', with double, creamy-white blooms; and 'Pearl Anniversary' – a semi-double, pearl-pink variety.

Groundcover roses

You can also have roses covering the ground at this time of the year and the county series are among the best: 'Kent', with slightly fragrant, semi-double, white flowers; 'Suffolk', a slightly fragrant cultivar with single, golden-centred, deep-scarlet flowers; 'Surrey', which bears cup-shaped,

Late summer shrubs to try

Shrubs
Abelia 'Edward Goucher'
Abelia x grandiflora
Aloysia triphylla
Ballota acetabulosa
Buddleja davidii 'Black Knight'
Buddleja davidii 'Dartmoor'
Buddleja davidii 'Nanho Blue'
Buddleja davidii 'White Profusion'
BBupleurum fruticosum
Callistemon citrinus 'Splendens'
Callistemon rigidus
Calluna vulgaris 'Alicia'
Calluna vulgaris 'Silver Knight'
Calluna vulgaris 'Silver Queen'
Calluna vulgaris 'Spring Cream'
Calluna vulgaris 'Wickwar Flame'
Caryopteris x clandonensis
Caryopteris x clandonensis 'First Choice'
Ceanothus 'Autumnal Blue'
Ceanothus 'Burkwoodii'
Ceratostigma griffithii
Ceratostigma willmottianum
Ceratostigma willmottianum 'Desert Skies'
Cistus x aguilarii 'Maculatus'
Cistus x argenteus 'Peggy Sammons'
Cistus x corbariensis
Cistus x skanbergii
Colutea arborescens
Colutea x media 'Copper Beauty'
Cotinus coggygria 'Royal Purple'
Cotinus 'Flame'
Cotinus 'Grace'
Cytisus battandieri
Desfontainia spinosa
Escallonia 'Iveyi'
Eucryphia x nymansensis 'Nymansay'
Hebe 'Great Orme'
Hebe 'Midsummer Beauty'
Hibiscus rosa-sinensis 'The President'
Hibiscus syriacus 'Blue Bird'
Hibiscus syriacus 'Woodbridge'
Hydrangea arborescens 'Annabelle'
Hydrangea aspera Villosa Group
Hydrangea macrophylla 'Blue Wave'
Hydrangea macrophylla 'Mariesii'
Hydrangea macrophylla 'Veitchii'
Hydrangea paniculata 'Floribunda'
Hydrangea 'Preziosa'
Hydrangea quercifolia 'Snow Queen'
Hydrangea serrata 'Bluebird'
Hypericum 'Hidcote'

Buddleja davidii 'Dartmoor'

Indigofera amblyantha
Itea ilicifolia
Justicia carnea
Lavandula angustifolia 'Hidcote'
Lavandula angustifolia 'Royal Purple'
Lavandula stoechas 'Rocky Road'
Lavandula x intermedia 'Grappenhall'
Lavandula x intermedia 'Grosso'
Leycesteria formosa
Myrtus communis
Myrtus communis subsp. tarentina
Nandina domestica 'Fire Power'
Olearia macrodonta
Olearia x haastii
Osmanthus heterophyllus 'Goshiki'
Romneya coulteri
Romneya coulteri 'White Cloud'
Rosa 'Amber Queen'
Rosa 'Arthur Bell'
Rosa 'Ballerina'
Rosa 'Blanche Double de Coubert'
Rosa 'Blessings'
Rosa 'Boule de Neige'
Rosa 'Buff Beauty'
Rosa 'Charles de Mills'
Rosa 'Congratulations'
Rosa 'Fragrant Cloud'
Rosa 'Golden Anniversary'
Rosa 'Golden Wedding'
Rosa 'Happy Anniversary'
Rosa 'Happy Birthday'
Rosa 'Heritage'
Rosa 'Iceberg'
Rosa 'Ingrid Bergman'

Rosa 'Just Joey'
Rosa 'Loving Memory'
Rosa 'Mary Rose'
Rosa 'Masquerade'
Rosa 'Peace'
Rosa 'Pearl Anniversary'
Rosa 'Polar Star'
Rosa 'Queen of Denmark'
Rosa 'Queen Elizabeth'
Rosa 'Rose de Rescht'
Rosa 'Roseraie de l'Haÿ'
Rosa 'Ruby Anniversary'
Rosa 'Ruby Wedding'
Rosa rugosa 'Rubra'
Rosa 'Silver Jubilee'
Rosa 'Southampton'
Rosa 'Suffolk'
Rosa 'Surrey'
Rosa 'Sussex'
Rosa 'Sweet Dream'
Rosa 'The Times Rose'
Rosa 'Winchester Cathedral'
Rubus 'Benenden'
Rubus biflorus
Rubus cockburnianus
Santolina chamaecyparissus 'Lambrook Silver'
Santolina chamaecyparissus var. nana
Spiraea japonica 'Anthony Waterer'
Spiraea japonica 'Golden Princess'
Tamarix ramosissima
Tamarix ramosissima 'Pink Cascade'
Tamarix ramosissima 'Rubra'
Tibouchina urvilleana

fragrant, double, rose-pink flowers; and 'Sussex', the slightly fragrant, double, apricot version.

Beneficial insects

Many other late-summer flowering shrubs provide a rich source of food for beneficial insects. Perhaps the most well known is the butterfly bush, *Buddleja davidii*, which bears dense terminal spikes of fragrant flowers that are a magnet to butterflies: 'Black Knight' (dark purple), 'Nanho Blue' (lilac-blue), 'Pink Delight' (orange-eyed, bright-pink flowers), 'White Profusion' (white) and the variegated 'Harlequin' (reddish-purple).

English lavenders are also covered in insects at this time of the year when they bear their very fragrant flowers in dense spikes. Cultivars to look out for include: 'Hidcote' (dark violet), 'Hidcote Pink' (pale pink), 'Lady' (mauve-blue) 'Nana Alba' (white) and 'Royal Purple' (bluish-purple).

Unusual shrubs

Slightly more unusual shrubs that are looking their best right now include the hare's ear, *Bupleurum*

Hydrangea macrophylla

fruticosum, which bears greenish-yellow, ball-shaped clusters of star-shaped flowers on a dense and spreading evergreen shrub with dark green leaves that are silvery on the underside. Another excellent choice is the bladder plant, *Colutea arborescens*, which has racemes of bright yellow flowers followed by green seed-pods that become bloated and translucent as they mature. Highly recommended is hibiscus, particularly the delightful 'Blue Bird', which bears violet-blue, trumpet-shaped flowers, each with a maroon eye, in succession throughout late summer.

Finally, consider the white, tissue paper-like flowers, each with a golden-yellow centre, of *Romneya coulteri* 'White Cloud'.

Flowering structures

Walls and fences can be covered in flowers at this time of year, many of them sweetly fragrant. You can choose from a huge range of late-

Oleria x haastii

Rosa 'Golden Showers'

Rosa 'Gloire de Dijon'

flowering, large-flowered clematis, climbing and rambler roses and sweetly fragrant honeysuckles, such as: 'Graham Thomas', with large, tubular white flowers that age to yellow; 'Dropmore Scarlet,' which bears a succession of long, trumpet-shaped, bright-scarlet flowers; and 'Serotina', the late Dutch honeysuckle, which bears tubular, purple-streaked, creamy-white blooms.

Late summer climbers to try

Campsis grandiflora
Campsis radicans 'Flamenco'
Campsis x *tagliabuana* 'Madame Galen'
Clematis 'Alba Luxurians'
Clematis 'Betty Corning'
Clematis 'Bill MacKenzie'
Clematis 'Comtesse de Bouchaud'
Clematis 'Ernest Markham'
Clematis 'Etoile Violette'
Clematis flammula
Clematis 'Gipsy Queen'
Clematis 'Hagley Hybrid'
Clematis 'Henryi'
Clematis 'Huldine'
Clematis 'Jackmanii'
Clematis 'Jackmanii Superba'
Clematis 'Niobe'
Clematis 'Perle d'Azur'
Clematis 'Polish Spirit'
Clematis 'Prince Charles'
Clematis 'Princess Diana'
Clematis 'Rouge Cardinal'
Clematis tangutica
Clematis 'Ville de Lyon'
Clematis viticella 'Purpurea Plena Elegans'
Fallopia baldschuanica
Jasminum officinale 'Devon Cream'
Lapageria rosea
Lonicera periclymenum 'Graham Thomas'
Lonicera periclymenum 'Serotina'
Lonicera x *brownii* 'Dropmore Scarlet'

Mandevilla boliviensis
Mandevilla splendens
Mandevilla x *amabilis* 'Alice du Pont'
Passiflora caerulea
Passiflora caerulea 'Constance Elliot'
Passiflora 'Eden'
Pileostegia viburnoides
Rosa 'Aloha'
Rosa 'Bantry Bay'
Rosa 'Breath of Life'
Rosa 'Climbing Iceberg'
Rosa 'Compassion'
Rosa 'Danse du Feu'
Rosa filipes 'Kiftsgate'
Rosa 'Gloire de Dijon'
Rosa 'Golden Showers'
Rosa 'Handel'
Rosa 'Laura Ford'
Rosa 'Madame Alfred Carrière'
Rosa 'Mermaid'
Rosa 'New Dawn'
Rosa 'Rambling Rector'
Rosa 'Schoolgirl'
Rosa 'Warm Welcome'
Rosa 'Wedding Day'
Schizophragma hydrangeoides
Schizophragma integrifolium
Trachelospermum asiaticum
Trachelospermum jasminoides

Clematis viticella 'Purpurea Plena Elegans'

Trachelospermum asiaticum

Passiflora caerulea

Plant selector: autumn

Although the summer can continue into early autumn in some years, this time of the year usually sees a dramatic change in both the weather and the appearance of the garden.

Shorter days and cool, longer nights are certain, causing plants to slow down and gradually become dormant. The autumn garden is briefly dominated by the fiery displays of many deciduous shrubs and climbers.

The acers
Some of the most spectacular autumn hues are offered by Japanese maples. Cultivars such as *Acer palmatum* 'Atropurpureum' make a graceful and slow-growing maple, with attractive palm-like, deeply lobed, dark purple leaves that are eye-catching all summer before turning brilliant shades of red in autumn. Another purple-leaved cultivar worth seeking out is 'Bloodgood', which turns brilliant red before falling. The startling red autumn colour of 'Osakazuki' is equally spectacular and would make a dramatic addition to any garden. If you prefer one of the cut-leaved varieties of Japanese

Abutilon megapotanicum 'Variegata'

maples, look out for *Acer palmatum* var. *d.* 'Dissectum Atropurpureum' Group, which makes a neat dome covered in particularly fine, deeply cut, red-purple, ferny foliage that turns fiery shades in autumn. 'Garnet' is similar, but the foliage is darker purple. Both these cultivars look good after leaf fall, too, as they reveal a tracery of fine twigs that provide winter interest.

Others that offer excellent autumn shades are the barberry (*Berberis*) cultivars, such as 'Atropurpurea Nana', which is grown for its dark purple leaves that turn a brilliant red in autumn accompanied by glossy red fruits; by contrast 'Aurea' offers brilliant acid-yellow spring growth that turns orange-red in autumn with conspicuous glossy red fruit; 'Bagatelle' is compact and easy to grow, with dark purple leaves that transform into a stunning red in autumn; 'Dart's Red Lady' is equally suitable for a confined space and has plum-red foliage that turns brilliant shades of red at this time of the year. If you're looking for a columnar version, try 'Helmond Pillar', which is clothed in plum-purple leaves that take truly eye-catching shades of red in autumn.

Brilliant autumn foliage is also the main ornamental feature of *Cotinus*, the smoke bush. Excellent purple-leaved versions include 'Grace' and 'Royal Purple', which spectacularly turn fiery shades of red and orange during the autumn.

Enkianthus perulatus

Cotinus coggygria 'Golden Spirit' is a relatively new and compact cultivar with golden-yellow leaves that take on eye-catching pink, orange and red coloration at this time of the year. The hardy plumbago, *Ceratostigma willmottianum*, is also worth considering because it makes a neat mound covered in clusters of pale blue summer flowers and brilliant fiery foliage effects in autumn. Look out for 'Forest Blue', which turns flaming shades of red and orange at the end of the growing season.

Fruits of autumn
Autumn is also a time for bountiful fruit production and few plants can match the startling displays offered by the beauty bush, *Callicarpa bodinieri* var. *giraldii* 'Profusion', which bears astonishingly vibrant violet, bead-like berries. *Hippophae rhamnoides* is equally dramatic, forming a large, bushy plant with sharp spines and silvery lance-shaped leaves that fall in autumn to reveal the clusters of bright orange berries, that last well into winter. Don't overlook contoneasters as they produce long-lasting, glossy, brightly coloured berries. *C.* 'Coral Beauty' makes excellent ground cover for sun or semi-shade and is covered in glossy, bright-orange berries during the autumn.

The popular herringbone cotoneaster, *Cotoneaster horizontalis*, is encrusted with spherical, bright-red berries during the autumn. *C.* 'Cornubia' is an upright, evergreen cultivar that is often trained as a single-stemmed tree and is covered in spherical, bright-red berries just as the leaves become bronze-tinted for the winter; while 'Hybridus Pendulus' is lower growing and produces glossy, bright red berries at this time of the year.

Autumn shrubs and climbers to try

Shrubs
Acer palmatum 'Atropurpureum'
Acer palmatum 'Bloodgood'
Acer palmatum 'Orange Dream'
Acer palmatum 'Osakazuki'
Acer palmatum var. d. Dissectum Atropurpureum Group
Acer palmatum 'Garnet'
Amelanchier lamarckii
Amelanchier x grandiflora 'Ballerina'
Aucuba japonica 'Rozannie'
Aucuba japonica 'Variegata'
Berberis julianae
Berberis thunbergii 'Atropurpurea Nana'
Berberis thunbergii 'Aurea'
Berberis thunbergii 'Bagatelle'
Berberis thunbergii 'Dart's Red Lady'
Berberis thunbergii 'Helmond Pillar'
Berberis thunbergii f. atropurpurea
Callicarpa bodinieri var. giraldii 'Profusion'
Callistemon rigidus
Calluna vulgaris 'Alicia'
Calluna vulgaris 'Amethyst'
Calluna vulgaris 'County Wicklow'
Calluna vulgaris 'Dark Star'
Calluna vulgaris 'H. E. Beale'
Calluna vulgaris 'Silver Knight'
Calluna vulgaris 'Spring Cream'
Camellia sasanqua 'Narumigata'
Caryopteris x clandonensis
Caryopteris x clandonensis 'First Choice'
Caryopteris x clandonensis 'Heavenly Blue'

Caryopteris x clandonensis 'Worcester Gold'
Ceanothus 'Autumnal Blue'
Ceratostigma griffithii
Ceratostigma willmottianum
Ceratostigma willmottianum 'Desert Skies'
Ceratostigma willmottianum 'Forest Blue'
Clerodendrum trichotomum var. fargesii
Colutea arborescens
Colutea x media 'Copper Beauty'
Cornus alba 'Spaethii'
Cornus 'Eddie's White Wonder'
Cornus sanguinea 'Midwinter Fire'
Cotinus coggygria 'Golden Spirit'
Cotinus coggygria' Royal Purple'
Cotinus 'Flame'
Cotinus 'Grace'
Enkianthus perulatus
Fothergilla gardenii
Gaultheria mucronata 'Mulberry Wine'
Gaultheria mucronata 'Wintertime'
Gaultheria procumbens
Hippophae rhamnoides
Viburnum x bodnantense 'Dawn'
Viburnum x bodnantense 'Charles Lamont'

Climbers
Although many summer-flowering climbers continue to bloom into autumn, none starts blooming at this time, so no entries are shown.

Foliage climbers
Some climbers also offer glorious autumnal foliage displays. For example, the ornamental grape vine, *Vitis* 'Brant' has apple-green leaves that turn rust-red between the main veins in autumn, while the crimson glory vine, *Vitis coignetiae*, is absolutely spectacular when its dark green leaves turn fiery shades of red during the autumn.

On the other hand, Chinese Virginia creeper, *Parthenocissus henryana*, offers handsome, deeply divided, dark green leaves with distinctive white and pink veins that turn fiery shades before falling at the end of the growing season. The related Virginia creeper (*P. quinquefloia*) is clothed in deeply divided, slightly puckered green leaves that transform themselves during the autumn when they take on brilliant shades of crimson and purple.

Other named varieties of creeper to look out for include 'Robusta' and 'Veitchii', both of which transform themselves at this time of the year and develop a spectacular cloak of red and purple.

Plant selector: winter

Winter-flowering shrubs and climbers are the gems of the garden during the dormant season. Although the flowers are not as spectacular as those produced by many spring- and summer-flowering plants, their intricate markings and delightful fragrance more than make up for it.

The Wintersweet, *Chimonanthus praecox*, is a prime example, with its waxy-looking, fragrant, sulphur-yellow flowers, often with a contrastingly tinted throat, that smother bare stems throughout this period. Named varieties worth seeking out include 'Grandiflorus', which is larger and of a darker yellow colour, as well as 'Luteus', with its clear yellow flowers. The winter-flowering shrubby honeysuckle, *Lonicera x purpusii* 'Winter Beauty' or the equally fragrant *Lonicera fragrantissima* are both a delight at this time of the year, bearing creamy-white flowers on naked stems during mild spells. Winter-flowering viburnums, such as *Viburnum tinus*

Winter shrubs and climbers to try

Shrubs

Acer palmatum 'Sango-kaku'
Bupleurum fruticosum
Calluna vulgaris 'Amethyst'
Calluna vulgaris 'Blazeaway'
Camellia japonica 'Nobilissima'
Camellia sasanqua 'Narumigata'
Chimonanthus praecox
Chimonanthus praecox 'Grandiflorus'
Chimonanthus praecox 'Luteus'
Cornus alba 'Aurea'
Cornus alba 'Kesselringii'
Cornus alba 'Sibirica'
Cornus alba Spaethii'
Cornus sanguinea 'Midwinter Fire'
Cornus stolonifera 'Flaviramea'
Corylus avellana 'Contorta'
Daphne bholua 'Jacqueline Postill'
Daphne odora 'Aureomarginata'
Erica carnea 'Ann Sparkes'
Erica carnea 'Challenger'
Erica carnea' December Red'
Erica carnea 'Foxhollow'
Erica carnea 'King George'
Erica carnea 'Myretoun Ruby'
Erica carnea 'Pink Spangles'
Erica carnea 'Springwood White'
Erica x darleyensis 'Furzey'
Erica x darleyensis 'Darley Dale'
Garrya elliptica

Garrya elliptica 'James Roof'
Hamamelis mollis
Hamamelis x intermedia 'Arnold Promise'
Hamamelis x intermedia 'Diane'
Hamamelis x intermedia 'Jelena'
Hamamelis x intermedia 'Moonlight'
Hamamelis x intermedia 'Pallida'
Jasminum nudiflorum
Lonicera fragrantissima
Lonicera x purpusii 'Winter Beauty'
Mahonia japonica Bealei Group
Mahonia x media 'Buckland'
Mahonia x media 'Charity'
Mahonia x media 'Lionel Fortescue'
Mahonia x media 'Winter Sun'
Rubus cockburnianus
Salix hastata 'Wehrhahnii'
Sarcococca confusa
Sarcococca hookeriana var. *digyna*
Sarcococca hookeriana var. *humulis*
Viburnum tinus 'Eve Price'
Viburnum tinus 'French White'
Viburnum tinus 'Gwenllian'

Climbers

Clematis cirrhosa 'Freckles'
Clematis cirrhosa 'Jingle Bells'
Clematis cirrhosa var. *balearica*
Clematis cirrhosa 'Wisley Cream'

Jasminum nudiflorum

'Eve Price', 'French White' or 'Gwenllian' bloom on bare, twiggy stems, producing highly fragrant flowers in dense clusters. Witch hazel, *Hamamelis*, is a winter essential for its bizarre sprays of sweetly scented, spidery flowers that are produced on bare stems. 'Arnold Promise' is a traditional favourite with golden flowers; 'Moonlight' is equally impressive when covered in its pale yellow blooms; or you could go for the coppery-red blooms of 'Diane' or 'Jelena'.

A dense, evergreen shrub that is covered in clusters of sweetly scented white flowers throughout the winter is *Sarcococca confusa*. *S. hookeriana* var. *digyna* and *S. hookeriana* var. *humulis* both have small, creamy-white or pink-tinged flowers. Another fragrant evergreen is the late-winter-flowering daphne. Cultivars worth looking out for include *Daphne bholua* 'Jacqueline Postill', with rose-pink flowers, and 'Aureomarginata' *D. odora*, which also has attractive yellow-edged, glossy, dark green foliage.

Stem colours

Brightly coloured stems are also of great ornamental value in the winter garden. The red-barked dogwoods, *Cornus alba* 'Sibirica' or 'Spaethii', are hard to beat when they both reveal brilliant red stems that look particularly impressive (especially adjacent to water features) when grown alongside the contrasting yellow-stemmed variety 'Flaviramea'. If you've only got room for one dogwood, go for the relatively new cultivar 'Midwinter Fire', which produces glowing red-tipped, orange and yellow winter stems that shine out in the winter gloom.

Berries

Most berries have been eaten by birds or shed by shrubs and climbers by the winter, but the hermaphrodite variety of *Skimmia japonica* called *reevesiana*, as well as its cultivar 'Robert Fortune', buck the trend by carrying their startling bright red berries throughout the winter. You can find them in garden centres as fully berried miniature shrubs and they are ideal for adding winter-long colour to containers and prominent borders around the garden.

At the back of a shrubbery or against a wall, the subtle charms of *Garrya elliptica* will be appreciated in the winter. While its lustrous, leathery leaves provide a year-round backdrop at other times, during the coldest months it becomes decorated

Saracococca confusa

with elegant, grey-green catkin tassels. Those of the cultivar 'James Roof' are impressive, with each silvery catkin up to 20cm (8in) long.

Clematis

Not to be forgotten are the clematis. Winter-flowering *Clematis cirrhosa* var. *balearica* will also provide winter interest when carrying its fragrant, creamy-white, bell-shaped, waxy-looking flowers that are heavily blotched with maroon inside the petals. Look out for the named cultivars, such as 'Freckles', with its distinctive red speckles, and 'Wisley Cream', which has attractively bronze-tinted leaves.

Hamamelis x *intermedia* 'Pallida'

Colour selector: orange

Colour is a critical ingredient in an overall garden design. Not only must the balance and blend of colours suit the plan you have in mind, but they will also have an impact on the final atmosphere that will be created.

Using colour in the garden

Knowing that different colours are perceived in particular ways enables the garden designer to reinforce the underlying mood – or even create illusions. For example, very strong, vibrant colours, such as oranges, reds and golden yellows, stand out like beacons in the border, seeming much nearer to the eye than they really are.

You can use these confident colours to create a more intimate atmosphere, even in a large garden. Plant them in bold groups at the furthest point of the vista to act as points of focus. From a distance, bright colours will have very much more impact than softer shades, such as blue and grey, which seem to recede into the background. You can also use this to your advantage in a small garden by planting bright colours close to the house and misty

HOW TO USE THE COLOUR WHEEL

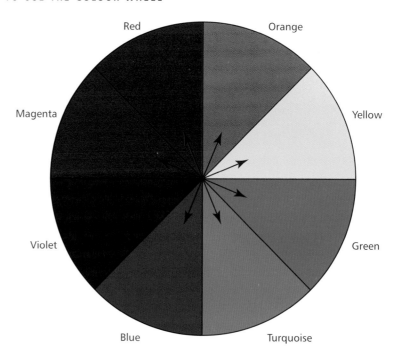

Colours that are next to each other on the colour wheel are complementary and will blend together well. Colours that are opposite are contrasting and will either look garish or stand out together. For example, orange and blue make a striking contrast but can't claim to blend with each other. It is usually wise to pick colours that are next to each other on the wheel. Select two or three colours and stick to plants within this range, knowing that they will harmonize well.

tones further afield to increase the sense of space and make the garden seem bigger than it really is.

There are many ways you can use hot colours in border schemes, creating a range of different effects.

You can combine them in a single scheme for a fiery display that will attract the eye. If you add lush foliage plants to the combination, the effect suddenly becomes more tropical, almost as if you were creating a steamy atmosphere. An even more dramatic effect can be achieved by combining these brilliant colours with complementary purple-leaved companions – producing a rich, sensual tapestry of texture and colour on which to feast the eye. You can also use contrast to add impact to hot colour schemes by combining a paler shade of a bright colour with a darker shade of a complementary dark colour, such as bright red with dark purple.

Brilliant orange

Orange is an intense colour that can be difficult to place in a border, as it tends to dominate all those colours

Attractive for much of the year, *Berberis linearifolia* 'Orange King' has spectacular deep orange flowers in spring, with a smaller flush of flowers appearing in late summer.

around it. Sitting between red and yellow in the colour wheel, it can be successfully combined with both these colours in a hot border scheme, or used in isolated blocks as a contrast to a soothing sea of green or silver, for example.

When used in mixed colour schemes, orange is much more difficult to accommodate and so is often avoided by gardeners. However, if flanked by less intense shades of peaches and cream, or apricot and bronze, it can help to create some harmony where otherwise there would be discord.

Striking orange

The range of orange-flowered shrubs and climbers is fairly limited, but most of them are strikingly orange and really do make a dramatic impact in the garden.

In spring, the deciduous azalea 'Gibraltar' is a beacon of colour, as the eye-catching, funnel-shaped flowers become the centre of attention. During early summer, *Berberis darwinii* and *Berberis linearifolia* 'Orange King' come to the fore, lighting up the border with their

burnt-orange blooms. They are useful fillers for borders or can be grown to make an informal flowering hedge, where their prickly stems will provide a deterrent against intruders.

Orange shrubs and climbers to try

Shrubs
Abutilon indicum 'Kentish Belle'
Acer palmatum 'Orange Dream'
Acer palmatum var. *dissectum* 'Green Globe'
Acer palmatum var. *dissectum* 'Inaba-shidare'
Amelanchier lamarckii
Amelanchier x *grandiflora* 'Ballerina'
Banksia coccinea
Berberis darwinii
Berberis linearifolia 'Orange King'
Berberis thunbergii 'Rose Glow'
Berberis x *stenophylla* 'Crawley Gem'
Berberis x *stenophylla* 'Irwinii'
Buddleja globosa
Cornus sanguinea 'Midwinter Fire'
Cotoneaster conspicuus 'Coral Beauty'
Fothergilla major
Hamamelis x *intermedia* 'Jelena'
Helianthemum 'Chocolate Blotch'
Hippophae rhamnoides
Lantana camara 'Radiation'
Nandina domestica 'Fire Power'
Parrotia persica

Parrotia persica 'Pendula'
Phygelius x *rectus* 'African Queen'
Phygelius x *rectus* 'Salmon Leap'
Potentilla fruticosa 'Sunset'
Potentilla fruticosa 'Tangerine'
Pyracantha 'Golden Charmer'
Pyracantha 'Orange Glow'
Pyracantha 'Saphyr Orange'
Rhododendron 'Gibraltar'
Rhododendron 'Glowing Embers'
Rhododendron 'Koster's Brilliant Red'
Rhododendron 'Persil'
Rhus typhina
Rhus typhina 'Dissecta'
Rosa 'Remember Me'
Rosa 'Southampton'
Stephanandra incisa 'Crispa'
Stephanandra tanakae

Climbers
Ampelopsis aconitifolia
Campsis grandiflora
Lonicera x *heckrottii* 'Gold Flame'
Lonicera x *tellmanniana*

Coppery orange

Later in the summer you can enjoy the large, fragrant, double, coppery-orange, flushed-yellow flowers of the rose 'Remember Me', as well as the large, double, slightly scented, red-flushed apricot clustered blooms of 'Southampton', with its distinctive ruffled petals.

By autumn, startling clusters of orange pyracantha berries, such as the cultivars 'Saphyr Orange' and 'Orange Glow', last well into winter and shine out against a backdrop of glossy, dark green leaves. There can be splashes of orange to see in the garden in even the coldest months, with the glowing bare stems of *Cornus sanguinea* 'Midwinter Fire', as well as the fragrant, coppery-orange, spidery flowers of *Hamamelis* x *intermedia* 'Jelena', which are borne on bare stems from Christmas onwards.

The many shades of orange combine to produce the lovely rose 'Miss Pam Ayres' – a very vigorous plant to have in the garden.

Colour selector: yellow

Warm and inviting, yellow is many a gardener's favourite flower colour. It seems to shine out in all weathers and at all times of the year.

Welcome yellow

In the spring, autumn and winter, yellow is a welcome relief on dreary days, radiating its cheerful disposition to all its neighbours. Then, in summer, it can be used to light up borders in both sun and dappled shade – contrasting the dark shadows where the sun is at its most fierce and reflecting light all around where it is not.

All yellows are fairly easy to accommodate into border schemes, combining well with oranges and reds to create hot, fiery displays, as well as providing startling contrasts to purples, violets and black. Yellow also partners browns and bronze shades to good effect, while white is a natural bedfellow.

Any yellow will happily partner green, which lies adjacent to it on the colour wheel, and some shades of yellow can be successfully added to schemes predominantly based on blue and silver tones. Even a monochrome display using a variety

Hypericum 'Hidcote'

of yellow hues can work particularly well. Choose two or three distinct, but complementary shades, such as the palest lemon-yellow, a clear butter-yellow and a rich bronzy-yellow. Being so accommodating, yellow is easy to take for granted. If it is used too liberally it dominates the whole garden display. However, there are so many shades of yellow that allow you to create subtly different effects around the garden without the effect being monotonous.

Yellow variegated foliage

Another way to introduce yellow into your garden is by using shrubs and climbers with yellow-variegated foliage. The effect you achieve will depend on the plants you choose and the plants that surround them. Yellow-variegated foliage ranges from the subtle greenish shades to the dramatic eye-catching tones of some all-yellow foliage plants. It is tempting to include yellow-variegated plants in monochrome schemes of yellow flowers, but this seldom works in practice because displays lack contrast and the various elements tend to cancel each other out. However, you can add a few pale yellow flowers to an all-yellow foliage scheme to good effect if you are aiming for a soothing, low-key combination.

Warm yellow

There is a huge range of plants that produce yellow flowers or foliage. You can start the year with the densely packed, arching spikes of the fragrant butter-yellow flowers of *Mahonia aquifolium* 'Apollo', which appear above the holly-like leaves that have a reddish tinge in winter. The stunning flower power of forsythias light up the spring with

Berberis 'Goldilocks'

their brilliant blooms produced *en masse* on bare stems. Among the best varieties are 'Beatrix Farrand' (orange-yellow), 'Lynwood' (golden-yellow), 'Spring Glory' (pale yellow), and 'Week End' (rich yellow). The deciduous azalea, *Rhododendron luteum*, is worth seeking out for its spectacular early summer, sweetly scented, yellow, funnel-shaped blooms. Another sought-after yellow is produced by *Fremontodendron* 'California Glory', which bears eye-catching, saucer-shaped, butter-yellow, waxy-looking flowers from late spring to autumn against a backdrop of leathery, lobed, dark green leaves.

Butter yellow

A spectacular seasonal highlight is produced by *Genista lydia*, when its arching stems are festooned in golden-yellow flowers throughout early summer. For larger, bright-yellow flowers at this time of year, you could opt for *Potentilla fruticosa* 'Goldfinger', which bears a crop of blooms against a mound of small, dark green leaves. You could also try *Hypericum* 'Hidcote', which bears impressive cup-shaped, golden-yellow flowers in succession from mid-

Yellow shrubs and climbers to try

Shrubs

Abelia x *grandiflora* 'Francis Mason'
Abelia x grandiflora 'Gold Spot'
Abutilon megapotamicum 'Variegatum'
Acer palmatum 'Sango-kaku'
Acer palmatum var. *dissectum* 'Ornatum'
Aucuba japonica 'Crotonifolia'
Aucuba japonica 'Picturata'
Azara dentata
Berberis aristata
Berberis thunbergii 'Aurea'
Berberis thunbergii 'Helmond Pillar'
Berberis x *stenophylla*
Berberis x *stenophylla* 'Claret Cascade'
Berberis x *stenophylla* 'Corallina Compacta'
Brachyglottis compacta 'Sunshine'
Buddleja davidii 'Harlequin'
Bupleurum fruticosum
Calluna vulgaris 'Wickwar Flame'
Caryopteris x *clandonensis* 'Worcester Gold'
Chimonanthus praecox
Chimonanthus praecox 'Grandiflorus'
Chimonanthus praecox 'Luteus'
Choisya 'Goldfingers'
Choisya ternata 'Sundance'
Colutea arborescens
Cornus alba 'Aurea'
Cornus stolonifera 'Flaviramea'
Coronilla valentina subsp. *glauca*
Cotinus coggygria 'Golden Spirit'
Cytisus battandieri
Cytisus x *praecox* 'Allgold'
Cytisus x *praecox* 'Warminster'
Diervilla x *splendens*
Elaeagnus pungens 'Maculata'
Elaeagnus x *ebbingei* 'Gilt Edge'
Elaeagnus x *ebbingei* 'Limelight'
Enkianthus campanulatus
Euonymus fortunei 'Emerald 'n' Gold'
Euonymus fortunei 'Sunspot'
Forsythia 'Beatrix Farrand'
Forsythia x *intermedia* 'Spring Glory'
Forsythia x *intermedia* 'Week End'
Fremontodendron 'California Glory'

Berberis aristata

Genista lydia
Genista pilosa 'Vancouver Gold'
Genista tinctoria 'Royal Gold'
Hamamelis x *intermedia* 'Moonlight'
Hamamelis x *intermedia* 'Pallida'
Hebe ochracea 'James Stirling'
Helianthemum 'Wisley Primrose'
Hypericum calycinum
Hypericum 'Hidcote'
Hypericum x *moserianum* 'Tricolor'
Ilex aquifolium 'Golden Queen'
Ilex x *altaclerensis* 'Golden King'
Jasminum nudiflorum
Kerria japonica 'Golden Guinea'
Kerria japonica 'Pleniflora'
Lantana camara 'Goldmine'
Lonicera nitida 'Baggesen's Gold'
Mahonia aquifolium 'Apollo'
Mahonia japonica Bealei Group
Mahonia x *media* 'Buckland'
Mahonia x *media* 'Charity'
Mahonia x *media* 'Lionel Fortescue'
Paeonia lutea var. *ludlowii*
Phlomis fruticosa
Phygelius aequalis 'Yellow Trumpet'
Potentilla fruticosa 'Abbotswood'
Potentilla fruticosa 'Goldfinger'
Pyracantha 'Soleil d'Or'
Rhododendron luteum
Rhododendron macabeanum
Ribes sanguineum 'Brocklebankii'
Rosa 'Felicia'

Rosa 'Golden Wedding'
Rosa 'Graham Thomas'
Rosa 'Masquerade'
Rosa 'Peace'
Rosa xanthina 'Canary Bird'
Salix lanata
Salvia officinalis 'Icterina'
Sambucus racemosa 'Plumosa Aurea'
Sambucus racemosa 'Sutherland Gold'
Santolina chamaecyparissus var. *nana*
Sophora microphylla 'Sun King'
Spartium junceum
Spiraea japonica 'Golden Princess'
Spiraea japonica 'Goldflame'
Viburnum rhytidophyllum

Climbers

Campsis radicans 'Flamenco'
Celastrus orbiculatus
Clematis 'Bill MacKenzie'
Clematis tangutica
Hedera colchica 'Sulphur Heart'
Hedera helix 'Buttercup'
Hedera helix 'Goldheart'
Hibbertia scandens
Humulus lupulus 'Aureas'
Jasminum officinale 'Fiona Sunrise'
Lonicera japonica 'Halliana'
Lonicera japonica 'Hall's Prolific'
Lonicera x *americana*
Lonicera x *italica* 'Harlequin'

Rhododendron macabeanum

summer onwards. Yellow roses are another popular choice and cultivars to look for include 'Amber Queen' (amber), 'Arthur Bell' (gold), 'Canary Bird' (clear yellow), 'Chinatown' (pink-edged yellow), 'Felicia' (apricot-yellow), 'Golden Wedding' (gold), 'Graham Thomas' (clear yellow), 'Masquerade' (clear yellow), 'Mountbatten' (gold) and 'Peace' (pink-flushed, deep yellow). *Clematis tangutica* and 'Bill MacKenzie' are two of the best yellow-flowered climbers, producing their blooms in succession from mid-summer.

Colour selector: white and green

Green is the predominant colour in most gardens and usually forms the canvas upon which all the other colours are added. However, you can create a garden using greens alone because there is such a wide range of shades and textures.

Atmospheric greens

The amazing variations of the tones of green and its variety of finishes, ranging from matt, through silk to high gloss, means that a real tapestry can be achieved with this colour.

Green also harmonizes with yellows and blues, which lie on each side of it on the colour wheel, so you can safely combine these, creating a calming atmosphere.

Alternatively, you can combine greens with contrasting reds and oranges, which lie opposite the green sector on the colour wheel. Green is an excellent foil for these strong colours, which would otherwise dominate the display.

In spring and summer, *Prostanthera cuneata* produces clusters of broadly tubular, pure white flowers.

Variegated green

Many ornamental shrubs and climbers have attractively variegated leaves: striped, splashed or edged with contrasting shades of green, yellow or white. These are particularly useful for adding light to darker corners and for providing interest all around the garden when other plants are out of season.

Monochrome plantings need a backdrop of green or silver to act as an effective foil, but they can also be used to striking effect in full sun, be eye-catching in dappled shade and glowing in full shade.

White

Like green, the importance of white within the garden palette is often overlooked. It is the universal colour that can be used in conjunction with any other colour in the colour wheel, or on its own.

When backlit in the twilight hours, white flowers can seem almost ghostly, shimmering above the border. Few flowers are pure white all over; most have a hint of green, pink, yellow or blue that makes them even more intriguing, while others may have pure white petals but combine with a contrasting colour, such as a splash of golden stamens. Even the purest of white flowers open from coloured buds that change the whole perception of the display.

There is a huge range of garden-worthy shrubs that bear brilliant white flowers in profusion. Among the best is *Amelanchier lamarckii*, a spectacular shrub in spring when smothered in star-shaped, white flowers accompanied by bronze-tinted emerging leaves. The flowering Chinese dogwood, *Cornus kousa* var. *chinensis*, is even more conspicuous when covered in its creamy-white flower bracts that fade

Choisya ternata

to white before turning red-pink during early summer, followed by strawberry-like fleshy fruit.

The star magnolia, *Magnolia stellata*, is equally dramatic, producing silky buds that open on bare branches in early spring to reveal stunning, lightly scented, white, star-shaped flowers. For sheer visual power, few shrubs can equal the floriferous *Exochorda x macrantha* 'The Bride', which produces elegant arching branches smothered in brilliant white flowers during late spring.

Roses should not be overlooked either, including 'Blanche Double de Coubert' (pure white), 'Boule de Neige' (pure white), 'Happy Birthday' (creamy-white), 'Ice Cream' (ivory), 'Iceberg' (pure white), 'Kent' (pure white) and 'Polar Star' (pure white).

Several climbers are noted for their sparkling white flowers. The *Clematis armandii* varieties 'Apple Blossom' and 'Snowdrift' bear their fragrant, star-shaped blooms in early spring against leathery, evergreen leaves. For early summer, *Solanum jasminoides* 'Album' is hard to beat, with its clusters of jasmine-scented flowers and glossy, dark green leaves.

White and green shrubs and climbers to try

Shrubs
Amelanchier lamarckii
Amelanchier x *grandiflora* 'Ballerina'
Brugmansia suaveolens
Buddleja davidii 'White Profusion'
Buxus sempervirens 'Suffruticosa'
Buxus sempervirens 'Elegantissima'
Calluna vulgaris 'Alicia'
Calluna vulgaris 'Spring Cream'
Camellia japonica 'Nobilissima'
Camellia x *williamsii* 'Jury's Yellow'
Carpenteria californica
Chaenomeles speciosa 'Nivalis'
Choisya 'Aztec Pearl'
Choisya 'Goldfingers'
Choisya ternata 'Sundance'
Cistus x *aguilarii* 'Maculatus'
Cistus x *corbariensis*
Clethra alnifolia
Clethra alnifolia 'Paniculata'
Colutea arborescens
Convolvulus cneorum
Cornus 'Eddie's White Wonder'
Cornus kousa var. *chinensis*
Cotoneaster salicifolius 'Gnom'
Cytisus multiflorus
Daboecia cantabrica f. *alba*
Deutzia gracilis
Drimys winteri
Erica carnea 'Springwood White'
Escallonia 'Iveyi'
Eucryphia x *intermedia* 'Rostrevor'
Eucryphia x *nymansensis* 'Nymansay'
Euonymus 'Emerald Gaiety'
Exochorda x *macrantha* 'The Bride'
Fatsia japonica 'Variegata'
Garrya elliptica

Gaultheria mucronata 'Wintertime'
Gaultheria procumbens
Griselinia littoralis
Hebe cupressoides 'Boughton Dome'
Hebe pinguifolia 'Pagei'
Helianthemum 'Wisley White'
Hydrangea arborescens 'Annabelle'
Ilex aquifolium 'Silver Queen'
Itea ilicifolia
Lantana camara 'Snow White'
Lavandula angustifolia 'Nana Alba'
Lavandula stoechas 'Snowman'
Ligustrum lucidum 'Excelsum Superbum'
Lonicera fragrantissima
Lonicera x *purpusii* 'Winter Beauty'
Magnolia stellata
Nerium oleander
Olearia ilicifolia
Olearia macrodonta
Olearia x *haastii*
Osmanthus delavayi
Osmanthus x *burkwoodii*
Pachysandra terminalis
Philadelphus 'Beauclerk'
Philadelphus 'Belle Etoile'
Philadelphus x 'Lemoinei'
Philadelphus 'Manteau d'Hermine'
Philadelphus microphyllus
Philadelphus 'Virginal'
Phoenix roebelenii
Phygelius x *rectus* 'Moonraker'
Pieris 'Forest Flame'
Pieris formosa var. *forrestii* 'Wakehurst'
Pieris japonica 'Purity'
Pieris japonica 'Variegata'
Pittosporum 'Garnettii'
Pittosporum tenuifolium 'Variegata'
Potentilla fruiticosa 'Abbotswood'
Rhododendron 'Cunningham's White'
Rosa 'Blanche Double de Coubert'
Rosa 'Boule de Neige'
Rosa 'Happy Birthday'
Rosa 'Ice Cream'
Rosa 'Iceberg'
Rosa 'Kent'
Rosa 'Polar Star'
Rubus 'Benenden'
Ruta graveolens 'Jackman's Blue'
Santolina chamaecyparissus var. *nana*
Sarcococca confusa
Sarcococca hookeriana var. *digyna*
Sarcococca hookeriana var. *humulis*
Spiraea 'Arguta'

Rosa 'Boule de Neige'

Spiraea nipponica 'Snowmound'
Spiraea prunifolia
Spiraea thunbergii 'Albovariegatum'
Syringa vulgaris 'Michael Buchner'
Viburnum davidii
Viburnum tinus 'French White'
Viburnum x *burkwoodii*
Viburnum x *carlesii*
x *fatshedera lizei* 'Variegata'

Climbers
Bougainvillea galabra 'Snow White'
Cissus antartica
Cissus rhombifolia
Clematis 'Alba Luxurians'
Clematis armandii 'Snowdrift'
Clematis 'Belle of Woking'
Clematis cirrhosa 'Wisley Cream'
Clematis 'Duchess of Edinburgh'
Clematis florida 'Seiboldii'
Clematis 'Henryi'
Clematis 'Huldine'
Clematis 'Lasurstern'
Clematis 'Marie Boisselot'
Clematis 'Miss Bateman'
Fallopia baldschuanica
Jasminum officinale
Jasminum officinale 'Clotted Cream'
Mandevilla boliviensis
Passiflora caerulea 'Constance Elliot'
Philodendron scandens
Solanum jasminoides 'Album'
Stephanotis floribunda
Trachelospermum jasminoides
Wisteria floribunda 'Alba'
Wisteria sinensis 'Alba'

Philadelphus 'Manteau d'Hermine'

Colour selector: pink

Pink is perhaps the most common flower colour, coming in a huge variety of shades, ranging from the most subtle of blush-whites to the quite startling shocking pinks.

Complex pink

Pink is the mongrel of the colour world and its complexity means it is not included on the colour wheel because pinks are viewed as a sort of watered-down red, with various amounts of other colours thrown in for good measure.

In fact, pinks are so varied that they could make up a colour wheel all of their own, with the purest clear pink at the core, made up of a splash of red and lots of white, flanked by heart-warming yellowish-pinks (including warm apricot-pink and vibrant salmon-pink) on one side and breezy bluish-pinks (such as shell-pink and lilac-pink) on the other, with white filling in between.

Pink is a chameleon colour too, as it seems to change with the intensity of light and the colours that surround it. The perception of pink also varies from one observer to another, so consider this when planning a planting scheme. Fortunately, pink is very easy to combine with other colours, provided you avoid saturated reds, with which it clashes terribly. As a rule, try to choose a shade of pink on the side of the spectrum from which its companions are derived. For example, if you want a pink to go with blue or purple, choose a cool lilac-pink or a clear pink as a companion. Similarly, if you want a pink to accompany a colour from the warmer side of the colour wheel, go for a yellowish-pink. Best of all, combine pink with white for a foolproof partnership that cannot fail to look impressive, as it offers a sense of romance and fun. Both these colours also combine well with other pastel shades and can be highlighted with splashes of deeper hues.

Soft pink

Pink looks its best in spring when light levels are not so intense. Early flowering plants are ideal choices for small gardens, such as *Rhododendron* 'Pink Pearl', with its white-edged, soft-pink, funnel-shaped flowers that age to white, 'Pink Drift', which bears rose-lavender flowers, and 'Homebush', which offers pretty pink, semi-double blooms.

Camellias come into their own at this time of the year, too, and there are many excellent pink-flowered forms, including *Camellia japonica* 'Elegans', 'Hagoromo' and 'Lady Vansittart', 'Leonard Messel', 'Debbie', 'Donation' and 'J. C. Williams'. Peonies are one of the features of early summer, including 'Duchess of Kent', with tulip-shaped buds that open in to reveal deep rose-pink, semi-double, cup-shaped flowers, and the exquisite 'Duchess of Marlborough', which bears huge, double, pale pink flowers with crinkle-edged petals that fade to silvery-white at the margins.

Rhododendron 'Pink Pearl'

The blush-pink to white sweetly scented blooms of *Rosa* 'Stanwell Perpetual'.

Other early summer favourites are the lavaterias, such as 'Burgundy Wine', 'Kew Rose' and 'Rosea', which all offer a succession of large, dark pink blooms.

Candy-floss pink

Of course, summer wouldn't be summer without the succession of candy-floss pink roses. Among the best are 'Ballerina' (white-centred, pale pink), 'Blessings' (coral-pink), 'Congratulations' (rose-pink), 'Fantin-Latour' (pale pink), 'Fru Dagmar Hastrup' (light pink), 'Happy Anniversary' (deep pink), 'Heritage' (pale pink), 'Louise Odier' (clear pink), 'Madame Pierre Oger' (pale silvery-pink), 'Mary Rose' (rose pink), 'Oxfordshire' (pale pink), 'Pearl Anniversary' (pearl-pink), 'Penelope' (pale creamy-pink), 'Queen Mother' (clear pink), 'Queen of Denmark' (deep to light pink) and 'Silver Jubilee' (rose-pink).

Early flowering clematis worth seeking out include 'Pink Flamingo', then later in the season the pinkish blooms of 'Bees' Jubilee', 'Doctor Ruppel', 'Markham's Pink', 'Pink Perfection', 'Tetrarose' and the flamboyant 'Nelly Moser' come to the fore. For a sun trap, consider the luminescent, cerise-pink *Bougainvillea* 'Raspberry Ice'.

Pink shrubs and climbers to try

Shrubs

Abelia 'Edward Goucher'
Abelia x *grandiflora* 'Confetti'
Abeliophyllum distichum Roseum Group
Buddleja alternifolia
Buddleja davidii 'Pink Delight'
Calluna vulgaris 'Blazeaway'
Calluna vulgaris 'County Wicklow'
Calluna vulgaris 'H. E. Beale'
Calluna vulgaris 'Silver Queen'
Camellia japonica 'Elegans'
Camellia japonica 'Hagoromo'
Camellia japonica 'Lady Vansittart'
Camellia 'Leonard Messel'
Camellia x *williamsii* 'Debbie'
Camellia x *williamsii* 'Donation'
Camellia x *williamsii* 'J. C. Williams'
Camellia x *williamsii* 'E.G. Waterhouse'
Chaenomeles speciosa 'Geisha Girl'
Chaenomeles x *superba* 'Pink Lady'
Cistus 'Silver Pink'
Cistus x *pulverulentus* 'Sunset'
Clethra alnifolia 'Pink Spire'
Clethra alnifolia 'Rosea'
Cornus florida 'Rainbow'
Cornus florida f. *rubra*
Daboecia cantabrica 'Bicolor'
Daphne bholua 'Jacqueline Postill'
Daphne odora 'Aureomarginata'
Deutzia x *elegantissima* 'Rosealind'
Deutzia x *hybrida* 'Mont Rose'
Erica carnea 'Foxhollow'
Erica carnea 'King George'
Erica carnea 'Pink Spangles'

Erica cinerea 'Pink Ice'
Erica x *darleyensis* 'Darley Dale'
Erica x *darleyensis* 'Furzey'
Grevillea 'Robyn Gordon'
Hebe 'Great Orme'
Hebe 'Midsummer Beauty'
Hebe 'Red Edge'
Hebe 'Rosie'
Hibiscus syriacus 'Woodbridge'
Hydrangea macrophylla 'Veitchii'
Hydrangea paniculata 'Floribunda'
Justicia carnea
Kalmia latifolia 'Ostbo Red'
Kolkwitzia amabilis 'Pink Cloud'
Lantana camara 'Fabiola'
Lavandula angustifolia 'Loddon Pink'
Lavandula angustifolia 'Rosea'
Lavatera x *clementii* 'Barnsley'
Lavatera x *clementii* 'Burgundy Wine'
Lavatera x *clementii* 'Kew Rose'
Magnolia 'Heaven Scent'
Magnolia stellata 'Royal Star'
Magnolia x *loebneri* 'Leonard Messel'
Magnolia x *soulangeana*
Paeonia suffruticosa 'Reine Elisabeth'
Phlomis italica
Phygelius x *rectus* 'Pink Elf'
Pieris japonica 'Valley Valentine'
Potentilla fruticosa 'Royal Flush'
Prunus tenella 'Fire Hill'
Prunus triloba
Rhododendron 'Debutante'
Rhododendron 'Grumpy'
Rhododendron 'Homebush'
Rhododendron 'Pink Drift'
Rhododendron 'Pink Pearl'
Rosa 'Buff Beauty'
Rosa 'Congratulations'
Rosa 'Cornelia'
Rosa 'Fantin-Latour'
Rosa 'Fru Dagmar Hastrup'
Rosa glauca
Rosa 'Golden Anniversary'
Rosa 'Happy Anniversary'
Rosa 'Heritage'
Rosa 'Louise Odier'
Rosa 'Madame Pierre Oger'
Rosa 'Many Happy Returns'
Rosa 'Mary Rose'
Rosa 'Oxfordshire'
Rosa 'Pearl Anniversary'
Rosa 'Queen of Denmark'
Rosa 'Sharifa Asma'

Rhodeodendron 'Homebush'

Rosa 'Silver Jubilee'
Rosa 'Surrey'
Rosa 'Sussex'
Rosa 'Sweet Dream'
Rosmarinus officinalis 'Majorca Pink'
Rubus odoratus
Salvia officinalis
Spiraea japonica 'Anthony Waterer'
Symphoricarpos x *chenaultii* 'Hancock'
Syringa vulgaris 'Madame Lemoine'
Viburnum tinus 'Eve Price'
Viburnum tinus 'Gwenllian'
Viburnum x *bodnantense* 'Dawn'
Viburnum x *juddii*
Weigela florida 'Foliis Purpureis'
Weigela 'Florida Variegata'

Climbers

Actinidia kolomikta
Bougainvillea 'Miss Manila'
Bougainvillea 'Raspberry Ice'
Bougainvillea glabra
Bougainvillea glabra 'Variegata'
Clematis alpina 'Pink Flamingo'
Clematis armandii 'Apple Blossom'
Clematis macropetala 'Markham's Pink'
Clematis montana var. *rubens* 'Elizabeth'
Clematis montana var. *rubens* 'Tetrarose'
Clematis 'Nelly Moser'
Clematis 'Princess Diana'
Hoya carnosa
Jasminum x *stephanense*
Mandevilla splendens
Wisteria floribunda 'Macrobotrytys'

Hebe 'Great Orme'

Colour selector: red

Plants with scarlet and vermillion flowers are often seen as the showgirls of the border, demanding attention as they cry out from the chorus of other more subtle shades all around them.

Hot reds

Reds fall on the hot side of the colour wheel, and so sit particularly happily alongside oranges and yellow in fiery combinations. However, reds have much more going for them than that.

The most saturated reds, which fall in the middle of the spectrum, have the most intense colour and can hold their own in any display. However, if they are used too liberally, they will dominate all the other colours surrounding them. For this reason, saturated red flowering plants with large blooms need to be used with care and reserved for creating distinctive points of focus in a border of more subtle shades, such as pale green.

Shrubs with scattered, small red flowers are much easier to accommodate in mixed planting schemes because their effect is moderated by the intermittent

Pieris 'Forest Flame'

backdrop of foliage that peeks through from behind the vibrantly coloured flowering display.

Velvet-reds

Rich velvet-reds that have just a hint of blue will add sensuality to a planting scheme and are particularly well suited to combining with plants of a purple tone. Many flowers offer plum-purple shades, which are now very popular. More subtle than the saturated reds, velvet-reds tend to add warmth and intimacy to a planting scheme.

Brilliant reds

Shades of red also can be introduced into the border by including plants with purple or red foliage. This can be a seasonal highlight, such as the brilliant red, glossy young leaves of *Photinia x fraseri* 'Red Robin' or, for longer-term display, *Berberis thunbergii* 'Atropurpurea Nana', with its dark purple leaves that turn a brilliant red in autumn, or *Cotinus coggygria* 'Royal Purple', another red-purple-leaved, bushy shrub that turns brilliant scarlet in autumn.

Japanese maples such as 'Atropurpureum', 'Bloodgood' and 'Garnet' make excellent specimens for small gardens, with their attractive palm-like, lobed or deeply cut dark purple leaves that look spectacular all summer before turning brilliant shades of red at the end of the growing season.

Crimson and scarlet

The ever-popular crimson and scarlet roses, such as 'Alec's Red' (crimson), 'Alexander' (vermilion), 'Charles de Mills', 'Fragrant Cloud' (deep-scarlet), 'Ingrid Bergman' (deep red), 'Just Joey' (coppery-red), 'Loving Memory' (dark red), 'Rose de Rescht' (deep mauve-red), 'Royal

Rosa 'Danse du Feu'

William' (deep-crimson), 'Ruby Anniversary' (ruby-red), 'Ruby Wedding' (ruby-red), 'Suffolk' (golden-centred, deep-scarlet) and 'The Times Rose' (dark-crimson), shouldn't be overlooked.

However, there are many other red-flowering shrubs worth considering, including the vermillion-red *Potentilla fruticosa* 'Red Ace', which blooms from late spring to autumn, or the stunning *Paeonia delavayi*, which bears single, cup-shaped, blood-red flowers from spring into early summer.

Red also makes a splash at the end of the growing season as shrubs and climbers take on their autumnal hues. Few sights are more spectacular than the blood-red foliage of the crimson glory vine, *Vitis coignetiae*, when its huge, heart-shaped leaves turn fiery shades, accompanied by bunches of small, blue-black, inedible grapes.

Equally impressive are the deeply divided, slightly puckered green leaves of the Virginia creeper, *Parthenocissus quinquefolia*, which transform in autumn as they take on brilliant shades of crimson and purple. When autumn turns to

Red shrubs and climbers to try

Shrubs

Abutilon megapotamicum
Acer palmatum 'Bloodgood'
Acer palmatum 'Fireglow'
Acer palmatum 'Osakazuki'
Acer palmatum 'Sango-kaku'
Acer palmatum var. *dissectum*
'Atropurpureum'
Amelanchier lamarckii
Amelanchier x *grandiflora* 'Ballerina'
Aucuba japonica 'Rozannie'
Aucuba japonica 'Variegata'
Berberis thunbergii 'Atropurpurea Nana'
Berberis thunbergii 'Bagatelle'
Berberis thunbergii 'Dart's Red Lady'
Berberis thunbergii 'Harlequin'
Berberis thunbergii 'Helmond Pillar'
Berberis thunbergii 'Red Chief'
Callistemon citrinus 'Splendens'
Calluna vulgaris 'Dark Star'
Calluna vulgaris 'Wickwar Flame'
Camellia japonica 'Adolphe Audusson'
Camellia japonica 'Mikenjaku'
Camellia x *williamsii* 'Anticipation'
Ceratostigma griffithii
Chaenomeles x *superba* 'Crimson and
Gold'
Chaenomeles x *superba* 'Nicoline'
Colutea x *media* 'Copper Beauty'
Cornus 'Eddie's White Wonder'
Cornus alba 'Sibirica'
Cornus alba 'Spaethii'
Cotinus 'Flame'
Cotinus 'Grace'
Cotoneaster dammeri
Cotoneaster frigidus 'Cornubia'
Cotoneaster horizontalis
Cotoneaster 'Hybridus Pendulus'
Cotoneaster salicifolius 'Gnom'

Cytisus 'Boskoop Ruby'
Daboecia cantabrica 'Bicolor'
Desfontainia spinosa
Enkianthus cernuus f. *rubens*
Erica carnea 'Ann Sparkes'
Erica carnea 'Challenger'
Erica carnea 'December Red'
Erica carnea 'Myretoun Ruby'
Escallonia rubra 'Crimson Spire'
Euonymus europaeus 'Red Cascade'
Fothergilla gardenii
Fuchsia 'Mrs Popple'
Fuchsia 'Pumila'
Fuchsia 'Riccartonii'
Gaultheria mucronata 'Mulberry Wine'
Gaultheria procumbens
Helianthemum 'Ben Heckla'
Helianthemum 'Ben Hope'
Helianthemum 'Henfield Brilliant'
Hibiscus rosa-sinensis 'The President'
Ilex aquifolium 'J.C. van Tol'
Leptospermum scoparium 'Red Damask'
Leucothoe 'Scarletta'
Leycesteria formosa
Paeonia delavayi
Photinia x *fraseri* 'Red Robin
Potentilla fruticosa 'Red Ace'
Pyracantha 'Saphyr Rouge'
Rhamnus alaternus 'Argenteovariegata'
Rhododendron 'Dopey'
Rhododendron 'Geisha Red'
Rhododendron 'Klondyke'
Rhododendron 'Lord Roberts'
Rhododendron 'Mother's Day'
Rhododendron 'Scarlet Wonder'
Ribes sanguineum 'King Edward VII'
Ribes sanguineum 'Pulborough Scarlet'
Rosa 'Alec's Red'
Rosa 'Alexander'

Viburnum betulifolium

Rosa 'Charles de Mills'
Rosa 'Fragrant Cloud'
Rosa 'Ingrid Bergman'
Rosa 'The Times Rose'
Rosa moyesii 'Geranium'
Skimmia japonica subsp. *reevesiana*
Virburnum betulifolium
Weigela 'Bristol Ruby'

Climbers

Berberidopsis corallina
Bougainvillea 'Scarlett O'Hara'
Campsis x *tagliabuana* 'Madame Galen'
Clematis 'Ernest Markham'
Clematis 'Niobe'
Clematis 'Rouge Cardinal'
Clematis 'Ville de Lyon'
Clianthus puniceus
Eccremocarpus scaber
Lonicera x *brownii* 'Dropmore Scarlet'
Parthenocissus quinquefolia
Parthenocissus tricuspidata 'Robusta'
Vitis 'Brant'
Vitis coignetiae

winter, sparking red stems stand out
from the dormant borders, with the
red-barked dogwood *Cornus alba*
'Sibirica' taking centre stage with its
brilliant red winter stems.

Coral

If you are looking for a shrub that
offers year-round interest then
seriously consider the coral-bark
maple, *Acer palmatum* 'Sango-kaku'.

This magnificent, ever-changing
plant offers startling coral-red young
shoots that dramatically set off the
emerging palm-shaped, orange-yellow
leaves in spring. The leaves gradually
turn green in summer, before taking
on fabulous shades of yellow in
autumn. When these lovely leaves
eventually fall, they reveal their
brilliantly coloured stems
throughout the winter.

Clematis reds

Clematis with flowers in shades of
red include the semi-double, reddish-
purple blooms of *Clematis viticella*
'Purpurea Plena Elegans', which are
produced *en masse* from mid-summer
onwards, and the ever-popular 'Ville
de Lyon', which offers large, cherry-
red flowers with contrasting golden
centres through the summer and into
the autumn.

Colour selector: purple, black and blue

Lying on the cool side of the colour wheel, purple, blue and black are all recessive colours and as such seem to sink back into the border – creating a subdued, almost brooding, edge to the garden atmosphere.

Purple

Despite its apparent richness and associations with opulence, purple is surprisingly calming and soothing. However, it doesn't take to competition all that well and will tend to get lost if it is included in a mixed scheme.

The best way to use purple is in isolated blocks, surrounded by greens and silvers, or combined with bluish-pinks such as lilac. Purples also associate well with cool blues and greens as well as hot reds, which lie either side of the purple sector in the colour wheel. For colour contrast, go for yellow, which lies opposite the purple sector on the colour wheel, or startling whites, which will help lift the mood and provide sensational highlights.

Softer mauves and lavenders are also part of the purple group and are even more subdued than their more vibrant, violet counterparts. They

Vitis vinifera 'Purpurea'

benefit from being used in bold swathes of single colours that lead the eye from one part of the garden to another, such as a lavender hedge alongside a path or a wisteria cascading over a boundary fence.

Black

By contrast, black (actually the darkest shade of purple) can be used for focal point plants when it is dotted within a planting of pale foliage plants. They look even better against a backdrop of silver or intermingled with the purest of whites. In blocks, black is too austere and will get overwhelmed in mixed colour schemes. Good examples of black plants include the lovely *Sambucus nigra* 'Black Lace and *S. nigra* 'Black Beauty.

Blue for illusion

Blue is perhaps the most tranquil colour in the garden palette, associating well with water and seating areas where its peaceful ambience can be best appreciated.

Although one of the least prominent colours, blue is also useful for creating illusions in a small garden where you want to increase the sense of space.

Like purple, blue associates well with white flowers and silver foliage, as these complement its introverted nature. It also harmonizes with other cool colours, such as bluish-purples and bluish-greens – both tones making an ideal antidote to the more flamboyant colour combinations often found elsewhere.

True blue

Pure blue flowers have a wonderfully luminescent quality about them, which means they often look their most spectacular at dusk and dawn, when other dominant colours seem

Cotinus coggygria

to recede and allow the blues to shimmer magnificently.

Perhaps the most reliable and impressive blue flowering shrub is the late spring-blooming Californian lilac (*Ceanothus*). Excellent varieties include: 'Burkwoodii', which bears clouds of sky-blue flowers above a compact evergreen shrub with bright green glossy leaves; 'Concha', which makes a dazzling mound of dark blue flowers; and the relatively new 'Italian Skies', which is covered in dense clusters of brilliant blue flowers. Other blue flowers that should not be forgotten are the popular 'Puget Blue' (dark blue) and 'Trewithen Blue', which bears fragrant, rich blue blooms. For a late show, go for 'Autumnal Blue', which bears clouds of bright blue flowers.

Vivid blue

Other shrubs that produce piercing, vivid blue flowers include the Chinese plumbago *Ceratostigma willmottianum* 'Forest Blue' and the ground-hugging periwinkles *Vinca major* (deep blue) and *Vinca minor* (pale blue). Alternatively, you might like to try *Caryopteris* x *clandonensis*

Purple, black and blue shrubs and climbers to try

Shrubs

Acer palmatum 'Atropurpureum'
Acer palmatum 'Garnet'
Ballota acetabulosa
Berberis thunbergii 'Atropurpurea Nana'
Berberis thunbergii 'Bagatelle'
Berberis thunbergii f. *atropurpurea*
Buddleja davidii 'Black Knight'
Buddleja davidii 'Nanho Blue'
Calluna vulgaris 'Amethyst'
Caryopteris x *clandonensis*
Caryopteris x *clandonensis* 'First Choice'
Ceanothus arboreus 'Trewithen Blue'
Ceanothus 'Autumnal Blue'
Ceanothus 'Burkwoodii'
Ceanothus 'Concha'
Ceanothus impressus 'Puget Blue'
Ceanothus 'Italian Skies'
Ceanothus thyrsiflorus var. *repens*
Ceratostigma griffithii
Ceratostigma willmottianum
Ceratostigma willmottianum 'Forest Blue'
Cistus x *argenteus* 'Peggy Sammons'
Clerodendrum trichotomum var. *fargesii*
Cordyline australis 'Atropurpurea'
Cordyline australis 'Purple Tower'
Cordyline australis Purpurea Group
Cordyline australis 'Red Star'
Cornus alba 'Kesselringii'
Corylus maxima 'Purpurea'
Cotinus 'Grace'
Cotinus coggygria 'Royal Purple'
Daboecia cantabrica 'Atropurpurea'
Fuchsia 'Mrs Popple'
Hibiscus syriacus 'Blue Bird'
Hydrangea macrophylla 'Blue Wave'
Hydrangea macrophylla 'Mariesii'
Hydrangea serrata 'Bluebird'
Hydrangea villosa
Indigofera heterantha
Lavandula angustifolia 'Hidcote'
Lavandula angustifolia 'Lady'
Lavandula angustifolia 'Munstead'
Lavandula angustifolia 'Royal Purple'
Lavandula 'Fathead'
Lavandula 'Helmsdale'

Lavandula stoechas 'Papillon'
Lavandula stoechas 'Rocky Road'
Lavandula x *intermedia* 'Grappenhall'
Lavandula x *intermedia* 'Grosso'
Magnolia 'Susan'
Magnolia x *soulangeana* 'Lennei'
Photinia x *fraseri* 'Birmingham'
Rhododendron 'Blue Danube'
Rhododendron 'Blue Diamond'
Rhododendron 'Blue Peter'
Rhododendron 'Purple Splendour'
Rhododendron 'Sapphire'
Rosa 'Cardinal de Richelieu'
Rosa 'Roseraie de l'Haÿ'
Rosa 'William Lobb'
Rosa rugosa 'Rubra'
Rosmarinus officinalis 'Severn Sea'
Salix hastata 'Wehrhahnii'
Salvia officinalis 'Purpurascens'
Salvia officinalis 'Tricolor'
Sambucus nigra 'Black Beauty'
Sambucus nigra 'Black Lace'
Syringa meyeri var. *spontanea* 'Palibin'
Syringa vulgaris 'Charles Joly'
Tamarix 'Rubra'
Tibouchina urvilleana
Vinca major
Vinca minor
Vinca minor 'Argenteovariegata'
Vinca minor 'Atropurpurea'
Vinca minor f. *alba* 'Gertrude Jekyll'

Climbers

Akebia quinata
Ampelopsis megalophylla
Aristolochia littoralis
Billardiera longiflora
Clematis alpina
Clematis alpina 'Frances Rivis'
Clematis alpina 'Frankie'
Clematis alpina 'Pamela Jackman'
Clematis 'Barbara Jackman'
Clematis 'Comtesse de Bouchaud'
Clematis 'Etoile Violette'
Clematis 'Fireworks'
Clematis 'General Sikorski'

Solanum laciniatum

Clematis 'Jackmanii'
Clematis 'Jackmanii Superba'
Clematis 'Mrs Cholmondeley'
Clematis 'Mrs N.Thompson'
Clematis 'Multi Blue'
Clematis 'Perle d'Azur'
Clematis 'Polish Spirit'
Clematis 'Prince Charles'
Clematis 'The President'
Clematis viticella 'Purpurea Plena Elegans'
Clematis 'Vyvyan Pennell'
Cobaea scandens
Lonicera henryi
Lonicera japonica var. *repens*
Lonicera periclymenum 'Belgica'
Parthenocissus henryana
Parthenocissus tricuspidata 'Veitchii'
Passiflora caerulea
Plumbago auriculata
Solanum laciniatum 'Glasnevin'
Sollya heterophylla
Vitis vinifera 'Purpurea'
Wisteria floribunda
Wisteria floribunda 'Royal Purple'
Wisteria sinensis
Wisteria x *formosa*

'Heavenly Blue', for its impressive dark blue flowers, or *Hibiscus syriacus* 'Blue Bird', for its exotic-looking, violet-blue, trumpet-shaped summer blooms, each with a maroon eye.

Blue clematis

Finally, there are a couple of clematis that are worth mentioning in the blue category. These are 'Perle d'Azur', for its beautiful yellow-centred, lilac-blue flowers, produced in succession from mid-summer onwards, and 'Prince Charles', which offers pale mauve-blue flowers with green centres.

Scent selector

Fragrance is an elusive quality that is almost impossibly difficult to define. Not only does each person's perception of scent vary from day to day, but atmospheric conditions, location and the blend of scents in the air all have an impact.

The fragrant garden

Although scent is a bonus to the gardener, its reason for existence is to attract insects for pollination. For this reason, many winter-flowering plants are aromatic. However, there are not many pollinators around at this time of year, so the flowers have to work particularly hard to attract them — and they do.

Some plants throw out their scent with gay abandon, and can be smelled over long distances. Others are much more discreet and can only be appreciated when you get up very close to them. Some are only noticable during the evening, as the light fades. Generally, a warm, sunny day brings out the scents of shrubs and climbers, but there are some that are much more noticable during or after a fall of rain.

Summer scent: *Rosa 'Zéphirine Drouhin'*.

Many gardeners believe that modern-day flowers have lost their delicate fragrance when compared to old-fashioned varieties. In a lot of cases, this is true. As breeders develop more and more hybrid plants, particularly roses, for even larger blooms, a wider range of colours and disease resistance, it is sometimes at the expense of their aromatic charms. However, breeders are now aware of this and are taking more care to preserve the other beauty that satisfies the gardener's senses — that of smell.

Fragrance or odour?

It is essential that you check out a plant's fragrance in person before you buy — because one gardener's pleasing fragrance is another gardener's bad odour.

Subtle fragrances are often the worst offenders: it seems the more delicate the scent, the greater the range of reactions it receives, with unusual scents the most likely to be perceived completely differently by different people.

The main reason for this is that a particular fragrance is made up of various layers. The first layer is the ephemeral part of the scent that the nose picks up initially and its influence on the appreciation of the whole scent varies from one person to another. This is the part of the scent that grabs your attention, for good or for bad.

Spring scent: *Viburnum x juddii*

Soon the nose becomes aware of a more representative part of the fragrance, which is the main body of the scent. Then finally, the experience transforms as you appreciate the underlying part of the fragrance that stays with you.

Scent structure

Perhaps the best way to picture the structure of a scent is as a pyramid, as described by the leading French rose breeder, Henri Delbard.

In his pyramid, the top is the 'spirit' of the fragrance and includes the citrus scents and more aromatic elements, such as aniseed and lavender. In the middle is the 'heart' of the scent, which includes floral, fruity, spicy and earthy fragrances. At the bottom is the 'base' scent, which comprises the woody elements. Examples of this are cedar or balsam.

Universal scents

There are some fragrances that are more or less universally liked. Vanilla is a case in point, with the spicy vanilla scent of the chocolate vine (*Akebia quinata*) or the sweet vanilla fragrance of *Clematis* 'Elizabeth' and *C. armandii*, as well as that of wisteria, very widely rated.

By contrast, other sweet scents, such as honey, are loved by some and despised by others. For example, the strong honey scent of most varieties of Butterfly bush (*Buddleja*) or that of *Viburnum carlesii* are not universally appreciated, nor is the sweet honey scent of the Californian lilac (*ceanothus*).

Many floral scents, such as jasmine, honeysuckle and lily-of-the-valley, are also widely acclaimed, as are those with fruity scents such as the peachy scents of *Coronilla glauca*, the fresh pineapple aroma of *Cytissus battanderi*, the spicy orange of

Spartium junceum and the perky lemon of *Eucalyptus citriodora*. Many roses have quite complex aromas, including the bananas-and-oranges smell of *Rosa* 'Bobbie James' and *R.* 'Polyanthus Grandiflorus'; the mix of lemon, peach, apricot and pears of

R. 'Nahema'; or very complex fragrance of mandarin, lemon, hyacinth, lilac, mango and lychee of *R.* 'Chartreuse De Parme'.

Many other climbers and shrubs have aromatic foliage, too, which can be resinous-smelling. Examples

Spring-scented shrubs and climbers to try

Shrubs
Abeliophyllum distichum
Aloysia triphylla
Choisya ternata
Choisya ternata 'Aztec Pearl'
Choisya ternata 'Goldfingers'
Choisya ternata 'Sundance'
Cytisus x praecox 'Warminster'
Daphne mezereum
Drimys winteri
Fothergilla gardenii
Fothergilla major
Magnolia 'Heaven Scent'
Magnolia stellata
Magnolia stellata 'Rosea'
Magnolia stellata 'Royal Star'
Magnolia stellata 'Waterlily'
Osmanthus delavayi
Pieris formosa var. *forrestii* 'Wakehurst'
Rhododendron luteum
Skimmia japonica 'Rubella'
Syringa meyeri var. *spontanea* 'Palibin'
Syringa pubescens subsp. *microphylla* 'Superba'

Syringa vulgaris 'Charles Joly'
Syringa vulgaris 'Katherine Havemeyer'
Syringa vulgaris 'Madame Lemoine'
Syringa vulgaris 'Michael Buchner'
Viburnum x burkwoodii
Viburnum x carlcephalum
Viburnum x carlesii
Viburnum x juddii

Climbers
Akebia quinata
Clematis armandii 'Apple Blossom'
Clematis armandii 'Snowdrift'
Clematis 'Betty Corning'
Clematis flammula
Clematis montana var. *rubens* 'Elizabeth'
Clematis montana var. *rubens* 'Pink Perfection'
Clematis montana var. *rubens* 'Tetrarose'
Clematis 'Mrs Cholmondeley'
Hoya carnosa
Jasminum polyanthum
Stephanotis floribunda

Spring scent: *Choisya ternata*

Summer scented shrubs and climbers to try

Shrubs

Abelia x *grandiflora*
Abelia x *grandiflora* 'Confetti'
Abelia x *grandiflora* 'Francis Mason'
Abelia x *grandiflora* 'Goldspot'
Aloysia triphylla
Azara dentate
Brugmansia suaveolens
Buddleja 'Lochinch'
Buddleja alternifolia
Buddleja davidii 'Black Knight'
Buddleja davidii 'Nanho Blue'
Buddleja davidii 'White Profusion'
Buddleja globosa
Carpenteria californica
Carpenteria californica 'Ladhams Variety'
Caryopteris x *clandonensis*
Ceanothus arboreus 'Trewithen Blue'
Clethra alnifolia
Clethra alnifolia 'Paniculata'
Clethra alnifolia 'Pink Spire'
Clethra alnifolia 'Rosea'
Cytisus battandieri
Cytisus x *praecox* 'Warminster'
Deutzia gracilis
Escallonia 'Iveyi'
Eucryphia x *intermedia* 'Rostrevor'
Eucryphia x *nymanensis* 'Nymansay'
Itea ilicifolia
Jasminum humile 'Revolutum'
Lavandula 'Helmsdale'
Lavandula angustifolia 'Munstead'
Lavandula angustifolia 'Hidcote Pink'
Lavandula angustifolia 'Hidcote'

Lavandula angustifolia 'Lady'
Lavandula angustifolia 'Loddon Pink'
Lavandula angustifolia 'Nana Alba'
Lavandula angustifolia 'Rosea'
Lavandula angustifolia 'Royal Purple'
Lavandula steochas 'Papillon'
Lavandula steochas 'Fathead'
Lavandula steochas 'Kew Red'
Lavandula steochas 'Rocky Road'
Myrtus communis
Myrtus communis subsp *tarentina*
Olearia ilicifolia
Philadelphus 'Beauclerk'
Philadelphus 'Belle Etoile'
Philadelphus 'Manteau d'Hermine'
Pittosporum tenuifolium 'Silver Queen'
Rosa 'Alec's Red'
Rosa 'Alexander'
Rosa 'Bantry Bay'
Rosa 'Blanche Double de Coubert'
Rosa 'Blessings'
Rosa 'Boule de Neige'
Rosa 'Buff Beauty'
Rosa 'Cardinal de Richelieu'
Rosa 'Charles de Mills'
Rosa 'Chinatown'
Rosa 'Congratulations'
Rosa 'Cornelia'
Rosa 'Felicia'
Rosa 'Fragrant Cloud'
Rosa 'Happy Anniversary'
Rosa 'Heritage'
Rosa 'Ice Cream'
Rosa 'Ingrid Bergman'

Rosa 'Just Joey'
Rosa 'L.D. Braithwaite'
Rosa 'Louise Odier'
Rosa 'Madame Pierre Oger'
Rosa 'Many Happy Returns'
Rosa 'Mary Rose'
Rosa 'Queen of Denmark'
Rosa 'Rosa de Rescht'
Rosa 'Roseraie de L'Hay'
Rosa 'Royal William'
Rosa 'Ruby Wedding'
Rosa 'Silver Jubilee'
Rosa 'Surrey'
Rosa 'Sussex'
Rosa 'Sweet Dream'
Rosa moyesii 'Geranium'
Rosa rugosa 'Rubra'
Rosa xanthina 'Canary Bird'
Rubus odoratus
Sambucus nigra 'Black Beauty'
Spartium junceum

Climbers

Actinidia kolomikta
Bougainvillea 'Raspberry Ice'
Cobaea scandens
Jasminum beesianum
Jasminum officinale
Jasminum officinale 'Clotted Cream'
Jasminum x *stephanense*
Lonicera japonica 'Halliana'
Lonicera japonica 'Halls Prolific'
Lonicera japonica var. *repens*
Lonicera periclymenum 'Belgica'
Lonicera periclymenum 'Serotina'
Lonicera x *americana*
Lonicera x *heckrottii* 'Goldflame'
Mandevilla x *amoena* 'Alice du Pont'
Passiflora caerulea 'Constance Elliot'
Rosa 'Alberic Barbier'
Rosa 'Albertine'
Rosa 'Aloha'
Rosa 'Bantry Bay'
Rosa 'Breath of Life'
Rosa 'Climbing Iceberg'
Rosa 'Compassion'
Rosa 'Emily Gray'

Rubus odoratus

Rosa 'Bantry Bay'

include cistus and escallonia; some can be camphorous, such as lavender, perovskia, and eucalyptus; while others are simply pungent, as with rue and ribes.

Siting fragrant plants

Aromatic plants are usually best positioned near places where you sit and relax. This could be in containers on the patio, by garden seats or by windows and doors, so that the scent wafts into the house during a warm day or evening. If you have a table and chairs for outdoor eating in the summer months, you

Summer scent: *Lavendula augustifolia*

Autumn- and winter-scented shrubs and climbers to try

Autumn Shrubs
Camellia sasanqua 'Narumigata'
Clerodendrum trichotomum 'Fargesii'
Jasminum nudiflorum
Mahonia x *media* 'Lionel Fortescue'
Mahonia x *media* 'Winter Sun'

Winter Shrubs
Abeliophyllum distichum
Chimonanthus praecox
Chimonanthus praecox 'Grandiflorus'
Chimonanthus praecox 'Luteus'
Coronilla valentia subsp. *glauca*
Coronilla valentia subsp. *glauca* 'Citrina'
Daphne bholua 'Jacqueline Postill'
Daphne odora 'Aureomarginata'
Hamamelis mollis
Hamamelis x *intermedia* 'Arnold Promise'
Hamamelis x *intermedia* 'Diane'

Hamamelis x *intermedia* 'Jelena'
Hamamelis x *intermedia* 'Pallida'
Hamamelis x *intermedia* 'Moonlight'
Lonicera fragrantissima
Lonicera x *purpusii* 'Winter Beauty'
Mahonia japonica 'Bealei'
Mahonia x *media* 'Buckland'
Sarcococca confusa
Skimmia x *confusa* 'Kew Green'
Viburnum x *bodnantense* 'Dawn'
Viburnum x *bodnantense* 'Charles Lamont'

Winter Climbers
Clematis cirrhosa 'Freckles'
Clematis cirrhosa var. *balearica*

may want to grow shrubs in containers so that you can site them nearby on the patio.

Fragrant foliage

Scent is not limited to the flowers of course, as several plants offer wonderfully aromatic foliage, including many herbs such as thyme, rosemary and bay. And not to be forgotten is the citrus-rich smell of lemon verbena (*Aloysia triphylla*).

In some cases, as with flowers, warmth brings out the fragrance, although in most cases it is necessary to crush the leaves or stems so that their aroma is released.

With scented foliage plants, it is best to site them near to a path so that you can run your fingers through them as you walk.

It is easy to run away with the idea of a fragrant garden. However, caution should be taken when planting, as some scents will vie with each other for attention, overwhelm their companions and not allow you to appreciate their individual fragrances. For this reason, when you are planning your purchases, try to smell your plants before you buy them, as some may not be as scented as you wish. Another reason for trying out scents, either in the garden or the plant nursery, is simply that you may not like the fragrance.

Summer fragrance: *Philiadelphus*

Autumn scent: *M.* x *media* 'Lionel Fortescue'

Winter fragrance: *Hamamelis mollis*

Using shrubs and climbers

Shrubs and climbers can be used in a number of different ways, depending on the effect you are trying to create. Over the following pages their various roles and uses are explored. Unlike bedding and perennials, the biggest challenge when selecting shrubs and climbers is to be able to visualize what they might look like five or ten years later and how you can take this into account when planning a new border.

Shrubs and climbers are permanent additions to the garden's overall design and so extra care must be given to placement and combinations. Many can be used to make strong points of focus in the garden that can draw the eye and add impact to the overall design, while others provide a much more subtle, but no less important, role as building blocks in the border that offer a suitable contrast to their more flamboyant neighbours. Bear in mind both the ultimate size and growth rates of the various shrubs and climbers you choose to combine in a single border to ensure that they continue to complement each other and the rest of the garden over time.

Even the most beautiful plants can benefit by being displayed well. Showing off plants relies on planting them in sympathy with their surroundings so that both landscape and plant are in harmony.

Specimens and focal points

There are many shrubs and climbers that make superb specimens and focal points in the garden. Some provide a constant point of reference, with their bold outline or foliage colour, while others offer a seasonal splash when in flower or take on autumnal hues when the blooms have finished.

Positioning specimens

The most attractively designed gardens use plants and structures to guide the visitor and casual viewer. Eye-catching features help to draw the attention to a particular spot or vista, and can also achieve the opposite by distracting the eye from less aesthetically pleasing aspects, such as a vegetable patch or a bed of spent daffodils.

A series of well-spaced and carefully positioned points of focus lead the eye around the garden and even subconsciously entice the visitor to explore further.

Good plants to try

Flowers	Bold foliage
Buddleja	Eucalyptus
Camellia	Fatsia
Carpenteria	Hedera
Ceanothus	Mahonia
Cistus	Paulownia
Clematis	Philadephus
Cytisus	Phormium
Forsythia	Sambucus
Genista	Vitis
Helianthemum	Yucca
Hibiscus	
Hydrangea	**Autumn colour**
Magnolia	Acer
Paeonia	Amelanchier
Rhododendron	Berberis
Syringa	Cornus
	Cotinus
	Cotoneaster
	Euonymus
	Rhus
	Viburnum

Create a blend of colours by planting different varieties of roses together. Here, the lovely soft red of *Rosa* 'American Pillar' and the gentle pink of *Rosa* 'Kew Rambler' grow up a supporting structure. Another growing season will see them mingling together at the top of the post.

When choosing a specimen shrub or climber, your first consideration should be its backdrop. If it is to stand out it needs to contrast in some way with its surroundings – by either its height, colour, form or texture. However, don't be tempted to overdo the contrast, as the specimen could result in totally dominating the scene, rather than simply drawing the eye. If the

attractive feature is only temporary, you should consider what the plant will look like when it is out of season. This is particularly important for specimens in prominent positions, such as next to the patio or set into a lawn.

When positioning a focal point or specimen, consider where it will be viewed from: windows overlooking the garden, the patio and seating areas or the entrance into the garden, for example. Specimens and focal points should be at home in their surroundings. The style of the plant should not be at odds with its neighbours, and should look like an intrinsic part of the overall design, rather than an after-thought. It should be sited so that it looks prominent among nearby features but not isolated from them.

Shape, colour and texture

Some plants have such a dramatic shape or outline that they provide a permanent focal point throughout the year. Others undergo dramatic makeovers with the changing of the seasons and so can be used to great effect within a garden design. You can even use seasonal specimens in pots and position them in different parts of the garden to change the point of focus from month to month, thereby constantly altering how the garden is viewed.

Bear in mind that colours vary in the way they are perceived. Hot, vibrant colours, such as red, orange and yellow, make a bigger impact on the eye and so the plant seems bigger, closer and larger than it really is. Conversely, cooler blues, greens and greys are more recessive to the eye and so have the opposite effect.

Texture also has an impact. Although much more subtle than using colours, plants with bold or glossy leaves create a more intimate atmosphere, while those plants with finely cut and matt foliage can help create the illusion of space.

Position trellis above a wall and grow a vigorous climbing rose to provide privacy as well as a beautiful backdrop to a border.

An enticing vista has been created by training *Rosa* 'Seagull' to drape over a hanging structure made of rope to provide a stunning focal point.

Beds and borders

Shrubs and climbers are the building blocks of the garden, providing a permanent framework that holds the design together in harmony. Try to use them in carefully considered groups rather than dotting them around individually. This will ensure that they provide structure and backbone to the overall design.

Using shrubs in borders

The usual way shrubs are used in the garden is in beds and borders — either in a special, dedicated shrubbery or combined with other types of plants, such as perennials and bulbs.

Shrubs that are being added to an existing display are the easiest to select because you already have a fixed reference point provided by the surrounding plants. You might want to choose a new addition to add height, form, texture or seasonal interest to the existing planting

The secret to planting a beautiful border is to design it with layers of colour and different textures, as well as planting shrubs and climbers that will grow at different heights.

The addition of the vibrant red perennial Maltese Cross (*Lychnis chalcedonica*) makes this combination of foliage shrubs come alive.

scheme, or it could be that you just want a more anonymous border plant to use as a background filler that doesn't upset the display.

New border planting

When planning a new shrub border from scratch, the options are seemingly endless. Unless you have a clear idea of what you want to achieve, you could spend a lot of time trying to make up your mind about the best plan to follow.

First-time planters and old gardening hands alike can be a bit nervous about border design, but a simple and effective method is to use a graduated growing scheme. Select small plants for the front of the border, medium-sized ones in the centre and tall shrubs at the back. This provides a slope effect, allowing the plants to be seen in all their glory.

Garden centres and plant nurseries can be very seductive places. One common pitfall is buying all your favourite shrubs and then trying to fit them into a border plan when you get home. This will inevitably end in disappointment. It is far better to decide what effect you are trying to achieve before you buy the plants and then draw up a list of potential candidates for each position in the border.

Factors that you need to take into account include the heights, spreads and growth rates of the larger specimen shrubs that are to go at the back. Also consider the same factors for the smaller ones that will go near the front. However, try not to over-regiment the border by size as this will look unnatural. As a rule of thumb, don't select any shrub that grows taller than the width of the border.

Next to consider are the foliage colours and textures of the plants on your shortlist. Successful planting is achieved when there is a combining of contrasting elements that provide a dramatic appearance or, conversely, a blend of similar elements that provide a soothing, mellow affect.

Combining plants

Combine evergreen and deciduous varieties in the ratio of about two to one, to give a continuity in the display, and mix different forms and outlines for added interest. Finally, consider the seasonal variations, including flowering periods, changes in foliage, berries, bark and scent.

Good plants to try

Backbone	Kolkwitzia
Abelia	*Lavatera*
Berberis	*Leycesteria*
Callicarpa	*Perovskia*
Carpenteria	*Rubus*
Ceanothus	*Sambucus*
Cotoneaster	*Syringa*
Deutzia	*Tamarix*
Erica	
Escallonia	**Dome shapes**
Euonymus	*Buxus*
Fuchsia	*Calluna*
Genista	*Cotoneaster*
Hebe	*Daboecia*
Helianthemum	*Daphne*
Hydrangea	*Erica*
Hypericum	*Euonymus*
Kerria	*Gaultheria*
Lavatera	*Genista*
Lavandula	*Hebe*
Pachysandra	*Helianthemum*
Potentilla	*Hypericum*
Ribes	*Lavandula*
Skimmia	*Potentilla*
Spiraea	*Santolina*
Weigela	*Senecio*
Fountains	**Spiky plants**
Buddleja	*Cordyline*
Itea	*Phormium*
Kerria	*Yucca*

The design of a bed or border will be largely influenced by the shape and size of the garden as well as the effect you are trying to achieve. Unless you are aiming to create a very formal design, most borders look best with sweeping curves rather than fussy shapes or sharp corners and straight lines.

If there is space, you may allow some of the border to form a peninsula so that part of the garden is hidden from view. This achieves the effect of sub-dividing the design and creating a sense of mystery. However, in smaller gardens it is usually best to keep the centre of the plot uncluttered, either laid to lawn or some form of hard landscaping. The deeper the bed, the more plants it will be able to accommodate, but try to avoid very deep beds over 4m (13ft) as they will be more difficult to maintain. On the other hand, very narrow beds (less than 1m/3ft) limit the scope for planting design.

Layering borders

Most borders can be designed in layers. The back layer should comprise most of the tallest plants: wall shrubs and climbers. It is best to choose plants that will provide an attractive, if somewhat plain, backdrop when out of season, so that they can set off the plants in the foreground to better effect.

If the plants are being used to cover ugly walls, fences or other structures, try to choose ones with evergreen foliage so that the disguise lasts all year round. Back-of-the-border plants shouldn't spread too much, otherwise they will tend to dominate the design. Avoid plants that need a lot of maintenance because pruning, spraying and deadheading will be more difficult to carry out in this area.

The low-growing bright blue flowers and dark foliage of *Lithodora diffusa* combine with *Salix repens* for spectacular ground cover.

The front layer should comprise most of the smallest plants. The job of this layer of planting is to provide a transition from the border to the lawn or path that runs along the front. If you choose the right plants, they can also be used to cover up the shortcomings of more spectacular but short-lived displays provided by plants behind. The middle layer of plants should offer most of the seasonal highlights, with colourful flowers at different times of the year and dramatic autumn colours to sustain the display.

Choose a few taller plants to break the regimented effect and give the design a more natural feel. You may prefer to choose plants that flower together in the most spectacular way, or combine plants that flower at different times to create a longer period of interest.

If space is restricted, try to choose plants that offer at least two seasonal features, as well as plants that flower for weeks or months, rather than days, so that the border can continue looking good for a longer period of time.

The silvery leaves of the shrub *Elaeagnus* 'Quicksilver' provide a beautiful foil for the showy flowers of *Erysimum* 'Bowles' Mauve'.

Using shapes for structure

A border simply made up of layers can be attractive, but often the effect seems to lack impact and contrast. For this reason it a good idea to take some time to consider what role each individual plant is to play in the border so that you can combine them to their best effect.

A few will be focal points that act as anchors to the overall display; other plants will be there to provide a backdrop and act as a foil for the more showy plants. They also help define boundaries and are essential in-between fillers that add structure and are generally restful on the eye. You can only have so many drama queens that provide flower power, eye-catching foliage and colourful berries or winter stems in your border, so don't underestimate the value of the less showy shrubs.

Making shapes

Another factor essential to consider is how all the different shapes of your chosen plants will work with each other, as well as the overall appearance of the border. For example, tall and columnar shapes draw the eye like living exclamation marks, while low-spreading shapes have the opposite effect. Add a sense of movement and gracefulness to a static border using fountain shapes, such as grasses. Further back, try weeping shapes, which tend to harmonize with their neighbours, or spiky shapes for added drama.

To get an impression of how these different shapes will work together, draw an outline of the plants and then cut them out and move them around as if you were designing a stage set until you achieve a combination that appeals to you.

Use the lists on the previous page and the opposite page to help you decide which plants to try. Bear in mind that the plants will grow and change shape over time, so ensure that you give them enough space to spread and develop their true outline. If you don't want it to spread, choose plants that will take well to being pruned.

Year-round interest

Unless you are trying to create a seasonal splash, try to combine plants to provide interest throughout the year. In a small garden it is particularly important that every plant contributes to the display during more than one season. Also, make the most of available space by under-planting shrubs with ground cover and bulbs that flower at other times.

The easiest way to visualize how these different plants will work together is to make a calendar of the plants and their main periods of interest. Use coloured pencils to indicate when their decorative features are on show so that you can see how the colours combine. You can also check how they overlap to achieve continuity in the display.

When planning your beds and borders, try to include a few plants that will add a bold splash at certain times of the year so that the border

A mix of the pink *Rosa* 'Zéphirine Drouhin', the purple *Clematis* 'Lady Betty Balfour' and the large-leaved *Vitis coignetiae* grow happily together in a border.

Great border design combines plants of different heights, textures and colours together to make a pleasing, unifying whole.

design ebbs and flows with the seasons. Equally, don't overlook the value of evergreens and variegated evergreens, as these will provide reliable winter interest as well as a constant setting for the more flamboyant jewels that sparkle at other times.

Using climbers in borders

Climbers are versatile plants that can be used in all three layers of the border design. At the back, they are a space-saving way of covering walls and fences (*see also* page 66); when planted in the middle, they can be trained over structures to add height to borders (*see* page 70) as well as through established plants (*see* page 72). For the front of the border, there are many climbers that will scramble over the ground between shrubs to provide attractive, weed-suppressing groundcover (*see* page 74). Climbers grown across the ground are also a useful way of disguising eyesores such as manhole covers, immovable rubble and old tree stumps.

Climbers for all situations

There are climbers and wall shrubs that can be grown in nearly every position in the garden. They not only take up very little space, but allow you take advantage of vertical surfaces that would otherwise remain bare. Perhaps the most challenging aspect is walls that face north and east, which remain cool in summer and cold in winter – bitterly so if exposed to northerly gales. The soil is usually dry because the wall casts a rain shadow over the area from the majority of rain-bearing weather systems that move in from the south and west.

Fences are less of a problem because water percolates naturally through the soil under the fence. However, walls do have the advantage in that they store warmth from the sun and improve a microclimate for the climbers and wall shrubs attached to it. Walls are also permanent structures and can generally carry a greater weight, which can be an issue over time as the plant matures and grows.

Shrubs and climbers for a north aspect must be very tough, able to cope with constant shade as well as biting winds during the winter months. Easterly aspects get more sunlight, but the plants must be able to withstand rapid thaws on sunny mornings after a severe frost. Shrubs to try for these planting positions include Japanese flowering quince (*Chaenomeles*), climbing hydrangea (*Hydrangea petiolaris*), *Cotoneaster horizontalis*, *Garrya elliptica*, winter jasmine (*Jasminum nudiflorum*) and firethorn (*Pyracantha*), which are all as tough as old boots and provide valuable seasonal interest.

Climbers to try include varieties of *Clematis macropetala*, *C. montana*, *C. orientalis* or *C. tangutica*; ivy such as *Hedera colchica* 'Dentata Variegata'; and Virginia creeper (*Parthenocissus henryana*). Easterly vertical surfaces that get some sun can be improved with the planting of climbing and rambler roses such as 'Albertine', 'Madame Alfred Carrière' and 'Maigold', as well as *Schizophragma hydrangeoides* and *Vitis coignetiae*.

Seasonal sensations

Colourful	Hibiscus	Choisya
Acer	Hippophae	Convolvulus
Amelanchier	Magnolia	Elaeagnus
Azalea	Nandina	Escallonia
Berberis	Olearia	Euonymus
Camellia	Paeonia	Fatsia
Chaenomeles	Pieris	Griselinia
Cistus	Pyracantha	Hebe
Cornus	Rhododendron	Mahonia
Cotinus	Rhus	Myrtus
Cytisus	Romneya	Olearia
Enkianthus	Rosa	Osmanthus
Eucryphia		Pachysandra
Exochorda	**Evergreens**	Photinia
Forsythia	Aucuba	Pittosporum
Fothergilla	Azalea	Pyracantha
Genista	Camellia	Rhododendron
Hamamelis	Ceanothus	Skimmia

Shrubs and climbers in containers

Many shrubs and climbers make excellent container plants and can be used to transform a patio, decorate a bleak wall or extend the range of plants you can grow in your garden. However, it is essential to choose the right plants, container and compost (soil mix) to ensure success.

Why grow in containers?

Growing shrubs and climbers in permanent containers allows you to grow plants that otherwise would not thrive in your garden soil. For example, if your soil is chalky, you can grow acid-loving shrubs such as pieris and azaleas in containers filled with a lime-rich ericaceous compost (soil mix). Similarly, plants that are too tender to survive outside in the garden during the winter months can be grown in containers and given protection or moved somewhere frost-free during the coldest weather.

Growing in containers also allows you to keep your plants where they'll get noticed so that you are able to see their delicate or intricately marked foliage and flowers close up. In addition, shrubs in containers make excellent mobile focal points,

Containers allow you to combine shrubs for colour and texture, such as this lavender and *Euonymous fortunei* 'Emerald Gaiety'.

Fuschias cope with being potted very well and make beautiful container plants. Tender varieties can be overwintered inside.

as they can be moved into a prominent position when they are looking their best. Once their season has finished, place them in a less noticeable position. You can also use pots to grow living screens to provide natural cover and privacy on the patio when you need it. Container-grown plants are also ideal for taking the limelight away from fading bedding plants.

As the seasons and the sun's position changes, you can move your plant to a sunnier or shady spot to prolong its flowering.

Choosing suitable plants

Before you choose the plants for your containers, you need to consider where they are to be positioned. If exposed to wind and cold on a roof garden, say, your choice of suitable candidates will be different than for a pot destined for a sheltered corner on a sunny patio. Unless the container is to be moved under cover in winter, it is the conditions during the coldest months that are most crucial.

If cut to the base each year, *Sambucus racemosa* 'Plumosa Aurea' will produce a stunning display of colourful foliage.

All container plants need to be able to cope with a restricted root growth, periods of drought between waterings and exposure to wind. Choose something that will look good for most of the year, either with attractive evergreen foliage and a neat silhouette, or a deciduous candidate that has attractive bark or outline when out of leaf. Slow-growing Japanese acers are a good example: many have colourful emerging spring foliage that is decorative all summer, before the leaves turn brilliant shades in autumn and then fall to reveal an appealing tracery of stems that last all winter long.

Growing tips

If you want to grow shrubs and climbers in pots for a long period, the pot will need to be quite large. Choose one with a circumference of at least 45cm (18in), as this will hold a sufficient amount of compost (soil mix) to allow for good root development. It will also provide a buffer against problems such as winter cold and inconsistent watering and feeding. The container also needs to be frost proof and should have drainage holes. The drainage holes should be covered with crocks and then about 3 cm (1 in) of stones or other drainage material can be added on top. Fill up the rest of the pot with either a loam-based compost (soil mix), which is suitable for most shrubs and climbers, or a lime-rich ericaceous compost (soil mix) for acid-loving plants, such as rhododendrons and camellias.

Watering pots

Plants in containers tend to dry out much quicker than those planted in the garden. For this reason, watering is critical. Expect to water at least once a week in spring and summer (maybe daily during warm spells) and occasionally during dry spells at other times. Use collected rainwater for acid-loving plants if you live in hard-water areas.

It is important to remember that frequent watering will wash the plant food out of the soil and the plant will use up the nutrients in the

Shrubs benefit from being grown in pots if the garden soil is unsuitable. Acid-loving plants such as rhodedendrons (*above*) can be successfully grown in pots in ericaceous compost.

limited amount of soil you have in the pot quite quickly. For this reason, regular feeding is essential. Do this by either inserting slow-release fertilizer pellets, which will last a whole season, into the compost (soil mix) in spring or add liquid feed to its weekly watering.

Good plants to try

Shrubs for containers
Acer japonica
Aucuba
Azalea (acid-loving)
Camellia (acid-loving)
Choisya
Convolvulus cneorum
Elaeagnus
Euonymus
Hebe pinguifolia 'Pagei'
Hydrangea macrophylla
Lavandula
Magnolia stellata
Nandina domestica
Pieris (acid-loving)

Phlomis fruticosa
Phormium tenax
Rhododendron (acid-loving)
Rosa, miniature
Santolina chamaecyparissus
Skimmia japonica 'Rubella' (acid-loving)
Viburnum davidii
Vinca
Weigela florida

Climbers for containers
Clematis
Hedera
Jasminum officinale
Passiflora

Pot-grown plants have their growth curtailed. This *Cornus mas* 'Aureoelegantissima' could grow to 6m (20ft) in garden soil.

Fragrant walkways and entrances

Climbers and shrubs are an ideal way of adding colour and scent to the air around a path or entrance, making what would normally be a functional area into a delightful visual and aromatic experience.

Scented climbers

You can make garden visitors feel really welcome by planting the entrance with deliciously scented varieties of climbers. Like other parts of the garden, the plants you choose will depend on how much sun the area gets, as well as how exposed it is to buffeting winds. The growing space available as well as the size of the support are also important factors to consider.

In sunny positions, there are many options. An early sweet-vanilla fragrance can be provided by *Clematis armandii* cultivars such as 'Snowdrift' or 'Apple Blossom', followed by the familiar and appealing scent of summer jasmine, which will last for much of the summer. Another jasmine-scented climber for a well-lit spot is *Trachelospurmum jasminoides*, which bears its creamy flowers from mid-summer onwards. Alternatively, you could try the spicy vanilla fragrance of the chocolate vine (*Akebia quinata*), which thrives in full sun or partial shade, and bears its unusual maroon-coloured flowers during early summer.

If you have space, you could try the wonderful fresh aroma of *Wisteria sinensis* cultivars, which put on a spectacular display at the same time.

Scented roses

If roses are your preference, there are quite a number you could try. 'New Dawn' offers a summer-long display of pale pink flowers with a sweet aroma as well as attractive foliage, while 'Gloire de Dijon' is peachier in

While the vivid red flowers of *Rosa* 'American Pillar' attempt to hog the limelight, the delicate *Clematis* 'Alba Luxurians' manages to make a highlighting contrast.

Good plants to try

Scented climbers
Actinidia chinensis
Akebia quinata
Clematis (many species/cultivars)
Jasminum officinale
Lonicera (many species/cultivars)
Rosa (many species/cultivars)
Trachelospermum jasminoides
Wisteria

Fragrant shrubs
Ceanothus
Chimonanthus praecox
Choisya ternata
Clerodendrum trichotomum
Corylopsis pauciflora
Cytisus battandieri
Daphne x burkwoodii
Daphne mezereum
Daphne odora
Elaeagnus x ebbingei
Lonicera fragrantissima
Osmanthus delavayi
Ribes odoratum
Sarcococca confusa
Syringa vulgaris
Viburnum x bodnantense
Viburnum carlesii
Viburnum fragrans

sticky honeydew over everything – including paths, seats and doorsteps. For this reason, you might prefer to site the plants at the back of a nearby border instead.

Also, all scented flowers will tend to attract hoards of pollinating insects – including bees – that might become a nuisance if they are lured by plants near a doorway or window.

Fragrant shrubs all year

Bring in the New Year with style by planting the very sweetly scented, yellow-flowered *Chimonanthus praecox*, following on with *Daphne odora* and *Sarcococca confusa*. Later on, add a bit of spice and zest in mid-spring with the aptly named Mexican orange blossom (*Choisya ternata*), followed by the heady perfume of the lilac varieties. For a mid-summer treat, add the honey-scented *Ceanothus* 'Gloire de Versaille', with the pungent *Clerodendrum trichotomum* following on. Next, blend in the

Golden hop (*Humulus lupulus* 'Aureus') and honeysuckle (*Lornicera periclymenum*).

autumn-flowering and sweetly fragrant *Elaeagnus x ebbingei*, and complete the year with the delicious perfume of *Viburnum fragrans*.

colour and has a rich tea fragrance. However, you may prefer near-thornless roses such as the very fragrant 'Blush Rambler' or the creamy-white aromatic 'Madame Alfred Carrière', which will flower reliably in sun or shade.

Insects and bees

Honeysuckles are another option, offering their heady, intoxicating fragrance wherever they are grown. Try combining the early red- and purple-flowered 'Belgica' with the later purple, red and cream blooms of 'Serotina' for a continuous display from late spring to mid-autumn. Honeysuckles are prone to aphid attack and so tend to drip

During the summer, the fragrance of the roses tumbling over the archway will intermingle with the scent of newly mown grass, providing the perfect garden perfume.

Hedging and screening

There are a number of shrubs that make excellent hedging plants, and which you choose should depend on how big you want it to grow and the amount of time you want to spend keeping it in shape.

Choosing a hedge

The choice of hedging is far wider than the ubiquitous privet. You can choose from flowering, fragrant and fruiting ones, to dwarf, herb and topiary hedges. However, before you choose a variety that meets your requirements, you can reduce the options available by asking yourself the following three questions:

• Do you want a deciduous or evergreen hedge? Evergreen hedges provide constant cover throughout the year, but are more susceptible to winter cold and some soil-borne diseases. Deciduous hedges offer a changing backdrop and are more wildlife friendly.

Before purchasing plants, bear in mind that deciduous shrubs will drop their leaves in the autumn, so if

privacy is your main consideration for a hedge, you would be better off choosing an evergreen shrub, as they provide good all-year screening.

• Do you want a formal or flowering hedge? Formal hedges provide a neat backdrop and complete privacy, but require regular trimming. Informal flowering hedges require little maintenance, but take up more space and aren't as dense.

• Do you want it to grow quickly? Quick-growing hedges provide privacy in a short period of time but will require more trimming once they have reached the desired height.

You also need to consider whether you want a secure boundary or simply a decorative screen. Hedging plants that make dense growth and are covered in vicious thorns make the best impenetrable boundary hedges, while evergreen hedges are an excellent backdrop for other garden features. Available space will also affect the choice you make. Most hedges occupy a strip at least 60cm (2ft) wide, while a few, including

A formal beech (*Fagus sylvatica*) hedge makes a neat garden boundary. Beech is a slow-growing plant and needs little attention.

beech and privet, can be kept half this width with regular trimming. Also consider that evergreen hedges tend to cast deep shade so that few plants will grow at the base on the north-facing side.

Wildlife hedges

Hedges can provide nesting and roosting sites for birds, and their flowers and berries are vital food sources for insects and butterflies.

Although all hedges offer some benefit to garden birds and other wildlife, a mixture of deciduous species, such as beech, hawthorn, hazel, holly and hornbeam, would be a good choice. Not only will they provide shelter and safe breeding sites, but if you get the mixture right, the hedge can also offer a year-

Buying hedging

Deciduous hedging plants are usually sold as barerooted plants in bundles, while evergreen varieties are available as young plants in small pots. Even though you can get much larger plants in containers, you will save a lot of money if you buy smaller ones. Such plants, about 30–45cm (12–18in) high, will establish themselves more quickly and soon catch up with the larger versions. Shop around, as prices can vary considerably between suppliers.

Low-growing hedges can be successfully made out of lavender bushes. Here, two rows of lavender border a narrow path. As you brush past, the aroma is spectacular.

Good plants to try

Evergreen hedges	Deciduous hedges	Flowering hedges	Hedges in shade
Aucuba japonica 'Variegata'	*Berberis thunbergii*	*Camellia x williamsii*	*Aucuba japonica* 'Variegata'
Berberis darwinii	*Carpinus betulus*	*Chaenomeles japonica*	*Buxus sempervirens*
Buxus sempervirens	*Chaenomeles japonica*	*Escallonia rubra* var. *macrantha*	*Chaenomeles japonica*
Chamaecyparis lawsoniana	*Corylus maxima* 'Purpurea'	*Forsythia x intermedia*	*Euonymus japonicus*
Elaeagnus pungens	*Crataegus monogyna*	*Fuchsia magellanica*	*Ilex aquifolium*
Escallonia rubra var. *macrantha*	*Fagus sylvatica*	*Hebe pinguifolia*	*Lonicera nitida*
Griselinia littorialis	*Forsythia x intermedia*	*Lavandula*	*Taxus baccata*
Hebe pinguifolia	*Fuchsia magellanica*	*Philadelphus coronarius*	*Viburnum tinus*
Lavandula	*Ligustrum ovalifolium*	*Potentilla fruticosa*	
Lonicera nitida	*Philadelphus coronarius*	*Pyracantha rogersiana*	**Thorny hedges**
Olearia x haastii	*Potentilla fruticosa*	*Ribes sanguineum*	*Berberis darwinii*
Prunus laurocerasus	*Ribes sanguineum*	*Rosa rugosa*	*Berberis thunbergii*
Pyracantha rogersiana	*Rosa rugosa*	*Weigela florida*	*Crataegus monogyna*
Taxus baccata	*Weigela florida*		*Olearia x haastii*
Thuja plicata			*Pyracantha rogersiana*
Viburnum tinus			

round larder of food for birds, butterflies and other beneficial insects looking for sustenance.

Garden dividers

Hedges can also be used to subdivide a garden or provide a neat edging to beds and borders. Although any type of hedge can be used in a large garden, for small gardens slow-growing, dwarf forms are best, such as the evergreen box, grey-leaved flowering lavender, potentilla, hebe and the red-leaved *Berberis thunbergii* 'Atropurpurea Nana'.

Planting hedges

Often, hedges are expected to thrive when planted in poor soil – or even subsoil dug up during house construction or renovation. Many hedges are planted too close to, or underneath, trees, making it difficult for them to get their fair share of nutrients from the soil as they compete with larger roots.

Preferably, hedges should be planted in spring or autumn when the plants are resting. They can be planted in exactly the same way as

PLANTING HEDGES

1 Start by digging a trench where you wish to plant the hedge. Turn over the soil and dig in some manure or compost (soil mix).

2 Fix a line taut across the centre of the trench and lay out the plants at regular intervals so they have equal growing space.

3 Remove the plants from their pots and position them in the trench, checking that they are accurately spaced.

4 Fill in the trench, firming the soil around each plant. Water throughly and mulch with well-rotted organic matter.

shrubs, but it is easier to excavate a trench along the line of the hedge, rather than digging individual planting holes.

The autumn before planting, dig a strip 60–90cm (2–3ft) wide, double-digging down its entire length. For less vigorous hedges and step-over hedges, you can get away with single digging. Plant each hedging plant as you would for shrubs, using a taut line as a guide to keep the hedge straight.

Hedges can be planted in single or staggered double rows. Unless you want a very thick, impenetrable hedge for security reasons, a single row should be sufficient. Planting distances depend on the vigour of your chosen hedge (*see* Hedge planting distances chart, below).

High or low maintenance?
Another essential consideration is how much time you are prepared to spend on keeping your hedge looking good. Formal hedges will need to be pruned several times a year if they are to remain attractive.

If you prefer a low-maintenance option, you would do better if you went for an informal, more natural-looking hedge. For the more ambitious gardener, topiary hedges look fantastic, but you really must be realistic. Are your pruning and trimming skills up to it?

Hedges should be cut in mid-summer and mid-winter, although if they need a little tidying up in between seasons, you can do this safely at any time. If more severe pruning is required, it is best done in late autumn.

The most common mistake when pruning is not cutting the plant back far enough, or cutting it too narrow at the base. This is especially true for young, growing plants. This condition becomes worse as the top grows and shades the lower portions. Cutting back is the only solution.

When to prune evergreen hedges

Name	when to prune
Berberis	late spring
Buxus sempervirens	early summer
Calluna	after flowering
Chamaecyparis lawsoniana	early summer and early autumn
Erica	after flowering
Escallonia	early summer
Euonymus	mid-summer
Griselinia	early summer
Ilex	mid-summer
Lavandula	early autumn
Ligustrum	late spring and late summer
Lonicera nitida	early summer
Prunus lusitanica	early summer
Rosmarinus	late-summer
Taxus	mid-summer
Thuja	mid-summer
x Cupressocyparis leylandii	early summer

Pruning and feeding your hedge
If you begin trimming hedges when they are first planted, they will respond well to shaping and training. Cut a few centimetres off the top of a hedge plant as soon as it has been planted to help form healthy, bushy plants. Try to shape the hedge so that it is wider at the bottom than it is at the top. This will allow sunlight to reach the lower leaves. Follow the steps on the right for maintaining hedges – these instructions will ensure you get an even-looking side, top and edge to your hedge.

Fast-growing hedges may require trimming two or three times a season to keep their shape. It is unwise to allow a hedge to grow rapidly to its desired height before you prune, as it will develop a thick top and open sides.

Prune your hedge during the active growing season, but only give it a light trimming at the end of the

Hedge planting distances

Deciduous hedges	vigour	planting distance
Beech	medium	60cm (2ft)
Hawthorn	medium	30cm (1ft)
Hornbeam	medium	45cm (18in)
Privet	high	25cm (10in)
Ribes	medium	45cm (18in)
Rose	medium	45cm (18in)
Evergreen hedges	**vigour**	**planting distance**
Berberis	medium	45cm (18in)
Box	low	25cm (10in)
Elaeagnus	low	45cm (18in)
Escallonia	medium	45cm (18in)
Holly	low	45cm (18in)
Lavender	low	30cm (1ft)
Laurel	medium	45cm (18in)
Lawson's cypress	high	45cm (18in)
Leyland cypress	high	60cm (2ft)
Photinia	medium	45cm (18in)
Portugal laurel	medium	45cm (18in)
Western red cedar	medium	45cm (18in)
Yew	low	45cm (18in)

growing season to keep your hedge looking good throughout the winter months. Evergreen hedges, such as juniper and cypress, should never be trimmed below the foliage because they will not grow back, so take care and clip only a few inches off the previous year's growth.

It should also be remembered that although your hedge may look like a room-divider or a screen, it is also a living shrub. Your hedge should be fed at least once a year, preferably in the early spring. Scatter the fertilizer along both sides of the hedge and work it well into the soil with a fork. A layer of mulch will help keep weeds at bay.

Good neighbours

The final factor to take into consideration when you are choosing a hedge is to take great care about where you site it. Will your hedge grow so big that it affects your neighbour's view, as well as their garden's light and shade? Do your research first, so you don't end up in a legal dispute, as a few unhappy owners of fast-growing *Leylandii* hedges have.

When buying your shrubs, choose those that will grow to the desired height – and no further. Planting a tall-maturing shrub where a short, informal hedge is desired creates unnecessary work.

Hedging alternatives

A solid barrier, such as a wall or fence, may seem like a good way to protect an exposed garden, but the wind is simply deflected over the top, creating damaging turbulence on the side that you are trying to protect. Hedges make excellent windbreaks because they filter the wind, rather than block it. However, you can also use other shrubs to achieve the same effect. Try tough, fast-growing shrubs such as berberis, viburnum, cotoneaster and elaeagnus in a mixed planting for a small garden, or combine un-pruned hedging plants such as laurel, photinia, holly and escallonia if there is enough space.

MAINTAINING HEDGES

1 Before you start trimming the hedge, lay down a cloth or plastic sheet under the area to make gathering up the clippings easier.

2 If you are using shears to trim the hedge, keep the blades flat against the plane of the hedge to achieve an even cut.

3 The top of a formal hedge looks neater if it is regularly trimmed flat. Stretch string against two poles to get an even cutting guide.

4 When cutting the top of a hedge, keep the blades flat. If it is a tall hedge, you will probably need steps to reach the top.

5 The job is done much quicker if you use a power trimmer – but things can go wrong much quicker, too. Always mind the cord.

6 Untidy growth on informal hedges is easier to trim to shape using secateurs (pruners). Large-leaved hedges are pruned this way.

Covering walls and fences

Climbers are an obvious choice for covering all types of vertical surfaces, from boundary fences to garage walls, but there are several wall shrubs that are worth considering, too.

Wall shrub or climber?

There are a number of factors to consider when choosing what to plant next to a particular wall or fence. The first is how much available space you have. Climbers generally require less border space than wall shrubs, but usually need a lot more wall space. So, for example, if you have a border under a window, a wall shrub would probably be the best option. But if you want to cover a large fence or wall in just a few seasons, there are quick-growing climbers that will fit the bill.

Some climbers also need to be given support, at least until they get established, whereas wall shrubs gradually cover the space with a framework of woody branches that are completely self-supporting. Different climbers hold on in

The combination of boundaries – the wooden fence supported on a low brick wall – is greatly softened in visual effect by an escallonia flowering hedge growing through it. The density of the hedge provides privacy and security.

different ways (*see* How climbers climb box, below). Twining climbers, such as the chocolate vine, need a support all the way up the vertical surface being covered, while self-clinging climbers, such as ivies, can scramble up the smoothest of surfaces without assistance.

Maintenance time can also vary. Most wall shrubs and some climbers need to be pruned annually to keep them neat and flowering well. If you want to avoid this, choose an easy-care variety. Furthermore, vigorous climbers that outgrow their allotted space may need trimming several times a year to keep them within bounds, so bear this in mind before you plant.

Planting next to walls and fences

The microclimate next to a vertical surface can be completely different to the surrounding garden, which offers a unique combination of challenges and opportunities. For

example, against a sheltered, south-facing wall you will be able to grow borderline hardy plants that wouldn't survive elsewhere. But to thrive, they will need to be able to cope with scorching summer days and water

Climbing roses not only cover the walls well, but have the added bonus of lovely fragrance.

How climbers climb

Different climbers cling on to their support in various ways. Some are self-clinging and are able to scramble up a vertical surface without any assistance. Ivies and climbing hydrangeas, for example, hold on to the wall or fence using modified roots along their stems that attach themselves to rough surfaces such as brick or wood. A few climbers, such as Virginia creeper, produce tiny suckers that will stick to any surface – even glass. Most climbers climb by twining stems (e.g. wisteria), leaf stalks (e.g. clematis) or tendrils (e.g. sweet peas) that literally wrap themselves around a support as the plant grows upwards.

Good plants to try for different aspects

South-facing aspect	North-facing aspect	East- or west-facing aspects
Acacia dealbata	Chaenomeles	Actinidia chinensis
Actinidia kolomikta	Clematis montana	Escallonia
Campsis grandiflora	Cotoneaster horizontalis	Holboellia coriacea
Carpenteria californica	Garrya elliptica	Humulus lupulus
Ceanothus	Hedera helix	Leptospermum
Cytisus battandieri	Hydrangea petiolaris	scoparium
Eccremocarpus scaber	Jasminum nudiflorum	Lonicera x tellmanniana
Fremontodendron	Parthenocissus	Myrtus communis
Hibiscus syriacus	Pyracantha	Phygelius capensis
Jasminum officinale		Ribes speciosum
Passiflora caerulea		Solanum crispum
Sollya heterophylla		Trachelospermum
Wisteria floribunda		jasminoides
		Vitis vinifera

Climbers and shrubs can help to soften the edges of brickwork and take the angularity away from modern structures.

shortages. On the other hand, plants on a north-facing wall will face the challenge offered by constant shade, cooler summers and colder winters than will be found in nearby borders.

Make sure you treat wooden fences and supports with preservative and repair loose mortar on walls before planting your chosen climber or wall shrub. Also, put up any supporting trellis, wires or netting at this stage. The soil at the base of walls and fences is usually dry and impoverished, so it needs to be improved before you plant by digging in plenty of well-rotted organic matter.

Making a feature

Although the standard advice is to put up trellis or wires as a support for climbers so that the trained plants eventually provide a complete cover-up, an alternative method is to use an attractively shaped trellis, such as a perspective panel, that creates the illusion of a tunnel. You can then train the climber tightly to the frame so that the overall shape is maintained. Not only is the trellis attractive in its own right, but the

eventual effect will be a living replica of the trellis and it will form an unusual and attractive garden feature all year round. This method works particularly well with small-leaved evergreen climbers such as ivies, and wall shrubs such as firethorns (Pyracantha). On a larger

scale, you can use twining climbers such as wisteria or a large-leaved ivy.

Another option is to create the pattern yourself using wires, so that the feature you design will fit the available space exactly. You can also design your structure to complement an existing feature in the architecture of the house or in a neighbouring part of the garden – helping to provide a linking theme to the garden's overall design.

Once established, most climbing roses like nothing better than to be given free rein over structures, weaving themselves in and out to face the sun.

Pergolas and arches

These structures make stunning garden features when covered in colourful climbers – and also provide the practical benefits of shade and privacy.

Using pergolas and arches

Pergolas and arches can be used in a variety of ways around the garden. Pergolas are ideal for providing a secluded hideaway halfway down the garden, or they can be combined with a sunny patio to create a shady retreat on hot sunny days.

Despite their size, they are also a handy design device for use in smaller gardens, where they can be positioned at an angle in a far corner to help disguise the boundary and create the illusion that the garden is bigger than it really is.

Arches have even more uses. Apart from framing an entrance over a gate or at the start of a garden path, they can also be used to highlight a particular feature, such as a bird bath or urn, to dramatically increase its impact. Similarly, if you have a particularly interesting view from your garden, for example an attractive church steeple, a stream or beautiful countryside, bring it to the attention of visitors by framing with an arch. In a small garden, an arch covered in scented climbers or surrounded by scented plants can be

used to create an intimate and intoxicating atmosphere around a garden bench.

Arches are also ideal for linking different elements within a garden together. For example, two borders separated by a path become a single feature with a central point of focus when linked by an arch. If you have an uninspiring straight path in your garden, add interest by spacing several identical arches at intervals. Cover them with the same climber and they will seem as one, like an old-fashioned arbour.

Good plants to try

Rambler roses
'Albéric Barbier'
'Albertine'
'American Pillar'
'Emily Gray'
'Rambling Rector'
'Veilchenblau'

Climbing roses
'Bantry Bay'
'Climbing Iceberg'
'Gloire de Dijon'
'Guinée'
'Madame Alfred Carrière'
'Madame Grégoire Staechelin'
'Mermaid'
'Zéphirine Drouhin' (thornless)

MAKING A HOOP FOR CLIMBERS

1 In early spring, make a series of hoops from pliable hazel (*Corylus avellana*) and push each end firmly into the ground.

2 As you bend the hazel, take care that you do not force the curve too sharply. If you do, the hazel might snap.

3 Tie in the long shoots of the climber (a climbing rose is shown here) along the length of the hoop.

4 The leaves of the plant will turn to face the light and new buds will be produced on the upper edges of the curved stems.

5 The plant will have filled out and produced blooms by mid-summer. Remove some of the older stems and tie in new ones annually.

GROWING CLIMBERS UP A TRIPOD

1 Dig a hole big enough to contain the roots of the climber. Position the plant in front of the tripod, not inside.

2 Fan out the stems of the plant and tie them in to the lowest rungs of the tripod, spreading them out to get an even coverage. Water well.

3 In another season the tripod will be covered in foliage and blooms. The structure will also weather down and look less obvious.

Plants for pergolas and arches

All but the biggest and most vigorous climbers can be used to cover pergolas and arches. However, it should be remembered that although leafy growth overhead will provide shade on sunny days, at other times the area may seem gloomy, and persistent drips falling on you after a rain shower can be a big nuisance.

Some climbers such as honeysuckle should be avoided as they are prone to pests that exude honeydew as they feed, resulting in everything underneath being covered with a sticky coating.

You can create the impression that a pergola is completely covered with climbers by training them up and over the outside edges, but leaving the hidden central portion free. Children will love being able to hide in it. Alternatively, you could grow smaller climbers that just cover the uprights and allow a glimpse inside.

The plants you select are a matter of choice and preference, but you do need to consider when you are most likely to use or view the structure, so that the climber is looking its best at that time. You can also combine different varieties to double the impact or plant pairs of plants that flower at different times in order to extend the show.

Temporary cover

When you first put up a pergola or arch, you will have to wait several seasons before the climbers provide dense cover. During this interim period, use quick-growing annual climbers to decorate the structure. Plants you could try include the cup-and-saucer plant (*Cobaea scandens*), sweet peas (*Lathyrus odoratus*) or black-eyed Susan (*Thunbergia alata*). If you have sited your structure in a sheltered spot, have a go with Chilean glory flower (*Eccremocarpus scaber*).

A welcome retreat from the sun is achieved by including the *Vitis vinefera* 'Purpurea' for foliage and grapes at the end of autumn and *Clematis montana* for colour in spring and early summer.

Adding height to borders

Whether you are planting a new garden or enhancing a more established one, simple garden structures, such as posts, obelisks and tripods, can add height and instant interest to borders – and are also ideal for transforming lifeless displays in tired borders.

Lifting displays

Although shrubs can grow to significant heights, sometimes borders need a little extra something to rejuvenate their appearance. This is where climbers show their true value: they can be used to either twine around existing shrubs, add colour when evergreens are not flowering, or provide structure within the garden.

As with trees and other tall focal points, structures have an important impact on the way a garden is viewed, instantly altering the garden's perspective.

Annual and perennial climbers can also be used to cloak obelisks, posts and tripods to obscure an

Essential maintenance

The main drawback to growing climbers in the middle or the back of a border is that access for essential maintenance can often be made difficult. For example, repeat-flowering roses need to be pruned and long shoots will need tying in to the support. Clematis may need pruning, depending on the variety you choose, and any wayward stems should be removed or tied in periodically throughout the growing season. Self-clinging ivies are the exception to this rule, as they require attention only when they start to outgrow their allotted space.

unattractive sight, such as a bed awaiting planting or one undergoing renovation. Even eyesore garden items – compost bins, water butts, oil storage tanks and the like – can be cunningly concealed with climber-clad structures.

When carefully sited, these structures can help to create a sense of intrigue, enticing the visitor to explore further. By combining these features with sweeping paths and peninsular borders, you can emphasize the effect, introducing a welcome sense of movement and purpose to the design.

The advantage of growing climbers up a pergola is that you can site the structure wherever you choose in your garden, ensuring that it has maximum impact.

Scrambling evergreen *Solanum jasminoides* 'Album' bears star-shaped white flowers.

The vigorous climber *Clematis* 'Lasurstern' is frost hardy. In summer it produces beautiful lavender-blue single flowers.

Simple posts can be used singly or in pairs, like sentries on duty at the entrance to the garden or at the end of a path, reinforcing the starting point or a change in direction. Further back in the border, a climber-clad post will draw the eye, providing height, colour and a change in pace. Several at intervals in a large border pull the viewer along as the eyes move from one vertical element to the next.

In a large garden, you can reinforce the sense of formality by using wrought-iron obelisks, which have the added advantage of providing a striking appearance even

Good plants to try

Climbing roses for pillars
'Aloha'
'Compassion'
'Golden Showers'
'Handel'
'Madame Alfred Carrière'
'New Dawn'
'Zéphirine Drouhin'

after the climber has retreated from view for the winter months.

At the back of a border, posts can be linked with lengths of rope to form a traditional colonnade. Once trained with climbers, the loops of rope will become festooned with flowers during the summer but also provide a strong, decorative backdrop at other times.

An even more powerful effect can be created by linking the posts with timber, rather like a one-dimensional pergola. This produces a look that can be relaxed and rustic or more ornate and regimented, depending on the style of the structure and the plants you use to decorate it.

Selecting a climber

If you are looking for a cheap and cheerful transformation, there are several vigorous annual climbers that will give any lacklustre border a makeover for the price of a packet of seeds. Try sweet peas (*Lathyrus odoratus*), black-eyed Susan

(*Thunbergia alata*), morning glory (*Convolvulus major*), canary creeper (*Tropaeolum canariensis*) or annual hop (*Humulus japonicus*).

For a permanent display, choose a climber that will not get too big. The variegated forms of common ivy (*Hedera helix*) provide year-round appeal, while flower power can be supplied by *Clematis alpina* or *C. macropetala* early in the season, with *C.* 'Marie Boisselot' and *C.* 'Niobe' later on. Summer jasmine (*Jasminum officinale*) should be close to the patio or seating area where you can appreciate the heady scent.

Climbing roses are useful in the middle or back of the border. Choose repeat-flowering varieties, such as 'Paul's Scarlet Climber', 'Handel', 'Compassion' and 'Madame Alfred Carrière'. For autumn tints, try Virginia creeper (*Parthenocissus quinquefolia*) and the early summer flowering potato vine (*Solanum jasminoides* 'Album'), which will continue on until early winter.

Shrubs are the backbone of a border and here you can see how the plants are positioned higher at the back and trail down to the lawn, making a beautiful vista along the path.

Combining climbers

Climbers are very sociable plants. They combine just as well with each other as they do with shrubs and hedges, which helps create an eye-catching display as well as extending the flowering season.

Choosing a perfect partner

When selecting a climber to combine with another plant, it is essential that you match the vigour of the climber with the host or companion plant you have in mind. If it is too vigorous, the climber will soon swamp its partner and need regular cutting back, but if it is not vigorous enough, the climber will never put on a decent show and may disappear without trace. Also bear in mind the climber's maintenance requirements. For example, it is a good idea to pair clematis that have the same pruning requirements, so they can be tackled at the same time and in the same way. Similarly, if you are planning to plant a clematis to scramble through a tall, inaccessible tree, choose one that needs the minimum of pruning.

Clematis are probably the most versatile climbers, combining well with both climbing and rambler roses as well as honeysuckles and other climbers. You can pair up clematis that will bloom at the same time for added impact or create a succession of colour by combining climbers with overlapping flowering periods. Flowers that are produced at the same time should blend or contrast, but not clash in colour. Of course, this is a matter of personal preference, so choose colour combinations that you find pleasing to the eye, but bear in mind how scented plants will intermingle.

On a large structure, such as a pergola, you could combine several different plants and varieties to provide colour and interest for much of the year. You can even achieve this with clematis alone (see Clematis all year box, below). Alternatively, you could plan the display so that it is at its best when you are most likely to be in the garden – during the summer and Easter holidays, for example.

In a shady spot, try combining a variegated ivy, such as *Hedera helix* 'Goldheart' or *H. colchica* 'Paddy's Pride', for year-round interest, with a shade-tolerant flowering climber, such as *Jasminum nudiflorum* (winter jasmine), which will combine to give an excellent winter display. For summer flowers, you could add a rose or vigorous clematis that can cope with partial shade.

Getting quick results

Climbers are an excellent way to improve the look of a new garden and to cover eyesores in an

GROWING A CLIMBER THOUGH A SHRUB

1 Choose a shrub that flowers at a different time to the climber. Here, a relatively low *Salix helvetica* will be planted with *Clematis alpina*.

2 Next to the shrub, start digging a planting area and add some well-rotted manure. For clematis, plant on the shady side of the shrub.

3 Use a cane to train the clematis into the shrub (remove when established). Spread the climber's shoots through the shrub's foliage.

4 Once planted, give both shrub and climber a good watering. Keep an eye on the climber's watering needs until it is established.

> ## Clematis all year
>
> **Winter into spring**: *Clematis alpina, C. armandii* and *C. macropetala*
> **Spring into summer**: *Clematis montana* and early-flowering hybrids
> **Summer into autumn**: *Clematis orientalis, C. tangutica, C. viticella* and large-flowered hybrids
> **Autumn into winter**: late-flowering hybrids and *Clematis cirrhosa*.

Clematis climbing partners

Try combining the following clematis with roses for beautiful effects:
C. 'Mrs Cholmondeley', which bears chocolate-centred, lavender-blue flowers (late spring–early summer), with R. 'New Dawn', which produces fragrant, double, pink flowers (early summer–early autumn). C. 'Marie Boisselot', which bears white flowers with golden centres (mid-summer–early autumn), with R. 'Madame Alfred Carrière' for its fragrant, double, pink-flushed white flowers from (mid-summer–early autumn). C. 'Niobe', which produces golden-centred, dark ruby-red flowers (mid-summer–early autumn) in combination with R. 'Zéphirine Drouhin', which has strongly fragrant, double, deep pink flowers (mid-summer–early autumn). C. 'Jackmanii Superba', which offers red-flushed, dark purple flowers with cream-coloured centres (mid-summer–early autumn), with R. 'Golden Showers', adding double, rich-yellow flowers (mid-summer–early autumn). C. 'Gipsy Queen', which bears red-centred, bright purple flowers (mid-summer–early autumn), alongside R. 'Climbing Iceberg', with its double, white flowers from (mid-summer–early autumn). C. 'Perle d'Azur', with yellow-centred, lilac-blue flowers (mid-summer–early autumn), paired with C. 'Purpurea Plena Elegans', which bears semi-double, reddish-purple flowers (mid-summer–early autumn).

established one. Fast-growing climbers will soon cover fence panels and walls with a cloak of foliage that softens the appearance and helps disguise the line of a boundary. In a small garden this will help to create the illusion of space, while in a larger one the effect can be the opposite – giving an area a sense of seclusion. Honeysuckles, such as 'Belgica' and 'Serotina', with their fragrant, tubular, reddish-purple flowers, are always worth considering, as are the vigorous clematis, such as C. montana and C. tangutica, which never disappoint with their masses of lantern-like flowers. Then there are the repeat-flowering climbing roses, such as Rosa 'Aloha', with its large, double, fragrant, rose-pink flowers; the double, rich-yellow blooms of 'Golden Showers'; and 'New Dawn', which bears fragrant, double, pink flowers in clusters. All bloom from mid-summer onwards.

Annual climbers are another option for small walls and garden dividers, especially if you are on a tight budget. They are an ideal stop-gap measure to provide colour and interest while slower-growing, more permanent climbers are getting established. Sow them under cover in the greenhouse, conservatory or kitchen windowsill to give them an early start or buy young plants in pots from garden centres in late spring. Nasturtiums are old favourites that are now back in vogue. The latest varieties offer more refined colour schemes than their rather garish predecessors. The related Canary creeper (Topaeolum peregrinum) is also worth a try for its attractive foliage and brilliant yellow, tubular flowers produced from mid-summer onwards.

The beautiful *Clematis* 'Marie Boisselot' combines with a small apple tree to provide a stunning display from early summer to late autumn.

Ground cover, edging and banks

Low-growing, well-behaved shrubs and some climbers are ideal for growing under the skirt of larger shrubs and trees to provide a weed-suppressing carpet of attractive foliage and colourful flowers. They are also useful elsewhere in the garden and for planting up problem areas where little else will grow.

What makes good ground cover?

A good ground cover shrub should be easy to look after, have a ground-hugging, uniform habit and should be quick to establish after planting. It should form a dense carpet of foliage over the ground, so there is no space for the weeds to grow. On the other hand, it should not be too invasive otherwise it will become the weed rather than the weed suppressor. Most good ground cover plants are evergreen and have attractive foliage, providing year-round cover, but there are one or two very good deciduous candidates worth considering. Ideally, the ground cover should bear colourful flowers, followed by berries as well as autumn and winter colour – but that's probably asking too much!

Genista lydia

Vinca minor 'Aureovariegata'

There are many shrubs and climbers recommended in books and catalogues for use as ground cover, but few actually make the grade in most situations. Ground cover roses are a good example. Although they do sprawl attractively across the ground and put on an excellent show during early summer, they don't produce enough leaf cover early in the season to smother the first flush of weed growth – and weeding between the thorny stems is a practical impossibility.

Using ground cover plants

While ground cover plants are ideal for filling in the gaps between large shrubs and trees, while providing a carpet of attractive foliage and suppressing weeds, they can also be used in other ways around the garden. Problem areas, such as narrow borders along the side of the house or under windows can be filled with suitable ground cover, as can that difficult-to-plant strip along evergreen hedges, where the soil is dry and there is almost constant shade. Similarly, some ground cover plants are an ideal way of covering awkward banks that would be difficult, if not dangerous, to mow if covered in grass. They can also be used to hide eyesores, such as manhole covers, ugly tree stumps, the footings of dismantled walls and old buildings that are too difficult to remove.

In the centre of the garden, ground cover plants make an easy-care alternative to grass, which can be particularly useful in areas that are well away from the main lawn or even in the front garden. Here, they will be on display, so you will need to choose plants that put on a show.

Planting ground cover

When you use plants as ground cover, plant them closer together than is usually recommended. This will ensure a complete cover more quickly, although it will cost more to achieve. The best time to plant is autumn or spring, so the plants will establish quickly. Ideally, plant through a sheet of landscape fabric into weed-free soil to prevent any new weeds appearing until the plants have carpeted the soil.

Budget ideas

Planting ground cover on any scale requires a great number of plants. As most ground cover plantings use swathes of the same variety, you can save money by propagating your own plants or buying in bulk direct from the grower.

Propagating plants doesn't mean waiting for years to get an effective cover on the ground, as many of the shrubs and climbers recommended here produce quick results if planted slightly closer.

If you know what type of ground cover you want, you could buy a large, well-established plant and divide it into many others. For example a 2-litre (3½ pint) pot of a periwinkle, such as *Vinca minor* 'Gertrude Jekyll', could yield up to five plants, while a 5-litre (9-pint) pot could produce ten new plants. Look for a stock plant that is well established in the pot and which has plenty of shoots and buds.

Other ground cover shrubs and climbers are easier to propagate from cuttings. Evergreen shrubs such as *Euonymus fortunei* 'Emerald 'n' Gold', conifers such as *Juniperus* x *media* 'Pfitzeriana Aurea' and climbers such as *Hedera helix* and its cultivars can all be increased easily in this way.

It is also worth visiting nurseries in your area or going to gardening shows to see if they will supply plants in bulk at a reduced cost. Small plants, known as liners, will be a fraction of the cost of a potted plant from the garden centre and will establish quicker. If you want larger plants, some nurseries will offer these at wholesale prices.

Using climbers as ground cover

Many climbers are as happy scrambling over the ground between shrubs and trees as they are covering walls and fences. If you match the vigour of the climber to the space available, it will also be largely maintenance free – requiring no tying in, pruning or training.

For example, in a large space between trees, a variety of the vigorous *Clematis montana* or a honeysuckle, such as 'Halliana', would be ideal. If the space is more restricted, for example in a shrubbery, then ornamental ivies or a less vigorous large-flowered clematis such as 'Lasurstern' or 'Perle d'Azur' would suit. Between flowering shrubs such as roses, choose a groundcover climber that will flower in early spring before the roses open. This will extend the season of

interest. Alternatively, choose a variety in a complementary colour that will bloom at the same time as the roses to create a really stunning floral display.

Climbers are often the best option for covering steep slopes or narrow borders at the base of a wall. The climber can be planted in the most favourable position at the top of the slope or at one end of the wall and allowed to cover the ground with its trailing stems. Ornamental vines such as the Boston Ivy (*Parthenocissus tricuspidata* 'Veitchii') will cover slopes with a neat bed of evergreen foliage, while varieties of the Alpine clematis look delightful scrambling along the front of a wall.

Good plants to try

Under shrubs
Clematis macropetala (cultivars)
Cotoneaster dammeri
Euonymus fortunei (varieties)
Gaultheria procumbens – acid-loving
Hebe pinguifolia 'Pagei'
Hedera colchica (varieties)
Hedera helix (varieties)
Stephanandra incisa 'Crispa'
Vinca major (varieties)
Vinca minor (varieties)

Under trees
Berberis thunbergii 'Atropurpurea Nana'
Clematis montana (varieties)
Cotoneaster conspicuus 'Coral Beauty'
Cotoneaster salicifolius 'Gnom'
Euonymus fortunei (varieties)
Hedera colchica (varieties)
Hedera helix (varieties)
Hypericum calycinum
Rubus cockburnianus
Santolina chamaecyparissus (varieties)

Over sunny banks
Calluna vulgaris (varieties) – acid-loving
Ceanothus thyrsiflorus 'Repens'
Eccremocarpus scaber
Erica carnea (varieties) – acid-loving
Genista lydia

Hedera colchica (varieties)
Hedera colchica (varieties)
Hedera helix (varieties)
Rubus cockburnianus
Santolina chamaecyparissus (varieties)
Tropaeolum tuberosum

Alternative to lawns
Calluna vulgaris (varieties)
Erica carnea (varieties)
Hedera helix (varieties)
Vinca major (varieties)
Vinca minor (varieties)

Hiding eyesores
Clematis macropetala (varieties)
Cotoneaster conspicuus 'Coral Beauty'
Cotoneaster horizontalis
Cotoneaster salicifolia 'Gnom'
Euonymus fortunei (varieties)
Humulus lupulus
Vitis coignetiae

In deep shade
Euonymus fortunei (varieties)
Hedera colchica (varieties)
Hedera helix (varieties)
Lonicera pileata
Pachysandra terminalis
Sarcococca hookeriana var. *humilis*
Vinca major (varieties)

Conservatory plants

A conservatory offers you the opportunity to grow a wide range of plants that would not thrive outside in the garden or in the relative gloom of indoor rooms.

Choosing the right plants

Many tropical and Mediterranean plants will appreciate the good light levels and high temperatures found in most conservatories. However, unless dedicated to plant raising, the conditions within the conservatory are usually a compromise between the needs of the plants and those of the owners.

For example, if you want to use your conservatory as an extension of the house and fill it with furniture and fabrics, you will not be able to provide the high humidity levels demanded by many tropical plants. Instead, you will have to confine your choice to climbers such as passion flowers, plumbago and

monstera, as well as flowering shrubs such as brugmansia and hibiscus, which can cope with the lower air-moisture levels and fluctuating temperatures in a conservatory that is in constant use. However, you will still need to heat your conservatory in winter in colder climates, with a minimum temperature of 8°C (45°F).

In a sunny conservatory, temperatures can rocket unless sufficient shade and ventilation are provided. Try to ensure there are opening vents in the roof and at the sides, so that a constant cooling flow of air can be achieved. This will also help prevent disease problems. In cool and damp weather, when the vents are closed, air movement can be maintained using an extractor fan.

By late spring, ventilation alone will not keep the temperature under control on sunny days, so you will need to provide shade. This can be achieved using internal or external

blinds, but internal blinds can easily become tangled with climbing stems. Instead, you might like to consider training a sun-loving climber, such as bougainvillaea, on wires inside the roof, so that it provides the shade for the other occupants and helps prevent sudden temperature rises.

Another option is to apply a shade wash to the roof of the conservatory, but this will cut down light levels severely on gloomy days.

In a cool conservatory that is just kept frost-free in winter, you can try a wide range of houseplants, as well as palms, bay, myrtle, olives and citrus, which can be placed outside during the summer months, plus half-hardy climbers such as *Jasminum polyanthum* and bougainvillaea.

Looking after plants

Watering All plants need to be regularly watered – possibly every day if they are in small pots. An alternative is to grow the plants in larger containers, such as raised beds or large troughs, so that they have a greater root run. You can also grow them in self-watering containers, which have in-built reservoirs that can be topped up regularly. There is also a range of automatic watering devices that you can use.

Misting Invest in a hand mister to spray the leaves of plants from time to time. It is also worth standing plants in groups on trays of moist gravel so that the air around the plants is kept as humid as possible. Wet the gravel periodically.

Feeding All actively growing conservatory plants need regular feeding. You can do this using a slow-release fertilizer stick pushed into the soil at planting time and at the beginning of each growing season, or you can add a houseplant liquid feed to the weekly waterings.

A year in the conservatory

Spring
Increase watering as necessary and feed only those plants growing strongly. Keep the conservatory glass clean to allow as much light in as possible. Clean leaves and remove yellowing and dead ones.

Summer
Maintain an even temperature by careful ventilation and use of shading. Water and feed all actively growing plants as necessary. Propagate from cuttings and layering. Mist plants and moisten gravel trays daily to maintain sufficient humidity around the plants. Pinch out trailing plants when they reach the floor and tie in new growth on climbers to their supports. Move plants outdoors for their summer holiday. Deadhead repeat-flowering shrubs, such as azaleas, to keep them blooming strongly.

Keep an eye open for signs of pest and disease attack and take the appropriate action to control it. Cut back permanent plants that outgrow their allotted space.

Autumn
Reduce watering and stop feeding all but strongly growing plants such as jasmine. Bring in shrubs and climbers from the summer break in the garden, but check them carefully for pests and diseases. Put up insulation. Clean glass to maximize light penetration. Keep an eye open for spider mite in a heated environment.

Winter
Water sparingly and feed only those plants that are actively growing. Routinely remove dead flowers and leaves and watch out for grey mould (botrytis) on leaves.

Good plants to try

Warm conservatory (min. temp. 5°C/41°F)

Abutilon megapotamicum
Aristolochia littoralis
Bougainvillaea glabra
Cissus antarctica
Cobaea scandens
Hoya carnosa
Jasminum polyanthum
Nerium oleander
Passiflora caerulea
Tibouchina urvilleana

Hot conservatory (min. temp. 10°C/50°F)

Brugmansia suaveolens
Clerodendrum thomsoniae
Hibiscus rosa-sinensis 'The President'
Justicia carnea
Lantana camara
Mandevilla x amabilis 'Alice du Pont'
Phoenix roebelenii
Rhapis excelsa

Problems Look out for any signs of pests and diseases and treat them immediately. Use suitable biological controls or chemical sprays as necessary. Check new plants carefully before adding them to your display, as this is the most likely way new pests and diseases are introduced.

Displaying conservatory plants

Plants in the conservatory look their best when displayed in groupings. Not only does this appear more natural than individual specimens, but there are practical benefits of keeping them in tight-knit communities, too: they are easier to look after and the microclimate surrounding each plant will be more humid, reducing the need for constant misting. Keep a display looking fresh and attractive by moving the plants within each group and between groups as they come in and out of flower.

Similarly, plants that are resting or are in less than pristine condition can be partially hidden behind those that are looking their best.

It is important to group plants with similar cultural requirements so that they will all need watering at the same time and be content with the common growing environment.

The best conservatory plant displays usually look natural in their setting and with the plants that surround them. You can bring out the best in neighbours by choosing complementary but contrasting features so that one emphasizes the attributes of the other. For example, a plain foliage plant is the perfect foil for a brash flowering plant.

You can also group plants to provide a bold splash at a particular time of the year, such as a colourful display of winter-flowering heathers at Christmas. Include props, such as wicker baskets and cast-iron planters, to highlight the plants that are looking their best. Plant stands, such as a tiered French *étagère*, are worth considering for large numbers of

plants in containers. Many modern versions come with built-in gravel trays to make providing a humid atmosphere easy. Stands are also ideal for showing off the cascading foliage of trailers and climbers to their best advantage, as well as bringing small plants and those with intricate makings closer to the eye.

On a table display, use a large container to provide a temporary home for plants as they come into flower. A basic planting of foliage trailers or a fern can be given a lift by introducing flowering plants as temporary bedfellows while they are in full bloom. Grow the seasonal highlights in one size of pot so that they are easy to slot in and out of the main display.

Some plants are worth using as solo specimens. Choose a suitable ornamental container to complement the plant's main features. As a rule of thumb, go for simple designs to show off vibrant and fussy shrubs and climbers and more ornate containers for feature plants with a strong but subtle appeal.

Having a conservatory or a greenhouse allows the gardener to grow shrubs and climbers that would not survive outside. It also allows you to prolong the season of others.

Gardening techniques

To get the best from your shrubs and climbers you will need to understand a few basic principles of gardening and master a number of straightforward techniques. In this section we guide you through all the essential tasks, using easy-to-follow instructions and clear, stage-by-stage photography and illustrations.

Before you can take steps to create a new garden or improve the appearance of an existing one, it is worth getting to know a little about your soil. Basic information such as pH and soil type are just two critical factors that will help determine which shrubs and climbers will thrive in your garden – as well as those that are likely to fail. Knowing more about your soil also enables you to take effective steps to improve it by adding well-rotted manure and, where appropriate, applying fertilizers.

Once the soil is in good heart, you will need to learn a few basic techniques, such as planting, watering, weeding and mulching, so that your new shrubs and climbers get off to the best possible start. You will find plenty of tips and advice here for improving the performance of established plants, too.

Beautiful, disease-resistant blooms are the pride and joy of every gardener, as they show that love, care and the proper gardening techniques have been successfully used.

Know your soil

The health of your soil is crucial to the types and quality of the plants you can grow. It is therefore essential that you have some understanding of the type of soil you have, and its advantages and limitations, before you can choose the correct plants for your garden. Once you know the basic facts about your soil, you can also set about improving it.

Identifying your soil

The quickest and easiest way to find out what type of soil you have in your garden is to handle it. Wet a small amount of soil and rub it between your finger and thumb and literally feel its consistency. By wetting the soil you will be able to assess more easily the types of particles it contains.
• **Gritty** If it feels gritty and the particles easily separate, then the soil has a high sand content. Then try rolling a small ball of the soil in the palm of your hand so you can estimate how much sand it contains: the easier the ball falls apart the greater the proportion is sand.
• **Gritty and cohesive** If the sample feels gritty but the particles hold together well, then it contains sand and loam. The ball of soil should hold together when rolled in the palm of the hand, but will break up when rolled into a sausage shape.

• **Gritty and sticky** If it feels gritty but is slightly sticky to the touch, it contains sand and clay particles. If the ball of soil becomes shiny when rubbed and can be rolled into a sausage shape and bent like a horseshoe without cracking or breaking, it contains sand, clay and also loam.
• **Smooth and silky** If the sample feels smooth and silky between finger and thumb and moulds into a ball and a sausage, but breaks when bent into a horseshoe shape, then it contains mainly loam and silt.
• **Sticky and malleable** If it feels sticky to the touch and the ball of soil is shiny and easy to roll into a sausage, but cracks when bent into a ring shape, then it contains mainly clay with some loam.
• **Very sticky** If the sample literally sticks your finger and thumb together and the ball of soil is shiny, easy to roll into a sausage and bend into a ring shape without breaking or cracking, then it contains mainly clay.

Soil types

All soils are made up of the same basic ingredients: sand, loam, clay, silt and organic matter. The proportions of each ingredient will determine the type of soil you have and how good the soil is for growing different plants. Sandy soil contains

Daphne bholua 'Darjeeling' prefers a well drained but not dry soil that is slightly alkaline.

a high proportion of large, irregularly shaped particles that have air spaces between them. This means that water drains freely so they tend to dry out quickly, which is a bonus in spring as they are easier to work and warm up earlier than other soils, but they are a problem in summer when they are more prone to drought during dry spells. Free-draining soils also tend to have essential soil nutrients washed out, known as leaching, leaving the soil impoverished unless given a regular application of fertilizer.

Clay soil contains a high proportion of tiny soil particles that pack very closely together, leaving very few air spaces. This prevents water from draining through the soil so it remains wet for longer. Clay soils are also heavy and sticky, and so very difficult to cultivate. They are easily damaged if walked on when wet, causing compaction of the surface, which just exacerbates the drainage problems. They are also slow to warm up in spring, and so planting has to be delayed. In

Soil type at-a-glance

Gritty to touch	Sticky to touch	Shines when rubbed	Rolls into ball	Rolls into sausage	Bends into ring	What's in your soil
√	x	x	x	x	x	Sand
√	x	x	√	x	x	Sand and loam
√	√	√	√	√	x	Sand, clay and loam
x	√	√	√	√	x	Clay and loam
x	√	√	√	√	√	Clay

Viburnum 'Eve Price' is easy going, but does best on clay or silty soil.

Plants for different soils

Sandy, chalky or alkaline soil	Peaty or acid soil	Clay or silty soil
Ceanothus	*Calluna*	*Abelia*
Ceratostigma	*Camellia*	*Alnus*
Clematis	*Corylopsis*	*Bergenia*
Cytisus	*Cryptomeria*	*Choisya*
Daphne	*Desfontainia*	*Corylus*
Euonymus	*Enkianthus*	*Crataegus*
Euphorbia	*Fothergilla*	*Kerria*
Genista	*Gaultheria*	*Laburnum*
Hypericum	*Halesia*	*Malus*
Ligustrum	*Hamamelis*	*Philadelphus*
Mahonia	*Kalmia*	*Potentilla*
Rosmarinus	*Larix*	*Pyracantha*
Spiraea	*Leucothoe*	*Pyrus*
Stachyurus	*Pieris*	*Rhamnus*
Weigela	*Pinus*	*Sedum*
Wisteria	*Rhododendron*	*Sorbus*
	Sarcococca	*Symphoricarpos*
	Skimmia	*Taxus*
	Staphylea	*Viburnum*
		Vinca

summer, clay soils can dry out to form a concrete-hard crust with a distinctive cracked surface as the soil shrinks. Clay soils are usually fertile.

Silty soil contains mainly medium-sized particles, and so tends to drain well in winter but retain soil moisture in summer. It is also usually fertile. Silty soils are easily damaged if walked on when wet, causing a compaction of the surface, known as 'capping'.

Loamy soil contains a mixture of particle sizes and so has the advantages of all the other soils, without the disadvantages. Loamy soils are usually easy to cultivate and have a robust and stable structure that drains well in winter and is still fairly moisture retentive in summer. They also generally warm up quickly in spring and are usually fertile.

Soil-testing laboratories

For really accurate soil analysis you will have to send off a soil sample to a specialist laboratory for testing. Set up for the agricultural and horticultural industries. Some local authorities also offer a soil analysis service for gardeners, for which there may be a nominal charge. Not only will they test your soil accurately for pH, but many will provide an analysis of the main plant nutrients: potassium, phosphate and nitrogen as well as some trace elements (magnesium, calcium, manganese, iron, copper and zinc, for example), and information about the organic matter content. The most comprehensive soil analysis services will give some recommendations for fertilizer and lime application rates in order to improve your soil.

This sort of professional analysis may be worth considering if you have just moved to a new house and don't know anything about the garden's history, or where you've had difficulties in the past and suspect the problem lies in the soil. You can also use this sort of soil analysis to test deliveries of topsoil to make sure they are up to standard, but bear in mind that results can take anything from a week to a month to get the results, so you may have to hold back on planting.

Hamamelis mollis prefers peaty or acid soil.

Assessing your soil

Once you are familiar with your soil type, there are two other key factors you need to find out so that you can take steps to improve the soil before planting: how acid the soil is and which nutrients it contains.

Testing your soil

Although the best way to find out about your soil in detail is to send a representative sample off to a specialist laboratory to have it analysed, you can find this out with reasonable certainty by carrying out a simple set of tests yourself.

There are cheap and reliable soil-testing kits widely available from garden centres and DIY stores that will tell you your soil's pH level as well as indicate the nutrient balance in your soil.

The pH level is a measure of your soil's acidity or alkalinity. Each plant has an ideal pH range in which it will thrive, which varies from plant to plant. To make the most of your plants' growing potential, it is

The rock rose (*Helianthemum*) is a dwarf shrub that is able to thrive on almost any soil that is reasonably fertile and well drained.

Checking drainage

Another important factor to establish when planting a new area is how well it drains. If the soil is poorly drained, you may wish to take steps to improve it before planting. To check how well your soil drains, dig several holes about 30cm (12in) deep spaced randomly across the plot. Fill each hole with water and see how quickly it drains. If there is still water in the hole after 24 hours, you may have a drainage problem. This can usually be overcome by digging deeply and incorporating plenty of well-rotted organic matter and grit into the soil, otherwise you will have to consider installing land drains, or building raised beds to improve drainage around the roots of the plants.

essential that you test a soil sample that's representative of the whole area you are planning on planting up. Make sure that you do not test contaminated areas, such as where a compost heap has been, otherwise the results will be invalid.

The easiest and most reliable way to select a representative soil sample is to lay out four canes on the soil surface in a large 'W' shape. Use a hand trowel to dig five small holes about 15cm (6in) deep at the points of the W. Scoop out a little soil from the bottom of each hole and place this in a sieve over a bucket. This will remove stones, pieces of chalk and organic matter that might skew the results. Mix the sieved soil samples together before testing.

Altering acidity

The best range of nutrients are provided when the soil has a pH value of about 6–7. It is possible to temporarily reduce the acidity of the soil by applying lime several weeks before planting. Choose either garden lime or ground

chalk that has been made for the purpose. The amount of lime you apply will be determined by the type of soil and its pH. For example, to change a clay soil from pH5 to pH6 will require about 1,200g of lime per square metre, while you would need only 800g per square metre on loamy soil and 400g per square metre on a sandy soil.

It is essential that you follow the guidance notes on the soil test kit and the instructions on the lime

A more high-tech soil-testing device is an electronic meter. When the probe is inserted in the soil, a reading of its pH level is given.

packaging to work out exactly how much you need to apply to your soil.

The best time to apply lime is during the autumn or early winter when soil conditions allow. Wear gloves and apply lime only in still, non-windy conditions. Rake the lime roughly into the surface after application. Bear in mind that liming is only a temporary solution, and so you will need to check the soil acidity every few years.

If you intend to add organic matter to your soil before planting, do this during early spring at least two months after liming to prevent the two reacting together and producing ammonia. Use acidic well-rotted farmyard manure on alkaline soil to help lower the pH and alkaline mushroom compost on acid soils to help raise the pH.

Tricky situations

Climbers and wall shrubs are often planted in borders next to walls where the soil is impoverished. In new gardens, the soil can be full of builders' rubble and so needs digging out to a depth of at least 30cm (12in) and replacing with good-quality topsoil from elsewhere in the garden or from a garden supplier. The soil will also be dry because the wall draws water from it via capillary action and, more often than not, prevents rain falling on the border. The best way to counteract this is to add lots of well-rotted organic matter to the soil before planting and to cover the soil surface with an organic mulch afterwards.

In the dappled shade under trees and the dense shade along evergreen hedges, ground cover shrubs can be difficult to establish. Give new plants the best start by planting in spring into well-prepared soil cleared of roots and mulching the soil surface after planting. Pay particular attention to all new plants in difficult situations to make sure they are kept weed-free and well watered through their first growing season.

TESTING YOUR SOIL FOR ITS NUTRIENT VALUES

1 Collect a soil sample from 10cm (4in) below the surface. Take several different samples and mix together for a representative test.

2 Follow the instructions on the kit. Usually, you mix 1 part soil with 5 parts water. Shake well and then allow the water to settle.

3 Using the pipette provided with the kit, draw off some of the settled liquid from the top of the jar.

4 Having drawn off about 5cm (2in) of the solution, transfer the sample to the test chamber in the plastic container.

5 Select a colour-coded capsule (one for each nutrient). Put the powder in the chamber, replace the cap and shake well.

6 After a few minutes, you can compare the colour of the liquid with the shade panel shown on the side of the container.

Improving your soil

If you know what your soil type is and have a good idea about its acidity and nutrient content, you can take steps to improve it by thorough cultivation as well as the application of well-rotted organic matter and fertilizers.

Soil conditioners

No matter whether your soil is predominantly clay, sand, loam or silt, it will benefit from the application of well-rotted farmyard manure or garden compost. In fact, all but peaty soils, which are already high in organic matter, can be improved in this way.

The organic matter works in different ways for different soils. In heavy clay, the fibrous organic particles improve the structure – creating air spaces and allowing water to drain more freely. In sandy soil, the same fibrous particles collectively act like a sponge, holding on to soil moisture so plants are less prone to drought.

In all soils, the organic matter provides food for plants and beneficial soil-borne creatures, such as ground beetles and earthworms,

which help break it down slowly, releasing more essential plant nutrients. The soil-borne creatures also help aerate the soil as they move around their subterranean habitat.

Well-rotted organic matter can be added to the soil when it is cultivated at planting time, and after planting as a mulch on the soil surface. Whenever it is applied it must be well rotted – tell-tale signs include a dark brown, even, crumbly structure that is practically odourless. If it is put on the soil before reaching this stage, it will continue to rot down once applied, and the soil-borne micro-organisms will use up nitrogen from the soil in the process. This could lead to plants running short of this vital nutrient.

Cultivating your soil

Soils are cultivated to remove weeds and to improve the soil structure and nutrient content by incorporating well-rotted organic matter. There are several ways this can be achieved:
Forking Light sandy soils and other soils that have been well cultivated in the recent past can be broken up

easily with a garden or border fork. Weed the area by hand, then cover the surface of the soil with a layer of organic matter. Cultivate the soil by simply plunging the fork to the full depth of its prongs and turn the soil over in more or less the same position so that the organic matter is roughly buried.
Digging There are three levels of digging with a spade. Which you choose should depend on how thoroughly and how deeply you want the cultivation. Simple digging is the most basic, with the soil being turned over and deposited in roughly the same place. Any annual weeds are buried and will rot down, while perennial weeds can be removed by hand. Repeat this process, moving across the plot. When the other side is reached, move back about 15cm (6in) and repeat, until the whole area has been cultivated. Organic matter can be incorporated at the same time or simply spread over the surface afterwards to allow earthworms and other beneficial soil-borne creatures to incorporate it for you.

Single digging is the best way to tackle heavier loamy, silty and clay soils, as it ensures that the organic matter is thoroughly incorporated into the upper soil layer. Excavate a trench about 30cm (12in) wide right across the plot, leaving the soil to one side. Fill the bottom of the trench with a 7cm- (3in-) deep layer of well-rotted organic matter.

Move back 30cm (12in) and dig another trench – using the excavated material to fill the previous trench with topsoil. Repeat until the entire plot has been dug. The excavated soil from the first trench can then be used to fill the last trench. Double digging cultivates the soil to about a depth of 30cm (12in) and is a

Autumn is the best time for digging over the soil. Fork in some organic matter afterwards, such as well-rotted garden compost or farmyard manure, to help improve the soil's structure.

the bottom of the planting hole. Improve the excavated soil and the soil in the planting hole with well-rotted organic matter and a little bonemeal. Water the climber thoroughly before planting and fill the planting hole with water and allow to drain. Remove the pot and tease out the roots from around the rootball before planting to encourage the roots to spread into the surrounding soil. Place the climber in the centre of the hole and angle it backwards at 45 degrees towards the support. Then backfill the excavated soil around the rootball in layers, carefully firming each layer to remove air pockets. Repeat the process until the hole is filled. After planting, level the surface and then water the climber thoroughly before applying a generous 8cm (3in) deep organic mulch around the plant, but take care not to pile it up against the stem.

Planting next to arches and pergolas

Freestanding supports should be erected and the soil allowed to settle before climbers are planted,

Ideal for growing up supports, *Clematis* 'Jackmanii' is a sun-seeker and will thrive in sunny spots.

Plant clematis deep

Clematis should be planted deeper than other climbers so that the base of their stems are underground. This means making the planting hole about 8cm (3in) deeper then normal. This technique is a precaution against clematis wilt disease, which is a serious problem with clematis – killing all the top-growth. However, any shoots underground are unaffected, so that any deeply planted clematis that suffer from this disease can recover by producing new shoots the following year from healthy buds that form at the base of the stems underground.

following the technique described above. You can plant right next to the support if space is limited, unless foundations were laid under the soil to support the structure. Once planted, untie the climber from its supporting cane in the pot and spread out the stems. Carefully tie them into the support. If there is only one stem, tie the cane into the support and pinch out the tip of the climber to encourage new side shoots to be produced.

Planting near shrubs and trees

Climbers can also be planted alongside established shrubs and trees that can be used as a natural

support. The soil is likely to be dry and full of roots, so choose a planting position at the edge of the host plant's canopy, where water will naturally run off when it rains – this is known as the 'drip zone'. Carefully excavate a hole and cut off any fibrous roots that have become exposed. If large roots are in the way, move the planting hole to another position. Improve the soil as before, then line the sides of the planting hole with old pieces of softwood. This will help prevent the surrounding roots from the host plant competing with the climber while it becomes established. In time, the timber will rot away.

Providing support: vertical surfaces

Although some climbers can scramble up, over and through supports without any assistance, all wall shrubs and some climbers require a helping hand. By providing wires, trellis or mesh supports, you can also train the climbers and wall shrubs to go exactly where you want them to grow.

Supporting climbers and wall shrubs

There are a number of ways you can support climbers and wall shrubs up a vertical wall or fence. It is essential that you choose a support that's robust and sufficiently large to match the vigour of the climber or wall shrub. For example, annual sweet peas can be supported on plastic mesh or wire netting loosely anchored to the vertical surface, while a vigorous clematis will need a substantial trellis that's been securely screwed into place. Indeed, some climbers, such as wisteria, can reach tree-like proportions and need a heavy-duty support to match. The support system you choose should

Some climbers can cling to brick, stone or wood by putting out modified roots.

Vigorous clematis varieties are ideal for clothing the walls, particularly if you want to hide eyesores, such as compost bins.

also be in keeping with its surroundings. For example, on a decorative wall, you may prefer to use a series of parallel wires that are invisible to the naked eye from a short distance. On the other hand, a less attractive structure can be camouflaged or enhanced by adding prominent decorative trellis as a support for a new climber.

Using wires

Most climbers and wall shrubs can be supported using wires. Wires are the most versatile support, covering any shape or size of surface. Choose a strong galvanized or plastic-coated wire, say 10 to 14 gauge. The wire needs to be held 5–8cm (2–3in) away from the wall or fence using special wall fixings called vine-eyes. This gap will allow air to flow around the plant and help prevent the wall remaining damp for long periods. There are two types of vine-eye: triangular pegs that are hammered into the mortar between courses, or screw-in eyelets that are

Clinging plants will cover any vertical surface without needing any support, as seen with this *Hydrangea peteolaris*.

secured in holes drilled into the wall and filled with wall plugs. Space parallel wires every 30cm (12in) up the wall for most climbers and wall shrubs, but use a fan-shaped or even vertical arrangement of wires for twining climbers. When training and tying in new growth to the support, make sure that it is in front of the wires, so that it helps to hide the wires, the plants are easy to prune and, if necessary, can be detached and lowered from the wall without removing the support system.

Using trellis

Wooden trellis is available in a range of decorative shapes and sizes, but you can also make your own from inexpensive wooden lathes, which can be bought from builders' merchants. These will have been pressure-treated against rot, so just need to be cut to length and fixed with screws. Making your own trellis won't work out any cheaper than buying ready made, but it can be tailored to fit any size or shape of wall or fence.

All types of trellis need to be attached to battens or wooden blocks on the wall so that the trellis is held 3–4cm (1–1½ in) away from the vertical surface. Ready-made trellis may look attractive, but the battens are actually spaced too close together. If you make you own, aim to space them 30cm (12in) apart for most climbers and wall shrubs. Expanding trellis is even worse. It isn't as strong as ready-made panels and is usually more expensive. However, it is easy to transport and can be expanded to fit the space available, so is worth considering for very restricted areas and lightweight climbers.

Ready-made trellis is also useful for extending the height of your boundary fence. Special post extensions are available, or you can make your own using 8cm- (3in-) wide exterior quality plywood. There is a wide range of trellis styles available, from simple squares to a diamond pattern or basket weave, so you can select one to suit your garden design.

Trellis can be used to break up the appearance of large walls and fences, too. For example, eye-catching perspective panels effectively draw the eye to the centre of the trellis and the climber it supports. Alternatively, use strips of standard trellis panels to hide a prominent downpipe or other eyesore or paint decorative trellis as an effective way of disguising ugly walls or fences, or even a garden shed. Choose from a wide range of coloured stains made for the purpose, or make your own by diluting oil-based exterior gloss paint in the colour of your choice with white spirit in the ratio of 1:3.

Using mesh

Plastic-coated wire mesh or plastic mesh panels are also available in a limited range of colours. They are easy to cut to size and can be shaped around doorways or windows, used

GROWING CLIMBERS UP WIRES

1 Drill holes where you want the vine-eyes, which will support the plant, to go. You can hammer them in, but a drill makes it easier.

2 If you are using vine-eyes with a screw fixing, insert a plastic plug into the wall first. Then screw the eye into the plug.

3 If you are using wedge vine-eyes, hammer them into the masonry .

4 Thread the wire through the hole in the vine-eye and then wrap the excess back on itself to keep it taut and secure.

5 Arrange the longest stems to the wire and tie in with plastic ties or string. Ensure that the stems lie flat against the wall.

6 The stems should be fanned so the plant can cover the wall as it grows and produce more buds on the top edges of the stems.

to cover downpipes or to fill in gaps in freestanding structures such as arches.

Like wires and trellis, they will also need supporting away from the wall using vine-eyes or wooden battens. However, mesh is less pleasing on the eye than trellis and plastic mesh isn't strong enough for vigorous climbers.

Access for maintenance

Both the vertical support and the trellis attached to it will need maintenance from time to time. Although most ready-made trellis has been pressure-treated against rot, which should protect it for at least

ten years, the trellis may need repairing every now and then as the staples may become loosened by wind-rock and the weight of the climber pulling on it.

Some climbers can be cut back to near ground level to free the trellis, which can be removed so that the supporting wall or fence can be maintained. With sufficient space and a flexible climber, you might prefer to unscrew the trellis and lay it down on the ground with the climber still attached while you carry out repairs. However, if the wall requires regular maintenance, painting for example, you can make the whole job easier if you attach the

Some climbers hold on by twining up their support as they grow, and so do not require routine tying in through the growing season.

ERECTING A TRELLIS

1 Start by digging a hole at least 60cm (2ft) deep. If your soil is light, you may need to dig an even deeper hole to secure the trellis.

2 Put the post in the hole and partly fill with a dry-mix concrete. Check the upright, adjust if necessary and then continue filling the hole.

3 When you fill the hole with concrete, make sure to ram it down very firmly. Once the concrete has 'cured' it will be solidly secure.

4 Lay the trellis next to the ground to work out where the next hole should be. Dig the next hole as for the first.

5 You now have two posts at the right position for the trellis. Offer up the trellis and nail the panel on to the supporting posts.

6 As you progress putting up the panels, stop and check the uprights regularly, ensuring they are level and at the right angle.

bottom of the trellis panel to the lower batten using galvanized hinges. You can then can lower the top of the panel away from the wall and replace it in exactly the right position in just a few seconds.

Next to doors and windows

Climbers and wall shrubs can look delightful when trained to frame a doorway or window and, as long as you choose the right plants, it is as easy to achieve as growing them against other vertical surfaces.

Aim to choose a plant that will provide year-round interest. This effect can be formal or informal, depending on the type of plant you choose. For example, a small-leaved evergreen could be used to create neat, leafy pillars if they are positioned on either side of the door, while a languid, scrambling clematis or rose can offer garlands of colour and scent throughout the summer months.

Plants to avoid around doors and windows include anything that is very vigorous, because it will need constant cutting back. Also steer clear of thorny climbers and wall shrubs, opting for the spineless varieties instead, as children and unaware visitors could get nasty scratches if they brush against them.

Plants that are prone to being attacked by sap-sucking insects, such as honeysuckle, are also worth avoiding, because the resultant honeydew excreted by such pests will make a mess on your windows, as well as making the ground around a doorway sticky underfoot.

Train your selected plants up the wall to the side of the window or doorway by tying them into a support. To do this, either use strong horizontal wires spaced 30cm (12in) apart up the wall, held taut

A fragrant honeysuckle will take just one or two seasons to clothe supporting trellis. The plant is ideal for growing up structures, as it is not too heavy and spreads well.

between vine-eyes, or install a trellis by screwing it to a series of battens. This will ensure good air circulation between the wall and the plant, helping to prevent disease problems. Make sure the battens are made from pressure-treated timber to prevent rot and that they are fixed with rust-resistant screws. You can either plant the climber or wall shrub straight into the soil at the base of the wall

or you may prefer to set it into a large, permanent container. Before you begin planting, make sure the soil has been improved with well-rotted organic matter and keep the plant well watered until it has become established.

Position the climber or wall shrub at least 18in (45cm) away from either side of the doorway so that there is room for growth.

Providing support: freestanding structures

Climbers can be used to cover vertical structures all around the garden. They are an ideal way of adding height to borders as well as creating living focal points that attract the eye.

Arches and pergolas

Although attractive features in their own right, arches and pergolas can be used to enhance the overall design of the garden: framing an entrance or feature; leading the eye farther down the garden; connecting separate elements within the garden; or creating the illusion of space by emphasizing an attractive view outside the garden. Pergolas are useful for creating secluded seating areas or a shady refuge in a hot sunny garden. Both pergolas and arches can also be used to create covered walkways.

Arches and pergolas are available in a wide range of styles and materials, so there should be one to suit your garden. For example, metal structures look most at home in modern or formal garden settings, while rustic wooden pergolas and

This metal archway provides medium support. The Golden hop (*Hummulus lupulus* 'Aureus') plant covers the arch with a mass of yellow leaves, which support themselves with curling stems.

arches are perfect for a more relaxed cottage-style garden. For best effect, choose a structure that fits in with its surroundings and select a combination of climbers to suit the position you have in mind as well as the size of the structure. Bear in mind what the structure will look like in winter. An ornate metal structure will tend to stand out and

To help climbers get a good coverage, tie in their stems, spreading them out so that they are near horizontal, to encourage flowering.

Repeat-flowering roses are ideal for growing up archways, as they will provide colour and cover for a longer season.

Creating a living arch

If you have hedges on either side of a pathway, you can create a living arch by training them together. To do this, first select two or three upright growing shoots on the hedging plants adjacent to the path, trimming the rest of the stems back. Insert a 3m (10ft) cane into the ground next to the stems so that they can be trained up vertically. Each year, trim the hedge as usual, leaving the selected stems un-pruned.

When the un-pruned shoots reach about 2.5m (8ft), remove the canes and tie a hoop of wire to the stems on either side of the path, so that the top of the hoop is about the right height for the arch. Then, bend the selected stems over the hoop and tie them in using soft string. If they are long enough to touch at the top of the hoop, tie them together.

Continue to tie in new shoots in subsequent years until the arch is thick enough and the desired shape has been achieved. In following years, keep in shape by regular trimming when you cut back the rest of the hedge. Any type of hedging plant can be trained in this way.

Even when it is not in flower, wisteria makes a good covering for structures because its foliage is abundant even when its characteristically beautiful lavender-coloured drooping blooms are over.

This simple arch is constructed using rustic poles and is covered with variegated ivy.

become a feature in its own right, while one made from wood is likely to blend in more with the rest of your garden.

Metal structures Metal arches and pergolas can be practically maintenance-free if well made. Make sure they are coated completely to prevent corrosion, especially around joints, welds and drilled holes. The structure should seem sturdy and rigid, with strong joints and welds. Have a small tin of matching exterior paint to hand to touch up any chips or unprotected areas after erection to ensure protection.

Wooden structures Most softwood arches and pergolas are pressure-treated to prevent rot, but if you have bought one from a local supplier it's worth checking this before you buy. If the wood was treated before it was cut, then untreated wood will be exposed to the elements and will need painting with preservative before you put the structure together. All wooden arches and pergolas should have strong joints and should not be warped.

Check that the structure is well braced with cross-members so that it will be rigid once put together.

Pergolas and arches are available in kit form, usually flat-packed, and are relatively easy to construct. However, it may require two people to put them together. The key to success is

to make sure that the posts are vertical and spaced correctly before securing them and that the crossbars are horizontal. The structure will have to bear the weight of the climbers it supports, which can be considerable after heavy rain. Climber-clad arches and pergolas

Sited in the middle of a wildflower meadow, this wonderfully romantic arch serves no purpose other than to support some roses and provide an absolutely beautiful scene.

A combination of sweet-scented roses, clematis and an overhanging fig makes an intimate, shady area for sitting and relaxing in the summer months.

A newly planted arbour will eventually be smothered in foliage and blooms, creating a tranquil spot for sitting.

also put up a lot of wind resistance when the climbers are in leaf, so check how rigid the structure is before you buy. All types of arches and pergolas need to be well anchored to keep them secure.

Mid-border structures

Simple garden structures such as single posts and tripods are much underrated and under-used. They are ideal for adding instant and inexpensive points of focus to a garden. There are many decorative obelisks now available that look attractive all year round without the need for a climber. Pots and tripods also make effective markers at the ends of paths – acting like sentries to emphasize a change in direction or a meeting point. Posts can also be effective when linked with timber crossbars or wire at the back of the border to provide a backdrop. When festooned with climbers, the simple structure becomes a cascade of colourful flowers and foliage that will add height to your borders and help provide privacy. Making mid-

border plant supports is very straightforward. For example, you can create an attractive obelisk from inexpensive wooden roofing lathes, available from builders' merchants, which come pressure treated against rot. First construct four 2.5m (8ft) high triangular frames that are 45cm (18in) wide at the base, then attach

horizontal battens on each triangle using the same wood, spacing them about 15cm (6in) apart. Fit the four sides together, securing them with weather-proof screws. Finally, add a fence post finial to the top as a finishing touch. You can also make a traditional colonnade out of posts and rope or lengths of plastic chain

A large arbour, built for entertaining, is covered by a variety of climbers, including a purple grapevine (*Vitis vinifera* 'Purpurea'), which needs a strong trellis or pergola to support it.

— an ideal way to make a feature out of your favourite climbing rose. You can also combine trellis with posts within the garden to divide the growing area into separate 'rooms' or to add height to beds and borders. The trellis needn't be a continuous screen — you can create the impression of separate areas using just a couple of matching screens on either side of a pathway and they won't make the garden seem too small or the divisions too claustrophobic. Ornate screens that have been stained in a colour that complements or contrasts with the colour scheme of the surrounding

A secluded spot tucked away in the garden allows you to view your gardening efforts in peace and quiet after a hard day of digging, weeding and pruning.

Growing climbers into established shrubs

Climbers look their most natural when climbing through other shrubs and trees. It is important that you match the vigour of the climber to its host plant and try to choose one that flowers at a different time so that the climber extends the period of interest. The host plant needs to be well established, but not so old that it is no longer growing vigorously.

Position the climber on the side of the prevailing wind so that any gusts will blow the climber as it grows into the host plant rather than away from it. After planting the climber (*see* pages 88–9), hammer a short stake into the ground nearby and attach a rope to the stake. The other end of the rope should be attached to a suitable low branch of the host plant. Untie the climber from its supporting cane, then tie it to the rope, and if the stems are long enough, train them into the canopy of the supporting plant. Do not, as is sometimes recommended, loop the bottom end of the rope under the rootball of the climber when planting, because the climber is likely to be pulled out of the ground by the first strong gust of wind.

plants are the most eye-catching. However, in a small garden you may prefer to give the screen a more neutral or rustic finish so that it is recessive on the eye and blends naturally into the garden. For those who have smaller gardens, siting a mirror surrounded by climbing

foliage will give the illusion of more space. Combine this with an arch and the optical effect is one of leading the viewer into another part of the garden, hitherto unseen. A similar effect can be achieved by siting a sculpture at the end of a vista to give a sense of space.

A romantic walkway is created from a series of arches along a path cut through long grass. The arches provide a tunnel effect, leading the eye to the end, where a statue completes the view.

Watering and mulching

Watering is one of the most important and time-consuming tasks around the garden. It makes sense, therefore, to be water-wise and use this increasingly precious resource as efficiently as possible.

Watering efficiently

How often your garden will need watering will be determined by the following factors: the type of plants you have (each plant grows at a different rate); the plant's absorption rate and ability to retain moisture; the site's exposure to sun and wind; the depth and type of mulch you use (if any); the amount of recent rainfall; the amount of hot, drying sunshine; and the amount of organic matter in the soil. Each of these factors will affect how quickly your garden dries out.

Saving water

You can collect your own water to use in your garden. A water butt plumbed into a downpipe off the house or an outbuilding can be in exactly the right place to water climbers and wall shrubs in dry borders alongside. There are many decorative versions now available, some shaped like terracotta pots and urns, so there is no need to hide them away. The butt should also be easy to use. Make sure it is raised so that you can get a watering can or hose to the drainage tap at the base. Choose a butt with a cover to keep the water 'sweet' and clean.

If you live in a hard-water area, saving rainwater is a good idea as it's slightly acidic and so is perfect for watering acid-loving shrubs and climbers grown in ericaceous soil. Waste water from washing or bathing can also be recycled in the garden. Known as 'grey-water', it is suitable for applying to established shrubs and climbers.

Plants lose water through their leaves all the time so it is essential to water regularly to make sure they have enough moisture to replenish the roots, otherwise they will die. Plants growing next to walls and fences tend to dry out more easily and so need extra watering.

That said, most shrubs and climbers do not need regular watering once they are established. However, on well-drained and shallow soils, and elsewhere during drought periods, it is a good idea to water judiciously.

Newly planted shrubs and climbers should be kept well watered throughout their first growing season until they have become well established. You might need to water them for longer if your soil is dry, which is often the case at the base of a wall or on a sunny slope.

Efficient watering

The key to watering efficiently is to water thoroughly when and where it is needed.

Watering a little and often is a common mistake made by novice gardeners. This not only wastes a lot more water through evaporation, but it means that only the surface layer of the soil is moistened. This encourages shallow rooting, which exacerbates the problems you will have during dry spells. Aim to

apply the equivalent of 2.5cm (1in) of water to drought-affected borders. It is best to water during the evening, especially in summer, as this will prevent unnecessary water loss through evaporation caused by the sun drying out the water you have just applied. Also, the hot sun acts like a magnifying glass on the watered leaves and can scorch them.

Rain is slightly acidic, so ericaceous plants like rhododendrons benefit from being watered with rainwater. Collect it in a water butt.

Watering systems

Apart from using a watering can, there are several different watering systems available to make the tedious task of watering plants easier.

Perforated hosing This consists of plastic tubing punctured with tiny holes through which the water slowly leaks out. This type of system can be quickly removed when it is no longer needed.

Seep or soak hosing A flexible, porous hose made from rubber is buried in the ground and left in for a season or more.

Drip irrigation This is a system professional growers use. One or more drip nozzles deliver water to individual plants or containers. It can be designed to cover any size and shape of garden.

Sprinklers Although mainly used by gardeners to water their lawns, sprinklers can be very helpful for dowsing beds and borders.

When watering, aim the water directly to the root areas of the plants rather than spreading it liberally all over the garden. You can avoid wetting the surface altogether by sinking a pot or pipe filled with gravel next to the plant and applying the water through this. If the soil surface remains dry, there is the added benefit of fewer weeds to deal with.

Applying a mulch

You can reduce the need for watering still further by applying a loose mulch or laying a proprietary mulch mat. These methods will stop water evaporating out of the soil surface and also help to prevent weed seeds germinating. They are best applied in spring when the soil is moist and also weed-free.

There are two main methods of mulching plants:

Loose mulches These are organic or inorganic mulches, and are the most popular because they not only help to reduce water loss and prevent weed competition, but they also provide food for soil-borne creatures such as ground beetles and earthworms.

These creatures incorporate the humus into the soil and improve its structure and fertility. However, the mulch will need to be topped up each year to remain effective. Aim to apply the mulch of organic matter at a thickness of 5–8cm (2–3in). Use a mulch of well-rotted garden compost, composted bark or cocoa shells and remember to keep topping it up each spring.

Inorganic loose mulches, such as pea gravel and pebbles, also reduce water loss and prevent weeds, but they do not help to feed the soil. On the plus side, however, they look attractive and do not require topping up each spring, so offering an easy-care alternative to organic mulches.

Sheet mulches When you are planting up specimen shrubs and climbers, specially made sheet mulches are an option that is well worth considering.

Also known as mulch matting or landscape fabric, these sheets are all weed-proof. They are more effective weed barriers than loose mulches, but do not look as attractive. However, they can be disguised with a thin layer of soil or mulch if used in a prominent position.

To apply a sheet mulch, lay it over the prepared soil and cut cross-shaped slits in the sheet for the climber to be slotted into. For planted shrubs, place the sheet around the bottom of the plant, surrounding the base of the plant by an area of at least 1 sq m (1 sq yard) of sheeting.

USING DIFFERENT TYPES OF MULCH

1 Bare soil is prone to weeds and loses water through evaporation. Before applying a mulch, remove any weeds in the bed.

2 Avoid using grass clippings as a mulch as they deplete the nitrogen in the soil. They may also root, causing a weed problem.

3 Composted bark is attractive as a mulch. However, don't use fresh bark as it may deplete the soil of nitrogen as it decomposes.

Weeding and feeding

Weeds not only spoil the display but they also compete with your plants for soil moisture and nutrients. Most gardeners find weeding a chore, but there are ways you can keep weeding to a minimum without sacrificing the appearance of your garden.

Keeping weeds at bay

The best way to prevent weeds becoming a problem is to thoroughly clear soil of all weeds, including the entire root system of perennial weeds such as dock, bindweed and couch grass, before planting. Thereafter, you can go a long way to prevent new weeds colonizing your garden by preventing them gaining a foothold. In practice, this means keeping bare soil to a minimum and tackling weeds as soon as they are noticed. You can cover bare soil by planting up all beds and borders, filling any gaps with ground cover plants or mulches (*see* page 97). Between well-established woody plants such as in a shrubbery, you can use a special chemical to treat the soil surface that inhibits any weed seed from germinating. However, such products cannot be used in borders with bulbs or herbaceous plants

since the new growth will be damaged as it pushes through the chemically treated soil.

Controlling weeds

Even in the best-kept gardens, weed problems can occur from time to time. The best strategy is to tackle them early, before they have a chance to flower and set seed. The old saying 'one year's seed means seven years' weed' is as true today as it has ever been.

Annual weeds, such as groundsel and chickweed, are easy to tackle, either by ripping them out by hand or hoeing them off between shrubs. Take care not to hoe too deeply and avoid hoeing between shallow-rooted shrubs or those prone to suckering, such as rhus.

Perennial weeds are more difficult, because you have to remove the whole of the root system from the soil to prevent it regrowing from below ground. With tap-rooted perennial weeds, such as dandelions and thistles, this can be difficult enough, but with brittle-rooted perennial weeds, such as couch grass and bindweed, it's nigh-on impossible! Indeed, if you have a widespread problem with the latter,

Use a spade to dig out large, unwanted plants and weeds before you prepare the ground for your shrubs and climbers.

you might be better off digging up all the plants so that you can painstakingly clear the soil of every bit of weed root, before replanting. If you do this, make sure there are no weed roots hidden in the rootball of the shrub or climber, otherwise all this effort will have been in vain.

Another method you can try is to kill perennial weeds by constantly cutting them back to ground level each time they re-sprout. Over time, they will gradually weaken and eventually die if they are unable to photosynthesize. However, you will have to be as tenacious as they are and be very thorough about removing them at all times.

The final option is to tackle the weeds using a chemical weedkiller. There are two types available: contact weedkillers, which kill the parts of the weed they touch; and systemic weedkillers, which are taken up by the weeds and transported inside it, killing all parts.

Take care when applying weedkillers as they will kill anything that they come into contact with — and that could mean your ornamental plants as well. For this reason, you will have to either use a dab-on-the-spot treatment, which you apply directly to the weed leaves by hand, or cover ornamental plants

Removing weeds by hand is a laborious task, but it is necessary when weeding larger annual weeds and perennial weeds.

Hoeing is a quick and simple weeding method. It is an ideal way of removing weed seedlings that have just emerged.

with plastic before spraying the weeds between them. Leave the plastic in position until the weedkiller has dried completely to avoid accidentally affecting the nearby shrubs or climbers.

Feeding shrubs and climbers

All plants need nutrients to keep them healthy and enable them to produce a magnificent display of blooms. Unfortunately, they have to compete with each other to get their fair share of food. This is especially true when the plants are crowded into beds and borders to make a lush display. The more crowded they are, the more they have to compete, particularly those that have been newly planted and are in need of extra care and support.

Get new shrubs and climbers to establish quickly by applying a slow-release fertilizer, such as blood, fish and bonemeal, over the rooting area during early spring. Thereafter, if your soil is in good condition, most well-established shrubs and climbers will need no regular feeding.

However, hungry shrubs, such as roses and lilacs, and floriferous climbers, such as clematis, do

Before planting, prepare the soil and then sprinkle a balanced fertilizer evenly over the planting area.

perform better if given an annual feed. On poor soils, use a general balanced fertilizer containing a 7-7-7 balance of NPK nutrients – nitrogen (N), phosphorus (P) and potassium (K) – to promote healthy growth throughout the garden (*see* page 85). These ready-made preparations are widely available at garden centres and DIY stores.

Apply the general fertilizer over the root area during early spring. Double this amount for hungry shrubs, such as roses. During the early summer months, you can also give your shrubbery a fillip by applying a foliar feed using a hose-end diluter, but do not feed after

Granular fertilizer can be applied by hand. Apply it as a top dressing according to the manufacturer's instructions.

mid-summer, otherwise you will promote soft new growth that won't have time to ripen before winter and will be liable to frost damage.

If your plants are already established, choose a slow-release or controlled-release fertilizer so that the plants will receive all the nutrients they need throughout the summer months.

Feeding container plants

Liquid feed is suitable for container-grown shrubs and climbers. Add the feed to the water and give to the plant every 1–3 weeks, depending on the type of plant and the manufacturer's recommendations.

FEEDING YOUR PLANTS

1 Add fertilizer at the rate recommended by the manufacturer. Use a controlled release fertilizer if planting in the autumn.

2 Gently hoe the fertilizer into the soil. This will help it penetrate the soil more easily and provide nutrients for the plant more quickly.

3 Water around the plant thoroughly to ensure the nutrients are taken down into the root system area.

Protecting vulnerable plants

Frosts, wind, heavy snowfalls and excessive rain can all kill vulnerable shrubs and climbers during the winter months, so take steps to protect them in autumn before the onset of the coldest weather.

Preventing weather damage

Frosty weather can cause water in plants' cells to freeze. When this happens, the cell walls of the plant are damaged. This makes the plants limp and they become distorted, with their leaves and stems wilting and blackening. If the ground is frozen, water lost through the leaves of evergreens cannot be replaced and so the leaves become scorched and unsightly. In severe cases, the whole plant can be killed.

Wind damage is also a problem. Evergreens in particular are susceptible to wind during the winter months. Newly planted evergreens are most at risk, so make sure these are protected with a screen of windbreak netting or hessian sacking material held taught between stout, securely anchored posts. Some deciduous shrubs are also susceptible

to wind damage. Japanese maples, for example, often suffer die-back at the tips of branches. Also, their emerging leaves in spring can be scorched before they have had a chance to unfurl. However, they can be protected in exactly the same way as evergreens.

Groups of susceptible low-growing shrubs, such as ground cover plants or dwarf shrubs such as hebes, are easier to protect by laying the windbreak netting directly over the top. If your garden gets a lot of snow in winter, lift the material clear of the shrubs using hoops or bamboo canes.

Climbers and wall shrubs can be protected by attaching a double sheet of fine-mesh netting or garden fleece on either side above the vulnerable plant and then stuffing between the sheets with insulating material for protection.

Preventing root damage

Many borderline-hardy shrubs, such as hardy fuchsia, *phygelius* and *romneya*, as well as borderline-hardy climbers, such as passionflower and potato

Climbers that are vulnerable to temperature damage can be protected by covering them with netting during the worst of the weather.

vine, will produce new shoots from the crown in spring even if all the top-growth is killed over the winter. The best way to protect these is to insulate the roots with a layer of insulation material before the cold weather starts. You can either pile on a 15cm- (6in-) deep layer of dry leaves, straw or bark chippings, or use prunings cut from evergreen hedges. If using dry leaves, ideally choose ones that don't rot down too quickly, such as oak, beech or chestnut tree leaves. In exposed gardens, keep the leaves in position by pegging down netting over the top or create a low fence around each plant with a piece of plastic or wire mesh. If your soil is very well drained, you can even protect vulnerable plants by mounding soil over the crowns in winter, clearing it away again before new shoots appear in spring.

To protect a tender shrub, you can provide a shield for it. To do this, insert three stout stakes firmly into the ground around the plant. Wrap bubble wrap, plastic sheeting or several layers of horticultural fleece around the outside of the stakes. Tie securely and peg down the bottom.

Avoiding winter wet

A few shrubs, such as *Convolvulus cneorum* and sage, are susceptible to winter wet, particularly if the soil is not well drained. Put an up-turned pot, slightly raised on stones to allow good air circulation, over the top to keep off the worst of the rain. Alternatively, you could use open-ended barn cloches. Another option is to grow these plants in containers and move them into a protected area, such as underneath the eaves of the house, for the winter.

Insulating containers

Even hardy plants in containers may need protection during the winter months. During spells with sub-zero temperatures the rootball is liable to freeze solid, damaging fine roots and preventing the plant from taking up any moisture.

You can help to prevent this by planting in frost-proof containers so that the pots don't crack when the temperature drops. Once the cold well and truly sets in, move small plants to a sheltered position at the base of a hedge or beside the house.

Conifers are particularly susceptible to damage caused by the weight of heavy snow, which can pull the plant out of shape or break its boughs. Prevent damage by tying up the shrub before winter. If you are too late and the snow has fallen, knock it off before any damage is caused.

A temporary method of protecting plants is to cover them with a large plastic bag or horticultural fleece sleeve.

Another method is to plunge them rim-deep into the border soil.

The easiest method is to insulate the pot with bubble wrap packaging material or improvise a protective 'duvet' made from a plastic bag stuffed with dry leaves or crumpled newspaper. Tie the insulating material securely right around the pot. If the plant is only borderline hardy for your area, you could protect this using bubble wrap or a double layer of garden fleece. Make sure there is an access flap to the pot, so the plant can be watered if necessary and allowed to breathe. If there isn't sufficient air, the plant will rot and die from condensation building up inside the plastic.

Vulnerable shrubs grown as standards, such as bay, can have their stem protected using a foam pipe insulating tube. Move them out of windy areas where they could be knocked over by high winds.

Despite all your efforts, excessive cold or chill, drying winds will almost certainly kill off one or two of your plants – but wait until spring before getting rid of them, as they could well surprise you and come back to life.

Moving established plants

No matter how good you are at planning your garden, at some stage you may change your mind about where a shrub or climber should go. Another reason for moving shrubs or climbers is that sometimes, despite your regular pruning efforts, a plant outgrows its allotted space and threatens to overwhelm the other plants. If a plant outgrows its welcome, it is time to move it on.

The best time to move

Moving established plants is hard work and requires careful planning. Rootballs will be difficult to dig up and heavy to move, so you will probably need help.

The best time to move established deciduous plants is during the dormant season (late autumn to early spring). Choose a time when the soil is not frozen or waterlogged. The transplants will establish more quickly if the soil is warm and moist, so the depths of winter are best avoided.

Evergreens, including conifers, are best moved in mid-spring when the soil is moist and warm so that they have time to re-establish themselves before the onset of winter. On heavy soils, delay moves until the soil dries out in late spring.

How to move established plants

Before you start, you should prepare the planting site to receive the transplanted plant. To do this, dig a hole about twice as wide and as deep as the rootball. Fork over the bottom of the hole and incorporate a bucketful of grit to improve drainage on heavy soils. If the rootball is large, make sure there is an easy access route to the new hole, so that the rootball can be dragged into position if necessary.

When preparing the rootball, first clear any weeds and loose soil from under the canopy of the plant. Then, use a sharp spade to mark out the circumference of the rootball. Cut a slit-trench, using the line as a guide, by pushing the spade in vertically to its full depth all the way round the established plant, severing any roots as you go. Move away about 30cm (12in) and make a second slit-trench running parallel to the first.

Dig out the soil between the two to create a moat-like trench right around the plant being moved. This trench should be as deep as the rootball you are trying to create.

Use the spade at an angle to undercut all the way around the rootball from the bottom of the trench, again severing any roots that are encountered. This should be sufficient to free rootballs under 45cm (18in) in diameter. The

Once you are happy about where your shrubs have been planted and they have enough room to reach their best growth and shape, you can relax and enjoy a spectacular display for years to come.

MOVING AN ESTABLISHED SHRUB

1 If possible, root-prune the shrub a few months before moving to encourage the formation of fibrous roots.

2 Dig a trench around the plant, leaving the rootball completely uncovered. Sever any roots, if necessary, to remove the rootball.

3 Dig under the shrub as far as you can. It may be necessary to cut through any tap roots that are stubbornly holding it in place.

4 Tilt the plant to one side and insert a sheet of sacking or plastic. Push several folds of the material under the rootball.

5 Rock the rootball in the opposite direction and pull the material through, so that it is completely underneath the plant.

6 Pull the material around the rootball to enclose the soil and tie it securely. The plant is now ready for moving.

7 Heavier plants require a joint effort. Slide a pole through the material. With one person on each end, lift the shrub out of the hole.

8 Having prepared the ground at the new site, follow the reverse procedure for planting the shrub in its new home.

rootball can then be carefully wrapped and secured with string. Larger rootballs may need further excavation to reveal any vertical roots at the centre of the rootball.

Wrap large rootballs by rocking the rootball over to one side and placing a folded piece of heavy-duty plastic or sacking underneath. By rocking the rootball the other way you can release the leading edge of the material, which can then be pulled through. Securely tie the corners of the material together over the rootball and tie these to the main stem. To keep the soil in position, use strong string to wrap up the rootball tightly on all sides as well as underneath.

Move the rootball by slipping a sturdy post or pole through the wrapping. Do not lift the rootball by the trunk because the soil will not be supported and it will crumble away. Very large rootballs are easier to drag from one place to the other. Create a ramp out of the hole using short, smooth planks to make it easier and lay plastic sacks over rough, level surfaces so that the rootball slides easily.

Once positioned in the new hole, carefully remove the wrapping and string, then backfill the excavated soil in layers, firming each layer to remove air pockets. Water thoroughly and cover the rootball with a thick organic mulch.

Aftercare

Spray the foliage of newly transplanted evergreens every few days to help prevent scorching. Provide shade if the weather is sunny and warm. On exposed sites, put up a windbreak to prevent wind scorch. With all transplanted shrubs, keep well watered during any dry spells throughout the first growing season.

Pruning techniques

One of the most common questions asked by a gardener when they buy a new shrub or climber is 'How do I prune it?' As there is often more than one correct answer to this simple query, pruning has gained an undeserved reputation for being a difficult and risky operation – especially for those new to gardening.

Fortunately, you can prune successfully to the standard of your gardening expertise without any risk to the plant. By being a little bit bolder, you can take the art of pruning a step farther by learning a little about each individual plant, so that you can tailor the pruning to suit them and keep them vigorous, looking natural and problem free. If you take a further step forwards, you can become an expert pruner, using your craft to increase the ornamental performance of a particular shrub or climber.

To show your plants off to their best advantage, pruning is essential. It need not be an arduous task, and many gardeners find it both rewarding and creative.

Pruning made easy

Pruning is an essential part of growing shrubs and climbers successfully. Although initially all shrubs and climbers will grow perfectly well without pruning, eventually the appearance and overall flowering performance of many will decline.

At its most basic, pruning is all about cutting out the three Ds: dead wood, diseased wood and damaged wood. Provided you do this using a suitable pruning tool that's been kept clean and sharp, you will only do good to your garden plants. Basic pruning also includes cutting back plants to keep them within bounds. The aim here should always be to maintain the plant's overall natural shape, not cutting back all wayward shoots to exactly the same length.

Shredder

When to prune

Some plants are best pruned at certain times of year because they have a tendency to 'bleed' sap or are particularly vulnerable to airborne diseases, so this is also worth knowing before you start. Initial pruning after planting, often called formative pruning, is important to get right since this sets up the shrub or climber for life. This involves the removal of damaged and weak shoots as well as creating a balanced framework to the desired shape for the plant. Thereafter, pruning should be confined to maintaining the health of the shrub or climber.

Pruning encourages larger and better flowering displays that last for longer as well as bigger, more dramatic and lush foliage. Shrubs and climbers that offer attractive bark, autumn colour or crops of eye-catching berries can all be enhanced by choosing the right pruning technique.

Creative pruning

You can graduate to be a master pruner by employing more creative pruning techniques that alter the plant's overall appearance. For example, you can have fun creating hedges on legs, known as pleaching, or lollipop trees, known as pollarding, trim suitable shrubs into intricate topiary shapes or train climbers to form screens, unusual ground cover or standards.

Pruning isn't essential, of course, as native shrubs and climbers in their natural habitat cope admirably without human intervention. Indeed, there are many shrubs and some climbers that don't require any routine pruning in the garden either, and these are often the ones recommended for beginner gardeners. The need for pruning can

Hand shears with wavy blade

Hand shears with straight blade

also be reduced by planting shrubs at the correct spacing and matching the vigour of the climber to the space available and size of support. Overcrowded plants not only have to compete for light, soil moisture and nutrients with their neighbours but will also be under more stress and less able to shrug off pest and disease attacks, as well as being more vulnerable in periods of drought.

After any significant pruning, always water your shrub or climber thoroughly and cover the ground with a 8–10cm (3–4in) thick organic mulch, keeping the immediate area around the trunk clear. The mulch will not only help to insulate the root area and prevent soil moisture from evaporating but will help prevent competition from weeds. The mulch will slowly rot down and add nutrients to the soil. In spring, it is also worth feeding the pruned plants with a balanced, slow-release fertilizer to promote new growth in the growing season.

BASIC TOOLS AND EQUIPMENT

Most gardeners manage with the minimum of equipment – a pruning saw and a pair of secateurs (pruners). However, to do the job more efficiently and more effectively, it really does make sense to invest in the proper tools, particularly if you have a large garden.

Long-arm pruners

Curved saw with hook for removing cut-off branches

Straight-bladed pruning saw

Long-handled pruners

Electric hedge trimmer

Secateurs (pruners)

Petrol hedge trimmer

Curved pruning saw

Petrol chainsaw

How and when to prune

Many gardeners find pruning daunting, but it is actually very straightforward, provided you follow a few simple rules that are easy to understand and put into practice in your garden.

How to prune

All pruning cuts should be made in the same way, whatever you are pruning. If you are shortening a stem, the cut should be made cleanly just above a healthy-looking bud, preferably facing outwards from the centre of the plant so that new growth does not increase congestion. If you are using secateurs (pruners) or loppers with just a single cutting blade, this should be cutting into the stem on the opposite side from the bud. Pruning cuts should be made at a slight angle, with the lowest point on the side opposite from the bud. If the stem produces pairs of buds that are opposite each other on the stem, make the cut square to the stem as close to the buds as possible, but without damaging them.

Always make sure your pruning tools are sharp and clean. They will cut more easily and so cause less bruising and other damage to the part of the plant left behind. This, in turn, ensures that the potential for disease infection is reduced. If you are cutting out diseased material, minimize the risk of spreading the infection to other healthy branches by cleaning the pruning blade between cuts with a suitable garden disinfectant. Large cuts can also be treated with special wound sealants to help prevent disease spores gaining access through the cut. Small pruning cuts do not need covering because they will soon heal naturally.

When to prune

It is essential that pruning is carried out at the right time. The exact timing will depend on which shoots the shrub or climber flowers on. Early flowering shrubs and climbers tend to produce their blooms on stems produced the previous year, and so need to be pruned directly after flowering is over. This will allow them sufficient time to produce new shoots that will mature and ripen sufficiently to bear flowers the following year. On the other hand, later-flowering shrubs and climbers, tend to produce the blooms on stems produced during the current season and so are best pruned before new growth is put on during early spring. This will maximize the number of flowering stems on the plant. There are exceptions to this rule, such as many repeat-flowering plants producing a first flush of blooms on the old wood and a second flush later in the season on older wood. Other plants produce flowers on spurs, like fruit trees, so the aim here is to promote as many spurs as possible on a permanent framework of branches. To check when specific plants need pruning, use the month-by-month pruning guide in the Calendar of Care section on pages 246–51.

Which pruning tool to use

If you buy good-quality pruning tools and keep them well maintained, they will make pruning easier and the tools will last a lot longer. Make sure that you find the handles comfortable before you buy and that the fully open position for secateurs (pruners) is not too wide for your hand. Do not use pruning tools for other jobs around the garden, such as cutting string or wire, because you will damage the blades. Also, avoid letting the blades come into contact with the soil, as this can dull the cutting edge. It is also important to choose the right tool for the specific pruning job.

A good pruning cut is made about 2mm (⅛in) just above a strong bud. If the stem has pairs of buds, make a horizontal cut (right).

If you use blunt secateurs (pruners), you will get an unhealthy, ragged cut (left). Instead, make sharp cuts not too far from the bud.

Cutting too close to the bud can damage it or allow disease to enter. Do not slope the cut backwards (right), as this could cause die-back.

Deadheading not only improves the appearance of the plant, but will encourage repeat-flowerers to produce more blooms later in the season.

start pruning, make sure your tetanus protection is up to date. If you haven't had a booster jab in the last ten years, make an appointment at your local doctor's surgery.

When pruning, always wear suitable clothing that won't get caught up in the plant or equipment. Thick, thorn-proof gloves are useful when pruning roses and other prickly plants, but it's wise to protect your forearms and eyes too. If you are dealing with stems above head height, consider investing in a pair of long-handled pruners. When cutting back plants that are high off the ground, such as trimming a large hedge or reducing the spread of a tall climber, make sure you work from a sturdy platform rather than balancing on a ladder.

Pruning new plants

Most shrubs and climbers do not need pruning during the first few years. However, a few benefit from being pruned during the first year after planting to encourage branching from low down the main stem and to establish more quickly.
Improved shape Shrubs, such as aucuba, box, elaeagnus, evergreen euonymus, griselinia, holly, bay, Portugal laurel and evergreen buckthorn, can be encouraged to produce a bushy, balanced shape by pruning back the previous year's growth by about one-third after planting. The shape of mahonias can also be enhanced by removing the uppermost rosette of leaves on each stem after flowering.
Quick establishment Shrubs such as buddleja, deciduous ceanothus, kerria, dogwoods, hypericum, lavatera, leycesteria and sambucus will establish quickly if the previous season's growth is cut back to within 5cm (2in) of the main framework during the early spring after planting.

• Use garden shears for trimming off wispy stems on climbers and flower-heads from shrubs such as lavender and heather.
• Use a pair of secateurs (pruners) for cutting woody stems up to 1cm (½in) thick.
• Use a pair of long-handled loppers for stems 1–3cm (½–1¼in) thick. Don't be tempted to cut stems larger than this with these pruning tools because you will end up damaging the plant you are pruning, leaving bruised tissue behind that is open to disease infection.
• Use a pruning saw for stems more than 3cm (1¼in) thick. Choose a curved Grecian saw with teeth on the lower edge, because this is easier to use and less likely to cause damage to other parts of the plant than other types of pruning saw. Don't use carpentry saws because their teeth will soon clog up with sawdust and sap and the blade will stick in the cut. A pruning knife with a curved blade is also useful for tidying up larger pruning cuts.

Prune safely

All pruning tasks should be carried out with safety in mind. Even deadheading can be hazardous if there are unprotected canes sticking out of the border that could poke you in the eye. Before you make a

Pruning popular deciduous shrubs

Most shrubs will flower reasonably well without pruning, but problems such as diseased wood, congested growth and non-flowering shoots will build up with time. This can all be rectified by pruning, but it must be carried out at the correct time of the year.

Pruning early-flowering shrubs

Many of the most popular deciduous garden shrubs, including deutzia, philadelphus, forsythia, flowering currant, some flowering spiraeas and weigelia, flower in spring or early summer – producing their blooms on wood produced the previous year. This means you have to wait until after flowering before you can prune.

No-prune shrubs

You can reduce the amount of time you spend maintaining your garden by choosing shrubs that flower perfectly well without routine annual pruning. They may need pruning to remove broken or dead stems or if they outgrow their allotted space, however. These include:

Abelia
Berberis
Choisya
Corylopsis
Cotoneaster (many)
Daphne
Elaeagnus
Euonymus (most)
Fatsia
Genista
Hamamelis
Hibiscus
Ilex
Mahonia
Olearia
Osmanthus
Phormium
Sacococca
Skimmia
Viburnum (most)
Yucca

It is important to prune directly after flowering so that the shrub has plenty of time to put on new growth and flower buds for the following season. If you prune later in the year, you risk losing the flowering display for the following season.

Prune out any dead or diseased material as well as crossing or rubbing branches that are congesting growth in the centre of the plant. Then cut out one in three stems, starting with the oldest, to a new side shoot lower down or a plump outward-facing bud. Most shrubs in this group do not need pruning every year – once every two or three years is ideal and will not noticeably reduce their overall performance. The exception is forsythia, which can become woody at the base and flower less well if it not pruned each year.

Pruning late-flowering shrubs

Deciduous shrubs that flower from mid-summer onwards, such as *Buddleja davidii*, hardy fuchsia, *Caryopteris*, *Hydrangea paniculata*, lavatera, *Potentilla fruiticosa* and late-flowering spireas, produce blooms on wood produced during the current season. These must be pruned before

HARD PRUNING

Several plants that have attractive coloured bark in the winter are best cut right back to the ground in the spring.

the new growth is produced during early spring. During mild years, especially with the impact of global warming, pruning may be required earlier than many traditional gardening books suggest. Be guided by the state of the shrubs in your garden and start pruning as growth buds start to break. All shrubs in this group are vigorous and should be pruned back every year. Some, such as hardy fuchsias, will shoot from below soil level and should be cut back to the ground. Others should have all the previous season's growth cut back to a low, stubby framework of stems.

1 Late-flowering shrubs that bear blooms on new growth perform better if pruned back hard during early spring.

2 Cut the shoots back almost to the ground to encourage the maximum new stems, which will bear blooms during the current season.

Pruning for colourful stems and foliage

Several deciduous shrubs, such as dogwoods, willows, white-stemmed brambles, cotinus, eucalyptus, *Sambucus nigra* and *Spiraea japonica* 'Goldflame', are grown more for their brightly coloured juvenile stems or enlarged, decorative foliage than for their flowers. To promote the type of growth you want, these shrubs need to be pruned in a different way from those that are grown for their flowers. Shrubs in this group do not need to be pruned every year, but annual pruning will produce the most dramatic displays.

Cut back all the previous growth to near ground level or to a low framework of woody stems during early spring. This will produce bright-coloured stems and larger, more brightly coloured foliage. Indeed, if you leave *Eucalyptus gunnii* without pruning, you will be disappointed by the rather lacklustre adult foliage that results rather than the plant producing dramatic elliptic foliage that is so sought-after by flower arrangers.

PRUNING FOR COLOURFUL STEMS

1 If left unpruned, the winter stems of *Salix alba* subsp. *vitellina* will produce its colourful new stems higher up where they cannot be seen – eventually forming a small tree.

2 To prune, cut back some of the older wood and any congested branches. This will allow the shrub to rejuvenate from the base of the plant. Use a saw on the thicker wood.

3 Remove any of the dead branches and shoots, cutting or sawing off until you reach healthy wood. Use a saw for thicker wood and clean up the cuts.

4 When you have finished thinning out the old and straggly wood, you are left with the basic framework of the shrub. This will give you an idea of how it will look next year.

5 Cut back any remaining shoots from last year's growth to a good, strong bud. This may seem very drastic but it will encourage strong and vigorous new growth.

6 If the shrub is planted at the front of the border or has another shrub situated behind it, try to ensure that the cutting back is sufficiently low so other plants can be seen.

Pruning popular evergreen shrubs

Most evergreens do not need routine pruning but can be cut back to restrict their overall size or as part of a remedial programme to restrict the spread of a pest attack or disease infection. Evergreens come in a huge variety of forms, from the dapper, dome-shaped shrubs to dramatic drama queens that dominate a garden with their huge flowers and monster foliage. Fortunately for the gardener, they can be grouped according to their pruning requirements.

Pruning small evergreen shrubs

Most small evergreens, such as cistus, heathers, hebe and rosemary, do not need regular pruning, unless grown as a hedge. In this situation, use shears to clip off spent flower-heads and to trim new growth to shape. Trim summer-flowering hedges in mid-autumn and winter-flowering hedges in mid-spring. Specimen plants do not need any serious pruning unless they have suffered die-back as the result of harsh winter weather. Inspect the shrubs during late spring or early summer to look for signs of growth on apparently dead stems before deciding what needs to be pruned out. If you need to cut back hard, aim to cut back to a healthy side shoot lower down on the branch. Do not cut back into old wood as this is unlikely to re-sprout.

Pruning large-flowered evergreens

Rhododendrons, camellias and evergreen azaleas all fall into this group. They are all acid-loving shrubs that require no routine pruning other than the removal of the seed-pods of spent flowering heads to tidy up the shrub after flowering. Removing the seed-pods before they swell also avoids the

The foliage of *Pieris japonica* alters its colour as it matures, providing a constantly changing appearance. This evergreen will grace any garden with acid soil.

shrub wasting energy producing seeds. This should be carried out very carefully since the next year's flower buds are carried just below this year's fading flowers. The best technique is to hold the bottom of the seed-head between finger and thumb, twist it and pull sharply.

Specimen shrubs with dead or diseased growth should have these cut out to a healthy side shoot lower down. Straggly shrubs can be cut back after flowering during mid-spring before new growth is put on.

Pruning large-leaved evergreens

Large-leaved evergreens, such as laurel, aucuba and holly, make excellent specimen shrubs as well as robust hedges. Specimen plants require little or no routine pruning, other than the removal of dead or diseased stems. In this situation, aim to cut back to a healthy side shoot lower down on the branch. However,

large-leaved evergreens grown as hedges will need annual pruning to maintain their neat shape and dense habit (see below). Ornamental forms with attractive variegated foliage can sometimes produce all-green reverted shoots. These should be cut out completely as soon as they are noticed to prevent them spoiling the overall appearance of the shrub.

Pruning grey-leaved evergreens

Many grey-leaved shrubs, such as artemesia, helichrysum and santolina, are grown solely for their attractive foliage. For this reason many gardeners trim the shrubs to prevent flowering stems being produced so that they do not detract from the overall appearance of the display. Other grey-leaved shrubs, notably lavenders, are valued for their flowering display, so these should not be trimmed until after flowering is over. All grey-leaved shrubs can be kept neat and compact by trimming new growth to within a couple of leaves of the main shrub during spring. Do not cut back into old wood, as this is unlikely to re-sprout.

Repairing weather damage

Evergreens are particularly susceptible to severe weather damage because they remain in full leaf throughout the winter months, when most storms occur. The weight from heavy snow, for example, can build up on the foliage, pulling the shrub out of shape and, in severe cases, causing branches to break. Even branches that remain intact do not 'close-up' again to the original position when the snow melts, exposing the brown areas underneath their dense outer covering of evergreen foliage. This is most noticeable on upright conifers that normally have a neat columnar habit.

Icy winds can be equally troublesome because they dry out the foliage through evaporation, just when the roots find it most difficult to draw water from the frozen ground. This leads to exposed conifers becoming scorched on the windward side. Fortunately, both these problems are easy to avoid. Protect particularly vulnerable plants by wrapping them in a straitjacket of fine mesh netting for the winter months. You can prevent scorch by protecting exposed conifers with a barrier of windbreak netting held up on stout posts fixed firmly into the ground. (see Protecting vulnerable plants, page 102).

Where damage does occur, you can persuade wayward branches back into their normal position by wrapping the plant in fine green or black netting. The netting can either be removed after a season or left in place, since the new foliage will grow

through it and hide it completely within a couple of years. Small, partially broken branches on other evergreen shrubs can be repaired by putting on a splint of bamboo canes and binding the break together with tape. The fracture will take at least two full growing seasons to mend and be strong enough for you to remove the splint. If the branches

are badly broken they will have to be removed. If this makes the evergreen shrub lopsided, try balancing it by removing a similar-sized unbroken stem from the other side. Where a hole has developed in the canopy of the evergreen, use soft string to pull neighbouring branches towards each other to fill it in and repair the look of the plant.

PRUNING EVERGREEN SHRUBS

1 Evergreen shrubs generally need little pruning. However, on occasion, as with this bay (*Laurus nobilis*), they may need to have their shape checked or smartened up.

2 Remove any dead or damaged wood and cut back any straggly stems at the top of the shrub to improve the overall shape. Keep stepping back to check on the shape.

3 The best time to carry out any pruning is during the spring, just before new growth appears. However, during the growing season they can be trimmed at any time.

4 Prune evergreens with secateurs (pruners) to avoid leaving damaged leaves on the plant. Make pruning cuts within the foliage so they do not detract from the shrub's appearance.

Pruning roses

Despite having a reputation for being complicated, rose pruning is no more difficult than pruning other garden shrubs. Indeed, recent research has suggested that the precise traditional methods might be a waste of time. So, how should you treat your roses?

Why do you need to prune roses?

Roses are so floriferous that after a few years of growing and flowering, an old stem becomes exhausted and flowering declines. The old shoot is more prone to pest and disease attack and often suffers from die-back. This prompts a newer shoot nearer the base to break and grow, eventually replacing the older shoot as it withers. Pruning is a good way of managing this natural process of renewal, helping to prevent any serious health problems while promoting vigorous new shoots that flower more profusely and for longer. Annual pruning also keeps large roses to a manageable size.

How to prune roses

If you follow all the basic rules of pruning you won't go far wrong:

Most gardeners would claim that without exception, there is no other plant to match the beauty of the rose. With careful pruning and nurturing, roses will reward you with beautiful blooms.

- use clean tools with a sharp blade
- prune to just above a healthy, outward-facing bud
- make the cut sloping to help protect the bud and shed water from the cut
- keep the centre of the shrub clear of crossing, weak and diseased stems

Wearing thorn-proof gloves and eye-protection is also a good idea when dealing with roses. Deadhead all repeat-flowering roses throughout the growing season to get better and longer-lasting flowering displays.

Miniature roses These require little or no pruning other than to keep growth neat and compact. On well-established plants you should remove all dead, damaged or weak growth to thin out the centre. Miniature roses

are a bit of a novelty and do not match the best of the other forms of roses for scent, colour and disease resistance. However, since they grow well in containers, miniature roses are becoming increasingly popular. See the Roses to try box on page 119 for miniature cultivars to try.

Patio and polyantha roses The patio rose is a compact, small bush that is usually covered in wide clusters of flowers throughout the summer. Polyantha roses are also small bushes and have a graceful habit. Pruning of these roses is easy. After planting, cut back the stems to 8–10cm (3–4in) above ground to a strong bud. Once established, the rose can be pruned to remove any dead, damaged or diseased wood. Also, cut

Pruning newly planted roses

Rose bushes should be pruned after planting to encourage them to establish quickly and produce a well-balanced shape. If too many shoots are left on the plant, the limited root system will not be able to cope.

Prune new roses by removing any dead or diseased stems completely. Then reduce the length of the shoots on bush roses and standard roses by about half their length. The top growth on miniature roses and shrub roses should be cut back by about a quarter at this stage.

To cut out crossed stems, try to do it when they are still young (before they start rubbing against each other) and free from damage and disease, as this will make it a lot easier. Use secateurs (pruners) to cut the stem at the base where it joins the main stem.

The tips of stems often die back and should be cut out to prevent the shoot dying. Cut back to good wood, just above a strong bud.

back all stems to about half to two-thirds of their length to an outward facing bud or a strong shoot. Every few years, take out one or two of the oldest stems to promote new growth.

Bush roses The traditional method of pruning bush roses is probably still the most reliable. Cut back all the stems of large-flowered (hybrid tea) roses by about half their length.

Cut back old stems of cluster-flowered (floribunda) roses to their base. The remaining younger stems of cluster-flowered roses should be pruned back to about 45cm (18in).

PRUNING A MINIATURE ROSE

PRUNING A PATIO ROSE

Remove all dead and damaged wood on miniature roses, along with any weak growth. Deadhead to prolong flowering. Well-established miniatures require little or no pruning, other than to keep their growth neat and compact.

Patio roses are initially pruned in the same way as miniature roses. Once established, they are generally pruned in the spring. Pruning involves removing any dead or weak wood and cutting back any remaining stems by up to two-thirds. Deadhead throughout the summer.

You should also remove all dead, damaged or weak growth and thin out the centre of the plant. Pruning should be carried out annually during early spring.

Rough pruning

There has always been a bit of a debate about pruning roses. Should you go carefully, or just hack away? It is now known that although the results won't be quite as good, all bush roses can be pruned roughly, cutting all stems back to 15–20cm (6–8in) once every few years without worrying about cutting to just above a bud. You can even use a hedge trimmer if you have a lot of roses and time is short.

Shrub roses

These comprise various roses that do not fit easily into other classes. This mix includes everything from hybrid rugosas and musks to floribundas and the modern landscape roses. They also include single-flowering and repeat-flowering roses.

That said, the advice is to give shrub roses a light prune each year or once every other year. Remove between a quarter and a half of the new growth and cut out any dead, diseased or congested stems. This will increase blooming and decrease disease and pest problems.

Disbudding

If you want to grow roses for a flower arrangement for or showing, you may want to encourage larger flowers on longer stems by removing the smaller side buds from hybrid tea roses. Remove the side buds by pinching them out between finger and thumb when they are small, taking care not to damage the main terminal bud.

Standard roses always look impressive, particularly when placed on either side of an entrance or doorway. These plants require the support of a stout stake, held with a tree or rose tie. Miniature roses planted in containers should be held secure with a cane.

Ground cover roses Prune repeat-flowering and creeping rambler ground cover roses to keep them within bounds by removing the growing tips of spreading stems. Remove upright shoots completely.

Rambler roses Cut out poor-flowering old stems to encourage floriferous new stems. If the growth is congested, cut out one old shoot for every new one being produced from the base. Cut back any side-shoots that have flowered to two or three leaves. Tie in all stems to their supports.

Standard roses Prune standard roses lightly, since cutting back severely will encourage over-vigorous shoots

Removing rose suckers

Vigorous new shoots from the base of the plant below the union on budded or grafted roses or emanating from roots underground, will produce flowers and foliage of inferior quality to the ornamental variety. Suckers are usually more vigorous and, if left to grow, will eventually swamp the desired variety, spoiling the overall appearance. Suckers should not be pruned off at soil level, since they will re-grow even more vigorously. Instead, excavate a hole to find the point at which the sucker is attached to the rootstock and then rip it off by hand as cleanly as you can. If this is not possible, cut it off at this point.

HOW TO PRUNE A STANDARD ROSE

1 When pruning, start by removing any dead, damaged or diseased growth. You also need to take out any weak stems.

2 Cut out any stems that cross over others, especially if they are rubbing and causing wounds. This will also reduce congestion.

3 Reduce the remaining shoots by about half to two-thirds of their length. Patio standards should just be tip-pruned.

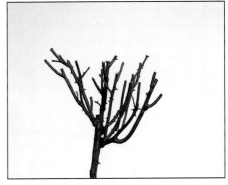

4 You are now left with the basic framework of the standard rose. Aim for an open, tulip shape that is not too crowded with stems.

that may spoil the shape. Shorten the main stems in the head of the standard as well as any side shoots. Prune standards during late winter or early spring, but prune weeping standards after flowering in summer.

Deadheading

It is not essential to deadhead roses but it is desirable if you want to maximize the number of flowers produced by repeat-flowering versions. If you don't deadhead, the rose will tend to put some of its energies into making seeds at the expense of new flowers. To ensure a succession of blooms, remove the fading flowers as soon as the petals start to fall. Pinch out the fading flower between finger and thumb for miniatures or use secateurs (pruners) to cut back the flowering stem to just above the next leaf joint, where new flowering shoots will emerge to bloom later in the season. It is also worth deadheading roses that have suffered from balling – where flower-buds fail to open after becoming waterlogged and infected with botrytis. Deadheading will not only improve the overall appearance of the rose but will also help to reduce the incidence of this disease.

Roses to try

Shrub	Miniature		Polyantha
'Cardinal de Richelieu'	'Amber Sunset'	'Red Bells'	'Ballerina'
'Chaucer'	'Angela Rippon'	'Robin Redbreast'	'Bashful'
'Constance Spry'	'Apricot Sunblaze'	'Sweet Magic'	'Cameo'
'Duc de Guiche'	'Baby Masquerade'		'Gloria Mundi'
'Fantin-Latour'	'Blue Peter'	**Patio**	'Lovely Fairy'
'Madame Hardy'	'Little Flirt'	'Amber Hit'	'Perle d'Or'
'William Lobb'	'New Penny'	'Bright Smile'	'White Pet'
	'Peach Sunblaze'	'Conservation'	
	'Peter Pan'	'Festival'	
		'Fond Memories'	

Pruning climbing and rambling roses

There are hundreds of varieties of climbing and rambler roses that have been bred from a wide range of rose hybrids and species, which means they vary greatly in how they grow and when they flower. Before you can prune your plant successfully, you really need to know a little bit about it.

Know your climbing rose

When it comes to climbing roses, terms such as 'climber', 'rambler' and 'repeat-flowering' are used very loosely in nursery catalogues, gardening magazines and books, so bear this in mind when deciding which way you are going to prune

When well cared for and pruned, climbing roses will reward you with spectacular displays of eyecatching – and often deliciously fragrant – blooms.

PRUNING A CLIMBING ROSE

1 When pruning a climbing rose, you can either prune it in situ or untie it, prune it and then tie it back up to the support.

2 Cut out dead and damaged wood and reduce one or two of the oldest stems to a point just above a new shoot.

3 After pruning, tie in the remaining shoots using rose ties or soft garden string. Tie the stems in firmly but not too tightly.

4 To keep your climbing rose tidy, deadhead any faded blooms. Do this by cutting the stem back to a leaf, shoot or bud.

your rose. For this reason, it is worth taking a little time to get to know your rose to see how vigorous it is, where new growth is produced (from underground, around the base or part-way up older stems), when it flowers and whether the blooms are produced on new growth or stems produced during previous seasons. Use the climbing rose checker (opposite) if you are unsure.

Pruning climbing species roses

Climbing species roses and their varieties, such as 'Bobbie James', 'Kiftsgate', 'Seagull', 'Wedding Day' and 'Rambing Rector', are extremely vigorous roses that need a lot of space, so they are not really suitable for most gardens. Sometimes known as wild roses, they can be trained to cover a large wall or even left to scramble through a well-established, healthy tree. They bloom during early summer in a single flush, producing sprays of cream, pink or white single flowers, often strongly fragrant. Flowers are borne on stems produced during previous seasons. Pruning is a matter of clearing out dead and damaged stems and thinning out congested growth during early spring. Tie in all stems to their supports.

Pruning rambler roses

Varieties such as 'American Pillar', 'Crimson Shower', 'Dorothy Perkins' and 'Sander's White Rambler', have a single flush of blooms during the summer, which are produced on growth that was formed the previous year. They produce long new shoots from the base. For each vigorous new young shoot, prune out an unproductive old one back to ground level after flowering. Do not prune out an old shoot unless there is a new one to replace it, but remove completely any very old, dead or diseased wood. Also cut back flowered side shoots on the remaining stems to two or three leaves. You can cut out poor-flowering old stems to encourage floriferous new stems. If growth is congested, cut out one old shoot for every new one being produced from the base. Tie in all stems securely to their supports.

Pruning single-flowering climbing roses

This group includes some of the best-loved varieties of climbing roses including 'Albéric Barbier', 'Albertine', 'Gloire de Dijon', 'May Queen', 'Madame Grégoire Staechelin', 'Paul's Scarlet Climber' and 'Veilchenblau', which produce large flowers in a single flush during early summer. Prune after flowering by removing up to one-third of the stems, starting with the oldest. Cut back to near to the base or to a new side shoot produced low down. If there isn't much new growth, cut back older branches to 30–45cm (12–18in) to encourage more next year. Trim back flowered side shoots on the remaining stems to two or three leaves.

Climbing rose checker

What is the growth habit of your rose?				
very vigorous	√	√	√	x
flowers once	√	√	√	x
flowers more than once	x	x	x	√
small flowers	√	√	x	x
large flowers	x	x	√	√
flowers on new wood	x	x	x	√
flowers on old wood	√	√	√	x
new shoots from the base	x	√	√	x
new shoots part-way up	√	x	√	√
What you've got:	species rose	rambler rose (single-flowering)	climbing rose	climbing rose (repeat-flowering)

Pruning repeat-flowering climbing roses

Flowering on and off all summer long, producing large blooms on new side shoots, these include some of the best value climbing roses such as 'Aloha', Bantry Bay', 'Climbing Iceberg', 'Compassion', 'Danse du Feu', ' 'Dublin Bay' and 'Golden Showers'. Little structural pruning is needed, but they benefit from regular deadheading to encourage further flushes of flowers. Further pruning is best done in winter, when the weakest and oldest stems can be removed. It is also necessary to cut back flowered side shoots on the remaining stems to two or three leaves. Since these roses tend to put all their energies into flowering after they have become established, rather than extension growth, light pruning and deadheading to remove the faded blooms will encourage further flower production. During the dormant season, dead, damaged or congested growth should be removed completely.

PRUNING CLIMBING ROSES

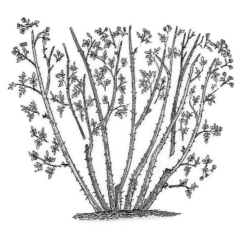

Cut out one or two of the oldest stems to just above a new shoot at the base of once-flowering climbers

PRUNING RAMBLING ROSES

Ramblers are easy to prune. Cut out old stems that have flowered, taking them back to a point where there is a replacement shoot.

Pruning clematis

Clematis are often thought to be difficult to prune because they are not all tackled in the same way, which leads many gardeners to neglect their plants so that they become a tangled mass of stems with the flowers out of sight at the top of the support. In fact, clematis are very easy to prune, provided you know when they flower.

Early spring-flowering varieties (Pruning Group 1)

Clematis that flower during the winter and into early spring bear their flowers on shoots produced during the previous growing season.

They produce single, nodding, bell-shaped flowers with ferny foliage or leaves divided into three leaflets. Some are deciduous, many are evergreen, but not all of them are fully hardy. Cut back vigorous species as necessary to keep them in check, but others in this group need

Group 1 clematis can largely be left alone in terms of pruning, apart from those that grow too vigorously for their allotted space.

Remove straggly new growth to keep your clematis under control and looking good. Prune harder if it is overgrowing its position.

little pruning other than the removal of dead, damaged or diseased stems. Prune back unwanted stems immediately after flowering (during late spring) to their point of origin

or to a pair of plump buds near to ground level. Keep mature plants flowering well and growing vigorously by cutting old stems back hard to encourage new growth from the base.

Early summer-flowering varieties (Pruning Group 2)

Clematis that flower during early summer do so on growth produced during the previous season and include many popular showy varieties with deciduous foliage.

The flowers are generally large, open, sometimes saucer-shaped and can be single, semi-double or fully double. Many also produce a second flush during late summer and early autumn of smaller flowers on the new wood produced during the current season.

They need little pruning other than the removal of dead, damaged or diseased stems. Congested growth can be thinned out by pruning back stems to their point of origin or to a pair of plump buds near to ground level. Alternatively, you can cut half

The flowers in this group are formed on the previous year's wood, so severe pruning will remove these – and its ability to flower in the current year. This group requires very little pruning other than that required to keep the plant under control and to remove any dead wood that has accumulated, which tends to build up and make the plant very congested.

PRUNING CLEMATIS GROUP 2

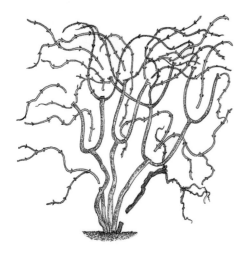

Pruning Group 2 Clematis require little or no pruning. However, the flowering wood tends to get higher and higher, as well as more congested, so it is better to prune lightly to keep them at bay. Take back the shoots to the topmost pair of strong buds. Damaged or dead wood should be removed.

the stems back to a pair of buds before growth starts to increase the number of blooms produced later in the year. Overgrown varieties can be cut back hard to a plump pair of buds about 30cm (12in) from the base immediately after the first flush of flowers.

Mid- and late-summer-flowering varieties (Pruning Group 3)

Flowering after mid-summer, this group of deciduous clematis includes varieties with flowers in a variety of shapes from open, pendulous bells, such as 'Bill MacKenzie', tight, tulip-shaped flowers, such as 'Gravetye Beauty', to open saucer-shaped flowers, such as those of 'Etiole Violette'. Many varieties continue to bloom well into the autumn. All flower on wood produced during the current season. Cut back all new growth during the winter or early spring to the lowest pair of buds. Group 3 clematis mainly flower on new wood produced in the current

PRUNING CLEMATIS GROUP 3

The previous year's growth of can often look like a tangled mess, but Group 3 Clematis is easy to prune. Cut all the stems back in late winter to the first pair of strong buds above where you cut the previous year. Cut out dead stems. New growth is almost immediate.

year and should be pruned back severely every year in late winter, when they are completely dormant.

Clematis Pruning Groups

Pruning group 1	Pruning group 2	Pruning group 3
Clematis alpina	Clematis 'Barbara Jackman'	Clematis 'Abundance'
Clematis alpina 'Constance'	Clematis 'Bees' Jubilee'	Clematis 'Betty Corning'
Clematis alpina 'Frances Rivis'	Clematis 'Belle of Woking'	Clematis 'Bill MacKenzie'
Clematis alpina 'Frankie'	Clematis 'Carnaby'	Clematis 'Comtesse de Bouchaud'
Clematis alpina 'Pamela Jackman'	Clematis 'Daniel Deronda'	Clematis 'Duchess of Albany'
Clematis alpina 'Pink Flamingo'	Clematis 'Doctor Ruppel'	Clematis 'Ernest Markham'
Clematis alpina 'Ruby'	Clematis 'Duchess of Edinburgh'	Clematis 'Etiole Violette'
Clematis alpina 'Willy'	Clematis 'Elsa Späth'	Clematis flammula
Clematis armandii	Clematis florida var. sieboldiana	Clematis 'Gipsy Queen'
Clematis armandii 'Apple Blossom'	Clematis 'General Sikorski'	Clematis 'Gravetye Beauty'
Clematis armandii 'Snowdrift'	Clematis 'Gillian Blades'	Clematis 'Hagley Hybrid'
Clematis cirrhosa	Clematis 'Guernsey Cream'	Clematis 'Huldine'
Clematis cirrhosa 'Freckles'	Clematis 'Henryi'	Clematis 'Jackmanii'
Clematis cirrhosa var. balearica	Clematis 'Lasurstern'	Clematis 'Jackmanii Superba'
Clematis 'Helsingborg'	Clematis 'Lincoln Star'	Clematis 'Lady Betty Balfour'
Clematis macropetala	Clematis 'Lord Nevill'	Clematis 'Perle d'Azur'
Clematis macropetala 'Jan Lindmark'	Clematis 'Marie Boisselot'	Clematis 'Polish Spirit'
Clematis macropetala 'Markham's Pink'	Clematis 'Miss Bateman'	Clematis rehderiana
Clematis montana	Clematis 'Mrs Cholmondeley'	Clematis 'Rouge Cardinal'
Clematis montana var. rubens	Clematis 'Nelly Moser'	Clematis 'Star of India'
Clematis montana var. rubens 'Elizabeth'	Clematis 'Niobe'	Clematis tangutica
Clematis montana var. rubens 'Pink Perfection'	Clematis 'The President'	Clematis 'Victoria'
	Clematis 'Vyvyan Pennell'	Clematis 'Ville de Lyon'

Pruning wisteria and honeysuckle

Wisteria and honeysuckle tend to become unruly, tangled masses of stems if they are allowed to grow unchecked. Wisteria need to be pruned twice annually, but honeysuckles can be left for two or three growing seasons before requiring attention.

Pruning and training wisteria

Wisterias are beautiful, dramatic and vigorous climbers that require a lot of space and a very sturdy support – as well as regular pruning – to be seen at their best.

Perhaps the most striking of wall-trained climbers, they're also an excellent choice for growing over a robust archway or pergola and can even be trained as an unusual and eyecatching standard.

Training wisteria

Against walls, wisteria should be trained rather like an espalier fruit tree on strong galvanized or plastic-coated horizontal wires (about 10–14 gauge) and spaced 25–30cm

To ensure successful flowering of wisteria, it needs to be pruned twice a year, in summer and winter. Careful pruning of a wisteria diverts its energies to flower production, rather than the ever-expanding new growth of stems and shoots, and will reward you with a magnificent display.

(10–12in) apart up the wall. The wire needs to be held 5–8cm (2–3in) away from the wall using vine-eyes. These allow air to flow around the plant and so help prevent the wall from becoming damp for long periods (*see* page 90).

Grow a standard wisteria

Wisteria can also be trained as an eye-catching focal point in the middle of a border. Although spectacular and unusual, it is surprisingly quick and easy to accomplish. After planting, insert a sturdy stake about 15cm (6in) shorter than the eventual height of the desired standard wisteria. Tie in the main shoot to the stake and cut off any side shoots completely. Keep tying in the leader as it grows and removing all side shoots each winter. When the main stem reaches beyond the top of the stake, cut it back to a plump bud. The following winter, select four or five well-spaced side shoots around the top of the main stem to form the head of the standard, then cut out completely all other side shoots lower down the stem. Also cut back the selected side shoots by about one-third – pruning to a healthy bud. Each summer thereafter trim the head of the standard to shape and shorten the side shoots to two or three buds from the main framework.

PRUNING WISTERIA

1 In spring and early summer, wisteria produces long, tendril-like new growth. Cut back leaving 4–6 leaves on each shoot.

2 In early- to mid-winter, cut back summer-pruned shoots even further to about half their length, leaving 2–3 buds on each shoot.

WISTERIA PRUNING CUTS

Cut back the new growth of wisteria each summer to about 4–6 leaves and reduce this even further with a winter pruning.

After planting the wisteria, cut back the main stem to a plump, healthy-looking bud about 90cm (36in) from the ground. Any side shoots should be completely removed. This will encourage new, vigorous side shoots to be produced.

During the first summer, tie in the top side shoot vertically to the horizontal wires to form the new leader. Also tie in the strongest side shoots on either side of the plant at about 45 degrees. Remove all other new side shoots.

During the second winter, untie the two side shoots and lower them to 90 degrees so they can be tied along the first horizontal wire on each side of the plant. Tip-prune the shoots back by about one-third, cutting just beyond a healthy bud. Also, cut the new leader back to a plump, healthy-looking bud about 90cm (36in) above the first tier of branches. Repeat this process until there are sideshoots trained along each of the horizontal wires.

Pruning wisteria

Once the main framework of the plant is complete, wisteria will continue to require pruning twice a year: during late summer and in winter. Any shoots that are required to extend the range or shape of the

wisteria should be left unpruned. The pruning is straightforward: cut back all the whippy new growth to four to six leaves during late summer and, when the leaves have fallen and it easier to see what you are doing, cut the same stumps to just two or three buds from the main framework.

Pruning honeysuckle

Honeysuckles are vigorous twining climbers that can be divided into two groups, according to their pruning requirements. The first group bear their flowers in pairs on wood produced during the current season, for example *Lonicera japonica*. They do not need regular pruning, unless the climber outgrows its allotted space. In this case, cut back all stems during the winter to allow for new growth the following season. Congested specimens can have one in three stems cut back to near ground level, starting with the oldest. The second group, which includes most of the popular varieties such as *Lonicera* x *italica*,

L. periclymenum, L. tellmanniana and *L. tragophylla*, bear their flowers in whorls on stems produced during the previous season. These should be cut back after flowering, pruning out all flowered stems to a newer shoot lower down on the stem.

Aftercare

Pruning inevitably removes part of the climber that provides the plant with energy, so it is a good idea to help the plant recover, especially after severe pruning. Feeding and watering are the most important factors because the climbers will need to put on new growth to replace what it has lost. Choose a balanced fertilizer that contains similar amounts of the main plant nutrients (nitrogen, potassium and phosphorus) as well as other trace elements. Feed in spring after pruning and mulch the ground with a generous layer of well-rotted organic matter to help keep the soil moist and prevent weeds. Water thoroughly during dry spells.

PRUNING HONEYSUCKLE

1 In late winter to early spring, when the stems are bare and you can see what you are doing, cut out any dead and congested stems.

2 Cut just above strong buds. You can be quite brutal when thinning, as honeysuckles are vigorous plants that will thrive on it.

Pruning and training other popular climbers

Provided you match the vigour of a climber to the size of the support and space available, little pruning should be necessary other than the removal of dead or damaged stems and thinning out congested growth. However, a few popular climbers do benefit from more routine pruning.

Climbing hydrangea

The climbing hydrangea, *Hydrangea petiolaris*, needs to be tied into its support until its self-clinging stems get a grip, which may take two or three years. Thereafter, it will climb happily without any help. No routine pruning is necessary unless you want to train the climber to a particular

shape, such as around a door frame or keep it on a fan-shaped trellis. Once established, to get the best flowering display, cut back about a quarter of the oldest flowering shoots that grow out horizontally from the support. Do this each year during the winter or early spring. Once the climber has filled its allotted space, it can be kept within bounds by cutting individual stems back to a healthy bud or to their point of origin on the main framework. Overgrown and neglected plants can be rejuvenated by cutting back all stems hard during early spring to the main framework. This is best done over a three-year

Climbers are born to reach for the sky, so make sure you prune them before they do damage to gutters, eaves and roof tiles.

period so that you don't miss out on the flowering display while the climber recovers.

Kolomikta vine

Unless the specimen is already well branched, *Actinidia kolomikta* benefits from being cut back after planting in spring to 30–45cm (12–18in). This encourages side shoots lower down that can then be trained up the support to form the main framework. Space these side shoots about 15cm (6in) apart up the support. During subsequent summers, side shoots can be cut back each year to an outward-facing bud about 15cm (6in) from the framework. In winter, shorten the same shoots to just two buds of the main framework. Once the climber has filled its allotted space, control it by cutting back new growth by about a half its length – cutting individual stems back to a healthy bud or to their point of origin on the main framework. Rejuvenate overgrown and neglected plants by cutting back all stems hard during early spring to the main framework.

REJUVENATING A CLIMBER

1 Climbing plants tend to grow with enthusiasm, criss-crossing their leaves and stems into densely tangled forms.

2 Untangle the old wood and trim away dead and excess shoots until you can see the basic structure of the climber.

3 Cut back the older wood to a strong shoot lower down to encourage strong, vigorous growth from the base.

4 Dead wood or stems that have died back should be cut back to a healthy shoot. This will encourage new growth.

Honeysuckles

Neglected honeysuckles become a huge mass of tangled, spindly, poorly flowering shoots that are prone to pest and disease attack. Often the new growth and the flowers are produced out of sight at the top of the plant. The best way to tackle an overgrown honeysuckle is to give it a hair cut with a pair of shears, removing most of the tangled top-growth. Then, when you can see the framework of stems underneath, identify which of the younger and vigorous stems you want to keep for a balanced shape and remove the rest. Alternatively, you can cut all the stems back to younger side shoots or plump pairs of buds about 30cm (12in) from the ground, but you will miss out on the flowering display for a year or two.

If neglected, honeysuckles will tend to become a tangled mess of stems with their flowers out of sight at the top of the plant.

Passion flower

Varieties of passion flower (*Passiflora caerulea*) all require careful training and pruning to get the best results. These evergreen or semi-evergreen tendril climbers are woody stemmed. The aim with pruning is to develop a permanent framework of branches that will produce a succession of flowering side shoots. If training against a flat surface such as a wall or fence, choose a plant with several stems that can be spaced about 15cm (6in) apart across the support. Unbranched specimens can be encouraged to produce side shoots by cutting back to 30–45cm (12–18in) after planting. If you are training the plant up the post of a pergola or arch, two or three stems will be sufficient. Tie in the stems until they reach the top of the support and then pinch out the growing tip to encourage the side shoots to grow.

On pergolas and arches, trim back all side shoots except those near the top, which can be trained over the support until the framework is completely covered, then simply cut back shoots that have flowered and fruited to two buds of the main framework. Overgrown and neglected plants can be rejuvenated by cutting back one or two of the older branches in the framework each year, to a younger side shoot lower down.

Actinidia kolomikta

Solanum crispum 'Glasnevin'

Potato vine

Solanum crispum 'Glasnevin' and the white form, *S. laxum* 'Album', which have just one or two stems, benefit from being cut back after planting in spring to encourage side shoots to be produced lower down which can then be trained up the support to form the main framework.

These should be spaced out and tied into the support as they grow. Once the climber is established, simply prune all the new growth to just two or three buds of the main framework during late spring after the threat of frost has passed.

Overgrown and neglected plants can be rejuvenated by cutting back one or two of the older branches in the framework each year.

Trumpet vine

Encourage *Campsis radicans* to bush out and produce new shoots from low down on the climber by pruning back to buds about 15cm (6in) from the ground during the spring after planting. If more than three or four side shoots are produced, remove the weakest first, before spreading out the rest and tying them into their support to form the main framework. Thereafter, once the climber is established, simply prune all new growth to two or three buds of the main framework during late winter or early spring. Overgrown and neglected plants can be rejuvenated by cutting back all stems hard in the winter.

Ornamental vines

Vigorous ornamental vines, such as *Vitis* and *Parthenocissus*, require very little routine pruning, other than the removal of any dead or damaged stems. If they outgrow their allotted space, cut back about half of the oldest shoots to the main framework and trim the remainder to keep them within bounds. Where space is very restricted, cut all new growth back to within two or three buds of the main framework each winter.

Ampelopsis

An increasingly popular climber, *Ampelopsis brevipedunculata* is a vigorous self-clinging plant that can be left to its own devices if you have the space. In a smaller garden it makes a lovely climber over a pergola, where it can be trained to produce a curtain of handsome leaves and attractive berries. Train the main stem along the pergola cross beam and allow the new shoots to cascade. Cut back all new growth to this framework each winter to keep it neat.

Chocolate vine

One of the 'must-have' plants of recent years, the chocolate vine (*Akebia quinata*) bears maroon-chocolate flowers with a hint of vanilla during late spring and early summer. Although regular pruning is not necessary, if they do need cutting back, do it in late spring after flowering – cutting back with shears to encourage fresh growth. Old plants can be rejuvenated by cutting back one or two of the oldest stems.

Dutchman's pipe

Easy to keep within bounds, the Dutchman's pipe (*Aristolochia*) responds well to hard pruning. If there is no need to keep it within bounds, let its twining stems spread freely. Prune either after flowering during summer or before buds break in early spring.

Coral plant

Do not hard-prune the Coral plant, *Berberidopsis corallina*, because it does not respond well to severe treatment. Instead, tidy it up by regular trimming to keep it within bounds. Prune in spring after the threat of frost has passed, removing only dead, damaged or wayward stems.

PRUNING ESTABLISHED CLIMBERS

1 Late autumn or early winter are the ideal times to prune overgrown deciduous climbers. Without the leaves, you can see the shape.

2 The first task is to remove all the dead and damaged wood so that you can regain a good shape and form to the climber.

3 Cut dead wood back to the healthy shoot or, if congested, take it back even farther, but always towards a shoot.

4 Once you have cut out the dead wood, take away congested wood, preferably the weakest and oldest growth.

5 Select some of the strongest and healthiest growths. These are most likely to be the youngest growth. Train them up the structure.

6 Tie in the healthy shoots to the supporting structure using garden twine. Distribute the younger shoots throughout the structure.

Virginia creeper

When the rampant growth of Virginia creeper, *Parthenocissus quinquefolia*, reaches the guttering or the roof, it is time to prune back hard to keep it under control. It climbs up surfaces by using its adhesive tendrils, so you may have to pull it away from its supporting structure to prune it. When established, this creeper can send out new growth up to 6m (20ft) in a year. Plants are very tolerant of trimming and can be cut right back to the base if required to rejuvenate the plant. Any pruning is best carried out in the spring.

Virginia creeper (*Parthenocissus quinquefolia*)

Pruning overgrown shrubs and climbers

If left unpruned for many years, most climbers will become woody and ugly at the base, with most of the ornamental flowers and leaves out of sight at the top of the plant. Fortunately, most climbers respond well to hard pruning and will produce vigorous new shoots that flower better if pruned in the right way and at the right time.

Getting started

Renovation pruning is best carried out during the dormant season when the sap is flowing slowly and there are no leaves in the way.

Choose a dry, mild day and arm yourself with a pair of secateurs (pruners), loppers for thicker stems and a pruning saw for woody growth over 3cm (1¼in) in diameter. A pruning knife is also useful for tidying up large cuts and if you are tackling thorny plants, wear stout gloves and goggles to protect your hands and eyes before you start.

Clematis

You can leave clematis unpruned for a few years, but if neglected for longer periods, it will gradually become a mass of unproductive woody stems at the base, with few flowers and little leaf cover. Any flowers that are produced tend to appear right at the top of the plant.

Clematis have a reputation for being difficult to prune (*see* page 123), but they all respond well to hard pruning. Clematis that flower on shoots produced during the current season respond to pruning back very severely to within 30cm (12in) of the base – cutting back to a newer side shoot or a pair of plump, healthy buds. Those that flower on older wood can also be cut back as severely, but you will miss out on the flowering display for a

HOW TO PRUNE OVERGROWN SHRUBS AND CLIMBERS

1 Tangled, congested stems need cutting out to encourage new, more vigorous and free-flowing growth.

2 Cut out the dead wood and take away congested growth, preferably the weakest and oldest, to allow new stems to flourish.

year or two. For this reason, you may prefer to cut them back over a three-year period, removing one in three of the stems during early spring, starting with the oldest.

Roses

Climbing and rambler roses will become less productive if they are left unpruned for many years. Large climbing roses can reach almost tree-like proportions, with large, gnarled, woody bases and sparse leaf cover, with all the green growth and flowers high up on the plant. They will have lost their vigour and often be plagued with diseases during the summer months. Fortunately, all but the most aged of climbing roses can be successfully renovated by severe pruning carried out during the early spring. When the stems are clear of leaves, it is easier to plan where to make the pruning cuts to maintain some sort of balanced shape. Aim to cut out one in three of the oldest stems – either right back to the base or to a younger side shoot close to the ground. Repeat over a three-year period to reinvigorate the plant.

Rambler roses are treated differently as they readily produce new shoots from underground or

very low down on the plant. This means that if they are neglected over a period of time, they will form an impenetrable thicket of stems that gradually loose their vigour. Improve flowering and reduce the overall size of the plant by cutting all the older stems right back to ground level during the dormant season.

Honeysuckles

Neglected honeysuckles can quickly become a huge mass of tangled, spindly, poorly flowering shoots, which makes them more prone to pest and disease attack when they are in this state. As for the blooms, the new growth and the flowers tend to be produced out of sight at the top of the plant.

The best way to tackle honeysuckle is to give it a haircut with a pair of shears, removing most of the tangled top growth. When you can see the framework of stems, identify which of the younger and vigorous stems you want to keep for a balanced shape and remove the rest.

You can cut all the stems back to younger side shoots or plump pairs of buds about 30cm (12in) from the ground, but you will miss out on the flowering display for a year or so.

Pruning other neglected shrubs

Vigorous shrubs can soon outgrow their space and will need trimming on a regular basis. If you haven't been able to carry out pruning for some years, you'll need to know which respond well to severe pruning and those best discarded.

Abelia
Responds well to severe pruning. Cut all the stems back to near ground level during early spring.

Artemesia
Responds well to severe pruning, so cut all the stems back to near ground level after the last frost in mid-spring.

Aucuba
Spotted laurels that have got too large or bare at the base can be cut back hard in spring. Remove one in three stems, starting with the oldest.

Berberis
Protect yourself with gloves and goggles before cutting back hard in early spring.

Buddleja
Responds well to severe pruning, so cut all the stems back to near ground level during early spring.

Camellia
Cut back oldest stems to a stubby framework 50cm (20in) from the ground after flowering in spring.

Ceanothus
Evergreen varieties are best replaced, but deciduous varieties can be cut back hard during spring.

Chaenomeles
Flowering quince can be cut back hard in spring after flowering. Remove one in three stems, starting with the oldest.

Choisya
Responds well to severe pruning, so cut all the stems back to near ground level during spring, after flowering.

Cistus
These do not respond well to severe pruning and so are best replaced.

Cornus
Dogwoods grown for stems and leaves can be cut back hard during early spring.

Corylus
Hazels respond well to severe pruning, so cut all the stems back to near ground level during winter.

Cotinus
Cut back to a stubby framework 50cm (20in) from the ground.

Cotoneaster
Fishbone cotoneaster (*C. horizontalis*) does not respond well to severe pruning, but individual shoots can be removed back to the main stem. Others can be cut back hard during spring.

Elaeagnus
Responds well to severe pruning, so cut all the stems back to near ground level during spring.

Escallonia
Responds well to hard pruning, so cut all the stems back to the main framework during spring.

Forsythia
Plants that are too large or bare at the base can be cut back hard in spring. Remove one in three stems, starting with the oldest.

Fuchsia
Hardy varieties respond well to severe pruning, so cut all the stems back to near ground level during early spring.

Garrya
Responds well to pruning over a period of three years, so cut one-third of the oldest stems back to the main framework each year during spring.

Hamamelis
These can struggle after hard pruning, with the more vigorous rootstock throwing up new shoots. Cut back during spring over three or four years and remove any new shoots from beneath the graft.

Helianthemum
These are short lived plants and are best replaced.

Kerria
Responds well to severe pruning, so cut all the stems back to near ground level during early spring.

Kolkwitzia
Responds well to severe pruning. Cut old stems to near ground level after spring flowering, leaving the youngest stems intact.

Lavender
Trim after the last frost in mid-spring, but don't cut back into bare wood.

Lavatera
Responds well to severe pruning. Cut stems back to near ground level during early spring.

Leycesteria
Responds well to hard pruning, so cut all the stems back to withing a few centimetres of the ground during spring.

Magnolia
Cut back oldest stems to 50cm (20in) from the ground after spring flowering.

Mahonia
Responds well to hard pruning, so cut all the old stems back to near ground level after flowering in spring, leaving the youngest to replace them.

Oleria
Responds well to severe pruning, so cut all the stems back to near ground level after flowering.

Osmanthus
Responds well to severe pruning, so cut all the stems back to near ground level after flowering.

Philadelphus
Mock oranges can be cut back hard by removing the oldest stems to ground level and cutting the youngest back by about half.

Photinia
Severe pruning is fine, so cut the stems back to near ground level during spring.

Pieris
Cut back oldest stems to 50cm (20in) from the ground after spring flowering.

Potentilla
Cut back hard to a stubby framework, but old plants are best replaced.

Rosemary
Cut back all stems by half or replace with a new one.

Sambucus
Can be cut back hard, but best replaced.

Santolina
Cut back hard to a stubby framework, or replace old plants with new ones.

Skimmia
Cut back hard to a stubby framework, but old plants are best replaced.

Weigela
Responds well to severe pruning, so cut all the stems back to near ground level during early spring.

Basic propagation

One of the joys of being a gardener is to grow your own plants from seed, cuttings or layering. Growing them on until they can be planted and become established in the beds or borders provides a tremendous sense of satisfaction.

Some gardeners, however, are put off or intimidated by growing plants from such an early stage, or have been unsuccessful in their attempts and prefer to spend much more money at a garden centre or nursery on plants that they believe they can grow more successfully.

If you follow the simple rules of propagation carefully and remember to water and shade plants as appropriate, your beds and borders will be flourishing with your own homegrown shrubs and climbers.

Growing your own plants from the beginning – either from seeds, cuttings or layering – is immensely satisfying. It isn't at all hard to do once you have learned a few basics.

Propagating plants

Many shrubs and climbers are easy to propagate and you can use a variety of different methods. Whichever technique you choose will depend on the type of plant you want to increase.

Raising your own shrubs and climbers from seed can be a worthwhile exercise if you want a lot of plants of the same type, such as for a hedge or for ground cover. It's also worth trying for plants, such as daphne, which are difficult to propagate in other ways. However, it is worth bearing in mind that you can raise only species from seed – results from named cultivars will be variable, with few being of real garden value.

Some plants are easy to raise using any one of a range of different methods, while others can only be propagated easily using only a single technique. Your success when propagating your own plants will also depend on timing and the equipment you have. It is very important to propagate plants at the right time of the year. Softwood cuttings taken in spring, for example,

If you don't have a propagator, cover a pot with a plastic bag. Inflate it to ensure that the bag is not in contact with the leaves. Remove the bag when the plants have rooted.

will often root in a matter of weeks, but delay that until the summer and some subject might not root at all.

Seeds will germinate and cuttings will root much more quickly if you can provide the right environment. It is essential that they do not run short of moisture and are kept at the optimum temperature for the plant you are trying to propagate.

Equipment

You don't need a lot of expensive equipment – a simple plastic bag cover and a snug spot on a warm, shaded windowsill will be sufficient for many shrubs and climbers. Others will germinate and root successfully in a coldframe or a basic border propagator made from old coat hangers and a supermarket carrier bag! Slightly more sophisticated versions of this can be made from kits or by buying the correct equipment (*see* Making a tunnel cloche, opposite).

However, for the best results it is worth investing in a thermostatically controlled, heated propagator if you want to raise plants from seeds or cuttings that germinate or root better in warm conditions.

Before you start propagating plants, it is worth thinking about where and how you are going to look after them once they have started to grow. There can be nothing more frustrating than raising a batch of new plants from seed or cuttings, only to find that you do not have sufficient shelf space in the greenhouse or enough room in the coldframe to accommodate them all.

You will also need to have the time to water, feed and pot the new plants on periodically so that they don't receive a check in growth, so bear this in mind before you start.

Harvesting seed from berries

Seeds in berries are often lost to the birds. It is, therefore, worthwhile protecting one or two selected branches with netting before the berries start to ripen. Although most harvested ripe berries can be sown as they are, you may prefer to clean the seed before sowing. The simplest way to do this is to place the berries in a polythene bag, squashing them thoroughly before tipping the pulp into a bowl of water and mixing well. The berry flesh will float and the seeds will sink. Collect the seed and sow or treat as necessary before sowing.

Collecting your own seed

It is perfectly possible to collect your own seed from shrubs and climbers. It is important to collect the seed as soon as they are ripe, but before they are eaten by birds and rodents. Ripe seed from your garden will often germinate more readily than shop-bought seed, but, depending on the plant, you may have to treat it first to overcome in-built germination inhibitors (see below).

Temperature treatments

Cold Many hardy shrubs and climbers that are native to areas prone to cold winters will germinate readily only after they have received a period of cold.

You can do this naturally by sowing during the autumn in a shaded position outside and waiting for seedlings to appear during the spring, but you will run the risk of some winter losses.

Alternatively, you can trick the seed into germinating more quickly by giving it a period of time at a temperature of 1–3°C (35–7°F),

The easiest way to do this is to place the seed in a sealed container with some moist peat or sand and put them in the crisper drawer at the bottom of the refrigerator for six to eight weeks before sowing. Some seed may require exposing to two 'fake' winters before germinating, so you will have to repeat this process before sowing the seed.

Hot and cold A few plants that come from areas that have warm autumns and cold winters produce seed that requires a period of warmth before the cold treatment. You can achieve this by placing the sealed container in a propagator set at 18–20°C (64–8°F) for about a month before subjecting it to the cold treatment.

Hard seed coats

Seeds with hard seed coats often take many years to germinate because they are unable to take up water until the seed coat has started to break down. However, you can speed up this process in several different ways, depending on the strength of the seed coat you are trying to breach.

Soaking Most seed can be encouraged to take up water by soaking them in tepid water for 24 hours. As a general rule of thumb, any seed that sinks after this period will be ready to sow.

Boiling If all the seed remains on the surface, try soaking in boiling water for 24 hours by placing the seed in a thermos flask and adding boiling water from the kettle. Again, any seed that sinks after this period will be ready to sow.

Rubbing Some seed has such a thick coat that soaking isn't sufficient to break down the seed coat. In this case, the coats can be worn away by rubbing. The easiest way to do this

is to line a jar with some fine-grade abrasive paper. Place the seed inside the jar, screw on the lid and shake or roll the jar for up to ten minutes. After this, give the seed the soaking treatment. Repeat the process, if necessary.

Nicking Larger seed can be tackled individually by cutting through the seed coat by using a sharp knife or scuffing them with an old nail file. Make the cut or abrasion on the opposite side of the seed from the scar.

Leave it to nature A few plants, such as crataegus, do not respond to these treatments and so have to be stratified naturally outside, which helps to break down their seed coat so that they can absorb moisture and germinate. This may take two winters to achieve.

To keep the seed safe while this happens, place them on layers of moist sand in a robust but ventilated container that is both bird- and rodent-proof. Place in a cool spot outside in permanent shade.

MAKING A TUNNEL CLOCHE

1 Prepare the soil thoroughly by digging over and removing all weeds. Lay out the cloche and space the supports along the plastic.

2 Carefully insert the hoops into the soil, ensuring that they are spaced sufficiently to hold the plastic taut over the prepared bed.

3 Pull the plastic sheeting taut over the frame. Gather the ends together and secure with sticks or pegs.

4 Heap a low bank of soil over the edge of the plastic sheeting to secure it in place and to stop any draughts getting inside.

Sowing seed

For successful plants, it is essential to provide the right conditions at the earliest possible moment – and that means when sowing.

Basic methods

How you sow your seed will depend on how many plants you are trying to raise. If you want a lot of shrubs for a hedge or are planning to run a charity stall at your local fair, you may be better off sowing into a prepared seedbed outside during the autumn, provided your soil is well drained.

You will need to protect the bed from birds and rodents. You also need to be prepared to protect early emerging seedlings during early spring with a floating mulch of garden fleece. Alternatively, sow medium quantities of seed in a coldframe, where they are easier to

look after and protect. Many shrubs and climbers will germinate and grow on more quickly if raised indoors, and all tender and borderline plants should be protected in this way.

Large seed can be sown individually during autumn in holes about 10cm (4in) apart, deep enough so that they are covered with about 1–2cm (½in) of soil.

Smaller seed is best left until late winter, when it should be scattered over the surface and lightly raked into the soil or covered in a thin layer of sharp sand. Very fine seed is best sown in spring on the surface and misted regularly to keep moist.

Small amounts of seed and all fine seed are easier to sow in pots or trays filled with potting mix and placed in the coldframe. Most spring-sown seed need a temperature of 15°C (60°F) to germinate and should be

sown in a container in a thermostatically controlled propagator or covered with plastic and placed on capillary matting in a heated greenhouse.

Once the seeds reach sufficent growth, they need to be thinned and potted on, a process called pricking out. This may be the first spring after an autumn sowing or during the following autumn, depending on how the seedlings are developing. Spring-sown seed should be pricked out into individual pots when large enough to handle.

All seedlings need a well-lit spot, out of direct sunlight, and need to be kept moist. All seed raised indoors or in a coldframe will need weaning off the warmer and more protected environment very gradually before planting outside, known as 'hardening off'.

SOWING SEED IN A POT

1 You will need a clean pot, sowing mix, seeds (your own or from a packet), plastic sheeting or a glass cover, a leveller and labels.

2 Fill the pot with the sowing mix. This mix deliberately has few nutrients, which could damage the little seedlings.

3 When the pot is full, level it off and then firm it down, either with a wooden block or the bottom of another pot.

4 Sprinkle the seeds over the top of the sowing mix very thinly. Very small seeds can be mixed with fine sand to make this easier.

5 Spread a fine layer of sowing mix or vermiculite over the surface of the pot. You can use a sifter to do this.

6 Label and lightly water them carefully. Cover with the plastic or glass. Keep inside or place in a heated propagator.

Shrubs and climbers to raise from collected seed

Abutilon Collect dry seed from seed-pods and sow immediately. No treatment necessary.

Amelanchier Pick ripe berries, remove seed and sow immediately. A warm and cold period is necessary for germination; alternatively, sow in spring.

Aucuba Pick ripe berries, remove seed and sow immediately. No treatment necessary.

Berberis Harvest ripe berries and sow after cold treatment to break dormancy; alternatively, leave outside during winter in a coldframe.

Callicarpa Collect seed from ripe fruits and sow immediately in a coldframe outside; alternatively, keep seed until spring and sow then.

Callistemon Collect seed and keep dry until spring. Sow on the surface of the potting mix.

Camellia Seed should be pre-soaked in warm water and its hard covering should be filed down to leave a thin covering. It usually germinates in 1–3 months at 23°c. Prick out into pots when they are large enough to handle. Grow them on in light shade in the greenhouse for at least their first winter.

Caryopteris Collect fruits and remove seed. Keep dry until spring and sow then. No treatment necessary.

Ceanothus Collect seed and soak in hot water before sowing to help break down the hard seed coat. Give cold treatment to break dormancy.

Chaenomeles Collect seed from ripe fruits and sow immediately in a coldframe outside, or keep seed to sow in spring.

Clematis Harvest seed and sow after cold treatment to break dormancy; alternatively, leave outside over winter in a coldframe.

Clianthus Collect dry seed from seed-pods and rub the seed coat or soak in water to break it down.

Leycesteria formosa

Colutea Collect dry seed from seed-pods and rub the seed coat or soak in water to break it down.

Cotinus Collect ripe seed and sow immediately outside or in a coldframe.

Cotoneaster Pick ripe berries, crush and remove seed. A warm and cold period is necessary for germination. Sow in spring.

Cytisus Collect seed and sow immediately outside or in a coldframe. Or store dry until spring, then soak in hot water before sowing to break down the hard seed coat.

Daphne Collect ripe fruit, remove seed and sow immediately after cold treatment to break dormancy. Some species may require two cold winters to germinate.

Enkianthus Surface-sow seed on lime-free potting mix immediately after collection and place in a heated propagator set at 15°C (60°F). Cover seed tray with clear film (plastic wrap) to prevent the seed from drying out.

Euonymus Collect ripe seed and sow immediately outside or in a coldframe.

Fatsia Collect ripe fruits and remove seed before sowing immediately. Place in a heated propagator set at 15°C (60°F).

Forsythia Harvest seed and sow after cold treatment to break dormancy, or leave outside during winter in a coldframe

Fuchsia Collect ripe fruits and remove seed and store for sowing in spring. Place in a heated propagator set at 20°C (68°F).

Genista Collect seed-pods and store dry until spring. Remove seed and sow after rubbing or soaking in hot water to break down the hard seed coat.

Hibiscus Collect seed-pods and store dry until spring. Extract seed and sow. No treatment necessary.

Hypericum Collect seed-pods and store dry until spring. Extract seed and sow. No treatment necessary.

Kalmia Surface-sow seed on lime-free soil mix immediately after collection and place in a heated propagator set at 15°C (60°F). Cover seed tray with clear film to prevent the seed from drying out.

Lavandula Collect and dry seedheads, remove seed and give cold treatment before sowing to break dormancy.

Leycesteria Collect ripe seed and sow immediately outside or in a coldframe.

Lonicera Harvest ripe berries, remove seed and sow after cold treatment to break dormancy; alternatively, leave outside during winter in a coldframe.

Paeonia Sow after two periods of cold treatment to break dormancy; alternatively, leave outside during winter in a coldframe for two years.

Philadelphus Collect ripe seed and sow after cold treatment to break dormancy; alternatively, leave outside during winter in a coldframe.

Pieris Surface-sow seed on lime-free compost immediately after collection and place in a heated propagator set at 15°C (60°F). Cover seed tray with clear film to prevent seed from drying out.

Euonymus elatus 'Compactus'

Seedling aftercare

Seeing your seedlings grow is a very satisfying experience. There is great pleasure to be had from seeing a tiny seed develop into a big plant that can climb up the side of a house or grow into a fully mature shrub, covered in beautiful flowers.

Seedling care

Growing shrubs from seed requires more patience than propagating climbers, as many shrubs take a number of years between sowing and growing to reach flowering size.

Once the seedlings emerge, they should be allowed to grow on in situ, provided there is sufficient room, and should be watered regularly. When the first set of true leaves appear, they are ready for pricking out. True leaves are usually the first set of leaves that emerge after the original germination leaves. The seedlings are ready for potting on when they have two or more sets of leaves large enough to handle. Pot up individually into pots that will provide plenty of root depth. However, it is important to water the seedlings an hour or so before pricking them out to make the roots easier to separate.

The most important aftercare task is to check how much watering your seedlings require so that you can keep them thriving.

Always handle the seedlings carefully by their leaves, never by the fragile stem that is so easily bruised or damaged.

Transfer the seedlings one by one into their own individual pots. You can do this by either filling a pot half way, holding the seedling in position and then filling up the pot with the remaining compost (*see* Pricking out seedlings, opposite), or you can hold the seedling gently by its leaves and loosen it from the seed tray with a dibber or just a pencil. Make a hole with your tool in the compost to accommodate the seedling, insert the seedling and gently push the compost towards the hole to fill it. Firm lightly with the dibber afterwards.

When to prick out seedlings

Prick them out as soon as possible, as the sowing mix is not very rich in nutrients and the seedlings will soon become starved. This may be the first spring after an autumn sowing or during the following autumn, depending on the rate of development of the seedlings.

Spring-sown seed should be pricked out into individual pots as soon as they are large enough to handle. Keep all seedlings in a well-lit position that is out of direct sunlight and never let them run short of moisture.

If the seedlings are left for any length of time, they will become overcrowded and consequently spindly and unable to grow properly.

Most seedlings are best pricked out into individual plant pots rather than seed trays as they will need to have space to grow. If they are overcrowded, the seedlings will fail to make sturdy young plants. As is more than likely, you will have many more seedlings than you need, so

some will have to be disposed of – either on to the compost heap for recycling or given to friends.

Compost types

Use a good potting compost (soil mix) that doesn't contain too much fertilizer. You can use a stronger one when you pot the seedlings on at a later stage.

Seed and potting composts are available in soil-based and soilless forms. Whichever you use will be a matter of personal preference. Seeds seem happy in either, but different composts seem to suit different regimes. Try some of each to see which suits your seeds.

Soilless composts are planting mixes that are based on fibrous material, such as peat or coir. The advantages are that they are lightweight and moisture-retentive, but they are a bit too easy to overwater and difficult to rewet if allowed to dry out.

Soil-based composts are heavier than soilless ones, are well-draining, difficult to overwater and absorb moisture easily when dry.

Damping off

If your seedlings keel over and wilt, this could be due to a condition known as damping off. This is caused by a range of soil- and water-borne fungi that attack the stem base of the seedling, making it become thin and brown. A white, fluffy fungus may also appear. This same fungus may also attack in the soil, causing the seed to fail to germinate. The disease is encouraged by cool, humid conditions and also by overwatering.

To prevent damping off, always be scrupulously vigilant about cleanliness. Use clean containers, fresh compost and clean water.

Creating a seedbed

Choose a sheltered site that does not suffer unduly from late or early frosts. Dig over the soil carefully and remove any weeds, including the roots of perennial weeds. Incorporate sharp sand into the soil if the ground is not free draining. Create a raised bed about 20cm (8in) higher than the surrounding soil to improve the drainage further. Level the top of the bed and remove any lumps by raking both along the bed and across it until the surface has a fine breadcrumb-like structure. Allow the soil to settle, then rake again before sowing.

Aftercare

Turn the plant pots every few days to stop the seedlings growing lopsided as they try to head towards the light. Water the compost when needed to stop them drying out. You might want to use a mist gun rather than a watering can to avoid accidentally washing out the seedlings. Keep the seedlings out of direct sunlight for a day or two after pricking out and water when needed.

Hardening off

Hardening off is a process that gradually acclimatizes the seedling to life outside. All seed raised indoors or in a coldframe will need weaning off the warmer and more protected environment very gradually before they can be planted outside.

Plants raised in protected environments need acclimatizing to cooler temperatures and increased air movement. If they are not, the shock at planting out can kill them. The time it takes to harden off plants varies, but generally it takes between two to six weeks. You will have to slowly increase ventilation

PRICKING OUT SEEDLINGS

1 Half fill the pot with a suitable potting compost (soil mix). Take care to hold the individual seedling only by the leaves, not the stem or the root. Suspend the seedling over the centre of the pot, resting your hand on the edge of the pot to steady it. With the other hand, fill the pot with more compost.

2 Gently tap the pot on the table to settle the compost mix and lightly firm it down with your thumbs, levelling off the surface. If you have had any problems in the past with seedlings rotting, add a 1cm (½in) layer of fine grit to the surface of the pot. Once potted up, water the seedlings well.

and reduce the ambient temperature. Greenhouse-raised plants will need to be moved to a cool coldframe. A couple of weeks before you want to move them outside, reduce the amount of water the seedlings get. You should not be keeping them constantly moist – let the soil become a bit dry-looking between waterings. This has the effect of making the roots more efficient at extracting water from the soil, a trait the plant will find very beneficial when it is planted in garden soil.

About a week before planting out, let the seedlings get used to the outdoors by leaving them out during the day. If the weather is suitable, you may be able to leave them out overnight – but check the weather forecast first. When the soil outside is warm enough, you can plant away.

Camellias can be grown from seed with success, as this *Camellia* 'Cornish Spring' bush shows. Grow the pricked out seedlings on in light shade in the greenhouse for at least their first winter.

Propagating from cuttings

Most shrubs and climbers can be propagated from cuttings. Many will root perfectly well from softwood cuttings, which are taken in spring when the plant is actively growing, but some will root better during the summer from material that has started to ripen at the base, or even in winter from fully ripened wood.

Taking softwood cuttings

Softwood cuttings are cut from new sappy growth taken from shrubs and climbers that are still in active growth. This is usually in mid- to late spring. Collect material while it is turgid and showing no signs of wilting – ideally choose an overcast day or collect early in the morning. Select healthy-looking material that shows no signs of pest or disease attack and is representative of the plant you are trying to propagate. Ideally, choose material that is not flowering or about to flower.

If this is not possible, remove any flowering stems from the material before trimming it into cuttings. When you remove the material from the parent plant, use a clean, sharp knife or pair of secateurs (pruners), cutting just above a leaf joint. Make a clean cut, which will help minimize the chance of infection, and then place the material directly into a labelled plastic bag to prevent them from wilting. You must keep the cuttings out of direct sunlight until you are ready to prepare them.

Prepare the cuttings

• Trim the stems using a clean sharp knife just below a leaf joint, so that the cuttings are 2.5–8cm (1–3in) long, depending on the type of growth that the plant produces.
• Remove the lowest pair of leaves from all the cuttings and the growing tip from longer cuttings. Most cuttings should then have two to four leaves.
• Dip the bottom cut end of the cuttings into a pot of hormone

TAKING ROSE CUTTINGS

1 Select a side shoot that is still green but beginning to turn woody at the base. Cut just above an outward-facing bud.

2 From the removed stem, trim an individual cutting from the base, making the cut just below a leaf joint.

3 Having made your lower cut, now trim back the soft tip to leave a length of stem about 10cm (4in) long.

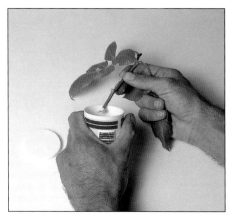

4 Remove the lower leaves and thorns of the cutting and dip the base in hormone rooting powder. Tap off any excess.

5 Using a dibble or a pencil, make a hole in the rooting medium and put the cutting into it, inserting it to two-thirds of its length.

6 Label the cutting and cover with a plastic bag 'tent' to ensure moisture retention. Don't allow the bag to touch the cutting.

POTTING UP AND POTTING ON CUTTINGS

1 Pot up the cuttings as soon as they have formed strong growth. Use an 8–10cm (3–4in) pot and a potting mix suitable for the young plants. Water thoroughly and keep out of direct sunlight for a couple of days while they recover from the root disturbance.

2 Cuttings that rooted earlier and have already been potted up for a month or more may need moving into larger pots. Check that the roots have filled the compost (soil mix) before you transfer them. If the compost has lots of white roots, pot on into a larger size.

3 When potting on, use a container a couple of sizes larger and put some compost in the bottom. Put the unpotted plant into the new container and trickle the same type of compost around the root ball. Firm well to remove air pockets.

rooting compound (also available as a gel), shaking off any excess, before inserting the prepared cuttings around the edge of a pot filled with moist, fresh cuttings compost.
• It is important to prevent softwood cuttings from wilting, so cover the container with a plastic bag, but make sure it is held clear of the cuttings by inserting short sticks or hoops of wire to hold it proud of

the cutting. Secure the bag in position around the pot using an elastic band. Alternatively, you can place the uncovered pot in a propagator with a lid.
• Place the pots of prepared cuttings in a warm, well-lit position that is out of direct sunlight. When the cuttings show signs of healthy growth, puncture the plastic bags to allow some air to enter and

surround the plant, or open the vents if they are being raised in a propagator.
• Gradually harden off the rooted cuttings by increasing ventilation and lowering the temperature. Once hardened off, they can be planted up individually into larger containers and filled with fresh, moist potting compost (soil mix) (*see* Potting on cuttings steps, above).

Avoiding disease problems

Softwood cuttings and the foliage of semi-ripe cuttings are susceptible to rot before the cuttings have had a chance to root. Apart from choosing healthy cuttings material, ensure that the propagation tools and equipment are clean and the compost fresh and sterile. You can help to prevent disease outbreaks by drenching the cuttings in a fungicidal solution once they are prepared. Check the information on the packaging for dilution rates and whether the fungicide can be used in conjunction with hormone rooting preparations.

ENCOURAGING BUSHY PLANTS

1 Bushy shrubs, such as the fuschia shown here, usually respond well to early 'pruning'. As soon as the cuttings have three pairs of leaves, pinch out the growing tip if you want a bushy shape.

2 New shoots will form after a few weeks. For really bushy plants, pinch out the tips of the side shoots as well. Repeat this process several times throughout the spring to encourage bushiness.

Summer cuttings

Many shrubs and climbers can be propagated from cuttings taken as growth slows down and new shoots start to ripen – turning woody at the base. Although rooting may take a little longer, the cuttings are generally easier to look after.

Types of cutting

Taking semi-ripe cuttings is largely the same as taking a softwood cutting (see below), except that the material is no longer growing vigorously and is starting to turn woody at the base. Where you make the bottom cut depends on the type of shrub or climber you are trying to propagate.

Nodal cutting Many shrubs and climbers can be raised from semi-ripe cuttings that are trimmed just below a leaf joint (or node). Simply make a straight cut across the stem just below the leaf joint so that the resulting cutting is about 8–10cm (3–4in) long. The leaves should then be trimmed off cleanly from the bottom half of the cutting.

Internodal cutting With this type of cutting, you will need to make a straight cut across the stem midway between leaf joints, so that the cutting is about 10cm (4in) long.

Stem cutting This an internodal or nodal cutting taken from part-way down a stem with the top of each cutting trimmed just above a leaf joint.

Basal cutting Trim off the cutting right at the base where it joins the previous year's growth – look for a slight swelling that is often present. Use a sharp knife or razor-blade to make the cut as close to the base of the material as possible.

Heeled cutting The cutting is removed from the parent tearing a short piece of woody material at the base from the previous year's growth – so that the cutting is 5–10cm (2–4in) long. Simply tidy up the 'heel' using a sharp knife so that it is 1–2cm (½–¾in) long before dipping in rooting hormone and inserting in compost.

Leaf-bud cutting A few shrub species, such as camellia, fatsia and mahonia, and many climbers, including campsis, clematis (see opposite), ivy and honeysuckle, root best if the cutting is simply a leaf joint. Make the top cut just above the leaf joint and the bottom cut about 3–5cm (1–2in) below it, using a straight cut made with a sharp knife. You should be able to get several cuttings from a single stem. These cuttings are best taken during the late summer.

TAKING SOFTWOOD CUTTINGS

1 Typically, a stem is taken from the new shoots produced in the current year. Cut off below the third or fourth pair of leaves.

2 Trim or pull off the lowest pair of leaves. Trim the base of the stem with a sharp knife, cutting just below a leaf joint.

3 Dip the end of the cutting into hormone rooting powder. Although not necessary, the powder will speed up rooting.

4 Make a hole in the compost with a dibber and insert the cutting, firming round it. Don't force the cutting, as you may damage it.

5 Water and place in a propagator or, as here, cover with a plastic bag – but don't let it touch the leaves. Secure with a tie twist.

Clematis cuttings

Clematis are easiest to root from double leaf-bud cuttings taken during early to mid-summer. Trim the top of the cutting just above a pair of leaves and the bottom cut about 3–5cm (1–2in) below it. If you are trying to get a lot of new plants from a single climber, you can double the number of cuttings by carefully cutting down through the middle of the main stem vertically so that each cutting has a half-thickness stem and one leaf.

Rooting summer cuttings

Although you can root summer cuttings in pots covered with plastic or in a heated propagator, they are just as easy to root in a simple border propagator in the garden.

Choose a position in a sheltered spot that is in light shade for most of the day. Dig a trench 5cm (2in) deep and about 25cm (10in) wide and fill it with sharp sand. Make hoops over the bed out of stiff wire such as an old coat hanger. Insert the prepared cuttings into the sand and water well. Push the wire hoops in every 15cm (6in) along the bed and cover with an opaque piece of plastic – such as an old supermarket carrier bag. This should be buried in the soil on one side and held down with bricks or stones at the ends and along the other side.

Check to see if the cuttings need watering from time to time and remove and discard any that show signs of disease.

Once most of the cuttings have rooted, cut some ventilation slashes in the cover to help harden them off, removing the cover completely after a couple of weeks. After this, you can then pot up or plant out the rooted cuttings.

Propagate clematis from double leafbud cuttings taken during early to mid-summer. You can also root cuttings later in the year but they will need to be kept humid and will take longer to root.

Autumn and winter cuttings

Many deciduous and a few evergreen shrubs can be propagated from hardwood cuttings using stems produced during the most recent season's growth. A few difficult-to-propagate shrubs can be increased from root cuttings taken during the dormant season.

Harwood cuttings

Once the current season's shoots have ripened fully and the leaves have fallen, it is an ideal time to take hardwood cuttings from many clump-forming deciduous shrubs. Select vigorous and healthy stems that are about the thickness of a pencil and typical of the plant you are trying to propagate. Remove the stems from the parent plant using secateurs (pruners), just above a bud. Trim the cutting to about 20–30cm (8–12in) with a straight cut just below a bud at the base and a sloping cut just above a bud at the top. This will help you identify which way up to insert the cuttings later on. Wound difficult-to-root subjects and dip the straight-cut ends in rooting hormone (*see* Improving box, right).

Hardwood cuttings are usually easy to root, but you will have to be patient as it can take up to a year. The simplest way to root them is in a slit trench 15–20cm (6–8in) deep that's been lined with sharp sand. Space the cuttings 8–10cm (3–4in) apart along the row, inserting each cutting into the sand so that about one-third is still above ground when the trench is refilled. Water and weed the area around the cutting throughout the following year and plant out the rooted cuttings or pot them up the following autumn.

Difficult-to-root subjects, such as this *Rhododendron* 'Loder's White', can be encouraged to root by cutting a thin sliver off the base of the stem of the prepared hardwood cutting.

Improving your chances of success

Some shrubs and climbers can be reluctant to root from softwood, semi-ripe and hardwood cuttings, but you can improve your chances of success with many by increasing the size of the cut and applying a specially formulated hormone to the cut surface.

Wounding Difficult-to-root subjects, such as rhododendrons and magnolias, can be encouraged to root by cutting a thin sliver off the base of the stem of the prepared cutting. Use a sharp knife on one side of the cutting a few centimetres (1in) from the base to remove a thin piece of material.

Rooting hormone Rooting hormone products are available as powders, liquids and gels that are simply applied to the base of the prepared cutting before it is inserted into the compost. They contain special chemicals that stimulate rooting, making difficult-to-root subjects easier to propagate and getting quicker results for most other cuttings. To avoid contaminating the hormone, tip a small amount into a saucer and use this. Throw away any unused rooting hormone that's left in the saucer once all cuttings have been completed. Bear in mind that rooting hormone deteriorates rapidly, so buy fresh stocks each year to make sure of its effectiveness.

Root cuttings

A few shrubs, including aralia, chaenomeles, clerodendron, rhus, romneya and rubus, can be increased from root cuttings taken during the dormant season. Excavate around the base of one side of the shrub to expose a few suitable large, fleshy roots. Select vigorous, healthy roots of about drinking-straw thickness if possible and sever them from the parent plant. Prepare the cuttings using a sharp knife so that they are

TAKING HARDWOOD CUTTINGS

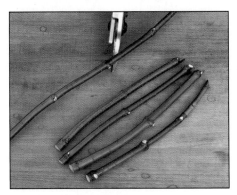

1 Select healthy, blemish-free pieces of wood about the thickness of a pencil. Cut each of these into sections about 20–25cm (8–10in long), angling the top cut.

2 Moisten the bases of the cuttings in water and then dip them in hormone rooting powder. Although not essential, the powder should increase the success rate.

3 Prepare a narrow slit-trench deep enough for the cuttings. Dig down enough so that the top 2.5–5cm (1–2in) of the cuttings will be proud of the earth surface.

4 Loosely fill the trench to about two-thirds with sharp sand or fine grit. This allows the passage of air around the bases of the cuttings and will help prevent rotting off.

5 Insert the cuttings about 8–10cm (3–4in) apart, making sure that the angled cut is uppermost, leaving about 5–10cm (2–4in) above the ground.

6 Firm the soil around the cuttings, ensuring that they are not over-compacted. Leave the cuttings for a whole growing season before lifting and planting out the next winter.

about 5–10cm (2–4in) long, making a straight cut nearest the end of the root nearest the crown and a sloping cut at the other end.

Dip the cuttings in a fungicidal solution to prevent rot setting in. Then, either insert the cuttings around the edge of a pot filled with a well-drained sowing compost (soil mix), with the straight cut just proud of the surface, or lay the cuttings horizontally on a tray of compost.

Cover the compost surface in either case with a thin layer of grit before watering well and allowing to drain. Place the prepared cuttings in a cool, sheltered spot, such as a cold frame or under a cloche in the garden.

Cornus kousa cuttings are taken in the dormant season after the leaves fall in autumn. However, it can be more successfully propagated by using seed, as this produces more vigorous plants.

Layering

Layering is perhaps the most underrated – and yet one of the easiest and most successful – methods of propagating many shrubs and climbers. There are several variations on a theme to layering, all of which involve wounding and partially covering a vigorous, healthy shoot to encourage it to root while it is still attached to the parent plant.

Layering explained

Some plants, notably magnolia and cornus, are very difficult to propagate by taking cuttings. Fortunately, layering is a very simple way of making new plants from old

ones. It involves promoting the development of new roots from a plant's stem, with the stem still attached to the plant. Once it has rooted, it is then severed from the main plant and planted up on its own. Layering can occur spontaneously, when branches of a plant touch the ground and decide to take root.

As the technique of layering is an asexual one, the plants that are produced always have the same flowers, foliage and fruit as the parent plant, which is very beneficial if you want to keep an old and favourite plant going. There are six different methods of layering:

LAYERING

1 Dig over the soil where you want to make the layer, incorporating some well rotted manure or compost.

2 Select a low stem and trim off side shoots Bend it down until it touches the ground. Make a small slit in the stem at that point.

3 Make a hole 10cm (4in) deep, and lay the stem in it, securing in place with a loop of wire. Cover with soil.

4 Additional security can be provided by placing a rock over the buried layer to prevent the stem from moving.

5 Approximately 16–18 months after layering, the shoot will have rooted. Cut it off from the parent plant, making a clean cut.

6 You should now have an independent plant with its own root system. Pot up and grow on until it is big enough to be planted out.

simple, serpentine, French, tip, mound and air, although simple and air are the most commonly used.

Simple layering

First, select a suitable vigorous, healthy stem low down on the plant. It should be flexible enough to bend down to ground level without snapping. If there are no suitable candidates, prune back one or two of the lowest branches to encourage new shoots in spring. These can be layered the following autumn.

Thoroughly dig over the area of soil under the potential layer and remove any weeds. If the soil is poor, incorporate old potting compost (soil mix) and grit. Use a pair of secateurs (pruners) to trim off any side shoots from the layer and then remove any leaves on the part of the shoot that is to be buried. Pull the layer down to the soil and make a

Cotinus coggygria 'Royal Purple'

shallow depression in the soil using a trowel along the line of the layer, about 30cm (12in) behind the tip of the layer. Carefully bend the stem to form a right-angle about 20cm (8in) behind the growing tip. Secure it into the bottom of the hole using a bent piece of stiff wire. Next, tie the growing tip vertically to a bamboo cane.

With difficult-to-root shrubs and climbers you can improve your chances of success by wounding the stem of the layer on the underside where it will be in contact with the soil using a sharp knife. You then dust the cut surface with rooting hormone before pegging the layer into position, as before.

Cover the portion of the layer that has been pegged to the soil with more soil and firm lightly before watering thoroughly. Water and weed as necessary during the following year, also checking that rooting is taking place. It will take anything from 6–18 months for the layer to root, depending on the species you

are layering, which can then be separated from the parent plant and moved to a suitable position elsewhere in the garden.

Serpentine layering

There are several variations on the layering theme, one of which is serpentine layering. This method is suitable for propagating climbers, such as clematis, wisteria and honeysuckle, which all produce long flexible shoots that can be layered several times along their length.

During early spring, bury a stem at intervals so that it loops in and out of the soil, making sure it has the growing tip poking out of the ground (as for simple layering). It is essential that each of the loops that are out of the ground has at least one leafbud so that it can produce new shoots once rooted.

By autumn of the same year, each of the loops should have rooted and can then be separated and planted out or potted up. Propagating in this way means that a single stem can produce several new plants in a single growing season.

Magnolia aquifolium 'Apollo'

Layering naturally

Many climbers, including ivies and ornamental vines as well as some thicket-forming shrubs, spread by producing roots on shoots that touch the ground. With climbers, the trailing shoots scramble horizontally, rooting as they grow, until they come across something to climb, while shrubs produce long pliable stems that arch out and root where the tip touches the ground. If this happens in your garden, use the self-layered shoots to propagate your plants. Simply cut off the rooted layer from the parent plant and then pot it up using fresh compost (soil mix) and cut back the top growth to a bud about 15cm (6in) from the ground. If the layer is established and has started to form a new plant, lift it with as much soil around the roots as possible and move it to a suitable position in the garden where it has room to grow and develop.

You can grow new plants of the *Amelanchier* species by mound layering. The *Amelanchier lamarckii* shown here produces coppery-red leaves that turn green in summer and then red, orange or yellow in autumn.

French layering

A few vigorous shrubs, such as cotinus, cornus and willow, can be layered by shallowly burying the whole shoot.

Prepare the selected shoot in autumn by pegging it into position. This will encourage all the buds along its length to break at the same

Heathers, such as *Calluna vulgaris* 'Wickwar Flame', are propagated by mound layering.

time in spring. Once this happens, prepare the soil as for simple layering and then peg the stem to the ground and carefully earth it up so that the stem is just below the surface and the top 5cm (2in) of the new side shoots can be seen.

As the side shoots grow, earth them up periodically to increase the depth of soil over the layered stem, until the ridge of soil is about 15cm (6in) high.

By the autumn, roots will have been produced along the length of the layered stem and each side shoot can be separated with its own portion of rooted layer.

Tip layering

A few shrubs, notably ornamental blackberries and winter jasmine, can be propagated by rooting the tips of their long, flexible shoots into the ground. This is how they would spread naturally if left to their own devices.

Mound layering

Also known as stooling or burying, this method of layering is suitable for small bushy shrubs, such as heathers, provided you have a well-drained soil.

As the name suggests, the whole plant is gradually covered in a 5–10cm (2–4in) deep mound of free-draining soil so that the roots are encouraged to form on the buried portion of each of the main stems. These can then be separated from the parent plant and potted up or replanted the following autumn.

Air layering

Air layering, often associated only with the propagation of house plants, is also a useful way of propagating some shrubs, such as rhododendron, magnolia, witch hazel and hydrangea, as well as woody climbers such as wisteria.

Air layering, also known as Chinese layering, as the technique was first devised by the Chinese

Layering aftercare

Once the newly rooted layers have been removed from the parent plant, they can either be replanted in the garden or potted up in a container and kept in the greenhouse until they are strong enough to survive being planted outside.

When they are ready to plant out in the garden, they are also ready to be pruned to promote new growth. Prune so that the leaf area is reduced to about one-third.

Plants outdoors should be shaded lightly through their first season. However, after the first winter the screens can be removed as the plants should be robust enough at this stage to survive outside without any additional protection.

many centuries ago, is a useful way of layering woody shrubs and climbers that don't produce pliable stems near to the ground that can be layered by other more conventional techniques. The best time to air layer is during the spring when new growth starts and sap rises.

Choose a healthy and vigorous stem that is representative of the plant as a whole. Trim off all its side shoots for about 30cm (12in) from the tip. Using a sharp knife, make a clean, shallow cut that is slanting upwards, towards the tip. The cut

should be about 5cm (2in) long and reach about halfway through the stem. Use a matchstick to hold the cut open while you dust both the cut surfaces with a hormone rooting compound.

Next, slide in a little moist sphagnum moss, peat or fresh cuttings compost into the cut before removing the matchstick. Tie a piece of black plastic around them, about 5cm (2in) below the cut, so that it can form a sleeve over the layer. Pack the plastic sleeve with moist sphagnum moss so that it forms a

5–8cm- (2–3in-) diameter bulge around the cut stem. Secure the tip end of the moss or the cuttings compost ball by tying the other end of the plastic to the stem and sealing it with tape. This will prevent any water running down the stem and waterlogging the moss or compost. It is important to use black plastic, rather than the clear type, because it will exclude any light and encourage rooting, while keeping the moss/compost moist but not too wet.

Inspect the layer every few months to see if it has rooted. The time this takes varies from plant to plant and with the time of year – taking anything from just three to 18 months. If there are insufficient roots, recover it after moistening, if required. Leave it for another period before inspecting again.

Once sufficient roots have formed, use a pair of secateurs (pruners) to sever the stem just below the roots. Remove the plastic and carefully tease out the roots before potting up into a container, using fresh potting mix. Don't forget to give it a good drink of water afterwards and to keep it well watered until well established.

AIR LAYERING

1 Layer the plant above the bare area of the stem, just below the leaves. If you are using the technique on a multi-stemmed plant to increase stock, remove a few leaves from the point where you want to make the cut.

2 Carefully make an upward slit about 3cm (1in) long, below the leaf joint. Use a sharp knife, particularly on woody plants, to get a clean cut. Do not cut more than halfway through the stem or the shoot may break.

3 Make a sleeve out of a sheet of black plastic, wrapping it around the stem (clear plastic is shown here to make the process easier to see) Fix the bottom of the sleeve using a twist tie or waterproof adhesive tape.

4 Brush a small amount of rooting hormone (either powder or gel) into the wound to speed up the rooting process. Pack a bit of spagnum moss into the wound to keep it open, or just use a matchstick.

5 Pack plenty of damp spagnum moss around the stem to enclose the wound. Cover with the plastic and secure at the top, as before. Keep the moss moist and check for rooting after a few months.

Common problems

Once well established and growing vigorously, shrubs and climbers will shrug off most pest and disease attacks. However, if they have recently been planted or are not growing well, they can fall victim to a wide range of problems. The most common pests to affect the ornamental garden are slugs and snails, aphids, whiteflies, caterpillars and vine weevils, while the most common diseases are blackspot, mildew, grey mould and rust. With the exception of blackspot, which attacks only roses, all the others can attack a wide range of garden plants.

Whether you want to take any steps to prevent and control pests and diseases on ornamental plants is largely a matter of personal choice. Some gardeners like to maintain a balance between pests and their natural predators, allowing a constant, low level of problems so that there is always sufficient food for the predators to keep them in the garden. Alternatively, you may prefer setting aside an area of the garden for this purpose – a wild corner where you can cultivate plants that are loved by common pests to act as a living larder for predatory birds and insects. You can also encourage natural predators to stay in your garden by providing them with shelter and suitable places to breed.

No matter how good a gardener you are, insects and diseases will affect your plants at some time. The best way to fight them is to understand what these invaders are and how they affect the plants.

Dealing with pests

The most common pests in most gardens are slugs and snails, but they do not cause any serious damage to shrubs and climbers once they are established and so are not covered here.

Catch them early

If a prominent or prized plant is attacked, you may prefer to take action to prevent the problem from spreading further. If you catch it early, you simply have to prune out the disease-affected parts of the plant or pick off individual pests, but if the problem becomes established, you may have to sacrifice affected plants to help protect their neighbours – either by cutting the affected plants back hard or removing them altogether. If you grow a lot of one plant in the same area, such as in a rose bed, pest and disease outbreaks are usually worse because the problem can spread easily from one plant to another. You can avoid this by mixing up plants in

Mammals

Mice, rabbits and deer can all be troublesome in some gardens. Although they are not widespread pests, where they do occur they can cause serious damage to shrubs and climbers. Mice are mainly a problem with new plants and seedlings; rabbits eat young shoots and strip bark from shrubs; while deer will cause similar damage higher up the plant. The best way to deal with mice is to set traps around vulnerable plants, such as in the coldframe or greenhouse. For rabbits, you'll need to erect a boundary barrier at least 90cm (3ft) high, with a further 30cm (12in) buried under the ground; while deer will require a fence at least 1.8m (6ft) high to keep them out of your garden.

Aphids appear quickly and in legions. They suck the sap out of the plants and spread viruses, causing plants to lose vigour or die.

borders or, in the case of roses, growing disease-resistant varieties. However, the following pests are all worth watching out for.

Aphids

Green, black, pink or brown insects attack actively growing shoot tips, quickly forming large colonies. Like other sap-sucking insects, aphids can transmit debilitating virus diseases. Be vigilant and pick off small colonies as soon as they are noticed. Where this is not possible, use a jet of water from a hose to dislodge them. Control with a suitable systemic insecticide.

Caterpillars

Voracious eaters of fresh new leaves, several common moth caterpillars can attack a wide range of ornamental plants. Caterpillars of the Angle Shades moth are green with V-shaped markings; Buff-Tip caterpillars are black and yellow; and grey-green caterpillars indicate that you have got the Small Ermine moth in residence. However, if silk webbing can be seen, you might have caterpillars of the web-forming Lackey moth or Hawthorn Webber moth. Fortunately, you don't need to identify the caterpillars to get rid of them. Simply pick off any that you

Caterpillars attack a wide range of plants. Pick them off leaves, let their natural predators deal with them, or use a pesticide.

The evidence of slugs and snails, which eat their way through stems. They are particularly troublesome during wet weather in spring.

see before they do too much damage. Those that produce webbing should have their 'tents' cut from the plant and opened out for birds. Severe infestations can be controlled using a biological control containing the bacterium *Bacillus thuringiensis*.

Vine weevil

Vine weevils seem to attack anything and everything. They can be a significant problem for anyone who grows a lot of shrubs and climbers in containers. Watch out for the tell-tale sign of notched leaves, which indicate the adult female is about, but it is the white grubs up to 8mm (⅜in) long that cause the real damage – feeding unnoticed on the roots. Vine weevils are flightless and so move around quite slowly. They

Pest-free shrubs and climbers

Abelia	Griselinia
Actinidia	Hebe
Aucuba	Hibiscus
Choisya	Jasminum
Cistus	Kerria
Cornus	Kolkwitzia
Corylus	Leptospermum
Cytisus	Myrtus
Deutzia	Parrotia
Escallonia	Phlomis
Euonymus	Photinia
Fatsia	Pittosporum
Fothergilla	Rosmarinus
Garrya	Santolina
Gaultheria	Skimmia

are usually introduced to an unaffected garden on new plants. Since vine weevils reproduce parthenogenically, it takes just a single female weevil to start off an infestation. Control is by catching the slow-moving adults at night, squashing any grubs that you find or applying biological controls. If you prefer to sleep at night, there is also a chemical control for vine weevil grubs that is applied as a drench to the compost of container plants.

Vine weevil larvae attack the roots while the parents eat holes in the leaves. They are becoming a big pest of shrubs and climbers.

Scale insects

These sap-sucking insects are immobile once they have found a suitable plant. Looking like round, raised spots on the stem or bark, they appear and hold on like miniature limpets.

Small numbers can be prised off individually. If you have a bad infestation, you can gain some control by rubbing over the affected stems with some soft soap. You can also use a suitable systemic insecticide to control these pests.

Galls

Many shrubs and climbers can be affected by galls, which appear as raised lumps on the upper or lower leaf surface and are caused by insects. The plant itself is stimulated by the insect to produce the odd-looking growths that can be either brightly coloured or well camouflaged. The main groups of insects that cause plants to produce galls are gall-wasps, gall-midges and gall-mites. They generally lay eggs inside the gall so that the hatching grub is protected by the plant as it feeds. In one particular type of attack by gall-mites, witches brooms are produced.

Control is unnecessary. If the galls are unsightly, cut off the affected foliage. On deciduous plants, rake up and bin the leaves at the end of the season in question.

Leaf-cutter bees

Semi-circular notches in the leaves of roses, privet and laburnums can be attributed to the activities of leaf-cutter bees, which collect material to build their nests.

The females get busy in early summer building individual cells out of pieces cut from suitable foliage.

The pest is a solitary bee that doesn't swarm or sting, and so is otherwise perfectly harmless. Little damaged is caused and no control is necessary. Unsightly leaves can be picked off if required.

Leaf miners

Tunnels, blotches and other leaf blemishes are caused by the grubs of certain insects. Different insects attack different types of plants. For example, the holly leaf miner causes unsightly tunnelling and brown areas in the fleshy leaves of this plant, which are caused by the grub of a fly. This can be a particular nuisance on hedges and hollies cut for indoor arrangements.

Different species of moth caterpillar cause similar damage to laburnums, gorse, lilac and other ornamental plants during early summer. Control is rarely called for because the plants are largely unaffected. However, if you want to stop further damage to hedges and prominent plants, dispose of hedge clippings and fallen leaves carefully, clear weeds that can harbour these pests and spray with a suitable systemic insecticide.

Box and bay sucker

These are two similar problems that affect two particular plants.

Box sucker attacks the Buxus species, causing the stunting of new growth so that the tips of the shoots often look like tiny cabbages.

Bay (Laurus nobilis) is attacked by tiny sap-sucking insects that cause the leaves to thicken and distort, often with yellow leaf margins.

In both cases, the control is a matter of removing the affected foliage or, in severe attacks, spraying with a suitable systemic insecticide.

Dealing with diseases

The most prevalent diseases affect a wide range of different plants. Their spread depends both on the vigour of the shrub or climber being attacked and also on the prevailing weather conditions.

Plant health

There are many different diseases that can affect your plants. Most of these are quite rare but every garden will suffer from its share of diseases at some point. In the main, most of these diseases are relatively easy to deal with, if you have made the correct diagnosis. As ever, it is best to be able to prevent disease rather than allowing it to take hold and spread in your garden.

The best way to control pests and diseases is to stay one step ahead of them and prevent them from becoming a problem in the first place. Stay vigilant at all times, so that when they do occur, you will be able to take decisive action quickly and effectively.

How to prevent pests and diseases

Practise good garden hygiene and you will go a long way to preventing outbreaks of pests and diseases. Clearing away fallen leaves and other debris and consigning any diseased material to the dustbin or bonfire, will help to prevent these problems carrying over from one year to the next.

It is also a good idea to keep weeds under control, which often act as a sink of infection. Always keep your eyes open for the first signs of pest and disease attack. When you are moving among your plants when watering, weeding or feeding, for instance, stay vigilant for tell-tale signs and symptoms of disease. Check them at night, too, since some serious pests, including slugs and vine weevils, are more active at night than they are at other times.

If you see anything untoward, take action quickly so that you can nip stop any problems before they spread and become more serious. Individual pests can be picked up and destroyed, while isolated outbreaks of disease can be pruned off the plant. Similarly, initial colonies of small insects such as aphids can be rubbed out between you finger and thumb. You can also stay one step ahead of the pests and diseases by putting down traps and barriers.

Powdery mildew

These are white, dusty-looking deposits that can be found on the young leaves and stems of plants, usually on the upper surface, causing their growth to become stunted and discoloured. It is caused by a range of fungi. Attacks are most acute during long, dry spells.

Treatment Remove and destroy any affected foliage and keep susceptible plants well watered during drought. Weed carefully, as the disease can be spread by weeds. Spray with a suitable systemic fungicide.

Downy mildew

Usually seen as yellow patches on the leaves, with grey or purple mould growing on the undersides, downy mildew is most prevalent in mild and damp weather.

Treatment Pick off and destroy any of the affected stems and try to encourage more air flow to flow between the plants by spacing them more widely. Spray healthy looking leaves with a suitable systemic fungicide to prevent a recurrence.

Powdery mildew looks like a dusty white-grey coating. It causes stunting and distortion of leaves, buds, growing tips and fruit.

Rust is a common fungal disease. Rusty patches or spots appear on the leaves, distorting growth and causing leaf drop.

Blackspot is a fungal disease that particularly affects roses. Black spots appear, primarily on the leaves, but sometimes on the stems.

The distinctive pinkish pustules of coral spot. The fungus enters through small wounds in the plant, usually caused by careless pruning.

Nutrient deficiencies

When plants run short of one or more particular nutrients, it can show up as leaf symptoms that are easy to confuse with disease symptoms. Magnesium and manganese deficiencies, for example, both cause yellowing between the leaf veins, while potash deficiency often causes the leaf edges to yellow or leaf tips to scorch.

The other two main plant nutrients, nitrogen and phosphorus, are more difficult to spot, causing poor, often pale, growth with small leaves that are sometimes discoloured. Fortunately, all these problems are easy to put right by feeding: use a balanced general fertilizer for the three main nutrients and one containing trace elements to supply your plants with extra magnesium and manganese.

Blackspot

This disease causes dark spots on the leaves, often with a yellow edge, which can lead to premature leaf drop. It is a serious disease when it affects roses, as it can severely weaken the plant if it is allowed to flourish year after year.

Treatment To control it, remove and destroy any affected foliage and clear fallen leaves in autumn to help prevent the continuation of the disease. This may mean hard-pruning infected plants. Spray healthy-looking leaves with a suitable systemic fungicide.

Rust

This is a common fungal disease that causes distinctive bright orange to brown spots on the undersides of leaves, with yellow flecks on the upper surface. The spots will eventually darken to black and the symptoms can sometimes spread to nearby plant stems.

Different species of rust attack different plants, with roses being particularly affected.

Treatment To control rust, remove and destroy any affected foliage and clear fallen leaves in autumn to help prevent the disease continuing. Try to avoid overhead watering, as the rust spores can be carried back up to the plant by the splashing water. Instead, apply the water at the base of the plant. Spray healthy-looking leaves with a suitable systemic fungicide as necessary.

Leaf spots

There are several types of leaf spot, some with dark green, brown or black spots, sometimes round, sometimes angular, on leaf surfaces. Coral spot, for example, has distinctive small, coral-coloured pustules. A host of fungi can be responsible, but the problem will only be temporary.

Treatment Prune out affected growth if you find it unsightly and feed the plant to encourage vigorous new shoots. Generally, it is not usually worth spraying for these spots, but if you want you can tackle them by using a suitable systemic fungicide.

Downy mildew appears as a white coating over leaves and causes distended growth, browning and wilting.

Grey mould

Also known as botrytis, this disease causes fluffy grey mould to appear on buds, flowers, leaves or stems and can occur on nearly any garden plant. However, it can be problematic with large flowers that 'ball' in wet weather and rot, as well as leaves and stems that have been damaged before the attack.

Treatment Pick off affected flowers and shoots and clear fallen ripe fruit, which can also be attacked. Make sure the plants are well spaced and ventilated to prevent a recurrence.

The tell-tail sign of powdery mildew is a dusty-looking coating appearing on the plant. It is often associated with humid conditions.

Keep plants well watered. Cut off any affected shoots and improve air circulation around the plant. Spray with a systemic fungicide.

Methods of control

All pests are preyed upon by natural predators in the garden, including birds, small mammals, amphibians, spiders and insects. One of the best ways of keeping pests under control is to encourage these natural predators to set up home.

Encourage natural predators

Welcome nature's way of controlling pests to your garden. For example, you can get frogs and toads, which feed on a wide range of insects, to remain by providing them with suitable places to hide and a small pond where they can breed. Similarly, many beneficial insects, such as hoverflies and lacewings, will be attracted by nectar-rich plants, such as buddleja, hawthorn and viburnum, and can be encouraged to overwinter by putting up bundles of bamboo where they can hibernate.

Other creatures to encourage include ladybirds (ladybugs), which eat aphids, scale insects, mealy bugs and caterpillars; ground beetles, which consume slugs, troublesome flatworms, vine weevils and spider mites; and centipedes, which eat slugs and snails.

The following are good predators to invite into your garden.

Ladybirds (Ladybugs) A single ladybird larva is able to eat more than 500 aphids while it is developing, so for this reason alone, ladybirds can have a dramatic impact on these pest numbers. Ladybird larvae look nothing like the familiar black-spotted red adult but look like a cross between a beetle and a caterpillar – so make sure you know what they look like so that you don't inadvertently think it's another pest to control.

Lacewings These are green flying insects that have translucent green wings, long antennae and bright,

Not all insects are pests in the garden. The ladybird is one of many that feed on garden problem pests and help keep their damaging populations under control.

golden eyes. Both the adults and larvae feed on aphids. The larvae are similar to ladybird larvae, but they are lighter in colour and often have dead aphids stuck to their bodies to act as camouflage.

Hover flies These are insects that mimic the appearance of wasps but are smaller and able to hover in one spot. They don't sting. As their name implies, they are true flies and their larvae eat aphids and other small sap-sucking insects.

Ground beetles Some beetles are troublesome in the garden, but the big black beetles that scurry about at night are ground beetles and they are definitely worth encouraging as they are voracious eaters of slugs and other insects.

Centipedes Often confused with millipedes, which can damage plants, centipedes eat insects and are worth encouraging into the garden. One simple way to tell them apart is to touch them: a centipede will scuttle away as fast as possible, while a millipede will tend to roll itself up for protection.

Amphibians Frogs, toads and newts are all useful predators in the garden,

as they gobble up slugs and insects. You will need a pond to encourage them into your garden, with suitable access and cover to provide a safe haven and breeding ground.

Hedgehogs Under the cover of darkness, hedgehogs are busy clearing gardens of slugs, caterpillars, beetles and other problem pests. Provide food and winter shelter to encourage them to set up home in your garden.

Birds Many garden birds eat pests. Starlings will eat worms and grubs; sparrows eat insects and weed seeds; thrushes love slugs and snails; robins favour spiders and weed seeds; and blue tits like caterpillars and aphids. Encourage them to stay in your garden by providing a plentiful supply of seed- and berry-producing plants, sheltered areas where they can build nests safely and rear their young, and a source of food and water during the winter months for resident species.

Using pesticides

If you choose to use pesticides to control pest and disease outbreaks, you must read the instructions carefully to ensure that the pest you are trying to control is featured on the label. Garden chemicals are broadly divided into three groups: fungicides, which control disease; insecticides, which control pests; and herbicides, which control weeds.

Some chemicals, called contact pesticides, work only when they are applied to the target. For this reason, if you are using contact insecticides it is essential that they are applied, sprayed or dusted where the pests are lurking – often in the shoot tips and on the undersides of the leaves. Some contact pesticides will remain active for a period of time to control pests and diseases that try to attack the plant for up to a fortnight after being applied. Others, known as systemic chemicals, are absorbed by the plant and transported throughout its structure via the sap. Such chemicals can be applied anywhere on the plant to control the pests and diseases attacking it. This means you can spray less accurately and do not need to cover all the foliage completely. A few chemical fungicidal sprays can be applied to

plants before the disease has attacked to provide protection. These are known as preventative fungicides. Like contact chemicals, they have to be applied thoroughly to give complete protection. Check the label carefully for instructions about how often the product should be reapplied and follow this diligently if you want it to be effective. Roses are a good example of how using a combined pesticide and fungicide produces healthy blooms.

Applying chemicals

Garden pesticides are available in various forms. Ready-to-use sprays that are already diluted are the most convenient form and, as their name suggests, can be applied immediately. They are an expensive way to buy pesticides, but they are useful if you are trying to control a small outbreak quickly, such as a pest outbreak in the greenhouse.

In the longer term, it might be preferable to invest in a small hand-pumped pressure sprayer in which to dilute concentrated chemicals. These work out much cheaper if you are applying a lot of the same chemical over the course of a season. Sprayers with a lance will also apply the chemical more quickly and accurately to border plants. For really large gardens, consider investing in a knapsack sprayer, which is much larger and enables you to spray for longer between refills.

Weedkillers are applied differently, depending on where the seeds are located. On a gravel path, for example, you could water the weedkiller using a watering can fitted with a dribble bar, but in the border you would be better off using a sprayer fitted with a spray hood to prevent any spray drift affecting neighbouring plants. Simply place

Using chemicals as a last resort

If all else fails and your plants are plagued by a damaging attack, you may want to resort to using a chemical spray. It is essential that you choose the right spray for the job and apply it exactly as described in the information on the packaging. However, you may also want to keep a few chemicals to hand, locked away safely in the garden shed or garage, that can be used in an emergency. It's worth having a packet of slug pellets if you want to protect vulnerable new plants, and a general systemic insecticide is handy for combating insect pests.

Healthy roses

The best way to keep roses healthy is to grow disease-resistant roses (see below). However, you can prevent the three common rose diseases of blackspot, mildew and rust on less robust varieties by following a regular spraying programme. If you use a combined pesticide and fungicide that is designed for the purpose, you can prevent outbreaks of pests such as aphids, too. Roses also benefit from a foliar feed containing trace elements to keep the foliage green and healthy.

The following varieties have all shown some resistance to blackspot, mildew and rust:

Large-flowered bush roses
'Alec's Red', 'Alexander', 'Blessings', 'Congratulations', 'Just Joey', 'Peace', 'Polar Star' (not rust), 'Remember Me', 'Royal William' and 'Silver Jubilee'.

Cluster-flowered bush rose
'Amber Queen', 'Mountbatten', 'Queen Elizabeth' (not blackspot) and 'Southampton'.

Climbing roses
'Aloha', 'Compassion', 'Golden Showers' and 'New Dawn'.

the hood over the weed, with the rim on the ground, before pressing the trigger to release the chemical spray. Set the spray nozel to produce a coarse spray to minimize any airborne droplets.

Safety first

Always read the label carefully before you buy or use a garden pesticide to make sure it will do what you want. Take great care to apply it at the right dilution and observe any precautions that are recommended. Always wear the protective clothing suggested when handling chemicals. Dispose of unwanted garden chemicals at your local authority's waste disposal centre.

Diagnosing problems

Most common pests and diseases are possible to diagnose from the tell-tale symptoms they cause. Use the following guide to help you identify the problem affecting the plants in your garden.

Identifying the problem

A pest is any living creature that causes damage to garden plants. Some are highly visible and easily recognized, while others can be microscopically small and therefore very difficult to spot and identify.

Recognizing that a pest or disease exists is the first stage in learning how to eradicate or control it. The damage created by insects can be infuriating, particularly if you are a gardener who has put many hours of work into the garden in order to enjoy watching your plants blossom and thrive.

Once you establish which plants are being attacked, you are on the way to recognizing the conditions in which the pests thrive. When this happens, you can take steps to remove them. However, many insects look similar, even though the damage they create can vary dramatically. Learning to recognize a beneficial insect from a pest is important. However, it is not just pests that attack plants. Other fungal conditions can develop in plants and stunt or ruin their growth. Bacteria is another important problem group. However, they are never seen and usually function within a plant's tissue. Many can be beneficial, and play an important role in breaking down dead plant material in order to return valuable nutrients to the soil. Most gardeners manage to control or live with a host of pests and diseases, but being able to produce strong and healthy plants is what gardening is all about.

The greyish-white spores of powdery mildew cover the leaves, making it look like a coating of powder. The problem is usually associated with humid conditions and root dryness.

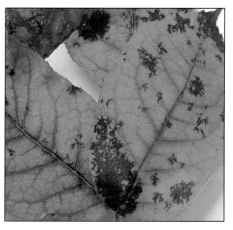

Black spot is the most common fungal disease of roses. It causes the rose to become lacking in vigour. It can be identified by the round brownish-black spots with ragged margins.

Rhododendron leafhoppers have distinctive reddish markings on their backs. They suck sap from the leaves and cause little harm, but it is thought they contribute to bud blast.

Capsid bugs damage leaves at the shoot tips. They suck sap and also secrete a toxic saliva that kills plant cells. Forsythias, fuchias, roses and hydrangeas are susceptible.

The distinctive pink pustules of coral spot indicate that this troublesome fungus has entered the plant through small wounds, usually caused by careless pruning.

These disfiguring masses are known as galls and they commonly affect forsythia plants. Cut back the affected growth, pruning to ground level. A good recovery should result.

Identifying common problems

LEAF SYMPTOMS

Are there spots on the leaves?
- Silver spots on privet = privet thrip
- White powdery covering = powdery mildew
- Dark green/brown scabby patches = pyracantha scab
- Grey or brown circular spots = fungal leaf spot
- Black spots with yellow edges on roses = blackspot
- Orange spots on leaf undersides = rust
- Transparent spots on roses = rose slugworm
- Yellow spots on rhododendron = rhododendron lacebug
- Translucent patches, often with darker spots = leaf miner

Are the leaves discoloured?
- Yellow leaves, brown spotting = chlorosis
- Yellow patches between veins = magnesium deficiency
- Pale green small leaves = nitrogen deficiency
- Purple small leaves = phosphorus deficiency
- Brown leaf edges = potash deficiency
- Pale green patches between the veins = manganese deficiency
- Furry white covering = downy mildew
- Silvery-grey sheen = silver leaf
- Discoloured leaves, wilt and die = eelworm

Are there holes in leaves?
- Semicircular cuts in leaf edges = leaf-cutter bee
- Small holes = shothole canker

Leaf-cutting bees take neat pieces from leaves, which they use to build their nests.

- Holes and notches = vine weevil
- Ragged holes with evidence of slime trails = slugs and snails

Are there misshapened leaves?
- Rough, often coloured lumps = galls
- Leaf surface grazed off on willow = willow leaf beetle
- Thick leaves, yellow margins = bay sucker
- Tightly rolled leaves on roses = leaf rolling sawfly
- Rolled or webbed leaves = caterpillars
- Distorted leaf clusters on box = box sucker

Are there insects on the leaves?
- Green, black, pink or brown insects = aphids
- White insects on rhododendron = rhododendron whitefly

Have variegated leaves turned green?
- Variegated leaves turn green = reversion

FLOWER SYMPTOMS

Were no flowers produced?
- No flowers = growing conditions (see pages 98–105)
- No flowers – incorrect pruning (see pages 106–115)

Did the flowers fail to open?
- Flowers fail to open and fall in early spring = frost damage
- Flower buds dry and harden on rhododendron = rhododendron leaf hopper
- White or brown fuzz on withered flowers = grey mould (botrytis)
- Withered flowers = blossom wilt

Are the flowers distorted?
- Flowers open unevenly = capsid bug

Are the flowers discoloured?
- Petal blight

Are there holes in the flowers?
- Holes at the base of flowers = bumble bee
- Irregular holes = moth caterpillars
- Ragged holes = earwigs

Whiteflies suck the sap of the plant and excrete honeydew.

Are the flowers covered in insects?
- Green, black, pink or brown insects = aphids
- Shiny black insects = pollen beetles

Did the flowers disappear?
- Flower buds scattered under plant = birds, squirrels and other wildlife

STEM AND TRUNK SYMPTOMS

Have stems and shoots wilted and died?
- Shoots wilt and die on clematis = clematis wilt
- Shoot tips dying back slowly = die-back
- Shoot tips dying back from flowers = fireblight

Are the stems broad and flattened?
- Flattened stems or flowers = fasciation

Are there spots or lumps on stems?
- Brown spots on bark = scale insects
- Pink or red spots on bark = coral spot
- Rough lumps on forsythia stems = gall
- Rough lumps on stems = crown gall
- Rough patches, sometimes concentric rings on bark = canker
- Unusually flat patches of bark = bacterial canker

Has the bark been stripped?
- Bark removed from right around the trunk = squirrels or rabbits
- Wood stems removed, leaving ragged edge = deer

Is the whole plant distorted?
- Stunted and distorted growth = virus

A directory of shrubs

This directory offers a comprehensive array of shrubs – including all the familiar favourites plus some rarer specimens. The selection here will help gardeners of all levels find the shrubs that will make the most of their garden space. The initial introduction for each entry is either for the whole genus or the main species grown. Beyond this, the entry is split between more common species and cultivars and those that are less common. The advent of the internet has meant that it is often possible to obtain rare shrubs from around the world. Growing rarer species can be rewarding, as they are often particularly beautiful.

However, there is also a joy in growing less exotic plants. If your garden centre does not have the ones you want, you can always try mail-order catalogues – and the internet – to find the perfect plant for your garden.

Shrubs are often viewed as the backbone of the garden, allowing other plants to look their best. However, shrubs in their own right make a delightful addition to beds and borders, with their stunning blooms, fruits, foliage and scents.

Abelia x grandiflora

ABELIA

A genus of about 30 species with a long flowering season that make excellent compact, garden plants. Their pretty, trumpet-like flowers are produced on arching stems throughout summer and into early autumn. Although hardy in milder areas, they will need protection elsewhere.

Cultivation They will grow in well-drained garden soil that is reasonably fertile. They need full sun and protection from cold winds. Most are not reliably hardy in colder areas and need the protection of a sheltered, south-facing wall or fence.

Pruning Prune established plants after flowering to encourage new growth. In colder areas, treat as a herbaceous plant and cut down the whole plant in autumn and protect roots with a layer of dry leaves or bark chippings held in place with wire netting.

Propagation Take softwood cuttings during early summer, semi-ripe cutting in late summer or hardwood cuttings in mid-autumn.

Abelia 'Edward Goucher'

Purple-pink trumpets are produced from early summer to early autumn along arching stems. The glossy, bronze-green leaves mature to dark green. H 1.5m (5ft) S 2m (6ft).
Aspect: sun
Hardiness: ✿✿ Zone: 9

Abelia x grandiflora (syn. A. rupestris)

Scented, trumpet-shaped, pale pink and white flowers are borne on arching stems from early summer to mid-autumn. Vigorous and long-flowering, this semi-evergreen shrub with glossy leaves makes a perfect focal-point plant for a well-drained border in sun. This plant is orderline frost hardy. H 3m (10ft) S 4m (13ft).
Named varieties: 'Confetti', with very compact, pink-tinged white flowers. Frost hardy. H 1m (3ft) S 1m (3ft). 'Francis Mason', variegated, glossy, yellow-edged leaves. More tender than other varieties. H 1.5m (5ft) S 2m (6ft). 'Gold Spot' (syn. 'Gold Strike', 'Aurea'), bright yellow foliage. H 1.5m (5ft) S 2m (6ft).
Aspect: sun
Hardiness: ✿✿ Zone: 9 (some borderline)

Abelia x grandiflora 'Gold Spot'

ABELIOPHYLLUM

A genus of just one species, that is grown for its masses of fragrant flowers borne on bare branches during late winter and early spring. A good alternative to forsythia, they can be grown in the border or trained against a wall or fence. To fully appreciate the almond-scented flowers, plant close to an entrance or path.

Cultivation Abeliophyllum will grow in well-drained garden soil that is reasonably fertile and in full sun.

Pruning No routine pruning is necessary. Neglected plants can be rejuvenated by cutting back one stem in three to near ground level after flowering, starting with the oldest stems.

Propagation Take softwood cuttings during early summer, semi-ripe cuttings in late summer or hardwood cuttings in mid-autumn.

Abeliophyllum distichum White forsythia

A much underrated, forsythia-like shrub that bears masses of fragrant, star-shaped, pink-tinged white flowers on bare branches during late winter and early spring. H 1.5m (5ft) S 1.5m (5ft).
Named varieties: 'Roseum Group', pale pink flowers on dark stems. H 1.5m (5ft) S 1.5m (5ft).
Aspect: sun
Hardiness: ✿✿✿ Zone: 9+

ABUTILON

A genus of about 150 species of graceful shrubs, many with spectacular, lantern-like flowers. Most are tender, but a few can be grown against a warm, sheltered wall or fence in mild areas, in a container on the patio or in the conservatory in colder areas.

Cultivation In the garden they will grow in well-drained garden soil that is reasonably fertile and in full sun. Indoors, grow in a soil-based compost (soil mix). Water freely during the spring and summer and sparingly at other times. Feed every fortnight during the growing season.

Pruning In the garden, prune out frosted shoots in early spring or mid-spring. Indoors, prune back established plants by half in mid-spring to restrict their size.

Propagation Take softwood cuttings in late spring or semi-ripe cuttings from early summer to late summer. They can also be raised from seed in mid-spring.

Abutilon 'Kentish Belle' Chinese lantern

This is a lax and graceful evergreen shrub with toothed, three- or five-lobed green leaves and delightful, long, pendent, bell-shaped flowers with pale yellow petals and burnt-orange base that are borne from late spring to mid-autumn. H 2.5m (8ft) S 2.5m (8ft).
Aspect: sun
Hardiness: ✿✿ Zone: 9+

Abutilon x suntense

Abutilon x suntense 'Geoffey Gorer'

Abutilon megapotamicum
Brazilian bell-flower, trailing abutilon

This is a graceful, frost-hardy evergreen shrub with slender stems that carry red and yellow lantern-like flowers from late spring to mid-autumn. The toothed, three-lobed bright green leaves form an attractive backdrop at other times. H 2m (6ft) S 2m (6ft).

Named varieties: 'Variegatum' (variegated trailing abutilon), wonderful yellow-blotched leaves on self-layering branches means that it can be grown as deep ground cover in mild areas, but it also makes an attractive shrub if trained against a warm, sheltered wall or fence in cooler areas. H 2m (6ft) S 2m (6ft).
Aspect: sun
Hardiness: ✿✿ Zone: 9+

ACER
Maple

This genus of about 150 species of deciduous trees and shrubs contain many that are grown for their ornamental bark and foliage, as well as brilliant autumnal tints. Only the shrubs are covered here.

The 'palmatum' group have distinctively lobed leaves and attractive bark, while the 'dissectum' group are generally more compact and have leaves that are much more deeply cut. Both are slow growing and make superb garden specimens – creating spectacular seasonal focal points in spring, summer and autumn. They also make excellent specimens in containers.
Cultivation In the garden, grow in well-drained garden soil that doesn't dry out in summer and is reasonably fertile. Acers will grow in sun or partial shade, where they are sheltered from cold winds and late frosts that can scorch the emerging leaves. In containers, grow in a soil-based compost (soil mix). Feed every fortnight throughout the growing season and water as necessary.
Pruning No routine pruning is necessary. Neglected plants can have any wayward branches removed to balance the overall shape of the canopy.
Propagation Can be raised from seed in mid-autumn, but results are variable. Named varieties must be grafted in early spring or budded in late summer on to seedling stock of the same species.

Acer palmatum 'Atropurpureum' (syn. *A. palmatum* f. *atropurpureum*)
Japanese maple

This is a graceful and slow-growing maple that makes an excellent specimen for a small garden or for growing in a large container. The plant's attractive palm-like, deeply lobed, dark purple leaves look spectacular through all of the summer before turning brilliant shades of red in autumn. H 8m (26ft) S 8m (26ft).
Aspect: semi-shade
Hardiness: ✿✿✿ Zone: 4+

Acer palmatum 'Bloodgood'
Japanese maple

This is one of the best purple-leaved varieties. It has attractive deeply lobed, palm-like leaves that are sumptuous all summer long, turning brilliant red in autumn. This is an ideal specimen or accent plant for a partially shaded spot. The autumn hues are particularly long lasting, making it the perfect choice for a seasonal display. When its leaves fall, dark purple twigs and stems add winter interest. Can be grown in a container. H 5.5m (18ft) S 5.5m (18ft).
Aspect: semi-shade
Hardiness: ✿✿✿ Zone: 5+

Acer palmatum var. *dissectum* 'Atropurpureum' (syn. *A. palmatum* var. *dissectum* 'Atropurpureum Group')
Japanese maple

Ideal for growing in a container or as a specimen plant on the patio, this compact Japanese maple has a neat dome-like habit and particularly fine, deeply cut, red-purple, ferny foliage. In autumn the leaves turn dramatic fiery shades. Protect from cold winds and late frosts. Its delicate foliage can burn in full sun. H 2m (6ft) S 3m (10ft).
Aspect: semi-shade
Hardiness: ✿✿✿ Zone: 4+

Acer palmatum 'Garnet'
Japanese maple

A popular form of Japanese maple with a mound-like habit and dark purple, finely cut leaves. It makes an excellent specimen or focal point in a small garden that gets some sun. In autumn the leaves turn brilliant red before falling to reveal a tracery of fine twigs that provide winter interest. Protect from cold winds and late frosts, which can burn the delicate foliage. H 5.5m (18ft) S 5.5m (18ft).
Aspect: sun to semi-shade
Hardiness: ✿✿✿ Zone: 4+

Acer palmatum 'Orange Dream'
Japanese maple

A wonderful new variety that forms an attractive specimen for a

Other good acers to look out for:

Acer palmatum 'Butterfly', pink-edged, grey-green leaves. H 3m (10ft) S 1.5m (5ft).
Acer palmatum var. *dissectum* 'Crimson Queen', finely dissected red-purple foliage turns gold in autumn. H 3m (10ft) S 4m (12ft).
Acer palmatum var. *dissectum* 'Green Globe', finely dissected apple-green foliage turns fiery shades of orange and red in autumn. H 5m (15ft) S 7m (22ft).
Acer palmatum var. *dissectum* 'Inaba-shidare', finely dissected red-purple foliage turns fiery shades of orange and red in autumn. H 3m (10ft) S 5m (15ft).
Acer palmatum var. *dissectum* 'Ornatum', finely dissected leaves emerge purple-red and mature to bronze-green, then turn gold during the autumn. H 3m (10ft) S 3m (10ft).
Acer palmatum 'Fireglow', deeply lobed, plum-purple leaves that turn brilliant red in autumn. H 7m (22ft) S 5m (15ft).
Acer palmatum 'Red Dragon', new variety with finely dissected burgundy-red leaves. H 6m (20ft) S 6m (20ft).

Acer palmatum 'Sango-kaku'

Acer palmatum 'Osakazuki'

small garden. The foliage emerges golden-yellow with pink edges in spring, slowly taking on a greenish hue in summer before transforming into a brilliant orange in the autumn. This plant is a good choice for a large container as its growth rate will be restricted. H 6m (20ft) S 1.5m (5ft).
Aspect: semi-shade
Hardiness: ✿✿✿ Zone: 5

Acer palmatum 'Osakazuki'
Japanese maple
Startling red autumn colour makes this slow-growing Japanese maple a dramatic addition to any garden. The large, palm-shaped leaves are rich green at other times and set off the hanging brilliant red fruits in summer. H 6m (20ft) S 6m (20ft).
Aspect: sun to semi-shade
Hardiness: ✿✿✿ Zone: 4+

Acer palmatum 'Sango-kaku' (syn. A. palmatum 'Senkaki')
Japanese maple, coral-bark maple
Perhaps the best maple for year-round interest, it is an ideal choice for small gardens. The brilliant coral-red young shoots dramatically set off the emerging palm-shaped, orange-yellow leaves in spring. The leaves gradually turn green in summer, before taking on fabulous shades of yellow in autumn. The leaves then fall to reveal the beautifully coloured stems that can be seen throughout the winter. Stem coloration is less pronounced on

A. palmatum var. *dissectum* 'Crimson Queen'

mature specimens. H 6m (20ft) S 5.5m (18ft).
Aspect: semi-shade
Hardiness: ✿✿✿ Zone: 4+

ALOYSIA
A genus of about 35 species of deciduous or evergreen flowering shrubs, only one of which is commonly cultivated for its distinctive lemon-scented foliage that is widely used for culinary purposes. Plant it in a convenient location in full sun, such as next to a path or outside the kitchen door, where you can harvest the leaves for adding to dishes, making lemon tea or pot-pourri.
Cultivation In the garden, grow in well-drained, poor, dry soil in full sun – the base of a sunny wall is ideal. Indoors, grow in a soil-based compost (soil mix). Water freely during the spring and summer, sparingly at other times.

Pruning In mild areas where the plant can form a permanent framework of branches, prune in mid-spring to keep within bounds. Elsewhere, cut back in autumn and protect roots with a layer of dry leaves or bark chippings held in place with wire netting.
Propagation Take softwood cuttings in mid-summer.

Aloysia triphylla (syn. A. citriodora, Lippia citriodora)
Lemon verbena
An upright, deciduous shrub with narrow, lemon-scented leaves, that is covered in clusters of pale lilac flowers from mid-summer to late summer. Tolerates poor, dry soils. H 3m (10ft) S 3m (10ft).
Aspect: sun
Hardiness: ✿✿ Zone: 5+

AMELANCHIER
Juneberry, snowy mespilus
A genus of over 25 species of deciduous multi-stemmed trees and shrubs that offer pretty spring flowers, attractive felted leaves that turn dramatic shades in autumn, accompanied by juicy fruit that are loved by birds. They make ideal specimens or seasonal focal points for use at the back of a mixed border in full sun or partial shade.
Cultivation Amelanchier will grow in any neutral to acid garden soil provided that it is reasonably fertile and positioned in full sun or partial shade.
Pruning No routine pruning is necessary. Neglected plants can

have wayward branches removed to open the canopy and maintain the overall balance.
Propagation Layer suckers in early spring and separate when well rooted in mid-autumn. Take softwood cuttings during mid-spring or semi-ripe cuttings in mid-summer. Sow seed as soon as ripe in summer.

Amelanchier x grandiflora 'Ballerina'
This compact and free-flowering deciduous shrub produces clouds of white, star-shaped flowers from early spring to mid-spring. Emerging bronze-tinted, the foliage matures to dark green before turning brilliant shades of red and orange during autumn. Sweet and juicy dark red fruits are produced in early summer.
H 6m (20ft) S 8m (26ft).
Aspect: sun or semi-shade
Hardiness: ✿✿✿ Zone: 4+

Amelanchier lamarckii
A spectacular shrub in spring and autumn, that is covered in a profusion of star-shaped, white flowers during early spring and mid-spring accompanied by bronze-tinted emerging leaves. By summer the leaves mature to dark green and then transform into a beacon of orange and red in autumn. Sweet and juicy dark red fruits are produced in early summer. H 10m (33ft) S 12m (40ft).
Aspect: sun or semi-shade
Hardiness: ✿✿✿ Zone: 4+

Aloysia triphylla

Amelanchier lamarckii

Aucuba japonica

Azara dentata

AUCUBA

A genus of three species of evergreen shrubs that offer robust, glossy foliage that is incredibly tough. Able to grow almost anywhere, including dry shade and wind tunnels found between buildings. Their tolerance of dry soil and urban pollution means they are widely used by landscapers in towns and cities. Their ability to cope with salt-laden air makes them ideal filler or hedging shrubs in coastal gardens. On female plants, bright red autumn berries are sometimes produced.
Cultivation Plant in almost any soil (except waterlogged soil), in sun or shade. To enhance berry production, plant one male to every five female plants. In containers, grow in a soil-based soil mix. Feed every fortnight throughout the growing season and water as necessary.
Pruning Prune in mid-spring to maintain the size and shape you require. Leave hedges until mid-summer or late summer. Use secateurs (pruners) so that you can avoid damaging any foliage that remains on the plant after trimming.
Propagation Take semi-ripe cuttings in late summer or hardwood cuttings in early autumn. Sow seed in early autumn or mid-autumn.

Aucuba japonica
Japanese laurel
Tough as old boots, this easy-to-please evergreen shrub is perfect for heavily shaded areas and wind tunnels found between buildings where little else will grow. However, its neat, domed habit and densely packed lustrous, dark green leaves means it is a bit on the boring side. On female plants, bright red autumn berries follow insignificant late spring flowers. H 3m (10ft) S 3m (10ft).
Named varieties: 'Crotonifolia' is the best spotted laurel with leathery, yellow-speckled, dark green leaves. Although female, it rarely produces fruit. H 3m (10ft) S 3m (10ft). 'Picturata' (spotted laurel), is the male variety, with yellow-splashed, dark green leaves that are yellow-speckled at the margins. H 3m (10ft) S 3m (10ft). 'Rozannie' is very compact, with glossy dark green leaves and large, bright red berries. H 1m (3ft) S 1m (3ft). 'Variegata' (spotted laurel) has yellow-speckled, dark green leaves and bright red berries. H 3m (10ft) S 3m (10ft).
Aspect: sun or deep shade
Hardiness: ✹✹✹ Zone: 4+

Azalea – see Rhododendron

AZARA

A genus of about 10 species of evergreen trees and shrubs, only one of which is widely grown. Frost-hardy, it should be given a sheltered position against a sunny wall or fence or among other hardier shrubs in the garden. In colder areas, try growing in a tub on the patio and move it into a cool greenhouse where the fragrant flowers can be best appreciated.
Cultivation Grow in any moist, garden soil that is reasonably fertile, in full sun or partial shade.
Pruning No routine pruning is necessary unless it is grown as a wall shrub, where selected shoots should be trained in a fan shape and subsequent side shoots thinned as necessary to maintain the overall shape.
Propagation Take semi-ripe cuttings in mid-summer.

Azara dentata
Unusual early summer-flowering evergreen shrub with serrated, glossy green leaves. It produces masses of fragrant, golden-yellow spidery flowers during early summer. H 3m (10ft) S 3m (10ft).
Aspect: sun or semi-shade
Hardiness: ✹✹ Zone: 5+

BALLOTA

Ballota comprises a genus of over 30 species of shrubs and also perennials but only one of the shrubs is featured here. This borderline hardy shrub has evergreen foliage covered in woolly hairs that give it a grey sheen. It is an ideal choice for a gravel or Mediterranean garden where it will appreciate the good drainage and full sun. Grow in a container on a sunny patio elsewhere.
Cultivation In the garden, grow in well-drained, poor, dry soil in full sun – the base of a sunny wall is an ideal spot for this plant. In containers, grow in a soil-based soil mix. Feed monthly throughout the growing season and water as necessary.
Pruning To promote a neat habit, established plants should be cut back by about half each mid-spring.
Propagation Take softwood cuttings in mid-spring or semi-ripe cuttings in late summer.

Ballota acetabulosa
A compact, aromatic, evergreen, drought-tolerant shrub that is generally pest- and disease-resistant. This grey-stemmed, evergreen shrub has felty, sage-green, heart-shaped leaves and silvery shoot tips. A bonus of pretty purple-pink flowers are produced in whorls during mid-summer and late summer. H 60cm (24in) S 75cm (30in).
Aspect: sun
Hardiness: ✹✹ Zone: 5+

Ballotta acetabulosa

Banksia coccinea

BANKSIA

Named after the botanist Sir Joseph Banks, who discovered this genus at Botany Bay, the plant is now known to contain about 70 species of evergreen shrubs and trees. The one featured here is grown for its dramatic dome-like flower-spikes produced from late spring and into summer. Ideal for cutting for use in indoor flower arrangements.

Cultivation Grow in neutral to acid, well-drained, poor, dry soil in full sun. In frost-prone areas, grow under glass in containers filled with a half-and-half mixture of ericaceous compost and a soil-based compost (soil mix). Feed every fortnight in the growing season and water as necessary.

Pruning Deadhead plants after flowering.

Propagation Raise from seed in mid-spring.

Banksia coccinea
Scarlet banksia

Wonderful spikes of bright orange-red flowers are produced in late spring and early summer from the tips of an open, upright shrub. The serrated, heart-shaped, dark green leaves have a felty covering underneath and make an excellent foil for the conspicuous flowers that appear from late spring to mid-summer. Can also be cut to use in flower arrangements. H 5m (16ft) S 3m (10ft).
Aspect: sun
Hardiness: ❋ Zone: 9+

BERBERIS
Barberry

A genus of over 450 species of evergreen or deciduous shrubs. Most are hardy, easy to grow and have vicious thorns and autumn berries. Deciduous species are also grown for their yellow-orange flowers and dramatic autumn colours, while the evergreen species have year-round, dense, glossy foliage, with some species offering eye-catching, spring flowers, too. They can be grown as border fillers and some make excellent hedging plants.

Cultivation They will grow in almost any well-drained garden soil that is reasonably fertile in full sun or partial shade. Deciduous varieties are best planted in a sunny position to get the best of their autumn colour and berries.

Pruning No routine pruning necessary, but you can trim lightly after flowering to maintain the overall shape.

Propagation Can be raised from seed in late autumn, but the results can be variable. Take softwood cuttings from evergreen varieties in mid-summer or semi-ripe cuttings of deciduous varieties in early autumn.

Berberis darwinii

An upright, evergreen shrub with prickly, holly-like leaves, which produces a profusion of pendent burnt-orange coloured flowers during mid-spring and late spring, followed in autumn by purple fruit with a bluish bloom. It is a useful filler for the shrub border or for growing as an informal flowering hedge where its prickly stems will provide a deterrent against intruders. H 3m (10ft) S 3m (10ft).
Aspect: sun or semi-shade
Hardiness: ❋❋❋ Zones: 7–8

Berberis julianae

This upright-growing, evergreen berberis has glossy, dark green leaves that turn red in autumn. A bonus of yellow flowers is produced during late spring, followed by black fruit with a bluish bloom. Although not as ornamental as some berberis, its dense growth and upright habit means it makes an excellent screen or hedge where its spiny leaves will provide an intruder deterrent to intruders. H 3m (10ft) S 1.2m (4ft).
Aspect: sun or semi-shade
Hardiness: ❋❋❋ Zones: 7–8

Berberis linearifolia 'Orange King'

This is an upright, carefree, evergreen shrub with viciously spiny, glossy, dark green leaves. Profuse burnt-orange coloured flowers are produced in clusters along stiffly arching stems during mid-spring, followed by rounded, blackish fruits. This vigorous evergreen makes an informal flowering hedge, as viciously thorny leaves provide a deterrent against intruders.

Berberis aristata

H 2.7m (9ft) S 2.7m (9ft).
Aspect: sun or semi-shade
Hardiness: ❋❋❋ Zones: 7–8

Berberis x stenophylla (syn. *B. darwinii* x *B. empetrifolia*)

The spiny, dark green leaves of this vigorous, evergreen barberry are the perfect foil for its dark yellow, double flowers, which are produced in arching clusters during mid-spring and late spring. A bonus of rounded, black fruits are produced in autumn. Easy to grow, it makes an excellent screen or hedge, where its spine-tipped leaves will provide a deterrent against intruders. H 3m (10ft) S 5m (16ft).
Named varieties: 'Claret Cascade', red shoots with bronze-green foliage, dark yellow flowers and

Berberis thunbergii f. *atropurpurea*

Other berberis plants to look out for:

Berberis thunbergii f. *atropurpurea*, purple leaves turn brilliant red in autumn; red-flushed pale yellow flowers are followed by glossy red fruit. H 1m (3ft) S 2.5m (8ft).
Berberis thunbergii 'Golden Ring', yellow-edged purple leaves turn brilliant red in autumn; red-flushed pale yellow flowers are followed by glossy red fruit. H 1m (3ft) S 2.5m (8ft).
Berberis thunbergii 'Red Chief', purple leaves turn fiery orange and red in autumn; purple stems provide winter interest. H 1.5m (5ft) S 1.5m (5ft).
Berberis thunbergii 'Red Pillar', purple leaves turn fiery orange and red in autumn; red-flushed pale yellow flowers. H 1.5m (5ft) S 1.5m (5ft).
Berberis thunbergii 'Rose Glow', pink-mottled, reddish-purple leaves turn fiery orange and red in autumn; red-flushed pale yellow flowers are followed by glossy red fruit. H 1m (3ft) S 2.5m (8ft).

black fruits. H 1.2m (4ft) S 1.2m (4ft). 'Corallina Compacta', very compact and slow growing with red-flushed yellow flowers that open from red buds. H 30cm (12in) S 30cm (12in). 'Crawley Gem', compact and very free flowering. Its orange blooms open from red buds. H 60cm (24in) S 60cm (24in). 'Irwinii', compact with spiky leaves and orange flowers. H 1.5m (5ft) S 1.5m (5ft). 'Lemon Queen' (syn. *B.* x *stenophylla* 'Cornish Cream', *B.* x *stenophylla* 'Cream Showers'), dark green leaves, creamy-white flowers and black fruits. H 3m (10ft) S 5m (16ft).
Aspect: sun or semi-shade
Hardiness: ✿✿✿ Zones: 7–8

Berberis thunbergii 'Atropurpurea Nana' (syn. *B. thunbergii* 'Crimson Pygmy', *B. thunbergii* 'Little Favourite')
Grown for its dark purple leaves, which turn a brilliant red in autumn, this compact deciduous shrub also bears pale yellow flowers with reddish highlights during mid-spring and late spring, followed by glossy red fruit in autumn. It is a useful filler for the front of a shrub border in sun or partial shade or for growing as a low, informal flowering hedge. It also makes a excellent foliage plant for containers. H 60cm (24in) S 75cm (30in).
Aspect: sun or semi-shade
Hardiness: ✿✿✿ Zones: 7–8

Berberis 'Georgii'

Berberis thunbergii 'Aurea'
Brilliant acid-yellow spring foliage is the main feature of this deciduous berberis with a neat rounded habit. The foliage colour deepens as the season progresses, eventually turning orange-red in autumn. Pale yellow flowers pass almost unnoticed during mid-spring and late spring, followed by more conspicuous glossy red fruit in autumn. An excellent choice for illuminating a shady corner. Avoid planting in full sun as it can scorch the foliage. H 1.5m (5ft) S 2m (6ft).
Aspect: semi-shade
Hardiness: ✿✿✿ Zones: 7–8

Berberis thunbergii 'Bagatelle'
Compact and easy to grow, this dwarf deciduous berberis has dark purple leaves that turn a brilliant red in autumn. It is ideal at the front of a border in sun or partial shade. The pale yellow flowers with reddish highlights are produced during mid-spring and late spring and are followed by glossy red fruit in autumn. H 30cm (12in) S 40cm (16in).
Aspect: sun or semi-shade
Hardiness: ✿✿✿ Zones: 7–8

Berberis thunbergii 'Dart's Red Lady'
This compact deciduous berberis has plum-red foliage that turns brilliant shades of red in autumn. The foliage is a perfect foil for the red-flushed, pale yellow flowers that are produced during mid-spring and late spring, followed by glossy red fruit in autumn. It is a useful specimen for a shrub border in sun or partial shade. H 1m (3ft) S 2.7m (9ft).
Aspect: sun or semi-shade
Hardiness: ✿✿✿ Zones: 7–8

Berberis thunbergii 'Harlequin'
An unusual deciduous berberis that has beetroot-red foliage marbled with pink and white, which turns pale crimson in the autumn. A bonus of pale yellow flowers with reddish highlights are produced during mid-spring and late spring, followed by glossy, red fruit in autumn. This compact, variegated

Berberis jamesiana

shrub makes a useful specimen for a shrub border in sun or partial shade. Lightly prune each winter to get the best foliage coloration. H 1.5m (5ft) S 2m (6ft).
Aspect: sun or semi-shade
Hardiness: ✿✿✿ Zones: 7–8

Berberis thunbergii 'Helmond Pillar'
A columnar, deciduous shrub with plum-purple leaves that take on brilliant shades of red in autumn. A bonus of red-tinged, pale yellow flowers are produced during mid-spring and late spring. This upright berberis makes a useful focal point or specimen for a shrub border in sun or partial shade, where it will add vertical interest to the planting scheme. H 150cm (5ft) S 60cm (2ft).
Aspect: sun or semi-shade
Hardiness: ✿✿✿ Zones: 7–8

Berberis valdiviana

Brachyglottis compacta 'Sunshine'

Brugmansia suaveolens

BRACHYGLOTTIS

A genus of about 30 species, including several evergreen shrubs. The one featured here has felty grey leaves that show off its brilliant yellow, daisy-like flowers during early summer. This sun-loving shrub is also tolerant of salt-laden air, so is an ideal choice for coastal gardens.

Cultivation It will grow in almost any well-drained garden soil that is reasonably fertile in full sun. It makes a suitable addition to a gravel or 'dry' garden, where it will appreciate the open site and well-drained soil.

Pruning No routine pruning is necessary, but you can trim it lightly after flowering to maintain overall shape.

Propagation Take semi-ripe cuttings in mid-summer.

Brachyglottis compacta 'Sunshine' (syn. *Senecio* 'Sunshine')

A popular evergreen, grey-leaved shrub that bears bright yellow, daisy-like flowers on wiry stems during early summer and mid-summer. The attractive felty leaves emerge silvery-white and mature to a darker green as the hairs are shed. H 1m (3ft) S 2m (6ft).
Aspect: sun
Hardiness: ✿✿ Zone: 9

BRUGMANSIA
Angels' trumpet

A genus of five species that includes the vigorous shrub featured here, which produces conspicuous, night-scented trumpets. Ideal for adding an exotic touch to a sheltered patio. Bear in mind that all parts of the plant are highly toxic if eaten, so it is not suitable if young children are around.

Cultivation In the garden, moisture-retentive, well-drained garden soil that is reasonably fertile suits this plant. It also prefers full sun. In containers, grow in a soil-based compost (soil mix). Feed every month throughout the growing season and water as necessary. The plant should be moved to a warm spot under cover when the temperature falls below 7°C, and watered sparingly throughout the winter.

Pruning No routine pruning is necessary, but you can trim lightly after flowering to maintain its overall shape. Neglected plants can be rejuvenated by cutting back one stem in three to near ground level after flowering, starting with the oldest stems.

Propagation Take semi-ripe cuttings in late summer or sow seed in mid-spring.

Brugmansia suaveolens

This night-scented tender shrub bears stunning, 30cm-(12in-) long, trumpet-shaped, white, yellow or pink flowers from early summer to early autumn, which appear against leathery, wavy-edged, mid-green leaves. H 5m (16ft) S 3m (10ft).
Aspect: sun
Hardiness: tender Zone: 10

BUDDLEJA

Over 100 species are in this genus, which includes the popular deciduous shrubs featured here. They are grown for their profusion of flowers, usually produced in terminal spikes, which are loved by butterflies and other beneficial insects. Buddlejas are also quick growing and easy to please and so are an ideal choice for a new garden.

Cultivation Grow in any well-drained, dry soil in full sun.

Pruning For best flowering displays, most should be cut back hard in early spring to encourage new, vigorous and free-flowering shoots from the base during early spring. The exceptions are *B. alternifolia* and *B. globosa*, which, once established, should have their flowered shoots cut back to a healthy shoot or a bud lower down in order to maintain a compact shape and encourage new flowering shoots. This should be done directly after flowering.

Propagation Take semi-ripe cuttings in late summer or hardwood cuttings during late autumn.

Buddleja alternifolia

An open, deciduous shrub with stiffly arching branches that are covered in dense clusters of very fragrant, lilac flowers during early summer. The gracefully arching branches look particularly effective when the shrub is grown as a standard to make a striking seasonal focal point in a sunny border. Train a single stem to 1.5m (5ft), then pinch out the growing tip. Progressively remove sideshoots from the base to create attractive weeping heads on a clear stem. The leaves also turn butter-yellow in autumn. H 4m (13ft) S 4m (13ft).
Aspect: sun
Hardiness: ✿✿✿ Zones: 7–8

Buddleja alternifolia

Buddleja davidii 'Black Night'

Buddleja davidii 'Nanho Blue'

Buddleja davidii 'Black Knight'
Butterfly bush

A dramatic, deciduous shrub that bears dense terminal spikes of fragrant, dark purple flowers from mid-summer to early autumn that are highly attractive to butterflies and other beneficial insects. The leaves also turn butter-yellow in autumn. H 3m (10ft) S 5m (16ft).
Aspect: sun
Hardiness: ✤✤✤ Zones: 7–8

Buddleja davidii 'Harlequin'
Variegated butterfly bush

Many gardeners would say that this is probably the best variegated version of this popular deciduous summer-flowering shrub. The lance-shaped, grey-green leaves are edged with yellow, maturing to cream, and provide added interest before the flowers appear. The dense spikes of fragrant, reddish-purple flowers are produced at the end of shoots in succession from mid-summer to early autumn and are a magnet for butterflies and other beneficial insects. H 3m (10ft) S 5m (16ft).
Aspect: sun
Hardiness: ✤✤✤ Zones: 7–8

Buddleja davidii 'Nanho Blue'
(syn. *B. davidii* 'Nanho Petite Indigo')
Butterfly bush

Slender, densely packed spikes of lilac-blue flowers are produced on the tips of gracefully arching branches on this deciduous shrub from mid-summer to early autumn. The fragrant flower spikes, up to 15cm (6in) long, are loved by butterflies and other beneficial insects. The leaves also turn butter-yellow in autumn. H 3m (10ft) S 5m (16ft).
Aspect: sun
Hardiness: ✤✤✤ Zones: 7–8

Buddleja davidii 'Pink Delight'
Butterfly bush

This splendid deciduous shrub bears densely packed, fragrant flower-spikes up to 30cm (12in) long at the end of arching shoots in succession from mid-summer to early autumn. Each flower-spike is made up of thousands of tiny orange-eyed, bright pink flowers that are a magnet for butterflies and other beneficial insects. The leaves are butter-yellow in autumn. H 3m (10ft) S 5m (16ft).
Aspect: sun
Hardiness: ✤✤✤ Zones: 7–8

Buddleja davidii 'White Profusion'
Butterfly bush

The best white form of the popular butterfly bush, this produces densely packed, fragrant terminal flower-spikes up to 40cm (15in) long in succession from mid-summer to early autumn. Each flower-spike is made up of thousands of tiny yellow-eyed, pure white flowers that become smothered in butterflies and other beneficial insects. The leaves also turn butter-yellow in autumn. For best displays, deadhead fading flower-spikes as they turn brown. H 3m (10ft) S 5m (16ft).
Aspect: sun
Hardiness: ✤✤✤ Zones: 7–8

Buddleja globosa
Orange ball tree

This is an unusual, semi-evergreen early summer-flowering shrub that bears ball-shaped clusters of fragrant, dark-orange and yellow flowers at the end of stiff stems from late spring to early summer. Although the plant is frost hardy (to –5°C/23°F), it prefers to be grown in the shelter of a warm wall or fence, where the deeply veined, dark green leaves are often retained over winter in mild areas. More protection will be required for this shrub in very cold areas. H 5m (16ft) S 5m (16ft).
Aspect: sun
Hardiness: ✤✤ Zone: 9+

Buddleja 'Lochinch'
Butterfly bush

This is a popular compact form of the butterfly bush that bears densely packed spikes of honey-scented flowers on arching stems in succession from mid-summer to early autumn. Each flower-spike is made up of thousands of tiny orange-eyed, lavender-blue flowers that are loved by butterflies and other beneficial insects. The fresh-cut flowers are popular in floral arrangements. The downy, grey-green leaves turn butter-yellow in autumn. For best displays, deadhead the fading flower-spikes to encourage further flowering. H 2.5m (8ft) S 3m (10ft).
Aspect: sun
Hardiness: ✤✤✤ Zones: 7–8

Buddleja davidii 'Dartmoor'

BUPLEURUM

A genus of over 100 species that includes the open, evergreen, summer-flowering shrub featured here. This useful filler for the mixed or shrub border can cope well with salt-laden air, and so makes a good choice for seaside gardens, where it can be used as an informal screen, too.

Cultivation Grow in any well-drained soil in full sun. Protect in exposed gardens, especially while it is getting established. In cold gardens it is only borderline hardy.

Pruning No routine pruning is necessary, but you can trim lightly after flowering to maintain its overall shape. Neglected plants can be rejuvenated by cutting back one stem in three to near ground level after flowering, starting with the oldest stems.

Propagation Take softwood cuttings in early summer or sow seed in mid-spring.

Bupleurum fruticosum
Shrubby hare's ear

A dense and spreading evergreen shrub with dark green leaves that are silvery on the underside. Greenish-yellow ball-shaped clusters of star-shaped flowers are produced at the end of new growth from mid-summer to early autumn, followed by brown seedheads that provide winter interest. H 2m (6ft) S 2.5m (8ft).

Aspect: sun
Hardiness: ❀❀❀ Zones: 7–8

Bupleurum fruticosum

Buxus sempervirens 'Suffruticosa'

BUXUS
Box

This genus of about 70 species includes the low-growing, hardy, evergreen shrubs featured here. These slow- and dense-growing shrubs are useful for adding structure to any size of garden. Left to their own devices in borders, they will form rounded shrubs that add a sense of permanence to the planting scheme, or can be clipped into a neat hedge or border edging. Alternatively, grow in containers and trim regularly to add a year-round sense of formality to shady patios, paths and entrances. Some can also be trained and trimmed into intricate topiary shapes.

Cultivation In the garden, grow in any well-drained soil that is reasonably fertile in partial shade. Trim hedges and topiary into shape during late summer or early autumn. In containers, grow in a soil-based soil mix. Water as necessary.

Pruning Trim before new growth appears in early spring. Clip intricately shaped plants in mid-summer to maintain the neat outline.

Propagation Take semi-ripe cuttings in late summer.

Buxus sempervirens

A slow-growing, bushy, evergreen shrub with densely packed, lustrous, dark green leaves. Its rate of growth and dense, compact habit make it ideal for clipping into a formal, low-growing hedge or shaping into topiary.

H 5m (16ft) S 5m (16ft). Named varieties: 'Elegantissima', compact, flame-shaped evergreen with densely packed tiny, white-margined, dark green leaves. Ideal for illuminating shady corners or adding light to other parts of the garden. Regular clipping may cause it to revert to green. H 1.5m (5ft) S 1.5m (5ft). 'Suffruticosa' is a very slow-growing, dwarf, evergreen with densely packed, tiny, lustrous, dark green leaves. It makes an excellent very low-growing cloud-like hedge if left unclipped. It also responds well to regular trimming and so is the best choice for clipping into a low, formal edging for beds and borders, or for framing seasonal planting schemes. It is also an ideal choice for growing in containers and for shaping into topiary. H 1m (3ft) S 1.5m (5ft).

Aspect: semi-shade
Hardiness: ❀❀❀ Zones: 7–8

CALLICARPA
Beauty berry

A large genus of over 140 species that includes the deciduous shrub featured here. Sought after by flower arrangers, the bare branches of this bushy, upright shrub are laden with eye-catching, violet berries that light up the autumn and winter garden if left by the birds.

Cultivation Grow in any well-drained soil that's reasonably fertile in sun or partial shade.

Pruning No routine pruning is necessary. Neglected plants can have awkwardly placed branches removed to maintain the overall balance of the canopy.

Propagation Take softwood cuttings in late spring or semi-ripe cuttings during mid-summer.

Callicarpa bodinieri var. giraldii 'Profusion'
Beauty bush

Aptly named, the beauty bush is a sight to behold when the garden becomes dormant. This upright, deciduous shrub bears astonishingly vibrant violet, bead-like berries during mid-autumn that last well after the autumn leaves have fallen. A bonus of small pink flowers are produced in July (mid-summer) and the dark green leaves emerge bronze tinted and turn yellow in autumn. H 3m (10ft) S 2.5m (8ft).

Aspect: sun or semi-shade
Hardiness: ❀❀❀ Zones: 7–8

CALLISTEMON

A genus of over 25 species that includes exotic-looking, half-hardy or frost-hardy evergreens that make excellent seasonal specimens for a sunny, sheltered spot on the patio. In frost-prone areas, grow in a large container and move into the protection of a greenhouse or conservatory over winter.

Cultivation In the garden, grow in any well-drained soil in sun that is sheltered from cold and winds – the base of a sunny wall is ideal. In containers, grow in a soil-based soil mix. Water as necessary.

Callicarpa bodinieri var. *giraldii* 'Profusion'

Callistemon citrinus

Pruning No routine pruning is necessary. Neglected plants can have old branches removed after flowering to encourage new shoots from the base.

Propagation Take semi-ripe cuttings during late summer or sow seeds in early spring.

Callistemon citrinus 'Splendens'
Crimson bottlebrush

Striking crimson, bottlebrush-shaped flower-spikes are produced at the tips of stiffly arching branches throughout early summer and mid-summer. The downy, pink-tinged young shoots mature to dark green and produce a distinctive lemon fragrance when lightly crushed. H 4m (13ft) S 3m (10ft).

Aspect: sun
Hardiness: ❀ Zone: 10

Callistemon rigidus
Stiff bottlebrush

A bit hardier and more compact than other species, this plant bears distinctive, rich red flower-spikes up to 15cm (6in) long at the tips of arching branches from early summer to late summer. H 1m (3ft) S 2.5m (8ft).

Aspect: sun
Hardiness: ❀ Zone: 10

CALLUNA
Ling, Scots heather

A genus of just one species of hardy, evergreen shrubs with colourful summer flowers, some of which offer autumn foliage tints, too. There are literally hundreds of named varieties, the best of which are featured here. All Scots heathers make excellent ground cover plants for open, sunny areas with acid soil. Many make useful permanent container plants, while others are used for cut-flower arrangements.

Cultivation In the garden, grow in any well-drained, but moisture-retentive acid soil in full sun. Add plenty of organic matter (but not alkaline mushroom soil mix) to the soil before planting. In containers, grow in an ericaceous soil mix on a sunny patio. Keep well watered.

Pruning Trim off flowering stems as they fade. Encourage bushy growth by trimming lightly before new growth appears in spring.

Propagation Take semi-ripe cuttings in mid-summer or layer side-shoots in early spring.

Calluna vulgaris 'Blazeaway'

Year-round colour is provided by the superb golden foliage that turns dark red in winter. A bonus of lilac flower-spikes are produced continuously from mid-summer to early autumn. Its neat habit and year-round display means it is a good choice for a permanent container. H 35cm (14in) S 60cm (24in).

Aspect: sun
Hardiness: ❀❀❀ Zones: 7–8

Calluna vulgaris 'Dark Star'

This compact evergreen produces dense spikes of semi-double, crimson flowers amid a neat mound of dark green leaves from mid-summer to mid-autumn. H 20cm (8in) S 35cm (14in).

Aspect: sun
Hardiness: ❀❀❀ Zones: 7–8

Calluna vulgaris 'H. E. Beale' (syn. *C. vulgaris* 'Pink Beale')

This old favourite produces slim spikes of double, shell-pink flowers from late summer to late autumn above a mound of dark green leaves. The long, tapering flower-spikes are ideal for cutting. H 30cm (12in) S 60cm (24in).

Aspect: sun
Hardiness: ❀❀❀ Zones: 7–8

Calluna vulgaris 'Silver Queen'

This is a wonderful, vigorous and spreading silver-leaved Scots heather with silky foliage that lasts throughout the year. An added bonus of lavender-pink flowers are produced on short spikes from late summer to early autumn. H 40cm (16in) S 55cm (22in).

Aspect: sun
Hardiness: ❀❀❀ Zones: 7–8

Calluna vulgaris 'Wickwar Flame'

You can use this colourful heather to add much-needed winter interest to the middle of sunny beds and borders. Its open mounds of golden foliage turn bright red in winter, with the bonus of upright, mauve flower-spikes from mid-summer to late summer. H 50cm (20in) S 65cm (26in).

Aspect: sun
Hardiness: ❀❀❀ Zones: 7–8

Other good cultivars to look out for:

Calluna vulgaris 'Alicia', large, pure white flowers open from late summer to early winter, over a mound of apple-green leaves. H 30cm (12in) S 40cm (16in).

Calluna vulgaris 'Amethyst', purplish-crimson flowers open from late summer to mid-winter, above a mound of dark-green leaves. H 30cm (12in) S 40cm (16in).

Calluna vulgaris 'County Wicklow', double, shell-pink flowers are produced from late summer to mid-autumn, above a mound of mid-green leaves. H 25cm (10in) S 35cm (14in).

Calluna vulgaris 'Silver Knight', mauve-pink flowers open from mid-summer to mid-autumn, above downy, grey leaves, that turn pale purple in winter. H 40cm (16in) S 50cm (20in).

Calluna vulgaris 'Wickwar Flame'

Camellia japonica 'Elegans'

CAMELLIA

This is a very large genus of over 250 species that includes many evergreen shrubs with beautiful, flamboyant blooms during the spring that stand out against the dark, glossy foliage. Generally slow growing and long lived, they make excellent border fillers, while some compact varieties are also suitable for growing in large containers.

Cultivation In the garden, grow in any well-drained acid soil in dappled shade, but in colder areas provide shelter and plant in a position that gets afternoon sun. Add plenty of organic matter (but not alkaline mushroom compost/soil mix) before planting. In pots, grow in ericaceous compost and keep well watered. Wherever the camellia is planted, bear in mind that the flowers are susceptible to damage by a frost that is followed by a rapid thaw, so avoid positioning in east-facing areas that get early morning sun in spring.

Pruning Deadhead after flowering. Prune straggly branches of established plants to maintain the overall shape during late winter or early spring.

Propagation Layer low branches in early spring or take semi-ripe cuttings in late summer.

Camellia japonica 'Adolphe Audusson'

A compact evergreen shrub that bears masses of large, semi-double, bright red flowers intermittently from early spring to late spring against a backdrop of glossy, dark green foliage. Reliable and free-flowering, it offers great garden value. H 5m (16ft) S 4m (13ft).
Aspect: semi-shade
Hardiness: ✿✿✿ Zones: 7–8

Camellia japonica 'Elegans' (syn. C. japonica 'Chandleri Elegans')

Superb, sugar-pink, anemone-like flowers are produced during mid-spring and late spring against a backdrop of lustrous, wavy-edged, dark green leaves. H 3.5m (12ft) S 3m (10ft).
Aspect: semi-shade
Hardiness: ✿✿✿ Zones: 7–8

Camellia japonica 'Nobilissima'

This is one of the earliest flowering camellias, bearing peony-shaped, yellow-centred, white flowers from mid-winter to early spring against a backdrop of glossy, dark green leaves. This tough evergreen shrub will survive cold and windy conditions and so is an ideal choice for colder areas. H 5m (16ft) S 3.5m (12ft).
Aspect: semi-shade
Hardiness: ✿✿✿ Zones: 7–8

Camellia x williamsii 'Anticipation'

This is a handsome evergreen camellia that is deservedly popular for its large, peony-like, bright red flowers during late winter and early spring. Its narrow habit makes it an ideal container camellia or for use as an informal flowering hedge. Fast growing. H 4m (13ft) S 2m (6ft).
Aspect: semi-shade
Hardiness: ✿✿✿ Zones: 7–8

Camellia x williamsii 'Debbie'

An excellent camellia that bears dark rose-pink, peony-shaped flowers during mid-spring and late spring that are reputed to have good weather resistance. This free-flowering, vigorous evergreen has a dense mound of

Other good cultivars to look out for:

Camellia 'Leonard Messel', large, semi-double peony-flowered variety with clear-pink blooms from early spring to May. H 4m (13ft) S 3m (10ft).
Camellia japonica 'Hagoromo', early flowering, semi-double, pale-pink flowers borne throughout late winter and early spring. H 5m (15ft) S 4m (13ft).
Camellia japonica 'Mikenjaku', early flowering, semi-double, rosy-red and white-marbled weather-resistant flowers are borne during late winter to early spring. H 4m (13ft) S 4.5m (14ft).
Camellia japonica 'Lady Vansittart', unusual holly-like leaves and semi-double, pink-striped, white flowers, which are borne from late winter to mid-spring. H 4m (13ft) S 3.5m (11ft).

Camellia x williamsii 'Jury's Yellow', anemone-flowered variety that bears yellow-centred white flowers from late winter to mid-spring. H 5m (15ft) S 3m (10ft).
Camellia x williamsii 'Mary Phoebe Taylor', this is a large, peony-flowered variety with semi-double, clear-pink flowers borne from late winter and early spring. H 4m (13ft) S 2m (6ft).
Camellia sasanqua 'Narumigata', scented, single, pink-tinged white flowers are borne from mid-autumn to early winter. H 6m (20ft) S 3m (10ft).
Camellia x williamsii 'E.G. Waterhouse', an upright camellia that bears double, sugar-pink flowers from late winter to mid-spring. H 5m (15ft) S 3m (10ft).

Camellia williamsii 'Anticipation'

Camellia williamsii 'Debbie'

Camellia x williamsii 'Donation'

Caryopteris x clandonensis

glossy, bright green foliage and tends to drop its blooms as they fade, so it always looks attractive. H 3m (10ft) S 2m (6ft).
Aspect: semi-shade
Hardiness: ❀❀❀ Zones: 7–8

Camellia x williamsii 'Donation'
A very long-flowering evergreen camellia, it produces its large, semi-double, sugar-pink flowers from late winter to late spring against lustrous, bright green leaves. Its compact, yet upright shape makes it an ideal choice for growing in a large container filled with ericaceous compost. H 5m (16ft) S 2.5m (8ft).
Aspect: semi-shade
Hardiness: ❀❀❀ Zones: 7–8

Camellia x williamsii 'J. C. Williams'
Beautiful single, rose-pink flowers are produced in early spring and mid-spring on open evergreen branches that can be trained effectively against a semi-shaded wall or fence. This free-flowering, fast-growing evergreen covered in lustrous, bright green foliage tends to drop its blooms as they fade and so always looks attractive. H 5m (16ft) S 3m (10ft).
Aspect: semi-shade
Hardiness: ❀❀❀ Zones: 7–8

CARPENTERIA
A genus of just one species of frost-hardy shrubs with beautiful, scented summer flowers. This upright, spreading evergreen is ideal for growing in the middle of a border in mild areas, but needs a sheltered wall or fence if grown elsewhere. *Carpenteria* can also be trained to grow effectively as a fan-shaped wall shrub.
Cultivation Grow this shrub in any well-drained, but moisture-retentive, soil in a sheltered spot in full sun.
Pruning Established plants can have one stem in three removed after flowering in late summer, starting with the oldest, to promote better flowering and a more compact shape.
Propagation Take softwood cuttings from new growth or semi-ripe cuttings in mid-summer, or sow seed in mid-spring.

Carpenteria californica
Brilliant white and fragrant anemone-like flowers, each with a pronounced central boss of yellow stamens, are produced in succession throughout early summer and mid-summer against a backdrop of lustrous, dark green leaves. H 2m (6ft) S 2m (6ft). Named varieties: 'Ladhams' Variety' has brilliant white flowers up to 8cm (3in) across. H 2m (6ft) S 2m (6ft).
Aspect: sun
Hardiness: ❀❀ Zone: 9+

CARYOPTERIS
A genus of over five species, including deciduous shrubs with aromatic foliage and late-summer flowers. The misty profusion of fragrant blooms are a magnet to bees and butterflies and provide much-needed colour to the late summer display. Ideal for growing alongside other shrubs or in a mixed border.
Cultivation Grow in any well-drained soil that is reasonably fertile and situate in full sun. In very cold areas, grow by a south-facing wall or fence.

Carpenteria californica

Pruning Once established, prune the shrub by cutting back to 5cm (2in) of the ground in early spring. This will help promote more vigorous flowering.
Propagation Take softwood cuttings from new growth in mid-summer or semi-ripe cuttings in late summer, or sow seed in early autumn.

Caryopteris x clandonensis Bluebeard
This is a mound-forming shrub that has grey-green, lance-shaped, aromatic leaves covered in silvery hairs on the underside. The leaves form the perfect foil for the whorls of purplish-blue flowers that are borne throughout late summer and early autumn and which are a valuable source of nectar for butterflies and other useful insects.
Named varieties: 'First Choice', a new variety bearing dark blue buds that open to reveal a haze of rich, cobalt-blue flowers. H 1m (3ft) S 1m (3ft). 'Heavenly Blue', upright deciduous variety with dark blue flowers. H 1m (3ft) S 1m (3ft). 'Worcester Gold' (golden bluebeard), glowing yellow, aromatic foliage and dense clusters of lavender-blue flowers. The fragrant flowers act almost as a magnet to beneficial insects such as bees and butterflies. H 1m (3ft) S 1m (3ft).
Aspect: sun
Hardiness: ❀❀❀ Zones: 7–8

Ceanothus 'Concha'

Ceanothus 'Julia Phelps'

CEANOTHUS

This genus of over 50 species includes both deciduous and evergreen shrubs that are covered in masses of blue flowers in either late spring or late summer. Quick growing, they make effective border fillers, or can be trained against walls and fences in colder areas, where they will help to extend the flowering season. The deciduous varieties tend to be hardier than the evergreen.
Cultivation Grow in any well-drained soil that is reasonably fertile in full sun, but sheltered from cold winds. In very cold areas, grow in the protection of a south-facing wall or fence.
Pruning Once the plant has become established, prune deciduous varieties in early spring by cutting back the previous year's growth to an outward-facing side shoot within a few centimetres of the base. Evergreen varieties should be pruned only lightly after flowering. Do not cut back into old wood as it is reluctant to resprout.
Propagation Take semi-ripe cuttings from deciduous varieties in early autumn, or take stem cuttings from evergreen varieties in mid-summer.

Ceanothus arboreus 'Trewithen Blue'
Blueblossom
This is a large, vigorous evergreen shrub with notched, dark green leaves that is smothered in fragrant, rich blue flowers from late spring to early summer. It is

less hardy than some other varieties and so is not a good choice for colder regions. H 6m (20ft) S 8m (26ft).
Aspect: sun
Hardiness: ✿✿ Zone: 9+

Ceanothus 'Autumnal Blue'
California lilac
A useful evergreen filler shrub with apple-green glossy leaves, and clouds of bright blue flowers borne from late summer to mid-autumn. Although it is hardier than other forms, it still needs protection in colder areas. H 3m (10ft) S 3m (10ft).
Aspect: sun
Hardiness: ✿✿✿ Zones: 7–8

Ceanothus 'Burkwoodii'
California lilac
Clouds of sky-blue flowers provide a dramatic seasonal accent to sunny beds and borders from late summer to early autumn above a compact evergreen shrub with bright green glossy leaves. H 1.5m (5ft) S 2m (6ft).
Aspect: sun
Hardiness: ✿✿ Zone: 9+

Ceanothus 'Concha'
California lilac
This dense, evergreen shrub with lustrous dark green foliage transforms into a dazzling mound of dark blue flowers during late spring and early summer. The flowers emerge dramatically from purple buds borne in dense clusters along arching stems to smother the entire shrub in a cloak of colour.

H 3m (10ft) S 3m (10ft).
Aspect: sun
Hardiness: ✿✿ Zone: 9+

Ceanothus 'Italian Skies'
California lilac
This is a relatively new variety with a spreading habit that is covered in dense clusters of brilliant blue flowers during late spring to early summer above glossy evergreen foliage. It is less hardy than some other varieties and so is not a good choice for colder regions. H 1.5m (5ft) S 3m (10ft).
Aspect: sun
Hardiness: ✿✿ Zone: 9+

Ceanothus 'Puget Blue'
Santa Barbara ceanothus
A vigorous spreading, evergreen shrub that is covered in masses of dark blue flowers from mid-spring to early summer above heavily veined, dark green leaves. Protect from cold winds as the leaves are easily scorched. H 3m (10ft) S 3m (10ft).
Aspect: sun
Hardiness: ✿✿ Zone: 9+

Ceanothus thyrsiflorus var. *repens* (syn. *C. repens*)
Creeping blueblossom
A steadfast, mound-forming, evergreen shrub that is excellent for covering sunny banks in mild areas where its profusion of pale blue flowers can be seen at their best during late spring and early summer. Although it is hardier

than other forms, it still needs protection in colder areas. H 1m (3ft) S 2.5m (8ft).
Aspect: sun
Hardiness: ✿✿ Zone: 9+

CERATOSTIGMA

A genus of eight species, including both deciduous and semi-evergreen shrubs with vivid late-summer flowers and brilliant autumn foliage colours. These spreading shrubs are perfect for a sunny, sheltered site positioned in a prominent position in the garden where they can be appreciated most.
Cultivation In the garden, grow in a moisture-retentive, but well-drained soil in full sun. Add plenty of organic matter to the soil before planting. When grown in containers, use a soil-based

Ceanothus thyrsiflorus 'Millerton Point'

Ceratostigma griffithii

compost (soil mix) and site on a sunny patio. Keep well watered.
Pruning In early spring, cut back straggly stems to a plump bud or side shoot near to ground level.
Propagation Take semi-ripe cuttings in mid-summer.

Ceratostigma griffithii
Excellent for autumn colour, this small, rounded semi-evergreen with purple-edged green leaves turns brilliant red in autumn and lasts well into winter. From late summer to mid-autumn the shrub is transformed by terminal clusters of large, purple-blue flowers. An ideal choice for the front of a sunny, sheltered border. H 1m (3ft) S 1.5m (5ft).
Aspect: sun
Hardiness: ❈❈ Zone: 9+

Ceratostigma willmottianum
Hardy plumbago
A spreading deciduous shrub that bears terminal clusters of pale blue flowers from late summer to mid-autumn over a mound of purple-edged, dark green leaves. The attractive foliage then turns brilliant fiery shades in autumn. H 1m (3ft) S 1.5m (5ft).
Named varieties: 'Desert Skies' (golden plumbago, syn. *C. willmottianum* 'Palmgold'), a new variety with brilliant yellow foliage that forms a dramatic foil for the cobalt-blue flowers

produced throughout late summer and early autumn. Slightly less hardy than the other varieties, so grow as a container plant in colder areas. H 1m (3ft) S 1.5m (5ft). 'Forest Blue' (Chinese plumbago), vivid blue flowers are produced in clusters over a mound of purple-edged, dark green leaves that turn flaming shades of red and orange in autumn. H 1m (3ft) S 1.5m (5ft).
Aspect: sun
Hardiness: ❈❈❈ Zones: 7–8

CHAENOMELES
Flowering quince
A genus of just three species that includes the deciduous, spring-flowering shrubs featured here. The yellow-tinged green fruit that follow the flowers are edible when cooked, and the flowering stems are valued in early spring and autumn by flower arrangers. The neat habit of these shrubs makes them particularly useful in the border or trained against a wall or fence. They are also ideal for growing as an informal flowering hedge in sun or shade, where their thorny branches form an impenetrable thicket.
Cultivation Grow in any well-drained soil that is reasonably fertile in full sun or dappled shade. Flowering and fruiting is reduced if planted in full shade.

Chaenomeles x superba 'Crimson and Gold'

Pruning In the border, no routine pruning is necessary. Informal hedges can be pruned after flowering to keep within bounds. You can also prune established shrubs grown against a wall or fence to enhance the overall display. Cut back all new stems to just after the main cluster of flower buds in early early spring, then prune again after flowering in late spring by cutting back the shoots to two or three buds from the main framework.
Propagation Take softwood cuttings in early summer or layer shoots in early autumn.

Chaenomeles speciosa 'Geisha Girl'
Apricot-pink and yellow double flowers add subtle charm to this compact, deciduous shrub from early spring to late spring, followed by aromatic, yellow-tinged green fruit. The twiggy, thorn-covered branches form a thicket, covered in lustrous, oval, dark green leaves. H 2m (6ft) S 1.2m (4ft).
Aspect: sun or semi-shade
Hardiness: ❈❈❈ Zones: 7–8

Chaenomeles speciosa 'Moerloosei' (syn. *C. speciosa* 'Apple Blossom')
Many gardeners consider this plant to be one of the most outstanding cultivars of this popular species. Beautiful large, white, apple blossom-like flowers that are delicately flushed with

pink cover the twiggy branches of this vigorous flowering quince and appear from early spring to late spring. H 2.5m (8ft) S 5m (16ft).
Aspect: sun or semi-shade
Hardiness: ❈❈❈ Zones: 7–8

Chaenomeles speciosa 'Nivalis'
Brilliant, snow-white flowers smother the twiggy, spine-covered stems of this vigorous flowering quince from early spring to late spring. H 2.5m (8ft) S 5m (16ft).
Aspect: sun or semi-shade
Hardiness: ❈❈❈ Zones: 7–8

Chaenomeles x superba 'Crimson and Gold'
Compact and easy to grow, this popular variety bears striking crimson flowers with contrasting golden anthers along twiggy, spine-covered branches from early spring to late spring. The aromatic, yellow-tinged, green fruit that follow are edible when cooked. H 1m (3ft) S 2m (6ft).
Aspect: sun or semi-shade
Hardiness: ❈❈❈ Zones: 7–8

Chaenomeles x superba 'Nicoline'
Striking scarlet flowers are produced in profusion along twiggy, thorn-covered stems from early spring to late spring. The branches form a thicket, covered in lustrous, oval, dark green leaves. H 1.5m (5ft) S 2m (6ft).
Aspect: sun or semi-shade
Hardiness: ❈❈❈ Zones: 7–8

Chaenomeles speciosa 'Geisha Girl'

Chamaedorea elegans

Chamaerops humilis

Chimonanthus praecox

CHAMAEDOREA

This large genus of over 100 species includes the parlour palm, which is a tender plant often grown as a house plant in frost-prone areas. Very small plants can be used successfully as temporary additions in bottle gardens, where they thrive in humid conditions.
Cultivation In areas where the temperature does not drop below 15°C (60°F), the tender parlour palm can be grown outside in neutral to acid, well-drained soil in shade. Elsewhere, it is best grown as a house plant, in a peat-based soil mix, and placed in a well-lit spot on a tray of moist gravel to increase humidity around the leaves. Feed every fortnight with a balanced fertilizer and water as necessary during the growing season. Water sparingly in the winter months.
Pruning No routine pruning is necessary, but remove damaged leaves as soon as they are noticed.
Propagation Sow seed in mid-spring.

Chamaedorea elegans (syn. Neanthe bella)
Parlour palm
This popular house plant has a suckering habit and produces upright bamboo-like stems and arching, leathery, dark green, divided fronds. Tiny yellow flowers appear on mature plants during the growing season, followed by small black berries. H 2m (6ft) S 1m (3ft).
Aspect: semi-shade to full shade
Hardiness: tender Zone: 10

CHAMAEROPS

A genus of just one species of suckering, half-hardy, bushy, palms that can be grown outside in full sun in mild areas to help create a tropical atmosphere. However, in frost-prone areas, grow in a large pot on the patio and move to a frost-free spot during the winter months. They also make handsome and easy-to-grow house plants.
Cultivation In frost-free areas this half-hardy fan palm can be grown outside in neutral to acid, well-drained soil in full sun. If grown as a house plant, use soil-based soil mix and stand the pot in a well-lit spot. Feed every fortnight with a balanced fertilizer and water as necessary during the growing season. Water sparingly during the winter months.
Pruning No routine pruning is necessary but remove damaged leaves as soon as they are noticed.
Propagation Sow seed in mid-spring. Separate and pot up rooted suckers in late spring.

Chamaerops humilis
Dwarf fan palm
This plant has spiky, glossy, fan-shaped, grey-green leaves that grow up to 1m (3ft) in length and are produced from suckering palm-like stems. On mature specimens of this plant, insignificant yellow flowers are produced in dense spikes throughout the growing season. H 2m (6ft) S 1m (3ft).
Aspect: sun
Hardiness: ❋ Zone: 10

CHIMONANTHUS

A genus of about five species that includes both deciduous and evergreen shrubs. The deciduous shrubs featured here are grown for their waxy-looking, fragrant yellow flowers that are borne on bare branches from late winter to early spring, when the garden needs them most. They make unassuming plants for the rest of the year and are most effective when planted in sun close to a path or entrance. The winter stems can be cut when in bud, so the superb sweetly scented flowers can be enjoyed inside over the Christmas period.
Cultivation Grow in any well-drained soil that is reasonably fertile in full sun.
Pruning Once established, prune out one stem in three, starting with the oldest, to encourage a continuous supply of young flowering stems. This should be done directly after flowering.
Propagation Take softwood cuttings in mid-summer. Layer lower stems in late summer.

Chimonanthus praecox
Wintersweet
A vigorous deciduous shrub that bears waxy-looking, fragrant, sulphur-yellow flowers, often with a contrastingly tinted throat, on branches from early winter to late winter. H 4m (13ft) S 3m (10ft).
Named varieties: 'Grandiflorus', large, slightly scented, dark yellow flowers, each with a purple-stained throat. H 4m (13ft) S 3m (10ft). var. *luteus* (syn. *C. praecox* 'Concolor'), waxy-looking, fragrant, clear-yellow flowers that open widely on bare stems from mid-winter to early spring. H 4m (13ft) S 3m (10ft).
Aspect: sun
Hardiness: ❋❋❋ Zones: 7–8

CHOISYA

A popular genus of over five species, including several compact, aromatic evergreen shrubs that produce star-like, white, flowers with a scent that is reminiscent of orange blossoms during late spring and again in late summer. The evergreen foliage is attractive all year round and provides the perfect foil for other flowers, too. It makes a good border filler and can be grown as a permanent container plant, and moved into a prominent position, such as the patio, while in flower.
Cultivation In the garden, grow in any well-drained soil that is reasonably fertile in full sun or dappled shade. In containers, grow in a soil-based compost (soil mix) on a sunny patio. Keep well watered. In colder gardens, plant in a sheltered spot, as cold winds can damage the foliage. Also, protect the less hardy yellow-leaved varieties in winter.
Pruning No routine pruning is required. Remove frost-damaged shoots in spring. Rejuvenate by cutting one stem in three to the ground, starting with the oldest.
Propagation Take semi-ripe cuttings in early summer or mid-autumn.

Choisya ternata

Choisya ternata 'Sundance'

Cistus x cyprius

Cistus x pulverulentus 'Sunset'

Named varieties: 'Aztec Pearl', starry, white flowers that open from pink-tinged buds. H 2.5m (8ft) S 2.5m (8ft). 'Goldfingers', a new introduction that forms a compact shrub with bold yellow foliage and sweetly scented white flowers during mid-spring and late spring. H 1.5m (5ft) S 1.5m (5ft). 'Sundance', a compact evergreen shrub with bright yellow, glossy young leaves that mature to yellow-green, especially when grown in deep shade. A bonus of pretty white flowers are sometimes produced during mid-spring and late spring. H 2.5m (8ft) S 2.5m (8ft).

Neither of the yellow-leaved forms are as hardy as the green-leaved varieties, and can also suffer from scorch if positioned in strong sunlight.

Choisya ternata
Mexican orange blossom
This is a compact evergreen shrub that bears masses of fragrant, starry white flowers in succession during mid-spring and late spring, often with a second flush from late summer to early autumn. The bright green, glossy leaves provide the perfect foil for the sweet and spicy-smelling flowers that give off a lovely aroma when lightly crushed.

H 2.5m (8ft) S 2.5m (8ft).
Aspect: sun and semi-shade
Hardiness: ✿✿✿ Zones: 7–8

CISTUS
Rock rose, sun rose
This genus of 20 species includes many compact evergreen shrubs with spectacular papery summer flowers that thrive in well-drained sun-baked sites. They are an ideal choice for a prominent dry border or bank in sun, or can be grown in a large container on the patio.
Cultivation In the garden, grow in any well-drained soil in full sun. In containers, grow in a soil-based compost (soil mix). Water as necessary.
Pruning Trim the shrub as the flowers fade, cutting back new growth by about two-thirds. Remove frost-damaged shoots in spring.
Propagation Take semi-ripe cuttings in early autumn.

Cistus x corbariensis (syn. C. x hybridus)
This is a bushy, evergreen shrub with delicate-looking, papery, white flowers that open from bright red buds during early summer and mid-summer, each with a central boss of yellow stamens. The wavy-edged, dark green leaves make it an attractive foil for other flowers at other times. H 1m (3ft) S 1.5m (5ft).
Aspect: sun
Hardiness: ✿✿ Zone: 9+

Cistus x pulverulentus 'Sunset' (syn. C. crispus 'Sunset')
This is a free-flowering variety that is covered in a succession of rose-pink blooms during early summer and mid-summer, each with a distinctive central boss of yellow stamens. The dense and spreading habit of this shrub makes it a useful ground cover plant. It tolerates salt-laden air. H 60cm (24in) S 90cm (36in).
Aspect: sun
Hardiness: ✿✿ Zone: 9+

Cistus 'Silver Pink' syn. C. 'Grayswood Pink'
Masses of delicate-looking, papery, silvery-pink flowers are produced on 'Silver Pink'. These gradually fade to white towards the middle of the petals, with each flower having a distinctive central boss of yellow stamens. The flowers are produced in succession throughout early summer and mid-summer on this compact, evergreen shrub that has narrow, dark green leaves, which have a grey underneath. H 75cm (30in) S 90cm (36in).
Aspect: sun
Hardiness: ✿✿ Zone: 9+

Other good cultivars to look out for:

Cistus x *aguilarii* 'Maculatus', yellow-centred white flowers with burgundy markings at the base of each petal during early summer and mid-summer H 1.2m (4ft) S 1.2m (4ft).

Cistus x *argenteus* 'Peggy Sammons', pale pinkish-purple, flowers are borne in early summer and mid-summer above grey-green, downy leaves, H 1m (3ft) S 1m (3ft).

Cistus x *dansereaui* 'Decumbens', white flowers with faint yellow and crimson marks at the base of each petal are produced during early summer and mid-summer. H 60cm (24in) S 90cm (36in).

Cistus 'Grayswood Pink', pale pink flowers that fade towards the centre are borne in early summer and mid-summer above wavy-edged, grey-green leaves. H 1m (3ft) S 1m (3ft).

Cistus x *skanbergii*, yellow-centred, pale pink flowers are produced in early summer and mid-summer above wavy-edged, grey-green leaves. H 75cm (30in) S 90cm (36in).

Clerodendrum trichotomum var. fargesii

CLERODENDRUM

A huge genus of over 400 species, including the deciduous shrub featured here, that bears white, star-like late-summer flowers, followed by striking bright blue berries in autumn. It makes a perfect filler for a shrub or mixed border next to an access point, where its unusual berries can be viewed at close quarters.
Cultivation Grow in well-drained, moisture-retentive soil that is reasonably fertile in full sun.
Pruning No routine pruning is required. Remove frost-damaged shoots in spring.
Propagation Take root cuttings in early winter. Remove rooted suckers in spring.

Clerodendrum trichotomum var. *fargesii*
An upright, deciduous shrub that is covered in striking turquoise-blue berries, surrounded by a contrasting, star-shaped, maroon calyx during mid-autumn and late autumn. The fruit follow pretty, pink-budded, scented, white, star-shaped flowers that are borne from late summer to early autumn. H 6m (20ft) S 6m (20ft).
Aspect: sun
Hardiness: ✿✿✿ Zones: 7–8

CLETHRA

This genus of over 60 species includes the deciduous summer-flowering shrubs featured here. They are useful, upright-growing shrubs for a shady border or for under-planting deciduous trees in a woodland garden with acid soil.
Cultivation Grow in any acidic well-drained, moisture-retentive soil that is reasonably fertile in dappled shade.
Pruning No routine pruning is required. Neglected shrubs can be rejuvenated in spring by cutting out one stem in three back to a side shoot lower down, starting with the oldest.
Propagation Take softwood cuttings from new shoots in mid-summer.

Clethra alnifolia
Sweet pepper bush
A delightful deciduous shrub that bears candle-like spikes of fragrant, bell-shaped white flowers throughout late summer and early autumn above the oval green foliage. H 2.5m (8ft) S 2.5m (8ft). **Named varieties:**
'Paniculata', H 10cm (4in) white flower spikes. H 2.5m (8ft) S 2.5m (8ft). 'Pink Spire', large pink flower-spikes. H 2.5m (8ft) S 2.5m (8ft). 'Rosea', large deep pink flower-spikes. H 2.5m (8ft) S 2.5m (8ft).
Aspect: semi-shade
Hardiness: ✿✿✿ Zones: 7–8

COLUTEA
Bladder senna
A genus of some 25 species, including the deciduous, summer-flowering shrubs featured here, that are loved by children – who take great pleasure in popping their bloated seed-pods that

Clethera areorea

follow. An unusual novelty shrub for a sunny spot.
Cultivation Grow in any well-drained soil that is reasonably fertile in full sun.
Pruning No routine pruning is required. Neglected shrubs can be rejuvenated in spring by cutting out one stem in three back to a side shoot lower down, starting with the oldest.
Propagation Take softwood cuttings from new shoots in mid-summer. Sow seed in late winter or early spring.

Colutea arborescens
A vigorous, rounded, deciduous shrub that bears 12cm- (4in-) long racemes of bright yellow flowers from early summer to early autumn above finely divided pale green foliage. Green seed-pods follow that become bloated and translucent as they mature. H 3m (10ft) S 3m (10ft).
Aspect: sun
Hardiness: ✿✿✿ Zones: 7–8

Colutea x media 'Copper Beauty'
A bushy deciduous shrub with finely divided, grey-green leaves that set off the 10cm- (4in-)

Colutea arborescens

long strings of attractive copper-red flowers from early summer to early autumn. Greenish-brown seed-pods (up to 8cm/3in long) follow that become bloated and turn increasingly copper-tinged and translucent as they mature. H 3m (10ft) S 3m (10ft).
Aspect: sun
Hardiness: ✿✿✿ Zones: 7–8

CONVOLVULUS

A huge genus of over 250 species, including the popular compact silver-leaved, evergreen, early summer flowering shrub featured here. A superb shrub for a hot, sunny rockery, bank or border edge with well-drained soil. Can be grown in a pot on the patio.
Cultivation Needs well-drained, reasonably fertile soil in full sun. If grown in containers, use a soil-based compost (soil mix). Water as necessary.
Pruning Trim as the flowers fade, cutting back new growth by about two-thirds. Remove frost-damaged shoots in spring.
Propagation Take softwood cuttings in late spring or early summer, or semi-ripe cuttings in early autumn.

Convolvulus cneorum

Convolvulus cneorum

Clusters of open, white, trumpet-shaped flowers, each with pinkish veins and a pale yellow centre, are produced in succession throughout late spring and early summer and intermittently thereafter. Silvery foliage looks good at other times. H 60cm (24in) S 90cm (36in).
Aspect: sun
Hardiness: ❀❀ Zone: 9+

CORDYLINE

A genus of around 15 species, including these palm-like shrubs that are grown for their delightfully elegant plumes of arching, lance-shaped, evergreen leaves produced in fountain-like clumps at ground level while the plants are young. These useful evergreens make eye-catching focal points, where they add a tropical touch to borders and in containers on the patio.
Cultivation In the garden, grow in any well-drained soil that is reasonably fertile in full sun or dappled shade. In containers, grow in a soil-based compost (soil mix). Water as necessary. Give winter protection in frost-prone areas.
Pruning No routine pruning is required. Remove dying or damaged leaves to tidy its appearance in spring.
Propagation Remove rooted suckers in spring.

Cordyline australis (syn. *Dracaena australis*)
New Zealand cabbage palm
This elegant plant forms a plume of arching, lance-shaped, evergreen leaves at ground level when young, eventually growing into a palm-like tree. Give winter protection in frost-prone areas. H 10m (33ft) S 4m (13ft).

Cordyline australis 'Red Star'

Named varieties: 'Atropurpurea', broad, strap-shaped leaves flushed with purple from the base. H 10m (33ft) S 4m (13ft). 'Purple Tower', broad, deep-purple, lance-shaped leaves. H 10m (33ft) S 4m (13ft). 'Purpurea Group', broad, plum-purple, lance-shaped leaves. H 10m (33ft) S 4m (13ft). 'Red Star', spiky fountain of bronze-purple, narrow, strap-like leaves. H 6m (20ft) S 7m (23ft). 'Torbay Dazzler', green leaves strikingly edged and striped with cream. H 10m (33ft) S 4m (13ft).
Aspect: sun
Hardiness: ❀ Zone: 10

CORNUS
Dogwood
Some 45 species make up this genus, including many useful garden shrubs offering a variety of features, including early summer flowers, attractive foliage, autumn tints and colourful winter stems. As they are very easy to grow, they offer great garden value – making them an ideal choice for the first-time gardener.
Cultivation Grow flowering dogwoods in any neutral to acid moisture-retentive, well-drained soil that is reasonably fertile in full sun or dappled shade. Most other varieties can be grown in any moist garden soil, but autumn colour and winter stems are best in full sun.
Pruning Flowering dogwoods require no routine pruning. Dogwoods grown for their decorative stems should be cut back to within a few centimetres of ground level in late winter or early spring every other year. Dogwoods with variegated foliage should have one stem in three removed each year, starting with the oldest.
Propagation Layer low shoots on all types of dogwood in mid-spring. Take hardwood cuttings from thicket-forming dogwoods in late autumn.

Cornus alba 'Aurea'
Red-barked dogwood
Superb golden-yellow leaves and stunning red new stems are the main features of this valuable garden shrub. The leaves also provide autumn colour and there is the bonus of small cream-coloured flowers during late spring and early summer, followed by bluish fruits. The leaf coloration is best in full sun. H 3m (10ft) S 3m (10ft).
Aspect: sun to semi-shade
Hardiness: ❀❀❀ Zones: 7–8

Cornus alba 'Kesselringii'
Grown for its dramatic, near-black, purple-brown winter stems and colourful autumn tints, this unusual dogwood looks particularly striking when planted in sun alongside yellow- or red-stemmed varieties, where it will help to transform the winter garden. Clusters of tiny, creamy-white flowers also appear during late spring and early summer. H 3m (10ft) S 3m (10ft).
Aspect: sun to semi-shade
Hardiness: ❀❀❀ Zones: 7–8

Cornus alba 'Sibirica'
Red-barked dogwood
Brilliant red winter stems make this red-barked dogwood ideal for growing alongside water features, where it will provide much-needed winter interest. Its dark green leaves take on reddish hues in autumn before falling to reveal the stem display. Clusters of tiny, creamy-white flowers also appear during late spring and early summer. H 3m (10ft) S 3m (10ft).
Aspect: sun to semi-shade
Hardiness: ❀❀❀ Zones: 7–8

Cornus alba 'Sibirica'

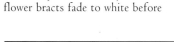

Cornus kousa

Cornus alba 'Spaethii'
Red-barked dogwood

The yellow-edged, bright green leaves on this plant look good all summer, after which they then take on striking autumn leaf tints before falling to reveal bright red stems that add much-needed interest throughout the winter. Clusters of tiny, creamy-white flowers also appear during late spring and early summer. H 3m (10ft) S 3m (10ft).
Aspect: sun to semi-shade
Hardiness: ❀❀❀ Zones: 7–8

Cornus 'Eddie's White Wonder'
Flowering dogwood

Striking white, petal-like bracts surround each insignificant purplish-green flower during late spring. Great value in a small garden, the green leaves of this bushy dogwood also turn brilliant fiery shades in autumn. Grows and flowers best in full sun, although it will tolerate dappled shade. H 6m (20ft) S 5m (16ft).
Aspect: sun to semi-shade
Hardiness: ❀❀❀ Zones: 7–8

Cornus florida
Flowering dogwood

A conical, deciduous shrub that produces insignificant yellow-tipped green flowers during late spring, surrounded by eye-catching white or pink bracts. The puckered green leaves look attractive during the summer and take on reddish-purple hues in autumn. Ideal for gardens with neutral to acid soil, but unsuitable for gardens with chalky soil. H 6m (20ft) S 8m (26ft).
Named varieties: 'Cherokee Chief', deepest pink bracts, red-purple autumn tints. H 6m (20ft) S 8m (26ft). 'Rainbow', compact shrub with white or pink bracts and yellow-edged green leaves turning red-purple in autumn with bright red margins. H 3m (10ft) S 2.5m (8ft). 'Rubra', dark pink bracts, red-purple autumn tints. H 6m (20ft) S 8m (26ft).
Aspect: sun to semi-shade
Hardiness: ❀❀❀ Zones: 7–8

Cornus kousa var. *chinensis*
Chinese dogwood

The conspicuous, creamy-white flower bracts fade to white before turning red-pink, surrounding insignificant green flowers during early summer, that are followed by strawberry-like fleshy fruit. This conical, deciduous shrub with dark green leaves takes on crimson-purple tints in autumn. The best leaf colour is achieved when grown in neutral to acid soil. H 7m (23ft) S 5m (16ft).
Aspect: sun to semi-shade
Hardiness: ❀❀❀ Zones: 7–8

Cornus sanguinea 'Midwinter Fire'

A relatively new variety, this shrub has glowing red-tipped orange and yellow winter stems that shine out in the garden. Clusters of tiny, creamy-white flowers also appear in early summer against green leaves that take on orange-yellow hues in autumn. Spherical bluish fruits are also produced. H 3m (10ft) S 2.5m (8ft).
Aspect: sun to semi-shade
Hardiness: ❀❀❀ Zones: 7–8

Cornus stolonifera 'Flaviramea'

Rich yellow stems provide winter interest and look striking planted in sun beside red-stemmed varieties. The dark green leaves take on reddish tints in autumn, before falling to reveal the eye-catching winter stems. Clusters of tiny, creamy-white flowers also appear during late spring and early summer. H 75cm (30in) S 150cm (60in).
Aspect: sun to semi-shade
Hardiness: ❀❀❀ Zones: 7–8

CORONILLA

This genus of about 20 species includes the following very long-flowering evergreen shrubs, with pretty, scented, yellow flowers that are borne from late winter until late summer. This shrub is ideal for planting in a container on the patio, where the flowers and foliage can be appreciated at close quarters.
Cultivation Grow in any well-drained soil that is reasonably fertile in full sun. Shelter from cold winds.
Pruning No routine pruning is required. Neglected shrubs can be rejuvenated by removing one stem in three each year in spring, starting with the oldest.
Propagation Take semi-ripe cuttings in mid-summer or late summer.

Coronilla valentia subsp. *glauca* (syn. *C.* 'Glauca')

This is an exceptionally long-flowering, rounded, bushy, evergreen shrub with dense evergreen growth and blue-green leaves. The scented, clear yellow pea-like flowers are produced throughout late winter and early spring and then intermittently all summer until a further flush in late summer and early autumn. H 80cm (33in) S 80cm (33in).
Named varieties: 'Citrina', pale yellow flowers. H 80cm (33in) S 80cm (33in).
Aspect: sun
Hardiness: ❀❀ Zone: 9

Coronilla valentina subsp. *glauca*

Corylus avellana 'Contorta'

CORYLUS

A genus of over ten species that includes native, deciduous trees and upright shrubs that can be grown as specimens or as an easy-to-grow hedge. Ornamental varieties offer attractive features including colourful spring catkins, good-looking foliage, autumn tints and winter stems. Ideal for growing in a sunny border or in a large permanent container on the patio.

Cultivation In the garden, grow in any well-drained soil that is reasonably fertile in full sun or dappled shade. In containers, grow in a soil-based compost (soil mix). Water as necessary.

Pruning No routine pruning is required for most types. Hazels grown for their colourful foliage should have one stem in three removed each year, starting with the oldest. Do this after flowering in early spring.

Propagation Layer low stems in mid-spring. Remove rooted suckers in early autumn.

Corylus avellana 'Contorta'
Corkscrew hazel, Harry Lauder's walking stick

The amazingly contorted bare stems carry golden catkins throughout late winter and early spring. The unusual stems of this slow-growing shrub are valued by flower arrangers. Will provide year-round interest in a large container. H 5m (16ft) S 5m (16ft).

Aspect: sun or semi-shade
Hardiness: ✤✤✤ Zones: 7–8

Corylus maxima 'Purpurea'

Glossy, dark purple, heart-shaped leaves cover this upright, deciduous shrub, which makes a superb specimen for a sunny garden. Reddish-purple catkins are produced during late winter and early spring and are followed by edible nuts ripening in late summer. This shrub makes a useful border filler. H 6m (20ft) S 5m (16ft).

Aspect: sun
Hardiness: ✤✤✤ Zones: 7–8

COTINUS
Smoke bush

A genus of two species, including the bushy deciduous shrubs featured here. Their airy plumes of flowers create a smoke-like illusion over the shrub during the summer, giving rise to its common name. Brilliant autumn foliage is the main ornamental feature of this plant. Grow in full sun for the most dramatic foliage effects.

Cultivation Grow in any moisture-retentive, well-drained soil that is reasonably fertile in full sun or dappled shade. Grow in full sun for the dramatic foliage effects.

Pruning Cotinus grown for their colourful foliage and smoke-like flowers should have one stem in

Cotinus obovatus

three removed each year, starting with the oldest. Do this in early spring.

Propagation Layer low stems in mid-spring. Remove rooted suckers in early autumn.

Cotinus coggygria 'Flame'
(syn. *C.* 'Flame')
Smoke bush

The plumes of pale pink flowers that appear on 'Flame' gradually darken during mid-summer and late summer. Later, the foliage spectacularly turns fiery shades of red and orange during the autumn months. H 6m (20ft)

S 5m (16ft).
Aspect: sun or semi-shade
Hardiness: ✤✤✤ Zones: 7–8

Cotinus coggygria 'Golden Spirit'

A relatively new and compact variety with golden-yellow leaves, that take on eye-catching pink, orange and red coloration in autumn. Plumes of green flowers appear during mid-summer and late summer. H 2m (6ft) S 2m (6ft).

Aspect: sun or semi-shade
Hardiness: ✤✤✤ Zones: 7–8

Cotinus 'Grace'
Smoke bush

The purple-tinged foliage of 'Grace' transforms in mid-summer and late summer when it is covered by airy plumes of pale pink flowers that darken with age. Stunning autumn colour appears as it turns a glowing shade of red. H 6m (20ft) S 5m (16ft).

Aspect: sun or semi-shade
Hardiness: ✤✤✤ Zones: 7–8

Cotinus coggygria 'Royal Purple'

This purple-leaved, bushy, deciduous shrub makes an impressive specimen in any size garden as it responds particularly well to hard pruning each spring. Airy plumes of pale pink flowers that darken with age are produced during mid-summer and late summer. The rich, red-purple leaves then turn brilliant scarlet in autumn. H 6m (20ft) S 5m (16ft).

Aspect: sun or semi-shade
Hardiness: ✤✤✤ Zones: 7–8

Cotinus coggygria 'Royal Purple'

Cotoneaster conspicuus 'Red Alert'

COTONEASTER

A large genus of over 200 species, including the deciduous, semi-evergreen and evergreen ornamental shrubs featured here. Larger varieties make useful border fillers, while low-growing types can be used to cover the ground or trained as a wall shrub. You can even train cascading varieties into unusual and attractive standards.
Cultivation Grow in any reasonably fertile, well-drained soil in full sun or dappled shade.
Pruning No routine pruning is required. Restrict the size of evergreen shrubs by trimming back to a new shoot lower down in mid-spring. Deciduous varieties can be kept within bounds by having one stem in three removed each year in late winter, starting with the oldest.
Propagation Take semi-ripe cuttings during mid-summer or hardwood cuttings in late autumn.

Cotoneaster dammeri

A prostrate evergreen that spreads vigorously, carpeting the ground with twiggy shoots covered in lustrous, dark green leaves. Dainty white flowers, borne during early summer, are followed by glossy, bright red berries in early autumn. It is a superb ground-cover shrub that will grow in most conditions, including the dry soil found at the base of evergreen hedges. H 20cm (8in) S 2m (6ft).
Aspect: sun or semi-shade
Hardiness: ❋❋❋ Zones: 7–8

Cotoneaster frigidus 'Cornubia'

An upright, evergreen shrub that is often trained as a single-stemmed tree, which makes an attractive specimen for a sunny spot. The dark green leaves provide the perfect backdrop for the dainty clusters of white flowers during early summer. Spherical bright red berries follow as the leaves become bronze-tinted for the winter. H 10m (33ft) S 10m (33ft).
Aspect: sun or semi-shade
Hardiness: ❋❋❋ Zones: 7–8

Cotoneaster horizontalis

This is a popular ground-cover deciduous shrub that has dainty pink-tinted white flowers that appear during the early summer and are followed by spherical, bright red berries in autumn. The twiggy branches are produced in an attractive herringbone pattern that make it easy to train over flat surfaces and provide winter interest. H 1m (3ft) S 1.5m (5ft).
Aspect: sun or semi-shade
Hardiness: ❋❋❋ Zones: 7–8

Cotoneaster 'Hybridus Pendulus'

A low-growing evergreen that bears dainty, small white flowers during early summer, followed by glossy, bright red berries in autumn. It can also be grown into a spectacular specimen when grown as a standard. Tolerant of a wide range of conditions. H 2m (6ft) S 2m (6ft).
Aspect: sun or semi-shade
Hardiness: ❋❋❋ Zones: 7–8

Cotoneaster salicifolius 'Gnom' (syn. C. 'Gnom' C. 'Gnome')

A prostrate, compact evergreen shrub with twiggy branches that are covered in dark green leaves. Dainty white flowers in early summer are followed by a limited number of rounded, glossy, bright red fruit. Excellent ground cover. H 30cm (1ft) S 2m (6ft).
Aspect: sun or semi-shade
Hardiness: ❋❋❋ Zones: 7–8

Cotoneaster x suecius 'Coral Beauty'

A low-growing evergreen with lustrous dark green leaves that bears dainty white flowers from late spring to early summer. It makes excellent ground cover for sun or semi-shade. Long-lasting glossy, bright-orange berries provide much-needed colour in early autumn and last until mid-winter or late winter. H 1m (3ft) S 2m (6ft).
Aspect: sun or semi-shade
Hardiness: ❋❋❋ Zones: 7–8

CYTISUS
Broom

A genus of over 50 species, including the busy deciduous summer-flowering shrubs featured here. They are a good choice for adding colour to a sunny border next to a wall, as they thrive in poor soils.
Cultivation Grow in any well-drained soil that is reasonably fertile in full sun. Shelter less hardy varieties from cold winds.
Pruning Pineapple broom requires no routine pruning. Keep most other brooms compact and free-flowering by cutting back new growth by about half directly after flowering. Do not prune back into the previous year's wood since this is unlikely to re-shoot.
Propagation Take semi-ripe cuttings in mid-summer. Sow seed in late winter.

Cytisus battandieri (syn. Argyrocytisus battandieri) Pineapple broom

Eyecatching, pineapple-scented, golden, cone-shaped flower-spikes are produced during mid-summer and late summer at the tips of silvery-grey shoots on this vigorous, deciduous shrub. Makes an ideal specimen in a sunny, but sheltered site next to a path or entrance, where its fruity scent can be appreciated. H 4m (13ft) S 4m (13ft).
Aspect: sun
Hardiness: ❋❋ Zone: 9

Cytisus 'Boskoop Ruby'

A compact deciduous shrub with arching stems that are covered in ruby-red, pea-like flowers throughout late spring and early summer. Downy green seed-pods follow. H 1.2m (4ft) S 1.2m (4ft).
Aspect: sun
Hardiness: ❋❋❋ Zones: 7–8

Cytisus multiflorus (syn. C. x praecox 'Albus', C. albus) Portuguese broom, white Spanish broom

Pure white, pea-like flowers are produced in masses along

Cytisus battandieri

Cytisus 'Boskoop Ruby'

elegantly arching stems from mid-spring to late spring on this upright, spreading, deciduous shrub. Reliable, early-flowering variety. H 1.2m (4ft) S 1.5m (5ft).
Aspect: sun
Hardiness: ❁❁❁ Zones: 7–8

Cytisus x praecox 'Allgold'
This is another popular variety that carries a profusion of rich-yellow, pea-like flowers along arching stems throughout mid-spring and late spring on a compact deciduous shrub. 'Allgold' is one of the earliest-flowering varieties. H 1.2m (4ft) S 1.5m (5ft).
Aspect: sun
Hardiness: ❁❁❁ Zones: 7–8

Cytisus x praecox 'Warminster'
Warminster broom
Creamy-yellow, pea-like flowers with an acid scent are produced in profusion along arching stems during mid-spring and late spring on this compact deciduous shrub. Easy to grow and early flowering. H 1.2m (4ft) S 1.5m (5ft).
Aspect: sun
Hardiness: ❁❁❁ Zones: 7–8

DABOECIA
A genus of just two species of hardy, evergreen shrubs with an exceptionally long flowering period, from early summer to mid-autumn. They look their best when planted in bold drifts and make excellent ground cover plants. They can also be grown in containers.

Cultivation In the garden, grow in open, sunny areas with well-drained acid soil. However, they will tolerate dappled shade and neutral soil. In containers, grow in ericaceous soil mix, feed monthly and water regularly to keep the compost (soil mix) moist.
Pruning Trim off flowering stems as they fade, using shears. Encourage bushy growth by trimming lightly before new growth appears in spring.
Propagation Take semi-ripe cuttings in mid-summer, or layer side shoots in early spring.

Daboecia cantabrica f. alba
Loose spikes of urn-shaped white flowers are produced from June (early summer) to October (mid-autumn) above glossy, dark green leaves that are silvery underneath. H 45cm (18in) S 75cm (30in).
Aspect: sun or semi-shade
Hardiness: ❁❁❁ Zones: 7–8

Daboecia cantabrica 'Atropurpurea'
The open spikes of dark purple urn-shaped flowers on this stunning shrub are produced from early summer to mid-autumn above glossy, dark green leaves that are silvery underneath. H 45cm (18in) S 75cm (30in).
Aspect: sun or semi-shade
Hardiness: ❁❁❁ Zones: 7–8

Daboecia cantabrica 'Bicolor'
This is an unusual plant that produces white, pink and dark red

Daboecia cantabrica f. alba

Daboecia cantabrica 'Atropurpurea'

urn-shaped flowers in loose spikes from early summer to mid-autumn. H 45cm (18in) S 75cm (30in).
Aspect: sun or semi-shade
Hardiness: ❁❁❁ Zone: 7–8

DAPHNE
This is a genus of 50 species, including upright-growing, evergreen and deciduous shrubs, that bear very fragrant flowers in winter and early spring. They are best grown in a sheltered corner in sun, next to a path or entrance, where their intoxicating fragrance can be best appreciated.
Cultivation This shrub can be grown in any moisture-retentive, well-drained garden soil provided it is reasonably fertile and it is positioned in full sun or partial shade. The less hardy varieties should be protected from cold winds in winter. This is a plant set in its ways, so avoid moving these plants, as they do not re-establish easily.
Pruning No routine pruning is necessary.
Propagation Sow seed in early autumn. Take semi-ripe cuttings in mid-summer.

Daphne bholua 'Jacqueline Postill'
This is an upright evergreen shrub that bears clusters of strongly fragrant rose-pink flowers during mid-winter and late winter above glossy, strap-shaped, dark green leaves. H 4m (13ft) S 1.5m (5ft).
Aspect: sun or semi-shade
Hardiness: ❁❁ Zone: 9

Daphne mezereum
Mezereon
Fragrant rose-pink flowers appear on bare branches during late winter and early spring. The upright habit of this deciduous shrub makes it a good choice for late winter interest. H 1.2m (4ft) S 1m (3ft).
Aspect: sun or semi-shade
Hardiness: ❁❁❁ Zones: 7–8

Daphne odora 'Aureomarginata' (syn. D. odora 'Marginata')
The attractive, evergreen, yellow-edged, glossy, dark green foliage provides interest during the winter. A bonus of fragrant, rose-pink flowers are produced from early winter to early spring. H 1.5m (5ft) S 1.5m (5ft).
Aspect: sun or semi-shade
Hardiness: ❁❁ Zone: 9

Daphne bholua 'Jacqueline Postill'

DESFONTAINIA

A genus of just one species of densely growing evergreen shrubs with eye-catching, tubular summer flowers. If you can provide the right growing conditions, it makes a useful and unusual border filler in all but the coldest areas, ideally at the base of a sheltered wall or fence.

Cultivation Grow in any moisture-retentive, humus-rich, acid or neutral soil in dappled shade. Provide a sheltered position where it is protected from drying and cold winds.

Pruning No routine pruning is necessary. Any frost-damaged growth should be removed in spring.

Propagation Take semi-ripe cuttings in mid-summer. Remove rooted suckers in early autumn.

Desfontainia spinosa

A bushy evergreen, with holly-like, glossy, dark green leaves. From mid-summer to mid-autumn it bears pendent tubular scarlet flowers with yellow-tipped petals. H 2m (6ft) S 2m (6ft).
Aspect: sun or semi-shade
Hardiness: ✿✿ Zone: 9

DEUTZIA

This genus of about 60 species includes the bushy deciduous shrubs featured here, grown for their early summer flowers that are borne in abundance. Plant in a shrubbery or in a mixed border to provide late spring and early summer colour. A good choice for small gardens.

Cultivation Grow in any moisture-

Deutzia x elegantissima

retentive, well-drained garden soil that is reasonably fertile and in full sun or dappled shade.

Pruning To encourage good displays year after year, cut back one stem in three to near ground level after flowering, starting with the oldest stems.

Propagation Take hardwood cuttings in mid-autumn.

Deutzia x elegantissima 'Rosealind'

Dark, pink-flushed, white star-like flowers are produced in clusters during late spring and early summer on this compact, rounded shrub. H 1.2m (4ft) S 1.5m (5ft).
Aspect: sun or semi-shade
Hardiness: ✿✿✿ Zones: 7–8

Deutzia gracilis

Fragrant, snow-white, star-like flowers are produced from late spring to early summer on

Diervilla x splendens

upright stems clothed in light green leaves. H 1m (3ft) S 1m (3ft).
Aspect: sun or semi-shade
Hardiness: ✿✿✿ Zones: 7–8

Deutzia x hybrida 'Mont Rose'

This elegant, upright shrub bears clusters of star-like, rose-pink flowers with yellow anthers during early summer. H 1.2m (4ft) S 1.2m (4ft).
Aspect: sun or semi-shade
Hardiness: ✿✿✿ Zones: 7–8

DIERVILLA
Bush honeysuckle

A genus of three species that includes the following deciduous shrub with colourful summer flowers and attractive autumn tints – a good choice for a shrubbery or mixed border, or for stabilizing soil on sunny banks.

Cultivation Grow in any well-drained garden soil that is

reasonably fertile and in full sun or dappled shade.

Pruning Maintain a compact shape by cutting back one stem in three to near ground level after flowering, starting with the oldest stems.

Propagation Take semi-ripe cuttings in mid-summer. Remove rooted suckers in early autumn.

Diervilla x splendens

Vibrant sulphur-yellow flowers are produced in clusters at the end of shoots from early summer to late summer on this thicket-forming deciduous shrub. The mid-green leaves take on purple-tints in autumn. H 1m (3ft) S 1.5m (5ft).
Aspect: sun or semi-shade
Hardiness: ✿✿✿ Zones: 7–8

DRIMYS

This is a genus of 30 species that includes the upright, evergreen

Desfontainia spinosa

Drimys winteri

Elaeagnus x ebbingei 'Limelight'

shrub with late spring and early summer flowers featured here. It is ideal for a shrubbery or situated in the dappled shade of a woodland edge.
Cultivation Grow in any moisture-retentive, well-drained garden soil that is reasonably fertile and in full sun or dappled shade. In colder regions, grow in a sheltered position where it is protected from cold winds.
Pruning No routine pruning is necessary. Any frost-damaged growth should be removed in spring.
Propagation Take semi-ripe cuttings in late summer. Layer lower stems in early spring.

Drimys winteri
Winter's bark
This shrub produces delightful jasmine-scented, creamy-white flowers from mid-spring to early summer and lance-shaped, leathery, dark green leaves. H 15m (50ft) S 10m (33ft).
Aspect: sun or semi-shade
Hardiness: ✿✿ Zone: 9

ELAEAGNUS
A genus of about 45 species, including the following brightly coloured variegated evergreens, that provide permanent interest

throughout the year. They make ideal border fillers, where they will help give lacklustre displays an uplift. They are all easy to grow and tolerate cold winds and salt-laden air – making them ideal for providing shelter and screens in coastal gardens. Their tolerance of dry soil and urban pollution means they are widely used by landscapers in towns and cities. Their handsome foliage is also popular with flower arrangers.
Cultivation They will grow in well-drained garden soil that is reasonably fertile and in full sun or dappled shade. However, leaf coloration will be best in full sun.
Pruning No routine pruning is necessary. Neglected plants can be rejuvenated by cutting back one stem in three to near ground level after flowering, starting with the oldest stems. Trim hedges in early summer and early autumn. Remove any reverted plain green shoots as soon as they are noticed.
Propagation Take hardwood cuttings during late winter.

Elaeagnus x ebbingei 'Gilt Edge'
The lustrous, golden-edged, dark green leaves make this a noticeable shrub in winter. Insignificant slightly scented white flowers

appear in mid-autumn. H 4m (13ft) S 4m (13ft).
Aspect: sun or semi-shade
Hardiness: ✿✿✿ Zones: 7–8

Elaeagnus x ebbingei 'Limelight'
Silvery when they emerge, the attractive lime-green and yellow-splashed dark green, leathery leaves are loved by flower arrangers. Insignificant, slightly scented, creamy-white flowers are also produced in mid-autumn. This really tough evergreen will tolerate dry soil too. H 3m (10ft) S 3m (10ft).
Aspect: sun or semi-shade
Hardiness: ✿✿✿ Zones: 7–8

Elaeagnus pungens 'Maculata'
Leathery dark green leaves are boldly marked with bright yellow in the centre and have a slightly frosted shine. Insignificant, slightly scented white flowers are also produced in mid-autumn, followed by brown fruit that ripen to red. H 4m (13ft) S 5m (16ft).
Aspect: sun or semi-shade
Hardiness: ✿✿✿ Zones: 7–8

ENKIANTHUS
This comprises a genus of about ten species, including the deciduous shrubs featured here, that offer early summer flowers and good autumn leaf tints. They are ideal for dappled shade, such as in a woodland-edge planting scheme. A useful and unusual border addition that is easy to

grow if you can provide the right growing conditions.
Cultivation Grow in any well-drained neutral to acid soil in full sun or dappled shade. In colder areas, shelter from winds. Add plenty of organic matter (but not alkaline mushroom compost/ soil mix) to the soil before planting.
Pruning No routine pruning is necessary. Any frost-damaged growth should be removed in spring.
Propagation Sow seed in early winter. Layer suitable stems in early autumn.

Enkianthus campanulatus
Spreading deciduous shrub that bears clusters of bell-shaped, pink-edged, pale yellow flowers during late spring and early summer. The toothed, matt-green leaves provide an attractive backdrop and take on vivid shades of orange and red in autumn. H 5m (16ft) S 5m (16ft).
Aspect: sun or semi-shade
Hardiness: ✿✿✿ Zones: 7–8

Enkianthus cernuus f. rubens
A bushy, deciduous shrub that is covered in pretty clusters of bell-shaped, red flowers during late spring and early summer. The leaves emerge bright green and turn plum-purple in summer, then take on blood-red hues in autumn. Protect in cold gardens. H 2.5m (8ft) S 2.5m (8ft).
Aspect: sun or semi-shade
Hardiness: ✿✿ Zone: 9

Enkianthus chinensis

ERICA

A huge genus of over 700 species of hardy evergreen shrubs with colourful winter flowers, some varieties of which offer autumn and winter foliage tints as well. There are literally thousands of named varieties. All winter-flowering heathers make excellent ground cover plants for open, sunny areas with acid soil. Some are tolerant of neutral or even slightly alkaline soil, as well as dappled shade. Many make useful permanent container plants.
Cultivation In the garden, grow in any well-drained, but moisture-retentive, acid soil in full sun. Add plenty of organic matter (but not alkaline mushroom compost/soil mix) before planting. In pots, grow in ericaceous compost on a sunny patio. Keep watered.
Pruning Trim flowering stems as they fade. Prune those grown for their colourful foliage in spring.
Propagation Take semi-ripe cuttings in mid-summer or layer side shoots in early spring.

Erica carnea 'Ann Sparkes'
Winter heath
Deep pink clusters of urn-shaped flowers that mature to blood-red as they age are produced from mid-winter to mid-spring. The burnished-gold foliage is bronze-tipped in spring. Tolerates slightly alkaline soils and dappled shade. H 25cm (10in) S 45cm (18in).
Aspect: sun or semi-shade
Hardiness: ❈❈❈ Zones: 7–8

Erica carnea 'Challenger'
Winter heath
Masses of urn-shaped flowers provide a splash of magenta from mid-winter to mid-spring above a mound of dark green foliage. Tolerates slightly alkaline soils and dappled shade. H 15cm (6in) S 45cm (18in).
Aspect: sun or semi-shade
Hardiness: ❈❈❈ Zones: 7–8

Erica carnea 'December Red'
Winter heath
Lilac-pink, urn-shaped flowers are produced in clusters from mid-winter to mid-spring above a mound of dark green foliage. Tolerates slightly alkaline soils and dappled shade. H 15cm (6in)

S 45cm (18in).
Aspect: sun or semi-shade
Hardiness: ❈❈❈ Zones: 7–8

Erica carnea 'Foxhollow'
Winter heath
Urn-shaped lilac flowers appear from mid-winter to mid-spring above mounds of yellow foliage that is bronze-tipped in spring, darkening to orange in winter. Tolerates slightly alkaline soils and dappled shade. H 15cm (6in) S 45cm (18in).
Aspect: sun or semi-shade
Hardiness: ❈❈❈ Zones: 7–8

Erica carnea 'King George'
Winter heath
Clusters of dark pink, urn-shaped flowers that darken as they mature are produced from early winter to early spring. Tolerates slightly alkaline soils and dappled shade. H 15cm (6in) S 25cm (10in).
Aspect: sun or semi-shade
Hardiness: ❈❈❈ Zones: 7–8

Erica carnea 'Myretoun Ruby'
Winter heath
Large, urn-shaped, ruby-red flowers that mature to crimson are produced from mid-winter to late spring above a mound of dark green foliage. Tolerates slightly alkaline soils and dappled shade. H 15cm (6in) S 45cm (18in).
Aspect: sun or semi-shade
Hardiness: ❈❈❈ Zones: 7–8

Erica carnea 'Pink Spangles'
Winter heath
Clusters of urn-shaped shell-pink flowers are produced from mid-

Erica x *veitchii* 'Exeter'

winter to mid-spring above a mound of dark green foliage. Tolerates slightly alkaline soils and dappled shade. H 15cm (6in) S 45cm (18in).
Aspect: sun or semi-shade
Hardiness: ❈❈❈ Zones: 7–8

Erica carnea 'Springwood White'
Winter heath
Long spikes of urn-shaped white flowers are produced from mid-winter to mid-spring above a mound of dark green foliage. Tolerates slightly alkaline soils and dappled shade. H 15cm (6in) S 45cm (18in).
Aspect: sun or semi-shade
Hardiness: ❈❈❈ Zones: 7–8

Erica cinerea f. alba 'Pink Ice'
Bell heather
Mini rosy-pink, bell-shaped flowers are produced in masses

from early summer to early autumn above a mound of dark green foliage that is bronze-tinted in spring and again during winter. H 20cm (8in) S 35cm (14in).
Aspect: sun
Hardiness: ❈❈❈ Zones: 7–8

Erica x darleyensis 'Darley Dale'
Clusters of urn-shaped, shell-pink flowers that darken with age are produced from mid-winter to mid-spring above a mound of green foliage that is cream-tipped in spring. H 15cm (6in) S 55cm (22in).
Aspect: sun
Hardiness: ❈❈❈ Zones: 7–8

Erica x darleyensis 'Furzey'
Urn-shaped, lilac-pink flowers are produced in clusters from early winter to late spring above a mound of lance-shaped green leaves that are pink-tipped in spring. H 35cm (14in) S 60cm (24in).
Aspect: sun
Hardiness: ❈❈❈ Zones: 7–8

ESCALLONIA

This genus of over 50 species includes several useful bushy evergreen shrubs with pretty summer flowers that shine out against a backdrop of glossy, dark green leaves. They make excellent border fillers but can be used to make an informal flowering hedge. They tolerate salt-laden air and so are ideal for providing shelter and screens in mild coastal gardens.
Cultivation Grow in well-drained garden soil that is reasonably

Erica x *darleyensis* 'Darley Dale'

Escallonia

Eucryphia x *nymansensis* 'Nymansay'

fertile and in full sun. Choose a sheltered position for the less-hardy varieties.
Pruning Cut back wayward shoots in spring to maintain a balanced shape. Trim flowered shoots after flowering to keep shrub compact. Trim hedges after flowering, if necessary, to keep in shape.
Propagation Take softwood cuttings in late spring or semi-ripe cuttings during mid-summer or late summer.

Escallonia 'Apple Blossom'
Masses of pretty, pale pink flowers are produced from early summer to late summer over a compact mound of glossy, dark green foliage. Good for growing as an informal, flowering hedge, but not on exposed sites. H 2.5m (8ft) S 2.5m (8ft).
Aspect: sun
Hardiness: ❀❀ Zones: 9

Escallonia 'Donard Seedling'
An open form of escallonia that produces arching shoots covered in blossom-like, pink-tinted white flowers from early summer to late summer. Very hardy, it is ideal for growing as an informal, flowering hedge even in cold areas. H 2.5m (8ft) S 2.5m (8ft).
Aspect: sun
Hardiness: ❀❀❀ Zones: 7–8

Escallonia 'Iveyi'
A vigorous, upright, evergreen shrub that is covered in clusters of fragrant, white flowers from mid-summer to early autumn. The glossy, dark green leaves

become bronze-tinted in winter. H 3m (10ft) S 3m (10ft).
Aspect: sun
Hardiness: ❀❀❀ Zones: 7–8

Escallonia rubra 'Crimson Spire'
Masses of tubular flowers provide a splash of pale crimson from early summer to late summer against a backdrop of glossy, dark green foliage. Good for growing as an informal, flowering hedge. H 2.5m (8ft) S 2.5m (8ft).
Aspect: sun
Hardiness: ❀❀ Zone: 9

EUCRYPHIA
A genus of about five species, including the following evergreen shrubs, grown for their late summer flowers. Rated among the most attractive summer-flowering shrubs, these shrubs are an ideal choice for planting in a sheltered woodland garden with acid soil, where there is plenty of room to spread, but they are borderline hardy in colder areas.
Cultivation Grow in any well-drained but moisture-retentive, acid to neutral soil in dappled shade. Add plenty of organic matter (but not alkaline mushroom soil mix) to the soil before planting to ensure that it gets a good start. Make sure the planting site is sheltered from cold winds.
Pruning No routine pruning is necessary. Any frost-damaged growth should be removed in spring.
Propagation Take semi-ripe cuttings in mid-summer or late summer.

Eucryphia x intermedia 'Rostrevor'
A large, evergreen, upright shrub that is covered in splendid white-scented, cup-shaped flowers up to 5cm (2in) across throughout late summer and early autumn. H 10m (33ft) S 3m (10ft).
Aspect: semi-shade
Hardiness: ❀❀❀ Zones: 7–8

Eucryphia x nymansensis 'Nymansay'
Very large, upright-growing, evergreen shrub with toothed, leathery foliage that is smothered in large, showy, white cup-shaped flowers throughout late summer and early autumn. H 15m (50ft) S 5m (16ft).
Aspect: semi-shade
Hardiness: ❀❀❀ Zones: 7–8

EUONYMUS
Spindle tree
This comprises a large genus of about 175 species that includes the useful and varied garden shrubs featured here. The evergreen varieties provide striking variegated foliage and make excellent ground cover and mid-border fillers anywhere in the garden, as well as attractive low hedges in mild areas. Some varieties will also make good wall shrubs, where they will produce aerial roots that are self-supporting. Deciduous euonymus

provide intense autumn colour and attractive berries.
Cultivation Grow in any well-drained soil that is reasonably fertile, in full sun or dappled shade. Make sure the planting site for evergreens is sheltered from cold winds.
Pruning No routine pruning is necessary. Any damaged growth should be removed in spring. Remove any plain green reverted shoots from variegated varieties. Rejuvenate neglected plants by cutting back one stem in three to near ground level after flowering, starting with the oldest stems. Evergreen hedges can be trimmed lightly in mid-spring to maintain a neat shape.
Propagation Take semi-ripe cuttings mid-summer or late summer or hardwood cuttings in mid-winter.

Euonymus europaeus 'Red Cascade'
The dark green leaves of this deciduous European native transform themselves into wonderfully vivid fiery shades during the autumn. Insignificant flowers produced during late spring and early summer are followed by eye-catching rosy-pink berries that last into the winter. Although it will grow in dappled shade, plant in full sun for the best

Euonymous europaeus 'Red Cascade'

Euonymous alatus

Euonymous fortunei 'Emerald 'n' Gold'

autumn colours. H 3m (10ft) S 2.5m (8ft).
Aspect: sun or semi-shade
Hardiness: ✿✿✿ Zones: 7–8

Euonymus fortunei 'Emerald Gaiety'

The white-edged, bright evergreen foliage on this compact, bushy shrub provides useful winter interest when there is little else happening in the garden. Insignificant clusters of tiny green flowers are produced during late spring and early summer. 'Emerald Gaiety' makes a useful ground cover and low hedging plant and does well in sun or shade. It is a good plant for training against a wall or fence. H 1m (3ft) S 1.5m (5ft).
Aspect: sun or shade
Hardiness: ✿✿✿ Zones: 7–8

Euonymus fortunei 'Emerald 'n' Gold'

A bushy, variegated evergreen with glossy, yellow-edged, bright green leaves that become pink-tinged in winter. Insignificant clusters of tiny green flowers are produced during late spring and early summer. It is a useful ground cover and low hedging plant in sun or light shade. H 60cm (24in) S 90cm (36in).
Aspect: sun or semi-shade
Hardiness: ✿✿✿ Zones: 7–8

Euonymus fortunei 'Silver Queen'

A low-growing, compact, busy evergreen with dark green leaves that have creamy-yellow or creamy-white margins that are pink-tinged in winter. Clusters of insignificant, tiny green flowers appear in late spring and early summer, followed by orange fruits. A good choice for training against a wall or fence in sun or light shade. H 3m (10ft) S 2m (6ft).
Aspect: sun or semi-shade
Hardiness: ✿✿✿ Zones: 7–8

Euonymus fortunei 'Sunspot'

A compact, bushy, evergreen shrub with glossy foliage splashed with gold and held on bright yellow stems. Excellent for winter colour. H 1m (3ft) S 1.5m (5ft).
Aspect: sun or semi-shade
Hardiness: ✿✿✿ Zones: 7–8

EXOCHORDA
Pearl bush

A genus of four species, including the graceful, deciduous shrub featured here, that is smothered with pretty blooms during late spring. Its lax habit makes it an ideal choice for a mixed border, but all look good covering banks or growing as a wall shrub.
Cultivation Grow in any moisture-retentive, well-drained soil that is reasonably fertile in full sun or dappled shade. Shelter evergreens from cold winds.
Pruning Cut back one stem in three to near ground level after flowering, starting with the oldest stems, to keep flowering profuse.
Propagation Take softwood cuttings in mid-spring.

Exochorda x macrantha 'The Bride'

Elegant arching branches are covered in brilliant white flowers during mid-spring and late spring. The delicate, bluish-green foliage makes a good foil for adjacent flowering plants at other times and then takes on yellow and orange shades in autumn. H 2m (6ft) S 3m (10ft).
Aspect: sun or semi-shade
Hardiness: ✿✿✿ Zones: 7–8

x FATSHEDERA

This bi-generic cross between a bushy evergreen shrub (*Fatsia*) and ivy (*Hedera*) is grown mainly for its handsome foliage. Can be grown as a shrub, trained up a wall or fence or left to sprawl as deep ground cover under deciduous trees. It is an excellent choice for town or coastal gardens since it can tolerate shade, urban pollution and salt-laden winds.
Cultivation Grow in any moisture-retentive well-drained garden soil that is reasonably fertile and in full sun or dappled shade. Grow at the base of a sunny wall in colder areas.
Pruning No routine pruning is necessary. Remove wayward or crossing shoots if necessary during early spring.
Propagation Take semi-ripe cuttings in mid-summer.

x fatshedera lizei

An open, branching shrub with glossy, evergreen, ivy-like leaves that are leathery to the touch. A bonus of creamy-white flowers are sometimes produced during in mid-autumn and late autumn. H 1.2m (4ft) S 3m (10ft).
Named varieties: 'Variegata', frost-hardy form with white-edged

Exochorda x macrantha 'The Bride'

leaves. H 1.2m (4ft) S 3m
(10ft).
Aspect: sun or semi-shade
Hardiness: ✸✸✸ Zones: 7–8

FATSIA

A genus of two species, including
the popular evergreen shrub
featured here. They make excellent
focal points when positioned in a
sheltered area of the garden, where
they will help to create a tropical
atmosphere. They can also be
grown as a permanent specimen in
a large container. This shrub is an
excellent choice for town or costal
gardens as it can tolerate shade,
urban pollution and salt-laden
winds.
Cultivation In the garden, grow
in any moisture-retentive, well-
drained soil that is reasonably
fertile in full sun or dappled
shade where it is sheltered from
cold winds. If planted in a
container, grow in a soil-based
compost (soil mix). Feed every
fortnight throughout the growing
season and water as necessary.
Pruning No routine pruning is
required. Keep plants compact by
cutting back one stem in three to
near ground level in mid-spring,
starting with the oldest stems.
Propagation Can be air layered in
mid-spring. Take softwood
cuttings in early summer.

Fatsia japonica
A tropical-looking shrub with
large, glossy, leathery, palmate
leaves that help to reflect light
into lacklustre corners. A bonus
of creamy-white flowers is
produced in ball-shaped flower-

heads in early autumn and mid-
autumn, followed by rounded
black fruit. H 4m (13ft) S 4m
(13ft). Named varieties:
'Variegata', half-hardy variegated
form with bright green leaves that
are cream-splashed at the margins.
Ideal for brightening up dark
corners. H 4m (13ft) S 4m
(13ft).
Aspect: sun or semi-shade
Hardiness: ✸✸✸ Zones: 7–8

FORSYTHIA

A genus of over five species,
including the following popular
and spring-flowering shrubs that
can be used as back-of-the-border
fillers, focal points or trimmed as
a deciduous flowering hedge.
They can even be trained into wall
shrubs, arches and standards.
Cultivation Grow in any moisture-
retentive, well-drained soil that is
reasonably fertile in full sun or
dappled shade.
Pruning Keep plants compact and
flowering well by cutting back one
stem in three to near ground level
during early spring, starting with
the oldest stems. Prune hedges
and other ornamental forms
lightly after flowering in mid-
spring.
Propagation Take softwood
cuttings in early summer or
hardwood cuttings in late
autumn.

Forsythia 'Beatrix Farrand'
Masses of 3cm- (1¼in-) wide
orange-yellow blooms are
produced on arching, bare stems
during early spring and mid-
spring. Sharply toothed leaves

Forsythia

provide a plain green backdrop
during the growing season. Very
good for training against a wall.
H 2m (6ft) S 2m (6ft).
Aspect: sun or semi-shade
Hardiness: ✸✸✸ Zones: 7–8

Forsythia x intermedia 'Lynwood'
Masses of delicate, golden-yellow
flowers are produced on bare
stems during mid-spring and late
spring. A dense crop of lobed,
mid-green leaves follows. H 3m
(10ft) S 2m (6ft).
Aspect: sun or semi-shade
Hardiness: ✸✸✸ Zones: 7–8

Forsythia x intermedia 'Spring Glory'
Pale yellow flowers smother the
branches of this deciduous shrub
during early spring and mid-
spring before the lance-shaped
leaves emerge. An excellent choice
for growing as a flowering hedge.
H 2m (6ft) S 3m (10ft).
Aspect: sun or semi-shade
Hardiness: ✸✸✸ Zones: 7–8

Forsythia x intermedia 'Week End'
Masses of rich yellow flowers are
produced on bare stems during
early spring and mid-spring as the
leaf buds break. H 3m (10ft) S
3m (10ft).
Aspect: sun or semi-shade
Hardiness: ✸✸✸ Zones: 7–8

FOTHERGILLA

A genus of just two species,
including the deciduous shrubs
featured here, grown for their
brilliant autumn colour. A bonus

of sweetly scented flowers are
borne from mid-spring before the
leaves emerge. They make good
border fillers and seasonal
specimens where suitable growing
conditions can be provided. A
good choice for a woodland-edge
planting on acid soil.
Cultivation Grow in any moisture-
retentive but well-drained acid
soil in full sun or partial shade.
Add plenty of organic matter (but
not alkaline mushroom compost/
soil mix) to the soil before
planting. Flowering and foliage
displays are best in full sun.
Pruning No routine pruning is
required.
Propagation Layer low branches
in early autumn.

Fothergilla gardenii
Witch alder
Upright deciduous shrub with
coarsely toothed green leaves that
turn brilliant crimson in autumn.
Sweetly scented clusters of white
flowers are produced on bare
stems during mid-spring and late
spring. H 1m (3ft) S 1m (3ft).
Aspect: sun or semi-shade
Hardiness: ✸✸✸ Zones: 7–8

Fothergilla major (syn. Fothergilla monticola)
Glossy, dark green leaves turn
fiery shades of orange, yellow and
red in autumn. Clusters of
sweetly scented white flowers are
produced on bare stems during
mid-spring and late spring.
H 2.5m (8ft) S 2m (6ft).
Aspect: sun or semi-shade
Hardiness: ✸✸✸ Zones: 7–8

Fatsia japonica

Fothergilla 'Huntsman'

Fremontodendron 'California Glory'

Fuchsia

Garrya elliptica

FREMONTODENDRON

A genus of just two species, including the long-flowering evergreen shrub featured here that is ideal for training against a sunny wall in mild areas but can also be grown as a free-standing shrub at the back of a sheltered border. It is mainly grown for its spectacular, waxy-looking flowers and handsome foliage.

Cultivation Grow in any well-drained neutral to alkaline soil in full sun that is sheltered from cold winds.

Pruning No routine pruning is required. Remove frost damaged and awkwardly positions stems in spring.

Propagation Sow seed in early spring.

Fremontodendron 'California Glory'

Eye-catching, saucer-shaped, butter-yellow and waxy-looking flowers are produced in succession from late spring to mid-autumn against a backdrop of leathery, lobed dark green leaves. H 6m (20ft) S 4m (13ft).
Aspect: sun
Hardiness: ✿✿ Zone: 9

FUCHSIA

A large genus of over 100 species, including the hardy types featured here that are grown for their superb summer flowers. In mild areas they can be treated as deciduous shrubs, making useful fillers in mixed borders and shrubberies, or even an unusual informal flowering hedge.

Cultivation Grow in any well-drained soil in full sun or dappled shade protected from cold winds. In colder areas, protect crowns with an insulating layer of leaves or similar material over the winter months.

Pruning In frost-free areas no routine pruning is required. They are more or less evergreen and grown with a permanent woody framework to make good border fillers or an informal long-flowering hedge. Remove any dead or damaged wood each spring. Hedges can be kept in shape by tipping back the new shoots in early spring or mid-spring to maintain dense growth. In colder areas, hardy fuchsias are treated more like herbaceous plants – the top cut back in early spring before new growth starts.

Propagation Take softwood cuttings from mid-spring to early autumn.

Fuchsia 'Mrs Popple'

Scarlet and purple single pendant flowers are produced from early summer to mid-autumn against a foil of dark green leaves. Borderline hardy. H 1.2m (4ft) S 1.2m (4ft).
Aspect: sun or semi-shade
Hardiness: ✿✿✿ Zones: 7–8

Fuchsia 'Pumila'

Scarlet and violet-blue single flowers are produced in succession from early summer to mid-autumn on this dwarf shrub. Borderline hardy. H 50cm (20in) S 50cm (20in).
Aspect: sun or semi-shade
Hardiness: ✿✿✿ Zones: 7–8

Fuchsia 'Riccartonii'

Red and dark purple single flowers are produced in succession from early summer to mid-autumn over bronze-tinted dark green leaves. Borderline hardy, it makes an excellent hedge in frost-free areas. H 3m (10ft) S 2m (6ft).
Aspect: sun or semi-shade
Hardiness: ✿✿✿ Zones: 7–8

GARRYA

This genus of over 10 species includes the tough, upright-growing, evergreen shrubs featured here, grown for their late-winter catkin-like flower tassels. They make an excellent choice for growing against a south- or west-facing wall or fence where they will provide valuable winter interest as well as an attractive foil for other plants throughout the year. This shrub makes a useful plant for town and coastal gardens as they tolerate both pollution and salt-laden air.

Cultivation Grow in well-drained, moderately fertile soil in full sun or dappled shade. In colder areas, protect from icy winds.

Pruning Keep plants in shape by cutting back one stem in three to near ground level in mid-spring, starting with the oldest stems.

Propagation Take semi-ripe cuttings in mid-summer, or hardwood cuttings in early autumn.

Garrya elliptica

A useful wall shrub with leathery, lustrous, wavy-edged evergreen leaves, that is decorated with elegant grey-green catkins tassels from early winter to late winter. H 4m (13ft) S 4m (13ft).
Named varieties: 'James Roof', dramatic silvery catkins up to 20cm long. H 4m (12ft) S 4m (13ft).
Aspect: sun or semi-shade
Hardiness: ✿✿✿ Zones: 7–8

GAULTHERIA

This is a large genus of 170 species, including the low-growing evergreen shrubs that are featured here The plants are mainly grown for their red berries and attractive winter tints. To ensure fruit production, it will be necessary to grow both male and female plants.

Cultivation Grow in a moisture-retentive, well-drained neutral to acid soil in full sun or dappled shade that is moderately fertile.

Pruning No routine pruning is required. Remove any dead or damaged stems each mid-spring.

Propagation Take semi-ripe cuttings in mid-summer or layer shoots in mid-spring.

Gaultheria mucronata 'Mulberry Wine'

Urn-shaped, pinkish-white flowers are produced during late spring and early summer, followed by aromatic, magenta fruit in early autumn that darken to purple. H 1.2m (4ft) S 1.2m (4ft).
Aspect: sun or semi-shade
Hardiness: ✿✿✿ Zones: 7–8

Gaultheria procumbens

Gaultheria mucronata 'Wintertime'

Aromatic, snow-white fruit in early autumn follow pink-flushed, urn-shaped white flowers that were produced during late spring and early summer. H 1.2m (4ft) S 1.2m (4ft).
Aspect: sun or semi-shade
Hardiness: ❀❀❀ Zones: 7–8

Gaultheria procumbens

Urn-shaped flowers in shades of white and pink are produced during late spring and early summer, followed by aromatic scarlet fruit in early autumn. The green leaves take on red and purple tints in winter. They are useful ground cover plants between acid-loving trees and shrubs. H 15cm (6in) S 1m (3ft).
Aspect: sun or semi-shade
Hardiness: ❀❀❀ Zones: 7–8

GENISTA

A genus of over 90 species, including the late-spring and early summer flowering spiny deciduous shrubs. They make excellent border specimens for providing a seasonal splash of colour and can be used to make informal flowering hedges in mild areas. Lower-growing forms also make useful ground cover on sunny banks or can be used to soften the edges of raised beds and rockeries.
Cultivation Grow in a well-drained poor soil in full sun.
Pruning No routine pruning is required. Keep plants bushy by pinching out shoot tips after flowering.
Propagation Sow seeds in early autumn. Take semi-ripe cuttings in mid-summer.

Genista hispanica
Spanish gorse
Golden-yellow flowers produced in clusters on spiny stems in late spring and early summer stand out against the mound of green leaves. Its prickles make it an excellent impenetrable hedging plant in mild areas. Borderline hardy. H 75cm (30in) S 1.5m (5ft).
Aspect: sun
Hardiness: ❀❀❀ Zones: 7–8

Genista lydia

The prickly, arching, grey-green leaves of this spreading shrub are festooned in golden-yellow flowers throughout late spring and early summer. H 60cm (24in) S 1m (3ft).
Aspect: sun
Hardiness: ❀❀❀ Zones: 7–8

Genista pilosa 'Vancouver Gold'

A spreading, mound-forming shrub that is covered in masses of golden-yellow flowers produced during late spring and early summer. H 45cm (18in) S 1m (3ft).
Aspect: sun
Hardiness: ❀❀❀ Zones: 7–8

Genista tinctoria 'Royal Gold'
Dyer's greenwood
An extremely long-flowering, upright-growing deciduous shrub that bears golden-yellow flowers intermittently from late spring to late summer. H 1m (3ft) S 1m (3ft).
Aspect: sun
Hardiness: ❀❀❀ Zones: 7–8

Grevillea 'Robyn Gordon'

GREVILLEA

A large genus of over 250 species, including the evergreen shrubs featured here, that are grown for their exotic-looking early summer flowers. If you have the right growing conditions, they make useful and unusual border fillers.
Cultivation In the garden, grow in any well-drained neutral to acid soil that is moderately fertile in full sun. Provide protection in frost-prone areas. Use ericaceous compost if grown in pots. Feed fortnightly in the growing season.
Pruning No routine pruning is required. Remove any dead or damaged stems each mid-spring.
Propagation Take semi-ripe cuttings in mid-summer.

Grevillea juniperina f. sulphurea

A rounded evergreen shrub with upright, branching stems that carry spiky yellow flowers from late spring to mid-summer. Although the plant is frost hardy, but it will need a sheltered site and winter protection in colder gardens. H 1m (3ft) S 1.8m (6ft).
Aspect: sun
Hardiness: ❀❀ Zone: 9

Grevillea 'Robyn Gordon'

This is a spreading evergreen shrub with upright branches that bear dark pink petal-less flowers produced intermittently all year round, but mainly during early summer. In frost-free areas, grow in a sunny, sheltered spot. Elsewhere, grow in a pot and move it inside during the winter. H 1m (3ft) S 1.8m (6ft).
Aspect: sun
Hardiness: ❀ Zones: 7–8

Genista lydia

HAMAMELIS
Witch hazel

This genus of about five species, including the hardy deciduous shrubs featured here, are grown for their fragrant, spidery winter flowers that look spectacular in the garden when illuminated by the low winter sun. Ideal for a sunny shrub border or woodland-edge planting.

Cultivation Grow in a moisture-retentive, well-drained, neutral to acid soil that is reasonably fertile in full sun or dappled shade.

Pruning No routine pruning is necessary. Neglected plants can have wayward branches removed to balance the overall shape of the canopy after flowering in early spring.

Propagation Difficult to propagate. Sow seeds when ripe in mid-autumn; graft named varieties in late winter.

Hamamelis x *intermedia* 'Arnold Promise'

This vase-shaped deciduous shrub bears clusters of large, sweetly scented, spidery golden flowers from early winter to late winter. The green leaves turn into brilliant autumnal colours in shades of rich yellow. H 4m (13ft) S 4m (13ft).
Aspect: sun or semi-shade
Hardiness: ✿✿✿ Zones: 7–8

Hamamelis x *intermedia* 'Diane'

Clusters of sweetly scented, spidery, dark copper-red flowers are produced on bare stems from early winter to late winter. The

Hamamelis mollis 'Pallida'

green leaves turn fiery shades of orange, red and yellow in autumn. H 4m (13ft) S 4m (13ft).
Aspect: sun or semi-shade
Hardiness: ✿✿✿ Zones: 7–8

Hamamelis x *intermedia* 'Jelena'

Large, fragrant, coppery-red or orange flowers are produced in clusters on bare stems from early winter to mid-winter. The green leaves transform into attractive autumnal colours with shades of rich orange and red. H 4m (13ft) S 4m (13ft).
Aspect: sun or semi-shade
Hardiness: ✿✿✿ Zones: 7–8

Hamamelis x *intermedia* 'Moonlight'

Clusters of sweetly scented, spidery, pale yellow flowers are produced on bare stems from early winter to late winter. Green leaves turn yellow in autumn.

H 4m (13ft) S 4m (13ft).
Aspect: sun or semi-shade
Hardiness: ✿✿✿ Zones: 7–8

Hamamelis x *intermedia* 'Pallida' (syn. *H. mollis* 'Pallida')

Bare branches from early winter to late winter carry clusters of large, sweetly scented, sulphur-yellow flowers. The green leaves transform into autumn colours with shades of rich orange and red. H 4m (13ft) S 4m (13ft).
Aspect: sun or semi-shade
Hardiness: ✿✿✿ Zones: 7–8

Hamamelis mollis

Clusters of sweetly scented, spidery, golden flowers are produced on bare stems from early winter to late winter. The slightly hairy mid-green leaves turn bright yellow in autumn. H 4m (13ft) S 4m (13ft).
Aspect: sun or semi-shade
Hardiness: ✿✿✿ Zones: 7–8

HEBE

A genus of around 100 species, including the evergreen shrubs featured here, that are grown for their colourful flowers and attractive foliage. Most are long flowering and make good filler shrubs for a border in sun or dappled shade. They are tolerant of pollution and salt-laden air, and so make a good choice for town and coastal gardens. Some also make excellent low hedges or edging in milder areas.

Cultivation Grow in a moisture-retentive, well-drained neutral to

slightly alkaline soil that is poor to reasonably fertile in full sun or dappled shade, but sheltered from cold winds and freezing temperatures. Borderline hardy, they need winter protection in colder areas.

Pruning No routine pruning is required. Straggly shoots on larger varieties can be pruned right back in mid-spring. Remove all-green reverted shoots from variegated varieties as soon as they are noticed. Trim hedges lightly after flowering to keep the plants dense and compact.

Propagation Take softwood cuttings in late spring or semi-ripe cuttings in early autumn.

Hebe cupressoides 'Boughton Dome'

An unusual hebe that looks more like a conifer, with its grey-green, scale-like evergreen leaves. Slow growing and hardy, it is an ideal choice for troughs and rock gardens. Small blue flowers in late spring are seldom produced.
H 30cm (12in) S 60cm (24in).
Aspect: sun or semi-shade
Hardiness: ✿✿✿ Zones: 7–8

Hebe 'Great Orme'

Slender spikes of bright pink flowers that fade to white are produced from mid-summer to mid-autumn above a mound of lustrous, evergreen leaves on this rounded shrub. Useful foil and gap filler. H 1.2m (4ft) S 1.2m (4ft).
Aspect: sun or semi-shade
Hardiness: ✿✿ Zones: 7–8

Hebe 'Marjorie'

A compact, rounded, evergreen shrub that bears long spikes of mauve flowers that gradually fade to white from mid-summer to early autumn. A useful foil and gap filler and for flower arranging. H 1.2m (4ft) S 1.5m (5ft).
Aspect: sun or semi-shade
Hardiness: ✿✿ Zones: 9

Hebe 'Midsummer Beauty'

The bright evergreen leaves emerge purple-tinged on this rounded shrub that produces dark lilac flower-spikes that fade to white from mid-summer to early

Hebe 'Great Orme'

Hebe pinguifolia 'Pagei'

autumn on purplish-brown stems. H 2m (6ft) S 1.5m (5ft).
Aspect: sun or semi-shade
Hardiness: ✿✿ Zone: 9

Hebe ochracea 'James Stirling'
The golden conifer-like foliage of this compact evergreen adds colour to the winter garden. Clusters of white flowers on arching stems are produced in early summer. H 45cm (18in) S 60cm (24in).
Aspect: sun or semi-shade
Hardiness: ✿✿✿ Zones: 7–8

Hebe pinguifolia 'Pagei'
A low-growing, compact but spreading evergreen that bears masses of snow-white flowers on purple stems throughout late spring and early summer above fleshy blue-green leaves. Good for edging beds and borders. H 30cm (12in) S 90cm (36in).
Aspect: sun or semi-shade
Hardiness: ✿✿✿ Zones: 7–8

Hebe rakaiensis
A neat, rounded shrub that bears clusters of large white flowers during early summer and mid-summer above glossy evergreen leaves. Its neat habit makes it a good choice for Japanese-style gardens. H 1m (3ft) S 1.2m (4ft).
Aspect: sun or semi-shade
Hardiness: ✿✿✿ Zones: 7–8

Hebe 'Red Edge'
A low-growing, spreading evergreen that bears lilac-blue flowers that fade to white throughout early summer and mid-summer. The grey-green leaves of young plants have attractive red margins and veining. Good for edging beds and borders. H 45cm (18in) S 60cm (24in).
Aspect: sun or semi-shade
Hardiness: ✿✿ Zone: 9

Hebe 'Rosie'
Its compact mound of evergreen foliage is decorated with pink flower-spikes from late spring to early autumn. H 60cm (24in) S 60cm (24in).
Aspect: sun or semi-shade
Hardiness: ✿✿ Zone: 9

HELIANTHEMUM
Rock rose, sun rose
A genus of over 100 species that includes the short-lived, spreading, evergreen shrubs featured here, grown for their early summer flowers. These low-growing shrubs are ideal for edging a sunny border and can be used in pots and for cascading over the edge of a raised bed. However, they tend to lose vigour as they age so are best replaced when they reach this stage.
Cultivation Grow in a well-drained neutral to slightly alkaline soil that is reasonably fertile in full sun.
Pruning Cut back hard after flowering to encourage a fresh mound of foliage and a second flush of flowers in late summer.
Propagation Take semi-ripe cuttings in early summer or mid-summer.

Helianthemum 'Ben Fhada'
A low-growing, spreading shrub that is covered in golden-yellow, cup-shaped flowers with orange centres from late spring to mid-summer. H 30cm (12in) S 30cm (12in).
Aspect: sun
Hardiness: ✿✿✿ Zone: 7–8

Helianthemum 'Ben Heckla'
Cup-shaped, brick-red flowers with orange centres are produced *en masse* from late spring to mid-summer above a spreading mound of grey-green leaves. H 30cm (12in) S 30cm (12in).
Aspect: sun
Hardiness: ✿✿✿ Zones: 7–8

Helianthemum 'Ben Hope'
A spreading shrub that bears bright red flowers with orange centres in succession from late spring to mid-summer over downy, silvery-green leaves. H 30cm (12in) S 30cm (12in).
Aspect: sun
Hardiness: ✿✿✿ Zones: 7–8

Helianthemum 'Chocolate Blotch'
Cup-shaped, pale orange flowers with chocolate-brown centres appear in succession from late spring to mid-summer above a spreading mound of grey-green leaves. H 30cm (12in) S 30cm (12in).
Aspect: sun
Hardiness: ✿✿✿ Zones: 7–8

Helianthemum 'Henfield Brilliant'
Bright-red, cup-shaped flowers are

Helianthemum 'Wisley Pink'

produced from late spring to mid-summer above a spreading mound of grey-green leaves. H 30cm (12in) S 30cm (12in).
Aspect: sun
Hardiness: ✿✿✿ Zones: 7–8

Helianthemum 'Wisley Pink'
Clear rose flowers are produced from late spring to mid-summer above a spreading mound of grey-green leaves. H 30cm (12in) S 45cm (18in).
Aspect: sun
Hardiness: ✿✿✿ Zones: 7–8

Helianthemum 'Wisley Primrose'
Primrose-yellow flowers with golden-yellow centres are produced from late spring to mid-summer above a spreading mound of grey-green leaves. H 30cm (12in) S 45cm (18in).
Aspect: sun
Hardiness: ✿✿✿ Zones: 7–8

Helianthemum

Hibiscus rosa-sinensis 'The President'

HIBISCUS

This large genus of over 200 species includes the exotic-looking shrubs featured here, grown for their eyecatching, colourful, trumpet-shaped, late-summer flowers. Useful for creating a tropical feel to a sunny corner or patio.

Cultivation In the garden, grow in a moisture-retentive, well-drained neutral to slightly alkaline soil that is reasonably fertile in full sun. In containers, use a soil-based compost (soil mix), water regularly and feed monthly during the growing season. Water as necessary during winter months.
Pruning No routine pruning is necessary. Remove any frost-damaged growth during spring.
Propagation Take semi-ripe cuttings in mid-summer.

Hibiscus rosa-sinensis 'The President'
Chinese hibiscus

Huge, red, ruffled-edged flowers with darker eyes across (up to 18cm/7in), are produced from mid-summer to early autumn. It is tender, so grow in a heated greenhouse or conservatory in cold areas (minimum temperature 10°C/ 50°F). H 3m (10ft) S 2m (6ft).
Aspect: sun
Hardiness: tender Zones: 9–10

Hibiscus syriacus 'Blue Bird' (syn. *H. syriacus* 'Oiseau Bleu')

Violet-blue, trumpet-shaped flowers with a maroon eye (up to 8cm/3in across) are produced in succession from late summer to mid-autumn against lobed, dark

green leaves. H 3m (10ft) S 2m (6ft).
Aspect: sun
Hardiness: ❀❀❀ Zones: 7–8

Hibiscus syriacus 'Woodbridge'

Large, deep pink, trumpet-shaped flowers with a maroon eye (up to 10cm/4in across) are produced in succession from late summer to mid-autumn against lobed, dark green leaves. H 3m (10ft) S 2m (6ft).
Aspect: sun
Hardiness: ❀❀❀ Zones: 7–8

HYDRANGEA

A genus of about 80 species, including the summer-flowering deciduous shrubs featured here, that are also grown for their autumn tints and winter seed-heads. Hydrangeas make useful border fillers where their late-summer displays can be appreciated.
Cultivation Grow in a moisture-retentive, well-drained reasonably fertile soil in full sun or dappled shade. Add plenty of organic matter to the soil before planting and mulch annually so that plants do not run short of moisture during the summer months. On shallow, chalky soils, some varieties show signs of chlorosis.
Pruning No pruning is necessary. Remove dead flower-heads in early spring. Remove any frost-damaged growth in spring.
Propagation Take softwood cuttings of deciduous varieties in early summer or mid-summer or hardwood cuttings in late autumn. Take semi-ripe cuttings of evergreen varieties in late summer.

Hydrangea arborescens 'Annabelle' Sevenbark

Large heads of creamy-white flowers are produced from mid-summer to early autumn. Pointed, dark green leaves. H 2.5m (8ft) S 2.5m (8ft).
Aspect: sun or semi-shade
Hardiness: ❀❀❀ Zones: 7–8

Hydrangea macrophylla 'Blue Wave'

From mid-summer to late summer flattened heads of dark blue to mauve flowers (lilac-pink

on chalky soils) are produced above a mound of coarsely toothed, lustrous, dark green leaves on this lacecap hydrangea. H 2m (6ft) S 2.5m (8ft).
Aspect: sun or semi-shade
Hardiness: ❀❀❀ Zones: 7–8

Hydrangea macrophylla 'Mariesii'

A rounded, lacecap hydrangea with coarsely toothed, glossy, dark green leaves that is covered in flattened heads of pale-blue flowers (rose-pink on chalky soils) from mid-summer to late summer. H 1.2m (4ft) S 1.2m (4ft).
Aspect: sun or semi-shade
Hardiness: ❀❀❀ Zones: 7–8

Hydrangea macrophylla 'Veitchii'

This is a lacecap hydrangea that bears large, somewhat flattened, heads of blue, pink and white flowers that darken to red with age from mid-summer to late summer. It is an ideal plant for a shady site. H 1.2m (4ft) S 1.2m (4ft).
Aspect: sun or semi-shade
Hardiness: ❀❀❀ Zones: 7–8

Hydrangea paniculata 'Floribunda'

This upright shrub has toothed, dark green leaves with white flower-heads that become pinkish in late summer and early autumn H 4m (13ft) S 2.5m (8ft).
Aspect: sun or semi-shade
Hardiness: ❀❀❀ Zones: 7–8

Hydrangea paniculata 'Tardiva'

A later bloomer, the 23cm- (9in-) white-coloured panicles begin to turn blush pink in autumn as the leaves begin to turn in mid-autumn. The dark green foliage is hairy to the touch. This can grow into a big plant if not pruned to remain contained. H 4m (13ft) S 2.5m (8ft).
Aspect: semi-shade
Hardiness: ❀❀❀ Zones: 7–8

Hydrangea quercifolia

White flowers that fade to pink are produced in conical clusters from mid-summer to early autumn. The foliage turns shades of bronze-purple in autumn. H 2m (6ft) S 2.5m (8ft).
Named varieties: 'Snow Queen', brilliant white conical flower clusters that fade to pink with age. H 2m (6ft) S 2m (6ft).
Aspect: sun or semi-shade
Hardiness: ❀❀❀ Zones: 7–8

Hydrangea serrata 'Bluebird' (syn. *H.* 'Acuminata')

A lacecap hydrangea that bears flattened heads of blue flowers (they appear as pink when grown on alkaline soil) from early summer to early autumn. It makes a compact mound of pointed green leaves that dramatically turn shades of red in autumn. Surprisingly resistant to drought. H 1.2m (4ft) S 1.2m (4ft).
Aspect: sun or semi-shade
Hardiness: ❀❀❀ Zones: 7–8

Hydrangea arborescens 'Annabelle'

Hydrangea paniculata 'Tardiva'

Hypericum 'Hidcote'

Hydrangea villosa (syn. *H. aspera* Villosa Group)

Flattened heads of dark blue flowers are produced throughout late summer and early autumn against lance-shaped dark-green leaves on this upright shrub. H 3m (10ft) S 3m (10ft).
Aspect: sun or semi-shade
Hardiness: ❀❀❀ Zones: 7–8

HYPERICUM
St John's wort

This huge genus of over 400 species contains the long-flowering shrubs featured here. Tough and easy to grow, they are ideal for covering dry banks and shady corners where little else will grow. In fertile soil they can be invasive.
Cultivation Grow in a well-drained soil that is reasonably fertile in full sun or dappled shade.
Pruning Keep plants in good shape by cutting back one stem in three to near ground level in mid-spring, starting with the oldest stems. Cut *Hypericum calycinum* right back to ground level each spring.
Propagation Take semi-ripe cuttings in early summer or mid-summer.

Hypericum 'Hidcote'

A semi-evergreen bushy shrub with pointed leaves that are decorated by large, cup-shaped, golden-yellow flowers produced in succession from mid-summer to early autumn. H 1.2m (4ft) S 1.5m (5ft).
Aspect: sun or semi-shade
Hardiness: ❀❀❀ Zone: 7–8

Hypericum calycinum
Rose of Sharon

A dwarf, vigorously spreading evergreen shrub with lance-shaped leaves that is covered in saucer-shaped bright yellow flowers, which are produced in succession from early summer to early autumn. Can be invasive, but makes excellent ground cover in shade. H 1.2m (4ft) S 3m (10ft).
Aspect: sun to shade
Hardiness: ❀❀❀ Zones: 7–8

Hypericum x moserianum 'Tricolor' (syn. *H.* 'Variegatum')

An attractive flowering shrub with green-and-white variegated foliage and distinct red margins. Grow only in shady areas as strong sunlight can scorch the foliage. Cup-shaped yellow flowers are produced from early summer to early autumn. H 30cm (12in) S 60cm (24in).
Aspect: semi-shade
Hardiness: ❀❀❀ Zones: 7–9

ILEX
Holly

This huge genus of over 400 species, including the large shrubs featured here, are grown for their handsome, evergreen foliage and colourful berries that appear in the winter, and greatly help in keeping the wildlife fed. These shrubs are very useful for using as specimens as they take well to being trimmed to form dense, slow-growing hedges or more eyecatching topiary.

Cultivation Grow in a moisture-retentive, well-drained soil that is reasonably fertile in full sun or dappled shade. Grow variegated varieties in sun for the best leaf coloration. Make sure you get a female variety if you want berries.
Pruning No routine pruning is necessary. All-green shoots on variegated varieties should be removed as soon as they are noticed. Trim hedges and topiary in late spring.
Propagation Take semi-ripe cuttings in late summer or early autumn.

Ilex x altaclerensis 'Golden King' (female form)

This compact evergreen carries a small crop of red autumn berries that stand out from the brilliant, yellow-edged, glossy, grey-green, spiny leaves. Good for hedging. H 6m (20ft) S 5m (16ft).
Aspect: sun or semi-shade
Hardiness: ❀❀❀ Zones: 7–8

Ilex aquifolium 'Argentea Marginata' (syn. *I. aquifolium* 'Argentea Variegata') (female form)

Thick and spiny, glossy, silver-edged, dark green leaves emerge pink-tinged. Brilliant red berries are produced *en masse* in autumn and last well into winter. This holly is a useful shrub for urban or coastal gardens as it copes well with pollution and salt-laden air. Good for hedging. H 14m (46ft) S 5m (16ft).
Aspect: sun or semi-shade
Hardiness: ❀❀❀ Zones 6–10

Ilex aquifolium 'Ferox Argentea' (male form)

A slow-growing upright shrub with cream-edged, leathery, dark green leaves that are covered with spines. No berries. H 8m (26ft) S 4m (13ft).
Aspect: sun or semi-shade
Hardiness: ❀❀❀ Zones: 7–8

Ilex aquifolium 'Golden Queen' (syn. *I. aquifolium* 'Aurea Regina') (male form)

A fruitless male variety of common English holly with spiny-edged dark green leaves that are decoratively splashed with gold. H 10m (33ft) S 6m (20ft).
Aspect: sun or semi-shade
Hardiness: ❀❀❀ Zones: 7–8

Ilex aquifolium 'J.C. van Tol' (female form)

The lustrous, dark green leaves on dark purple stems are almost prickle-free. Masses of bright red berries are produced from autumn and into winter. Good for hedging. H 6m (20ft) S 4m (13ft).
Aspect: sun or semi-shade
Hardiness: ❀❀❀ Zones: 7–8

Ilex aquifolium 'Silver Queen' (syn. *I. aquifolium* 'Silver King') (male form)

This slow-growing male variety of holly carries cream-edged, spiny, dark green leaves that emerge pink-tinged on purple stems. It does not produce berries. Good for a large pot. H 10m (33ft) S 4m (13ft).
Aspect: sun or semi-shade
Hardiness: ❀❀❀ Zones: 7–8

Ilex 'J. C. van Tol'

Indigofera amblyantha

INDIGOFERA

A huge genus of over 700 species, including the exotic deciduous shrubs featured here, valued for their sprays of pink, pea-like late-summer flowers. Excellent choice for growing as a wall shrub. It is very late coming into leaf and so is ideal for under-planting with spring-flowering bulbs and bedding or pairing it with an early flowering climber.
Cultivation Grow in a moisture-retentive, well-drained soil that is reasonably fertile in full sun.
Pruning No routine pruning is necessary. Frost-damaged growth should be removed in spring. If grown as a wall shrub, prune back new growth from the established framework by about two-thirds in mid-spring to late spring.
Propagation Take softwood cuttings in mid-spring or semi-ripe cuttings in mid-summer.

Indigofera amblyantha
Delicate-looking deciduous shrub with light green leaflets. Slender, arching flower-spikes of pea-like, shrimp-pink flowers are produced from mid-summer to early autumn. H 2m (6ft) S 2.5m (8ft).
Aspect: sun
Hardiness: ❀❀❀ Zones: 7–8

Indigofera heterantha (syn. I. gerardiana)
A spreading shrub with delicate-looking light green leaflets that provide a foil for the dense flower-spikes of pea-like,

Itea ilicifolia

purplish-pink flowers from early summer to early autumn. H 2.5m (8ft) S 2.5m (8ft).
Aspect: sun
Hardiness: ❀❀❀ Zones: 7–8

ITEA

A genus of some 10 species grown for its handsome foliage and dramatic catkin-like late-summer flowers. It is a useful shrub for growing against sheltered walls and fences. It can also be grown in a large, permanent container, but you will need to wrap up both the top-growth and the container during the winter in colder gardens.
Cultivation Grow in a moisture-retentive, well-drained soil that is reasonably fertile in full sun, but sheltered from cold winds.
Pruning No routine pruning is necessary. Any frost-damaged growth should be removed in spring.
Propagation Take semi-ripe cuttings in mid-summer.

Itea ilicifolia
This shrub has lustrous, dark green, holly-like leaves that provide the perfect backdrop for the 30cm- (12in-) long catkins of vanilla-scented, greenish-white flowers borne throughout late summer and early autumn. Although the shrub is frost hardy, it will require siting where it will get the protection of a sunny wall or fence in colder areas. H 5m (16ft) S 3m (10ft).
Aspect: sun
Hardiness: ❀❀ Zone: 9

JASMINUM
Jasmine
A large genus of over 200 species, including the useful wall shrubs featured here, grown for their fragrant yellow flowers. An excellent choice for providing winter colour near to a well-used entrance or path. It can be allowed to sprawl over banks, or be trained up walls and fences where space is limited.
Cultivation Grow in a well-drained soil that is reasonably fertile in full sun or dappled shade.
Pruning Keep established plants in good shape by cutting back one stem in three to near ground level in mid-spring, starting with the oldest stems.
Propagation Take semi-ripe cuttings in mid-summer. Layer suitable stems in early autumn.

Jasminum humile 'Revolutum' (syn. J. reevesii)
A semi-evergreen bushy, spreading shrub with bright green leaves that is exceptionally long-flowering, producing its pretty yellow fragrant flowers in succession from late spring to early autumn. H 2.5m (8ft)

S 3m (10ft).
Aspect: sun or semi-shade
Hardiness: ❀❀ Zone: 9

Jasminum nudiflorum
Winter jasmine
A popular deciduous shrub with bright green arching shoots that are decorated by scented yellow trumpet flowers from late autumn to late winter before the dark green leaves emerge in spring. H 3m (10ft) S 3m (10ft).
Aspect: sun or semi-shade
Hardiness: ❀❀❀ Zones: 7–8

JUSTICIA

A huge genus of over 400 species, including the tender evergreen shrub featured here, they are grown for their exotic-looking, late-summer flowers. This is an ideal, flamboyant border shrub in mild gardens or can be grown as a conservatory or greenhouse exotic in colder areas.
Cultivation In the garden, grow in a moisture-retentive, well-drained garden soil that is reasonably fertile in dappled shade, but protected from cold winds. In containers, grow in a soil-based compost (soil mix). Feed every

Jasminum nudiflorum

Justicia carnea

month throughout the growing season and water as necessary. Move to a warm spot undercover when the temperature falls below 7°C (45°F) and water sparingly during the winter.
Pruning No routine pruning is required. Pinch out the growing tips of shoots to keep the shrub compact.
Propagation Take softwood cuttings in late spring or semi-ripe cuttings in mid-summer.

Justicia carnea (syn. Jacobinia carnea, Justicia pohliana) Flamingo plant
A stiffly branching evergreen shrub with leathery green leaves and flamboyant conical clusters of tubular, lipped, rose-pink flowers from mid-summer to early autumn. H 2m (6ft) S 1m (3ft).
Aspect: semi-shade
Hardiness: tender Zone: 10+

KALMIA
This genus contains around five species, including the evergreen shrubs featured here, grown for their bright pink early summer flowers. An excellent seasonal focal point and border filler if you can provide the right growing conditions. Elsewhere, they can be grown in larger, permanent containers.
Cultivation In the garden, grow in a moisture-retentive, well-drained acid soil in sun or dappled shade. In containers, grow in ericaceous compost (soil mix). Feed monthly during the growing season and water as and when necessary.

Pruning No routine pruning is required. Neglected shrubs can be smartened up and reduced in size by cutting back one stem in three to near ground level in mid-spring, starting with the oldest stems first.
Propagation Take softwood cuttings in late spring or semi-ripe cuttings in mid-summer. Suitable shoots can be layered in mid-spring.

Kalmia angustifolia f. rubra
This mound-forming, evergreen shrub has dark green leaves and is covered in clusters of dark rosy-red, saucer-shaped flowers that appear throughout early summer. H 60cm (24in) S 150cm (60in).
Aspect: sun or semi-shade
Hardiness: ❋❋❋ Zones: 7–8

Kalmia latifolia 'Ostbo Red'
Clusters of bright red buds open to reveal pale-pink saucer-shaped flowers from late spring to mid-summer on this mound-forming evergreen shrub with dark green leaves. H 3m (10ft) S 3m (10ft).
Aspect: sun or semi-shade
Hardiness: ❋❋❋ Zones: 7–8

KERRIA
A genus of just one species of deciduous suckering shrubs that bear golden-yellow late-spring flowers. Easy to grow, it is an ideal choice for the first-time gardener and is ideal for filling gaps at the back of a border.
Cultivation Grow in well-drained

Kalmia latifolia

soil that is reasonably fertile in sun or dappled shade.
Pruning You can encourage a continuous supply of flowering shoots by cutting back one stem in three to near ground level in early summer, starting with the oldest stems. Remove any all-green reverted shoots on variegated varieties as soon as they are noticed.
Propagation Take hardwood cuttings in late autumn. Rooted suckers can be separated in mid-spring.

Kerria japonica 'Golden Guinea'
Masses of large, single, golden-yellow flowers are produced in succession on graceful arching stems during early spring and mid-spring on this upright shrub. H 2m (6ft) S 2.5m (8ft).
Aspect: sun or semi-shade
Hardiness: ❋❋❋ Zones: 7–8

Kerria japonica 'Picta' (syn. K. japonica 'Variegata')
The sharply toothed cream-and-green variegated foliage on this compact and less invasive shrub is a good choice for the smaller garden. Single golden yellow flowers are produced during early spring and mid-spring. H 1m (3ft) S 1.5m (5ft).
Aspect: sun or semi-shade
Hardiness: ❋❋❋ Zones: 7–8

Kerria japonica 'Pleniflora'
Pompon-like, double, golden-yellow early spring flowers are produced in succession during

Kerria japonica 'Golden Guinea'

Kolkwitzia amabilis 'Pink Cloud'

early spring and mid-spring on graceful arching stems with sharply toothed green leaves. Good wall shrub. H 3m (10ft) S 3m (10ft).
Aspect: sun or semi-shade
Hardiness: ❋❋❋ Zones: 7–8

KOLKWITZIA
A genus of just one species of deciduous suckering shrubs that bear masses of bell-shaped pink early summer flowers. It is an undemanding shrub that provides a useful splash of late spring colour when planted in a sunny border. It can also be used as a filler shrub in a mixed border or planted to grow up against walls and fences.
Cultivation Grow in any well-drained soil that is reasonably fertile in sun.
Pruning Encourage a continuous supply of flowering shoots by cutting back one stem in three to near ground level in early summer, starting with the oldest stems first.
Propagation Take semi-ripe cuttings in late summer. Rooted suckers can be separated in mid-spring.

Kolkwitzia amabilis 'Pink Cloud'
Masses of dark pink flowers are produced on arching stems during late spring and early summer. They appear against a backdrop of pointed dark green leaves that turn yellow in autumn. H 4m (13ft) S 3m (10ft).
Aspect: sun
Hardiness: ❋❋❋ Zones: 7–8

Lantana camara

LANTANA
This genus of about 150 species includes the long-flowering evergreen shrub featured here that is loved by butterflies and other beneficial insects. Ideal for growing as a specimen or in a sunny border, or in a large container in a heated conservatory or greenhouse in cold areas.
Cultivation In the garden, grow in any moisture-retentive, well-drained garden soil that is reasonably fertile and in full sun. In containers, grow in a soil-based compost (soil mix). Feed every month throughout the growing season and water as necessary. Move to a warm spot under cover when the temperature falls below 10°C (50°F) and water sparingly during the winter.
Pruning No routine pruning is necessary. Any damaged growth should be removed in spring. In the conservatory or greenhouse, prune back new growth on established plants to 10cm (4in) of the permanent framework during late winter.
Propagation Take semi-ripe cuttings in mid-summer.

Lantana camara
The attractively wrinkled dark green leaves of this tender evergreen shrub provide the perfect foil for clusters of vibrant flowers borne from late spring to late autumn in different colours ranging from white to pink. H 2m (6ft) S 2m (6ft).
Named varieties: 'Fabiola', pink and yellow flowers. H 2m (6ft)

S 2m (6ft). 'Goldmine' (syn. 'Mine d'Or'), bright yellow flowers. H 2m (6ft) S 2m (6ft). 'Radiation', red and orange flowers. H 2m (6ft) S 2m (6ft). 'Snow White', pure white flowers. H 2m (6ft) S 2m (6ft).
Aspect: sun
Hardiness: tender Zone: 10

LAVANDULA
Lavender
A genus of over 20 species, including the popular long-flowering, mostly fragrant and nectar-rich evergreen shrubs with aromatic foliage featured here. Lavender makes a useful specimen plant on the patio or in pots. The more compact varieties also make excellent low hedges. In the border, plant in groups of three or five for impact, although larger varieties can be used as single specimens. The flowers can also be used to make pot pouris.
Cultivation In the garden, grow in any well-drained garden soil that is reasonably fertile and in full sun. In colder regions, grow less hardy varieties in a sheltered position, protected from cold winds and excessive wet. In containers, grow in a soil-based compost (soil mix). Feed monthly throughout the growing season and water as necessary.
Pruning Trim off any flowering stems as they fade. Encourage bushy growth by trimming lightly before the new growth appears in the spring. Be careful not to cut back into old wood. Trim hedges lightly during early spring or mid-

spring to maintain shape.
Propagation Take semi-ripe cuttings in early autumn.

Lavandula augustifolia
Very fragrant purple flowers are produced in dense spikes from mid-summer to early autumn above a mound of grey-green aromatic foliage. Excellent for hedging and pot pourri. H 1m (3ft) S 1.2m (4ft).
Named varieties: 'Hidcote', dark violet flowers. H 60cm (24in) S 75cm (30in). 'Hidcote Pink', pale pink flowers. H 60cm (24in) S 75cm (30in). 'Lady', mauve-blue flowers. H 25cm (10in) S 25cm (10in). 'Loddon Pink', soft pink flowers. H 45cm (18in) S 60cm (24in). 'Munstead', purplish-blue flowers. H 45cm (18in) S 60cm (24in). 'Nana Alba', white flowers. H 30cm (12in) S 30cm (12in). 'Rosea', rose-pink flowers. H 75cm (30in) S 75cm (30in). 'Royal Purple', bluish-purple flowers. H 75cm (30in) S 75cm (30in).
Aspect: sun
Hardiness: ❀❀❀ Zones: 7–8

Lavandula 'Fathead'
French lavender
A recent introduction with very broad, almost rounded, midnight-purple flower-heads from late spring to mid-summer each topped by plum-purple wing-like bracts. Borderline hardy. H 40cm (16in) S 40cm (16in).
Aspect: sun
Hardiness: ❀❀❀ Zones: 7–8

Lavandula augustifolia

Lavandula stoechas

Lavandula 'Helmsdale'
French lavender
Plump spikes of fragrant dark purple flowers topped by purple wing-like bracts are produced from late spring to mid-summer above a compact mound of grey-green aromatic foliage. Borderline hardy. H 60cm (24in) S 60cm (24in).
Aspect: sun
Hardiness: ❀❀❀ Zones: 7–8

Lavandula x intermedia 'Grappenhall'
Slightly fragrant purplish-blue flowers appear on slender spikes from mid-summer to late summer above large grey-green, aromatic leaves. It is only frost hardy, so it is best grown in a container and moved indoors in cold areas. H 1m (3ft) S 1.5m (5ft).
Aspect: sun
Hardiness: ❀❀ Zones: 9

Lavandula x intermedia 'Grosso'
Dense spikes of fragrant, deep violet flowers on slender stems are produced *en masse* from mid-summer to early autumn above a mound of grey-green aromatic foliage. H 30cm (12in) S 40cm (16in).
Aspect: sun
Hardiness: ❀❀❀

Lavandula stoechas 'Kew Red'
French lavender
A recent introduction with plump, fragrant, cerise-pink flower-heads that are borne from early summer to late summer, topped by pale pink wing-like bracts. Borderline

hardy. H 60cm (24in) S 60cm (24in).
Aspect: sun
Hardiness: ✤✤✤ Zones: 7–8

Lavandula stoechas 'Papillon' French lavender

Tufted spikes of lavender-purple flowers, with long, wing-like bracts, are produced during early summer and mid-summer above a mound of grey-green aromatic foliage. Borderline hardy. H 60cm (24in) S 60cm (24in).
Aspect: sun
Hardiness: ✤✤✤ Zones: 7–8

Lavandula stoechas 'Rocky Road' French lavender

A new variety that bears goblet-shaped purple flower-spikes topped by large, pale-violet, wing-like bracts from mid-summer to late summer above a mound of grey-green aromatic foliage. Borderline hardy. H 50cm (20in) S 50cm (20in).
Aspect: sun
Hardiness: ✤✤✤ Zones: 7–8

Lavandula stoechas 'Snowman' French lavender

Slender spikes of white flowers, topped by snow-white wing-like bracts throughout early summer and mid-summer above a mound of grey-green aromatic foliage. Only frost hardy, so best grown in a pot and moved indoors in cold areas. H 60cm (24in) S 60cm (24in).
Aspect: sun
Hardiness: ✤✤ Zones: 7–8

LAVATERA

A genus of about 25 species, including the fast-growing, deciduous summer-flowering shrubs featured here, grown for their speed of growth and eye-catching, hibiscus-like, trumpet-shaped flowers. Quick to establish and flowering well, they are ideal for new borders. They also make useful gap fillers.
Cultivation Grow in any well-drained garden soil (preferably sandy) that is reasonably fertile and in full sun. In colder regions, protect from cold winds.
Pruning For best flowering, cut back all stems to within a few centimetres of ground level in mid-spring. Remove reverted shoots with the wrong colour flowers.
Propagation Take semi-ripe cuttings in mid-summer. Take hardwood cuttings in late autumn.

Lavatera x clementii 'Barnsley'

Large white blooms, each with a red eye, are produced from early summer to early autumn. The blooms gracefully age to pale pink. H 2m (6ft) S 2m (6ft).
Aspect: sun
Hardiness: ✤✤✤ Zones: 7–8

Lavatera x clementii 'Burgundy Wine'

A succession of dark pink flowers that are attractively veined are produced from early summer to early autumn on this compact variety with dark foliage. H 1.5m (5ft) S 1.5m (5ft).
Aspect: sun
Hardiness: ✤✤✤ Zones: 7–8

Lavatera x clementii 'Kew Rose'

A succession of attractively veined, frilly, dark pink blooms appear from early summer to early autumn. H 2m (6ft) S 2m (6ft).
Aspect: sun
Hardiness: ✤✤✤ Zones: 7–8

Lavatera olbia 'Rosea' (syn. L. x clementii 'Rosea')

A succession of large dark pink blooms are produced from early summer to early autumn on this vigorous-growing variety. H 2m (6ft) S 2m (6ft).
Aspect: sun
Hardiness: ✤✤✤ Zones: 7–8

Lavatera

LEPTOSPERMUM

A genus of about 80 species, including the slightly tender, early summer flowering shrub featured here. It makes a good back-of-the-border seasonal focal point.
Cultivation In the garden, grow in any well-drained garden soil that is reasonably fertile and in full sun or dappled shade. In colder regions, grow in pots of soil-based mix. Feed monthly and water as necessary during the growing season. Before frosts, move under cover, stop feeding and water sparingly in winter.
Pruning No routine pruning is required.
Propagation Take semi-ripe cuttings in mid-summer.

Leptospermum scoparium 'Red Damask'

A compact shrub with arching stems and narrow, pointed, aromatic, green leaves. During late spring and early summer it is covered in masses of double, dark red flowers. H 3m (10ft) S 3m (10ft).
Aspect: sun or semi-shade
Hardiness: ✤ Zone: 10

LEUCOTHOE

A genus of about 50 species, including the versatile evergreen shrub featured here, that are grown for their eye-catching foliage and clusters of pretty, urn-shaped spring flowers. They are ideal for a shady shrub or mixed border that offers suitable growing conditions. It can also be used as a deep

Leptospernum

Leucothoe fontanesiana 'Rainbow'

groundcover plant between deciduous trees in a woodland-edge planting.
Cultivation Grow in any moisture-retentive, well-drained acid soil in deep or dappled shade. Add plenty of organic matter (but not alkaline mushroom compost/soil mix) to the soil before planting.
Pruning To get the best foliage displays and maintain a compact shape, cut back one stem in three to near ground level during mid-spring, starting with the oldest stems first.
Propagation Layer low branches in early spring or take semi-ripe cuttings in late summer.

Leucothoe fontanesiana 'Rainbow'

A spectacular shrub with glossy, lance-shaped, dark green variegated foliage splashed with cream and pink. A bonus of white, urn-shaped flowers are produced in clusters during mid-spring and late spring. H 1.5m (5ft) S 2m (6ft).
Aspect: semi-shade or deep shade
Hardiness: ✤✤✤ Zones: 7–8

Leucothoe fontanesiana 'Scarletta'

Although first emerging red-purple, the dark evergreen foliage turns bronze during the winter. A bonus of white, urn-shaped flowers are produced in clusters during early spring and mid-spring. H 150cm (60in) S 40cm (16in).
Aspect: semi-shade or deep shade
Hardiness: ✤✤✤

Leycesteria formosa

LEYCESTERIA

A genus of about five species, including the fast-growing and suckering deciduous shrub featured here, that is grown for its unusual pendent, Chinese-lantern-shaped bracts, tipped with summer flowers, followed by autumn berries. A useful shrub for extending the season of interest in the garden and for filling a space at the back of a border.

Cultivation Grow in any well-drained garden soil that is reasonably fertile and site in full sun or dappled shade. In colder regions, these shrubs need to be protected from cold winds. In addition, you will need to cover its roots with a deep insulating mulch, which should be applied during the autumn.

Pruning For best flowering performance, cut back one stem in three to near ground level during mid-spring, starting with the oldest stems.

Propagation Take softwood cuttings in early summer or take hardwood cuttings in late autumn.

Leycesteria formosa
Himalayan honeysuckle
Long-lasting clusters of pendent, wine-coloured bracts, tipped with white flowers, are produced in succession from mid-summer to early autumn, followed by eye-catching purple berries. Borderline hardy. H 2m (6ft) S 2m (6ft).
Aspect: sun or semi-shade
Hardiness: ✿✿✿ Zones: 7–8

Ligustrum lucidum 'Tricolor'

LIGUSTRUM
Privet

This genus of about 50 species includes the deciduous and evergreen shrubs featured here, grown for their foliage and dense growing habit. These shrubs are very useful back-of-the-border fillers and make very popular hedging plants.

Cultivation Grow in any well-drained garden soil that is reasonably fertile and in full sun or dappled shade. However, for best foliage coloration, grow in full sun.

Pruning No routine pruning is necessary. Clip occasionally to maintain the plant's shape or to keep it compact. Neglected or overgrown plants can be rejuvenated by cutting back all the stems to within 10cm (4in) of ground level. All-green reverted shoots on variegated varieties should be removed completely when they are noticed. Trim hedges into shape in late spring and early autumn.

Propagation Take semi-ripe cuttings in mid-summer or take hardwood cuttings in late autumn.

Ligustrum japonicam 'Rotundifolium'
A compact and slow-growing evergreen with glossy, dark green, leathery leaves. Insignificant white flowers are produced in mid-summer and late summer. H 1.5m (5ft) S 1m (3ft).
Aspect: sun or semi-shade
Hardiness: ✿✿✿ Zones: 7–8

Ligustrum lucidum 'Excelsum Superbum'
A variegated evergreen with cream-edged, bright green leaves. Insignificant white flowers are produced in late summer and early autumn. H 10m (33ft) S 10m (33ft).
Aspect: sun or semi-shade
Hardiness: ✿✿✿ Zones: 7–8

Ligustrum lucidum 'Tricolor'
A variegated evergreen with white-edged, grey-green leaves that emerge pink-tinged. Insignificant white flowers are produced in late summer and early autumn. H 10m (33ft) S 10m (33ft).
Aspect: sun or semi-shade
Hardiness: ✿✿✿ Zones: 7–8

Ligustrum ovalifolium
The glossy, dark green, evergreen foliage of the oval leaf privet makes an excellent hedge in urban areas as it is particularly pollution-tolerant. Insignificant white flowers are produced in mid-summer and late summer, followed by shiny black berries. H 4m (13ft) S 4m (13ft).
Aspect: sun or semi-shade
Hardiness: ✿✿✿ Zones: 7–8

Ligustrum ovalifolium 'Aureum' (syn. L. ovalifolium 'Aureomarginatum')
Golden privet
The yellow-margined, broad green leaves are retained all winter in all but the coldest of gardens. Makes a useful hedge in urban areas as it is particularly pollution-tolerant. Insignificant white flowers are produced in mid-summer and late summer, followed by shiny black berries. H 4m (13ft) S 4m (13ft).
Aspect: sun or semi-shade
Hardiness: ✿✿✿ Zones: 7–8

LONICERA

A varied genus of over 180 species, including the deciduous and evergreen shrubs featured here, grown for either its fragrant winter flowers or colourful evergreen leaves. Plant winter-flowering varieties with fragrant blooms next to much-used paths and sheltered entrances, where they will be appreciated most. Evergreen types make excellent border fillers or edging plants and can be trimmed into low hedges.

Cultivation Grow in any well-drained garden soil that is

Lonicera nitida 'Baggesen's Gold'

Philadelphus 'Belle Etoile'

Propagation Take semi-ripe cuttings in early summer or take hardwood cuttings in late autumn.

Philadelphus 'Beauclerk'
A stiffly arching deciduous shrub that bears scented, cup-shaped, single white flowers that are flushed pink in the centre during early summer and mid-summer. H 2.5m (8ft) S 2.5m (8ft).
Aspect: sun or semi-shade
Hardiness: ✺✺✺ Zones: 7–8

Philadelphus 'Belle Etoile'
Very fragrant, single, cup-shaped white flowers with contrasting pinky-purple centres are carried throughout early summer and mid-summer on arching branches. H 1.2m (4ft) S 2.5m (8ft).
Aspect: sun or semi-shade
Hardiness: ✺✺✺ Zones: 7–8

Philadelphus coronarius 'Aureus'
Single, fragrant, creamy-white, cup-shaped flowers are carried throughout early summer on upright stems with golden-yellow leaves that become greenish-yellow in summer. Grow in dappled shade. H 2.5m (8ft) S 1.5m (5ft).
Aspect: semi-shade
Hardiness: ✺✺✺ Zones: 7–8

Philadelphus coronarius 'Variegatus'
Pure white, fragrant, cup-shaped flowers are carried throughout early summer on upright stems with white-edged, apple-green variegated foliage.

H 2.5m (8ft) S 2m (6ft).
Aspect: sun or semi-shade
Hardiness: ✺✺✺ Zones: 7–8

Philadelphus x lemoinei 'Lemoinei'
The arching branches of this upright mock orange are covered by masses of very fragrant clusters of single, cup-shaped white flowers throughout early summer and mid-summer. H 1.5m (5ft) S 1.5m (5ft).
Aspect: sun or semi-shade
Hardiness: ✺✺✺ Zones: 7–8

Philadelphus 'Manteau d'Hermine'
Elegantly arching shoots are festooned with very fragrant, double, creamy-white flowers throughout early summer and mid-summer on this compact, bushy, deciduous shrub. An ideal choice for a small garden. H 75cm (30in) S 150cm (60in).
Aspect: sun or semi-shade
Hardiness: ✺✺✺ Zones: 7–8

Philadelphus microphyllus
Single, white, fragrant, flowers are carried in clusters throughout early summer and mid-summer against a backdrop of glossy green leaves on this compact plant. H 1m (3ft) S 1m (3ft).
Aspect: sun or semi-shade
Hardiness: ✺✺✺ Zones: 7–8

Philadelphus 'Virginal'
Fully double, white, fragrant flowers festoon upright branches

throughout early summer and mid-summer on this vigorous mock orange. Its dark green leaves go yellow in autumn. H 3m (10ft) S 2.5m (8ft).
Aspect: sun or semi-shade
Hardiness: ✺✺✺

PHLOMIS
A genus of about 100 species, grown for their unusual tiered summer flowers on upright stems and woolly grey foliage.
Cultivation Grow in any well-drained garden soil that is reasonably fertile and in full sun. Grow in the protection of a sunny wall in colder areas.
Pruning In spring, cut back the previous year's growth to about 10cm (4in) of the ground as new shoots emerge from the base.
Propagation Take softwood cuttings in early summer, or semi-ripe cuttings in early autumn.

Phlomis fruticosa
A spreading evergreen shrub, with sage-like, aromatic, grey-green leaves that throws up vertical spikes that carry whorls of hooded, golden-yellow flowers in tiers throughout early summer and mid-summer. Borderline hardy. H 1m (3ft) S 1.5m (5ft).
Aspect: sun
Hardiness: ✺✺✺ Zones: 7–8

Phlomis italica
Upright spikes carry whorls of hooded lilac-pink flowers during early summer and mid-summer

above this compact evergreen shrub with silvery-grey woolly leaves. H 30cm (12in) S 60cm (24in).
Aspect: sun
Hardiness: ✺✺ Zone: 9

PHOENIX
A genus of over 15 species, including the tender miniature date palm featured here, grown for their handsome foliage. Ideal border plant in milder areas or for an exotic touch to the patio.
Cultivation Grow in a reasonably fertile, moisture-retentive, well-drained soil in full sun. In pots, use a soil-based mix, water regularly and feed monthly in the growing season. Water sparingly in winter. Needs a warm spot if the temperature falls below 10°C (50°F) and water sparingly.
Pruning No routine pruning is necessary.
Propagation Sow seed in mid-spring.

Phoenix roebelenii
Miniature date palm
This stemless palm has narrow, dark green leaflets that are grey-green when young. Mature plants carry clusters of cream flowers in early summer and mid-summer, followed by edible black fruit. Move to a heated greenhouse or conservatory in cold areas (min 10°C/50°F) over winter. H 2m (6ft) S 2.5m (8ft).
Aspect: sun
Hardiness: tender Zones: 10+

Philadelphus 'Manteau d'Hermine'

Phlomis italica

Pheonix roebelenii

Photinia x fraseri 'Birmingham'

PHOTINIA

A genus of about 60 species grown for their colourful new shoots in spring. It is useful for adding much-needed colour to mixed borders and shrubberies early in the year and for providing an attractive foil at other times.
Cultivation Grow in any moisture-retentive, well-drained soil that is reasonably fertile and in full sun. Train against a sheltered, sunny wall in colder areas.
Pruning No routine pruning is necessary. Cut back straggly plants by about one-third to rejuvenate them and encourage more foliage.
Propagation Take semi-ripe cuttings in mid-summer.

Photinia x fraseri 'Birmingham'
Eye-catching purple-red young foliage is the main feature of this handsome evergreen shrub.

Clusters of insignificant white flowers are carried in mid-spring and late spring, followed by red berries. H 5m (16ft) S 5m (16ft).
Aspect: sun
Hardiness: ❋❋ Zone: 9

Photinia x fraseri 'Red Robin'
A compact evergreen shrub with brilliant red glossy young foliage and clusters of insignificant white flowers carried in mid-spring and late spring, followed by red berries. H 5m (16ft) S 5m (16ft).
Aspect: sun
Hardiness: ❋❋ Zone: 9

PHYGELIUS

A genus of just two species, grown for their elegant summer flowers. A good choice for adding late colour in borders.
Cultivation Grow in any reasonably fertile, moisture-retentive, well-drained soil in full sun. Shelter from cold winds and apply a mulch in autumn.
Pruning No routine pruning is necessary. Deadhead for the best flowering displays. In cold areas, cut back to near ground level in early spring.
Propagation Take softwood cuttings in late spring.

Phygelius aequalis 'Yellow Trumpet'
An upright, suckering evergreen shrub that bears clusters of pale creamy-yellow tubular flowers on slender stems from early summer to late summer.

Phygelius x rectus 'Moonraker'

H 90cm (36in) S 90cm (36in).
Aspect: sun
Hardiness: ❋❋ Zone: 9

Phygelius x rectus
Tubular pale red flowers are produced in loose open sprays on the slender stems of this upright, suckering evergreen shrub from early summer to late summer on this shrub. H 1.2m (4ft) S 1.5m (5ft).
Named varieties: 'African Queen', red and orange flowers, H 1m (3ft) S 1.2m (4ft). 'Devil's Tears', red flowers, H 1m (3ft) S 1.2m (4ft). 'Moonraker', cream-coloured flowers, H 1m (3ft) S 1.2m (4ft). 'Pink Elf', pink flowers, H 75cm (30in) S 90cm (36in). 'Salmon Leap', pale orange flowers, H 1.2m (4ft) S 1.5m (5ft).
Aspect: sun
Hardiness: ❋❋ Zone: 9

PIERIS

A genus of over five species, including the evergreen shrubs featured here, grown for their fragrant clusters of lily-of-the-valley-like spring flowers and colourful new foliage. They make excellent border fillers, while some compact varieties are also suitable for growing in large containers.
Cultivation In the garden, grow in any well-drained acid soil in dappled shade, but in colder areas shelter from cold winds. Add plenty of organic matter (but not alkaline mushroom compost/soil mix) to the soil before planting. In containers, grow in ericaceous soil mix and keep well watered.
Pruning No routine pruning is necessary. Remove any frost-damaged stems in early summer.
Propagation Take semi-ripe cuttings in late summer, or layer low branches in mid-autumn.

Pieris formosa var. forrestii 'Wakehurst'
An upright, evergreen shrub that bears pendent clusters of fragrant, white, urn-shaped flowers during mid-spring and late spring when the glossy, brilliant red young foliage emerges. H 5m (16ft) S 4m (13ft).
Aspect: semi-shade
Hardiness: ❋❋❋ Zones: 7–8

Pieris 'Forest Flame'
The fiery red new foliage of this upright evergreen turns pink and cream before maturing to dark green. Clusters of white, urn-

Photinia x fraseri 'Red Robin'

Pieris 'Forest Flame'

shaped flowers festoon the shrub during mid-spring and late spring. H 4m (13ft) S 2m (6ft). Aspect: semi-shade Hardiness: ❁❁❁ Zones: 7–8

Pieris japonica 'Purity'

Clusters of white, urn-shaped flowers are borne in abundance during mid-spring and late spring and stand out against the lustrous young, pale green foliage that darkens with age on this compact evergreen. H 1m (3ft) S 1m (3ft). Aspect: semi-shade Hardiness: ❁❁❁ Zones: 7–8

Pieris japonica 'Valley Valentine'

An early and long-flowering compact variety that produces dark pink flowers from early spring until late spring against lustrous dark green leaves. H 4m (13ft) S 3m (10ft). Aspect: semi-shade Hardiness: ❁❁❁ Zones: 7–8

Pieris japonica 'Variegata'

New foliage is flushed pink, maturing to green with white margins on this variegated variety. Clusters of white, bell-shaped flowers are produced throughout mid-spring and late spring. H 80cm (32in) S 80cm (32in). Aspect: semi-shade Hardiness: ❁❁❁ Zones: 7–8

PITTOSPORUM

A genus of around 200 species, including the handsome, bushy evergreens featured here. They make good border fillers or specimens with year-round interest and can be trimmed into an attractive hedge in mild areas.
Cultivation Grow in reasonably fertile, moisture-retentive, well-drained soil in full sun or dappled shade. Grow against a sheltered, sunny wall in colder areas.
Pruning No routine pruning is necessary. Shrubs can be clipped to keep them compact during mid-spring. Trim hedges in mid-spring and early summer.
Propagation Take semi-ripe cuttings in mid-autumn.

Pittosporum 'Garnettii'

Half-hardy variegated evergreen with pink-spotted grey-green

leaves that have creamy-white, wavy edges. Purple, bell-shaped flowers are borne in late spring and early summer. H 4m (13ft) S 3m (10ft). Aspect: sun or semi-shade Hardiness: ❁ Zone: 10

Pittosporum tenuifolium 'Silver Queen'

This is a large, ornamental shrub that has handsome, white-variegated, wavy-edged, grey-green leaves that appear on contrasting near-black young stems. Honey-scented dark purple flowers are sometimes produced during late spring and early summer. H 4m (13ft) S 2m (6ft). Aspect: sun or semi-shade Hardiness: ❁❁ Zones: 9

Pittosporum tenuifolium 'Tom Thumb'

As its names suggests, this is a compact, rounded evergreen with wavy-edged, purple-bronze leaves and near-black young stems. Honey-scented dark purple flowers are sometimes produced during late spring and early summer. H 90cm (36in) S 60cm (24in). Aspect: sun or semi-shade Hardiness: ❁❁ Zone: 9

Pittosporum tenuifolium 'Variegatum'

A large bushy evergreen with creamy-white, variegated, wavy-edged, grey-green leaves on near-black young stems. It makes an attractive, variegated windbreak or hedge in mild coastal areas.

H 4m (13ft) S 2m (6ft). Aspect: sun or semi-shade Hardiness: ❁❁ Zone: 9

POTENTILLA
Cinquefoil

A large genus of over 500 species, including the summer-flowering, deciduous shrubs featured here. Smaller, compact varieties are useful for adding summer-long colour in confined spaces and all can be grown on poor soils. Ideal for rock gardens, sunny banks or the sunny base of hedges.
Cultivation Grow in any well-drained soil in full sun.
Pruning For good flowering, trim new growth by one-third each mid-spring. Rejuvenate neglected plants by cutting the plant back to ground level in mid-spring.
Propagation Take semi-ripe cuttings in early autumn.

Potentilla fruticosa 'Abbotswood'

Compact, bushy, deciduous shrub with blue-green foliage that bears masses of brilliant white flowers from late spring to mid-autumn. H 75cm (30in) S 120cm (48in). Aspect: sun Hardiness: ❁❁❁ Zones: 7–8

Potentilla fruticosa 'Goldfinger'

Large, bright yellow flowers are produced in abundance from late spring to mid-autumn against a backdrop of small, dark green leaves on this mound-forming deciduous shrub. H 1m (3ft) S 1.5m (5ft). Aspect: sun Hardiness: ❁❁❁ Zones: 7–8

Potentilla fruticosa 'Primrose Beauty'

Primrose-yellow flowers resembling wild roses appear from late spring to mid-autumn above a compact mound of deciduous grey-green leaves. Pest- and disease-free, it tolerates partial shade but flowers best in full sun. H 1m (3ft) S 1.5m (5ft). Aspect: sun Hardiness: ❁❁❁ Zones: 7–8

Potentilla fruticosa 'Red Ace'

Vermilion-red flowers each with a yellow centre and undersides are borne *en masse* from late spring to mid-autumn and stand out against the dark green leaves. H 1m (3ft) S 1.5m (5ft). Aspect: sun Hardiness: ❁❁❁ Zones: 7–8

Potentilla fruticosa 'Royal Flush'

Masses of rich pink flowers, each with a yellow centre that fades to white with age, cover this compact, busy, deciduous shrub from late spring to mid-autumn. H 45cm (18in) S 75cm (30in). Aspect: sun Hardiness: ❁❁❁ Zones: 7–8

Potentilla fruticosa 'Sunset'

The unusual, burnt-orange flowers that appear on this shrub are produced in succession from late spring to mid-autumn and appear above a mound of dark green deciduous foliage. H 1m (3ft) S 1m (3ft). Aspect: sun Hardiness: ❁❁❁ Zones: 7–8

Pittosporum tenuifolium 'Variegatum'

Potentilla fruticosa 'Abbotswood'

Prostanthera cuneata

Prunus 'Hirtipes'

PROSTANTHERA
Mint bush

A genus of some 50 species, including the bushy evergreen shrub featured here, grown for their eye-catching summer flowers. It is a useful front-of-the-border filler and for adding continuity to the garden display.
Cultivation Grow in any moisture-retentive, well-drained soil that is reasonably fertile and in full sun. Grow against a sheltered, sunny wall in colder areas.
Pruning No routine pruning is necessary. Deadhead to keep neat and help prolong flowering. Trim lightly after flowering to keep compact.
Propagation Take semi-ripe cuttings in mid-summer.

Prostanthera cuneata
Alpine mint bush
Tubular white flowers with distinctive purple and yellow flecks in the throat are produced in clusters from early summer to late summer on this small, bushy, evergreen shrub. H 1m (3ft) S 1m (3ft).
Aspect: sun
Hardiness: ❀❀ Zone: 9

PRUNUS

A large and varied genus of over 200 species, including the bushy evergreen shrubs featured here, grown for their handsome foliage and spring flowers, as well as deciduous shrubs grown for their spring blossom. Plant spring-flowering varieties as seasonal focal points where they will be appreciated most; evergreen types make excellent border fillers, ground cover and hedges, depending on the variety.
Cultivation Grow in any moisture-retentive, well-drained soil that is reasonably fertile and in full sun, dappled shade, even deep shade.
Pruning No routine pruning is necessary. Formal evergreen hedges and screens can be trimmed during early spring and late summer. Neglected or straggly evergreen shrubs can be cut back hard into old wood during early spring. Deciduous shrubs can be kept compact and flowering well by cutting back one stem in three during early summer, starting with the oldest.
Propagation Take semi-ripe cuttings in early autumn.

Prunus laurocerasus 'Otto Luyken'
A compact, bushy, evergreen shrub with narrow, pointed, dark green leaves. Candle-like spikes of small white flowers appear during mid-spring, followed by cherry-red berries. Good ground cover. H 1m (3ft) S 1.5m (5ft).
Aspect: sun, semi-shade to deep shade
Hardiness: ❀❀❀ Zones: 7–8

Prunus laurocerasus 'Rotundifolia'
A large, dense and bushy evergreen shrub with big, glossy, dark green leaves. Candle-like spikes of small white flowers are produced during mid-spring, followed by cherry-red berries. Good hedging plant.

H 5m (16ft). S 4m (13ft).
Aspect: sun, semi-shade to deep shade
Hardiness: ❀❀❀ Zones: 7–8

Prunus laurocerasus 'Zabeliana'
A low-growing, spreading, evergreen shrub with very narrow, pointed, dark green leaves. Candle-like spikes of small white flowers are produced during mid-spring, followed by cherry-red berries. Good ground cover. H 1m (3ft) S 2.5m (8ft).
Aspect: sun, semi-shade to deep shade
Hardiness: ❀❀❀ Zones: 7–8

Prunus lusitanica
Portugal laurel
A large, dense, evergreen shrub with dark green leaves that have red stalks. Candle-like spikes of small white flowers are produced during mid-spring, followed by red berries that mature to purple. Good hedging plant and can tolerate chalky soils. H 20m (70ft) S 20m (70ft).
Aspect: sun, semi-shade to deep shade
Hardiness: ❀❀❀ Zones: 7–8

Prunus tenella 'Fire Hill'
Dwarf Russian almond
An upright-growing, compact and bushy deciduous shrub with narrow, glossy, dark green leaves. The bare stems are smothered with bright pink blossom-like flowers during early spring and mid-spring as the leaves emerge, followed by velvety fruits. H 1.5m (5ft) S 1.5m (5ft).
Aspect: sun or semi-shade
Hardiness: ❀❀❀ Zones: 7–8

Prunus triloba
Flowering almond
Peach-pink, blossom-like flowers are borne on the bare stems of this dense, twiggy, deciduous shrub during early spring and mid-spring as the leaves emerge, followed by red berries. H 3m (10ft) S 3m (10ft).
Aspect: sun or semi-shade
Hardiness: ❀❀❀ Zones: 7–8

PYRACANTHA

A genus of over five species, including the spreading, spiny evergreen shrubs featured here, grown for their intruder-resistant properties, spring flowers and colourful autumn fruit that are loved by birds. They can be used as freestanding shrubs or hedges or be trained against a wall or fence. They make useful town garden plants, as they are very tolerant of urban pollution.
Cultivation Grow in any well-drained soil that is reasonably fertile in full sun or dappled shade, sheltered from cold winds. Grow less hardy varieties against a sunny wall in colder areas.
Pruning No routine pruning is necessary. Hedges and screens can be trimmed between late spring and mid-summer to keep in shape. Wall-trained specimens should be trimmed back at this time in summer. Cut back all the new shoots after they have flowered, to expose the developing berries.
Propagation Take semi-ripe cuttings in early autumn.

Pyracantha 'Golden Charmer'
A vigorous and bushy shrub that produces masses of small white flowers on arching branches during early summer, followed by clusters of dark orange berries that are resistant to disease. H 3m (10ft) S 3m (10ft).
Aspect: sun or semi-shade
Hardiness: ❀❀❀ Zones: 7–8

Pyracantha 'Mohave'
Masses of small white flowers are produced in clusters during early summer, followed by clusters of long-lasting bright red berries on this vigorous, bushy shrub. H 4m (13ft) S 5m (16ft).

Pyracantha 'Saphyr Orange'

Aspect: sun or semi-shade
Hardiness: ❀❀ Zone: 9

Pyracantha 'Orange Glow'

Clusters of small white flowers are produced in late spring against lustrous, dark green leaves, followed by brilliant orange berries that last well into winter on this open, spreading shrub. H 3m (10ft) S 3m (10ft).
Aspect: sun or semi-shade
Hardiness: ❀❀❀ Zones: 7–8

Pyracantha 'Saphyr Orange'

This vigorous, evergreen shrub is a recent introduction that bears sprays of small white flowers during early summer, followed by clusters of disease-resistant, orange berries that last well into winter against a backdrop of glossy, dark green leaves. *Pyracantha* 'Saphyr Rouge' is similar but bears carmine-red berries that mature to orange. H 4m (13ft) S 3m (10ft).
Aspect: sun or semi-shade
Hardiness: ❀❀❀ Zones: 7–8

Pyracantha 'Soleil d'Or'

Large clusters of long-lasting, disease-resistant, golden-yellow berries follow masses of white flowers produced in early summer on red-tinged spiny shoots of this upright evergreen shrub. H 3m (10ft) S 2.5m (8ft).
Aspect: sun or semi-shade
Hardiness: ❀❀❀ Zones: 7–8

RHAMNUS

A genus of around 125 species, including the variegated evergreen shrub featured here, grown for their handsome foliage. It makes an attractive freestanding shrub or hedge, but in cold areas it is best trained against a large sunny wall or fence. It also makes an excellent permanent container shrub that provides year-round interest.
Cultivation In the garden, grow in any garden soil that is reasonably fertile and in full sun. In colder regions, grow in a sheltered position, protected from cold winds. In containers, use a soil-based mix, feed monthly and water as necessary.
Pruning No routine pruning is necessary.
Propagation Take semi-ripe cuttings in mid-summer.

Rhamnus alaternus 'Argenteovariegata' (syn. R. alaternus 'Variegata')

A variegated evergreen shrub, grown for its white-edged grey-green leaves. Small, insignificant mustard-coloured flowers are produced in late spring and early summer, followed by red fruits that ripen to black. H 5m (16ft) S 4m (13ft).
Aspect: sun
Hardiness: ❀❀ Zones: 7–8

RHAPIS

A genus of over ten species of multi-stemmed palms, including the miniature fan palm featured here, that will add a tropical touch to mild gardens or can be grown as a house plant in colder regions.
Cultivation Grow in a well-drained soil that is reasonably fertile in dappled shade. In containers, use a soil-based compost (soil mix), water regularly and feed monthly during the growing season. Move to a warm spot undercover when the temperature falls below 10°C (50°F) and water sparingly throughout the winter.
Pruning No routine pruning is necessary.
Propagation Sow seed or divide large clumps in mid-spring.

Rhapis excelsa (syn. R. flabelliformis) Miniature fan palm

A tender dwarf palm that forms a clump of bamboo-like stems with large, deeply lobed, matt green, palm-like leaves. Insignificant cream flowers are produced in early summer and mid-summer. H 1.5m (5ft) S 5m (16ft).
Aspect: semi-shade
Hardiness: tender Zones: 10+

RHODODENDRON
(including azalea)

A huge genus of nearly 1,000 species, including the medium-sized and dwarf forms of evergreen azaleas and rhododendrons and the deciduous azaleas featured here, all grown for their spectacular flowering displays. Use according to their size: all make wonderful seasonal focal points, with smaller varieties best suited at the front or middle of borders, while bigger forms with larger, eye-catching flowers can be best accommodated towards the back of the scheme. Compact varieties also make excellent permanent container plants.
Cultivation Shallow-plant in any well-drained acid soil in dappled shade, but in colder areas provide shelter and plant where it gets afternoon sun. Some varieties are best grown in full sun. Add plenty of organic matter to the soil before planting. In containers, grow in ericaceous soil mix and keep well watered. Wherever the shrub is planted, bear in mind that the flowers are susceptible to damage by a frost that is followed by rapid thaw, so avoid positioning in east-facing areas that get early morning spring sun.

Pruning Deadhead after flowering. Prune straggly branches of established plants to maintain the overall shape during late winter or early spring.
Propagation Layer low branches in early spring or take semi-ripe cuttings in late summer.

EVERGREEN RHODODENDRONS
Rhododendron 'Blue Diamond'

Violet-blue funnel-shaped flowers that age to lavender-blue are borne during mid-spring and early spring. It has small, aromatic, dark, evergreen leaves. Best in full sun. H 1.5m (5ft) S 1.5m (5ft).
Aspect: sun
Hardiness: ❀❀❀ Zones: 7–8

Rhododendron 'Blue Peter'

Frilly edged, lavender-blue flowers with purple markings are produced in clusters throughout early summer. Large, dark, evergreen leaves. H 3m (10ft) S 3m (10ft).
Aspect: semi-shade
Hardiness: ❀❀❀ Zones: 7–8

Rhododendron 'Cilpinense'

Clusters of pale pink, funnel-shaped flowers are produced in profusion during early spring on this compact evergreen rhododendron, which has small, dark leaves. H 1.1m (3½ft) S 1.1m (3½ft).
Aspect: sun or semi-shade
Hardiness: ❀❀❀ Zones: 7–8

Rhododendron 'Cunningham's White'

Trusses of white, funnel-shaped flowers with brown or purple markings are produced throughout late spring. Compact evergreen with dark green leaves. H 2.2m (7ft) S 2.2m (7ft).
Aspect: semi-shade
Hardiness: ❀❀❀ Zones: 7–8

Rhododendron 'Dopey'

Masses of long-lasting, glossy, red, bell-shaped flowers, spotted dark-brown inside, are produced throughout late spring on this compact evergreen rhododendron. H 2m (6ft) S 2m (6ft).
Aspect: semi-shade
Hardiness: ❀❀❀ Zones: 7–8

Rhamnus alaternus 'Argenteovariegata'

Rhapis excelsa

Rhododrendron 'Dopey'

Rhododendron 'Grumpy'
Funnel-shaped, pink-flushed, cream flowers are produced in flat-topped trusses during mid-spring and late spring. The glossy, dark green leaves are woolly underneath. H 1.2m (4ft) S 1m (3ft).
Aspect: semi-shade
Hardiness: ❁❁❁ Zones: 7–8

Rhododendron 'Lord Roberts'
Dark crimson, funnel-shaped flowers with black markings are produced in clusters during early summer. Compact evergreen with dark green leaves. H 1.5m (5ft) S 1.5m (5ft).
Aspect: semi-shade
Hardiness: ❁❁❁ Zones: 7–8

Rhododendron 'Pink Drift'
Funnel-shaped, rose-lavender flowers are produced *en masse* throughout mid-spring and late spring on this very compact, dwarf evergreen rhododendron, which has small, pale green leaves. Good choice for small gardens. H 50cm (20in) S 50cm (20in).
Aspect: semi-shade
Hardiness: ❁❁❁ Zones: 7–8

Rhododendron 'Pink Pearl'
White-edged, soft-pink, funnel-shaped flowers that age to white are produced during mid-spring and late spring. Large, pale, evergreen leaves. H 4m (13ft) S 4m (13ft).
Aspect: sun
Hardiness: ❁❁❁ Zones: 7–8

Rhododendron 'Purple Splendor'
Frilly edged, funnel-shaped, deep purple flowers, each with a blackish-purple throat, are produced during late spring and early summer on this late-flowering variety. H 3m (10ft) S 3m (10ft).
Aspect: semi-shade
Hardiness: ❁❁❁ Zones: 7–8

Rhododendron 'Sapphire'
Masses of small, pale blue, funnel-shaped flowers are produced *en masse* during mid-spring and late spring on this compact evergreen, which has small, dark leaves. H 50cm (20in) S 50cm (20in).
Aspect: semi-shade
Hardiness: ❁❁❁ Zones: 7–8

Rhododendron 'Scarlet Wonder'
Wavy-margined, ruby-red, funnel-shaped flowers are produced *en masse* throughout mid-spring on this compact evergreen, which has small, dark leaves. H 2m (6ft) S 2m (6ft).
Aspect: semi-shade
Hardiness: ❁❁❁ Zones: 7–8

DECIDUOUS AZALEAS
Rhododendron luteum
Sweetly scented, the yellow, funnel-shaped blooms appear throughout late spring and early summer on this vigorous-growing deciduous azalea. Mid-green leaves turn fiery shades in autumn.
H 4m (13ft) S 4m (13ft).

Aspect: sun or semi-shade
Hardiness: ❁❁❁ Zones: 7–8

Rhododendron 'Debutante'
Pink, funnel-shaped flowers with orange markings are produced en masse throughout late spring. Mid-green leaves turn fiery shades in autumn. H 2m (6ft) S 2m (6ft).
Aspect: semi-shade
Hardiness: ❁❁❁ Zones: 7–8

Rhododendron 'Gibraltar'
Frilly, bright orange, funnel-shaped flowers appear in late spring on this deciduous azalea. A useful pot specimen on the patio. H 1.5m (5ft) S 1.5m (5ft).
Aspect: sun or semi-shade
Hardiness: ❁❁❁ Zones: 7–8

Rhododendron 'Glowing Embers'
Flaming reddish-orange, funnel-shaped flowers are produced in conical clusters during mid-spring and late spring. H 2m (6ft) S 2m (6ft).
Aspect: semi-shade
Hardiness: ❁❁❁ Zones: 7–8

Rhododendron 'Homebush'
Pretty pink, semi-double, funnel-shaped flowers are borne throughout late spring. A good pink variety for small gardens. H 1.5m (5ft) S 1.5m (5ft).
Aspect: semi-shade
Hardiness: ❁❁❁ Zones: 7–8

Rhododendron 'Klondyke'
Coppery-red flower buds open to reveal flaming red-flushed, golden-orange, funnel-shaped flowers throughout late spring. The mid-green leaves turn fiery shades in autumn. H 2m (6ft) S 2m (6ft).
Aspect: semi-shade
Hardiness: ❁❁❁ Zones: 7–8

Rhododendron 'Koster's Brilliant Red'
Vivid, orange-red, funnel-shaped flowers are produced during mid-spring and late spring on this early-flowering variety. Mid-green leaves turn fiery shades in autumn. H 2m (6ft) S 2m (6ft).
Aspect: semi-shade
Hardiness: ❁❁❁ Zones: 7–8

Rhododendron 'Persil'
Large clusters of orange-flushed, white funnel-shaped flowers are borne throughout April (mid-spring) on this bushy, deciduous azalea. The mid-green leaves turn fiery shades in autumn.
H 2m (6ft) S 2m (6ft).
Aspect: semi-shade
Hardiness: ❁❁❁ Zones: 7–8

EVERGREEN AZALEAS
Rhododendron 'Blue Danube'
Clusters of small, funnel-shaped, violet-blue flowers are produced *en masse* during late spring and early summer on this compact evergreen azalea. Very hardy. H 80cm (32in) S 100cm (36in).
Aspect: semi-shade
Hardiness: ❁❁❁ Zones: 7–8

Rhododendron 'Geisha Red'
Masses of small, funnel-shaped, pillar-box-red flowers are produced during late spring and

Rhododendron 'Persil'

Rhododendron luteum

early summer on this compact evergreen azalea. It makes a useful container specimen on the patio. H 60cm (24in) S 100cm (36in). Aspect: semi-shade Hardiness: ✹✹✹

Rhododendron 'Gumpo White'
Wavy-edged, funnel-shaped, white flowers are produced *en masse* throughout early summer on this dwarf, evergreen azalea. It makes a useful container specimen on the patio. H 1m (3ft) S 1m (3ft). Aspect: semi-shade Hardiness: ✹✹✹ Zones: 7–8

Rhododendron 'Mother's Day'
Small, funnel-shaped, semi-double, rose-red flowers are produced in profusion during late spring and early summer. H 80cm (32in) S 100cm (36in). Aspect: semi-shade Hardiness: ✹✹✹ Zones: 7–8

RHUS
A large genus of over 200 species, including the upright, suckering shrub featured here, grown for their handsome foliage that turns fiery shades in autumn. They make spectacular specimen plants for a sunny shrub or mixed border, providing an ever-changing year-round point of interest. *Cultivation* Grow in a moisture-retentive, well-drained garden soil that is reasonably fertile and in full sun or dappled shade. Grow in full sun for the best autumn tints. Remove suckers by digging

a hole to expose their point of origin and ripping them from the root. Do not prune off as this will just exacerbate the problem. *Pruning* No routine pruning is necessary. Neglected plants can be cut back hard in mid-spring. *Propagation* Take semi-ripe cuttings in mid-summer.

Rhus typhina
Stag's horn sumach
The velvet-covered red winter shoots gave rise to the common name, but it is the finely cut dark green foliage, which turns fiery shades of orange-red in autumn, that is the highlight. Mustard flowers on conical spikes appear in early summer and mid-summer, followed by dark red autumn fruits on female shrubs that make a useful food source for birds in winter. Prone to throwing up suckers, so avoid planting next to a lawn or driveway, or restrict its spread with a sucker-proof barrier. Named varieties: 'Dissecta' (syn. *R. typhina* 'Laciniata'), has more finely cut leaves and rarely produces suckers. H 2m (6ft) S 3m (10ft). Aspect: sun or semi-shade Hardiness: ✹✹✹ Zones: 7–8

RIBES
Flowering currants
A genus of some 150 species, including the deciduous, quick-growing shrubs here, are grown for their spring flowers and autumn fruit. Useful shrubs for filling gaps and for providing quick results in new gardens.

Cultivation Grow in any reasonably fertile, well-drained soil in full sun or dappled shade. *Pruning* Encourage better flowering by pruning annually, cutting out one stem in three after flowering in late spring. *Propagation* Take hardwood cuttings in mid-autumn.

Ribes sanguineum 'Brocklebankii'
A compact and upright deciduous shrub, with aromatic, golden-yellow leaves, that carries clusters of pink flowers during mid-spring, followed by blue-black fruit in autumn. Hot midday sun can scorch the foliage. H 1.2m (4ft) S 1.2m (4ft). Aspect: semi-shade Hardiness: ✹✹✹ Zones: 7–8

Ribes sanguineum 'King Edward VII'
Clusters of dark red flowers in mid-spring are followed by blue-black fruit during the autumn on this upright deciduous shrub with aromatic dark green leaves. H 2m (6ft) S 2m (6ft). Aspect: sun Hardiness: ✹✹✹ Zones: 7–8

Ribes sanguineum 'Pulborough Scarlet'
Clusters of white-centred red flowers appear in mid-spring, followed by blue-black fruit in autumn, on this vigorous shrub with dark green leaves. H 3m (10ft) S 2.5m (18ft). Aspect: sun Hardiness: ✹✹✹ Zones: 7–8

Rhododendron 'Pink Pearl'

Rhus typhina

Ribes sanguineum

Rosa 'Alec's Red'

ROSA
Rose

A large genus of over 150 species that includes the varied collection of popular, deciduous, summer-flowering shrubs featured here. Grow roses in traditional blocks to provide a stunning display, or use single specimens in between other shrubs and flowers for a summer-long splash of colour. Combine different varieties to get a succession of flowers and hips.
Cultivation Grow in any garden soil that is reasonably fertile and in full sun. They prefer the soil to remain moist in summer, so incorporate plenty of organic matter before planting. Avoid siting new rose plants in soil that has recently been used for growing other roses.
Pruning To keep neat, open and healthy, prune annually by cutting back the previous season's growth to within 10–15cm (4–6in) of a permanent twiggy framework before new growth starts in late winter or early spring. Traditionally, this was carried out using secateurs (pruners), but recent trials have shown rough pruning with a hedge trimmer to be equally effective. The sizes for individual varieties given here assume regular pruning. Ground-cover roses should have unwanted stems cut back to an outward-facing bud. In containers, use a soil-based compost (soil mix), water regularly and feed monthly during the growing season. Water as necessary during the winter months.

Propagation Take hardwood cuttings in mid-autumn.
Aspect: sun
Hardiness: ✵✵✵ Zones: 7–8

LARGE-FLOWERED BUSH ROSE
Includes the long-flowering hybrid tea roses with large, shapely blooms on long stems and attractive foliage that make them ideal for cutting.

Rosa 'Alec's Red'
Large, double, sweetly fragrant, crimson flowers are borne in succession from mid-summer to early autumn. Glossy, mid-green leaves. H 100cm (36in) S 60cm (24in).

Rosa 'Alexander'
Double, slightly fragrant, vermilion-red flowers with scalloped petals are produced from mid-summer to early autumn. Lustrous, dark green leaves. H 200cm (72in) S 80cm (32in).

Rosa 'Blessings'
Double, slightly fragrant, coral-pink flowers are borne in succession from mid-summer to early autumn. Glossy, dark green leaves. H 110cm (42in) S 75cm (30in).

Rosa 'Congratulations'
Double, slightly fragrant, rose-pink flowers on long stems are borne from mid-summer to early autumn. Glossy, mid-green leaves. H 1.5m (5ft) S 1m (3ft).

Rosa 'Fragrant Cloud'
Strongly fragrant, double, deep-scarlet flowers are produced from mid-summer to early autumn. Lustrous, dark green leaves. H 75cm (30in) S 60cm (24in).

Rosa 'Ice Cream'
Large, fragrant, ivory-white flowers are borne in succession from mid-summer to early autumn. Lustrous, bronze-tinted, dark green leaves. H 100cm (36in) S 70cm (28in).

Rosa 'Ingrid Bergman'
Fragrant, double, deep red flowers are borne from mid-summer to

Rosa 'Ingrid Bergman'

early autumn. Lustrous, dark green leaves. H 80cm (32in) S 65cm (26in).

Rosa 'Just Joey'
Fragrant, double, coppery-red flowers with wavy-margined petals are borne from mid-summer to early autumn. Matt, dark-green leaves. H 75cm (30in) S 70cm (28in).

Rosa 'Loving Memory'
Double, slightly scented, dark red flowers are borne in succession from mid-summer to early autumn. Matt, dark-green leaves. H 110cm (42in) S 75cm (30in).

Rosa 'Peace'
Double, pink-flushed, deep yellow, slightly fragrant flowers are borne from mid-summer to early autumn. Glossy, dark green leaves. H 1.2m (4ft) S 1m (3ft).

Rosa 'Just Joey'

Rosa 'Peace'

Rosa 'Polar Star'
Large, double, white flowers are borne in succession from mid-summer to early autumn. Matt, dark green leaves. H 100cm (36in) S 70cm (28in).

Rosa 'Remember Me'
Large, fragrant, double, coppery-orange, flushed-yellow flowers are borne from mid-summer to early autumn. Glossy, dark green leaves. H 100cm (36in) S 60cm (24in).

Rosa 'Royal William'
Double, deep-crimson flowers with a spicy fragrance are borne from mid-summer to early autumn. Matt, dark green leaves. H 100cm (36in) S 75cm (30in).

Rosa 'Ruby Wedding'
Slightly fragrant, double, ruby-red flowers are borne in succession from mid-summer to early autumn. Glossy, dark green leaves. H 75cm (30in) S 70cm (28in).

Rosa 'Silver Jubilee'
Fragrant, double, rose-pink flowers flushed salmon-pink are borne from mid-summer to early autumn. Matt, dark green leaves. H 100cm (36in) S 60cm (24in).

CLUSTER-FLOWERED BUSH ROSE
Including floribunda roses, which produce masses of flowers throughout the summer and autumn. They tend to be hardier and more disease-resistant than large-flowered varieties.

Rosa 'Amber Queen'
Fragrant, double, amber-yellow flowers are borne in succession from mid-summer to early autumn. Glossy, leathery, dark green leaves emerge reddish-green. H 50cm (20in) S 60cm (24in).

Rosa 'Arthur Bell'
Large, semi-double, very fragrant, golden-yellow flowers are borne from mid-summer to early autumn. Glossy, mid-green leaves. H 100cm (36in) S 60cm (24in).

Rosa 'Chinatown'
Fragrant, double, pink-edged yellow flowers are produced by 'Chinatown' from mid-summer to early autumn. Glossy, dark green leaves. H 1.2m (4ft) S 1m (3ft).

Rosa 'Golden Wedding'
Double, slightly fragrant, golden-yellow flowers are produced from mid-summer to early autumn. Glossy, dark green leaves. H 75cm (30in) S 60cm (24in).

Rosa 'Iceberg'
Double, slightly fragrant, white flowers are produced from mid-summer to early autumn. Glossy, mid-green leaves. H 80cm (32in) S 65cm (26in).

Rosa 'Many Happy Returns'
Cup-shaped, fragrant, semi-double, pale pink flowers are borne in succession from mid-summer to early autumn. Glossy, mid-green leaves. H 75cm (30in) S 75cm (30in).

Rosa 'Arthur Bell'

Rosa 'Mountbatten'

Rosa 'Masquerade'
Lightly fragrant, semi-double, yellow flowers that age to salmon-pink and red are borne from mid-summer to early autumn. Glossy, dark green leaves. H 80cm (32in) S 60cm (24in).

Rosa 'Mountbatten'
Large, fragrant, double, golden-yellow flowers are produced from mid-summer to early autumn. Glossy, mid-green leaves. H 120cm (48in) S 75cm (30in).

Rosa 'Queen Elizabeth'
Double, slightly fragrant, pale pink flowers are produced in succession and appear from mid-summer to early autumn. Glossy, dark-green leaves. H 2.2m (7ft) S 1m (3ft).

Rosa 'Ruby Anniversary'
Double, slightly scented, ruby-red flowers are produced in succession from mid-summer to early autumn. Glossy, mid-green leaves. H 60cm (24in) S 45cm (18in).

Rosa 'Southampton'
Large, double, slightly scented, red-flushed apricot flowers with ruffled petals from mid-summer to early autumn. Glossy, dark green leaves. H 100cm (36in) S 70cm (28in).

Rosa 'The Times Rose'
Double, slightly fragrant, dark crimson flowers are produced in succession from mid-summer to early autumn.

Glossy, purplish-tinged green leaves. H 60cm (24in) S 75cm (30in).

SHRUB ROSE
A varied collection of roses that grow in bushy, informal plants with spectacular displays of flowers. Many are sweetly scented and some have hips. All are useful for growing in a mixed border with other shrubs. Many old varieties and species roses bloom only in early summer but most modern varieties repeat bloom.

Rosa 'Ballerina'
Slightly scented, white-centred, pale pink flowers are produced from mid-summer to early autumn. Mid-green leaves. H 1.5m (5ft) S 1.2m (48in).

Rosa 'Blanche Double de Coubert'
Large semi-double, very fragrant, white flowers are borne from mid-summer to early autumn, followed by red rose-hips. H 1.5m (5ft) S 1.2m (48in).

Rosa 'Bonica'
Small semi-double, slightly fragrant, rose-pink flowers are borne from mid-summer to early autumn. Glossy, dark green leaves. H 85cm (34in) S 110cm (42in).

Rosa 'Boule de Neige'
Pink-tinged buds open to produce fragrant, double, white flowers from mid-summer to early autumn. Matt, dark green foliage. H 1.5m (5ft) S 1.2m (4ft).

Rosa 'Buff Beauty'
Double, fragrant, pale apricot-yellow flowers are borne from mid-summer to early autumn. Purple-tinged, dark green leaves. H 1.2m (4ft) S 1.2m (4ft).

Rosa 'Cardinal de Richelieu'
Fragrant, double, deep purple flowers are borne in clusters during early summer and mid-summer. Lustrous, dark green leaves. H 1m (3ft) S 1.2m (4ft).

Rosa 'Charles de Mills'
Double, fragrant, magenta-pink flowers are produced in a single flush during mid-summer. Mid-green leaves. H 1m (3ft) S 1.2m (4ft).

Rosa 'Cornelia'
Very fragrant, double, apricot-pink flowers are produced from early summer to early autumn. Matt, dark green leaves. H 1.5m (5ft) S 1.5m (5ft).

Rosa 'Fantin-Latour'
Slightly fragrant, double, pale pink flowers are produced throughout early summer and mid-summer. Glossy, dark green leaves. H 1.5m (5ft) S 1.2m (4ft).

Rosa 'Felicia'
Sweetly fragrant, double, apricot-yellow flowers that are flushed with pale pink from early summer to early autumn. Matt, mid-green leaves. H 1.5m (5ft) S 2.2m (7ft).

Rosa 'Iceberg'

Rosa 'Felicia'

Rosa **'Fru Dagmar Hastrup'**
Clove-scented, single, light-pink flowers are produced in succession from mid-summer to early autumn, followed by dark red autumn hips. Matt, dark green leaves. H 1m (3ft) S 1.2m (4ft).

Rosa glauca
Clusters of single, cerise-pink flowers with pale-pink centres are produced during early summer and mid-summer on almost thornless stems, followed by spherical red rosehips.
H 2m (6ft) S 1.5m (5ft).

Rosa **'Graham Thomas'**
Double, fragrant, yellow flowers are produced in succession from mid-summer to early autumn. Matt, bright green leaves.
H 1.5m (5ft) S 1.2m (4ft).

Rosa **'Heritage'**
Cup-shaped, fragrant, double, pale pink flowers that age to white are produced from mid-summer to early autumn. Matt, dark green leaves. H 1.2m (4ft)
S 1.2m (4ft).

Rosa **'L.D. Braithwaite'**
Large, double, fragrant, bright-crimson flowers are produced in succession from mid-summer to early autumn. Matt, grey-green leaves. H 1m (3ft)
S 1.2m (4ft).

Rosa **'Louise Odier'**
Fragrant, double, mauve-tinged pink flowers are borne from mid-

summer to early autumn. Matt, pale green leaves. H 2m (6ft) S 1.2m (4ft).

Rosa **'Mary Rose'**
Cup-shaped, double, fragrant, rose-pink flowers are borne in succession from mid-summer to early autumn. Matt, mid-green leaves. H 1.2m (4ft) S 1m (3ft).

Rosa **'Madame Pierre Oger'**
Very fragrant, double, pale silvery-pink flowers are produced in succession from mid-summer to early autumn. Matt, pale green leaves. H 2m (6ft) S 1.2m (4ft).

Rosa moyesii **'Geranium'**
Scented, single, cream-centred, bright red flowers are produced during late spring and early summer. Matt, dark-green leaves. H 2.5m (8ft) S 1.5m (5ft).

Rosa **'Penelope'**
Semi-double, fragrant, pale creamy-pink flowers are produced from early summer to early autumn. Matt, dark green, bronze-tinged leaves. H 1m (3ft)
S 1m (3ft).

Rosa **'Queen of Denmark'**
Double, very fragrant, deep to light pink flowers in a single flush appear in mid-summer. Matt, grey-green foliage. H 1.5 (5ft)
S 1.2m (4ft).

Rosa **'Rose de Rescht'**
Double, mauve-red flowers that age to magenta-pink are produced

in a single flush in mid-summer. Matt, mid-green leaves. H 90cm (32in) S 75cm (30in).

Rosa **'Roseraie de l'Haÿ'**
Strongly fragrant, double, red-purple flowers are borne in succession from mid-summer to early autumn. H 2.2m (7ft)
S 2m (6ft).

Rosa rugosa **'Rubra'**
Fragrant, single, yellow-centred, purple-red flowers are produced in succession from mid-summer to early autumn, followed by attractive red or orange-red rosehips. H 2.5m (8ft)
S 2.5m (8ft).

Rosa **'Sharifa Asma'**
Rose-pink, fragrant, double flowers are borne from mid-summer to early autumn. Matt, mid-green leaves. H 100cm (36in) S 75cm (30in).

Rosa **'William Lobb'**
Fragrant, semi-double, purple-magenta flowers that age to lavender are produced during early summer and mid-summer. Matt, dark green leaves. H 2m (6ft)
S 2m (6ft).

Rosa **'Winchester Cathedral'**
Double, cup-shaped, white flowers are produced in succession from mid-summer to early autumn. Matt, mid-green leaves.
H 1.2m (4ft) S 1.2m (4ft).

Rosa xanthina **'Canary Bird'**
Musk-scented, single, yellow flowers are produced in a single flush during late spring. Matt, fern-like, grey-green leaves.
H 3m (10ft) S 4m (13ft).

PATIO ROSE
These are compact floribunda roses that produce masses of flowers throughout the summer and autumn months and can be used at the front of the border or in containers.

Rosa **'Golden Anniversary'**
Large, semi-double, fragrant, apricot-pink flowers are produced from mid-summer to early autumn. Glossy, mid-green leaves. H 45cm (18in) S 45cm (18in).

Rosa **'Happy Anniversary'**
Sweetly fragrant, deep-pink flowers appear in succession from mid-summer to early autumn. Glossy, dark green leaves.
H 80cm (32in) S 75cm (30in).

Rosa **'Happy Birthday'**
Double, creamy-white flowers are produced in succession from mid-summer to early autumn and Glossy, mid-green leaves.
H 45cm (18in) S 45cm (18in).

Rosa **'Pearl Anniversary'**
Semi-double, pearl-pink flowers are produced in succession from mid-summer to early autumn. Glossy, mid-green leaves.
H 60cm (24in) S 60cm (24in).

Rosa **'Queen Mother'**
Cup-shaped, semi-double, pink flowers appear in succession from mid-summer to early autumn. Glossy, mid-green leaves.
H 40cm (16in) S 60cm (24in).

Rosa **'Sweet Dream'**
Fragrant, cup-shaped, double, peach-apricot flowers are produced in succession from mid-summer to early autumn. Glossy, dark-green leaves. H 40cm (16in)
S 35cm (14in).

GROUND-COVER ROSE
These are low-growing and spreading roses that produce masses of small blooms and offer good disease resistance. As this category name suggests, they are very useful for covering the ground and also preventing weeds.

Rosa **'Kent'**
Slightly fragrant, semi-double, white flowers appear from mid-summer to early autumn, followed by small red hips. H 45cm (18in)
S 100cm (36in).

Rosa **'Oxfordshire'**
Slightly fragrant, semi-double, pale pink flowers are produced in succession from mid-summer to early autumn. H 60cm (24in)
S 150cm (60in).

Rosa **'Suffolk'**
Single, slightly fragrant, golden-centred, deep-scarlet flowers are borne in succession from

Rosa 'Queen Mother'

mid-summer to early autumn, followed by orange-red rosehips. H 45cm (18in) S 100cm (36in).

Rosa 'Surrey'
The cup-shaped, fragrant, double rose-pink flowers of 'Surrey' are produced in succession from mid-summer to early autumn. Matt, dark green leaves. H 80cm (32in) S 120cm (48in).

Rosa 'Sussex'
The slightly fragrant, double, apricot flowers of 'Sussex' are borne in succession from mid-summer to early autumn. The flowers are borne above, mid-green leaves. H 60cm (24in) S 100cm (36in).

ROSMARINIUS
Rosemary
A small genus of just two species, grown for their early summer flowers and aromatic foliage. Widely used in culinary dishes. Good for a sunny border or can be trimmed into a dense hedge.
Cultivation Grow in any well-drained garden soil that is poor or reasonably fertile and in full sun. In colder areas, choose a sunny spot that is sheltered from cold winds or grow in a pot. Use a soil-based mix. Feed monthly during the growing season and water as necessary.
Pruning To keep neat and bushy, cut back the previous year's growth to within 10cm (4in) of the main framework or the ground during mid-spring. Trim hedges after flowering.
Propagation Take semi-ripe cuttings in mid-summer or late summer.

Rosmarinus officinalis
Common rosemary
An evergreen culinary herb that forms a dense and rounded bush bearing purple-blue flowers during late spring and early summer along the stems of evergreen, strongly aromatic, dark green leaves. Good choice for growing as a hedge. H 1.5m (5ft) S 1.5m (5ft).
Named varieties: 'Miss Jessopp's Upright', vigorous, upright-growing rosemary, purple-blue flowers. H 2m (6ft) S 2m (6ft). 'Majorca Pink', compact, pale pink flowers. H 1m (3ft) S 1m (3ft). 'Severn Sea', arching stems carry bright blue flowers. H 1m (3ft) S 1.5m (5ft).
Aspect: sun
Hardiness: ✽✽ Zone: 9

RUBUS
A genus of about 250 species, including the tough, thicket-forming deciduous shrubs here, grown for their summer flowers and striking winter stems.
Cultivation Grow in any well-drained, reasonably fertile soil in full sun or dappled shade. Site those grown for winter stems where they will catch winter sun.
Pruning For the best flowering and stems cut back one in three stems near to ground level during early spring. Rejuvenate neglected plants by cutting back stems to near ground level in early spring.
Propagation Layer shoots or dig up rooted suckers in mid-spring.

Rubus biflorus
A prickly-stemmed, deciduous shrub with a brilliant white bloom when young. Small white flowers appear during late summer and early autumn, followed by yellow fruits. H 3m (10ft) S 3m (10ft).
Aspect: sun
Hardiness: ✽✽✽ Zones: 7–8

Rubus cockburnianus
Thicket-forming deciduous shrub with prickly purple stems that have a brilliant white bloom when young. Insignificant purple flowers are produced during late summer and early autumn, followed by black, inedible fruits. H 2.5m (8ft) S 2.5m (8ft).
Aspect: sun
Hardiness: ✽✽✽ Zones: 7–8

Rubus odoratus
Flowering raspberry
Fragrant, rose-pink, cup-shaped flowers appear from early summer to early autumn on this vigorous thicket-forming, deciduous shrub. H 2.5m (8ft) S 2.5m (8ft).
Aspect: sun or semi-shade
Hardiness: ✽✽✽ Zones: 7–8

Rosa 'Sussex'

Rosmarinus officinalis

Rubus odoratus

Ruta

RUTA
Rue

A genus of over five species that includes the evergreen shrub featured here, grown for their summer flowers and feathery aromatic foliage. An ideal choice for a sunny mixed border or can be trimmed to make a low hedge.
Cultivation Grow in any reasonably fertile, well-drained garden soil in full sun or dappled shade. Wear gloves and long sleeves when working with rue, as contact with the leaves can cause painful skin blistering in sunlight.
Pruning To keep plants neat and compact, cut back hard during mid-spring. Trim hedges after flowering.
Propagation Sow seed in early spring. Take semi-ripe cuttings in late summer.

Ruta graveolens 'Jackman's Blue'
This compact, rounded form has aromatic, steel-blue feathery leaves and tiny, mustard-coloured flowers from early summer to late summer). H 60cm (24in) S 75cm (30in).
Aspect: sun or semi-shade
Hardiness: ✿✿✿ Zones: 7–8

SALIX
Willow

This is a large and varied genus of some 300 species, including the low-growing deciduous shrubs featured here. They are grown for their silvery catkins and colourful bark. Compact and slow-growing varieties make excellent specimen plants for a small, sunny garden.

Willow trees to grow as shrubs

A few willow trees can be kept to shrub-like proportions by annual pruning. Cut all stems to near-ground level in March (early spring) every year.
Salix alba 'Chermesina'
Bright red winter stems. H 3m (10ft) S 3m (10ft).

Salix alba subsp. *vitellina* 'Britzensis'

Fiery orange-red winter stems. H 3m (10ft) S 3m (10ft).

Salix daphnoides
Violet-purple young stems with a white bloom. H 3m (10ft) S 3m (10ft).

Salix irrorata
Purple young stems with a white bloom. H 3m (10ft) S 3m (10ft).

Cultivation Grow in any moisture-retentive, well-drained garden soil in full sun.
Pruning No routine pruning is necessary other than removing wayward or damaged stems in early spring.
Propagation Take hardwood cuttings in late winter.

Salix hastata 'Wehrhahnii'
A neat, slow-growing shrub with dark purple shoots and bright green leaves that turn yellow in autumn. Large, silvery catkins appear in early spring on bare stems before the leaves emerge. H 1m (3ft) S 1m (3ft).
Aspect: sun
Hardiness: ✿✿✿ Zones: 7–8

Salix lanata
Woolly willow
This compact, slow-growing and bushy shrub produces stumpy shoots that are white and woolly when young. Small yellow catkins are borne in mid-spring as the leaves emerge. H 1m (3ft) S 1.5m (5ft).
Aspect: sun
Hardiness: ✿✿✿ Zones: 7–8

SALVIA
Sage

This huge genus of around 900 species, includes the evergreen sub-shrubs featured here, are grown for their handsome aromatic foliage and widely used in culinary dishes. Grow in a mixed or herb border or in a container on a sunny patio.
Cultivation In the garden, grow in a moisture-retentive, well-drained soil that is reasonably fertile and in full sun or dappled shade. In pots, grow in any fresh general-purpose compost (soil mix).
Pruning To keep plants neat and compact, cut back hard to near ground level during mid-spring.

Replace neglected plants.
Propagation Sow seed in early spring. Take semi-ripe cuttings in early autumn.

Salvia officinalis
Common sage
An evergreen culinary herb with grey-green aromatic foliage that carries spikes of lilac-blue flowers borne from late spring to mid-summer. H 80cm (32in) S 100cm (36in).
Named varieties: 'Icterina', variegated form with yellow-edged green leaves, mauve-blue flowers. H 80cm (32in) S 100cm (36in). 'Purpurascens', bright purple young leaves age to grey-green, mauve-blue flowers. H 80cm (32in) S 100cm (36in). 'Tricolor', grey-green leaves, splashed with cream and reddish-purple, mauve-blue flowers. H 80cm (32in) S 100cm (36in).
Aspect: sun or semi-shade
Hardiness: ✿✿✿ Zones: 7–8

SAMBUCUS
Elder

A genus of about 25 species grown for their handsome foliage and summer flowers. Useful back-of-the-border plants. They are ideal for filling gaps.
Cultivation Grow in a moisture-retentive, well-drained garden soil that is reasonably fertile in full sun or dappled shade.
Pruning To get the best foliage displays, cut back hard to near ground level during early spring each year. For flowers and berries, cut back one stem in three during the dormant season, starting with the oldest.
Propagation Take hardwood cuttings in late winter.

Sambucus nigra 'Black Beauty'
A new variety with near-black, darkest burgundy foliage that contrasts with the flat heads of lemon-scented pale-pink flowers during early summer, followed by purple-black berries in autumn. H 3m (10ft) S 3m (10ft).
Aspect: sun or semi-shade
Hardiness: ✿✿✿ Zones: 7–8

Sambucus nigra 'Black Lace'
An exciting recent introduction with near-black, finely cut foliage

Salix vitellina 'Britzensis'

Salvia officinalis

Sambucus racemosa 'Plumosa Aurea'

that provides a foil for the flat heads of pale-pink flowers that open from cream-coloured buds during late spring and early summer. Good choice for small gardens. H 3m (10ft) S 2m (6ft).
Aspect: sun or semi-shade
Hardiness: ❋❋❋ Zones: 7–8

Sambucus racemosa 'Plumosa Aurea'

Emerging bronze-tinted, the deeply cut, almost feathery, foliage turns golden yellow as it matures. Arching shoots bear conical clusters of creamy-yellow flowers during mid-spring. Grow in dappled shade to avoid scorching the delicate foliage. H 3m (10ft) S 3m (10ft).
Aspect: sun or semi-shade
Hardiness: ❋❋❋ Zones: 7–8

Sambucus racemosa 'Sutherland Gold'

The deeply cut, almost feathery, foliage emerges bronze-tinted before turning golden yellow with age. Conical clusters of creamy-yellow flowers during mid-spring are followed by glossy red fruits. H 3m (10ft) S 3m (10ft).
Aspect: sun or semi-shade
Hardiness: ❋❋❋ Zones: 7–8

SANTOLINA

A genus of nearly 20 species, including the compact evergreen

shrubs featured here, grown for their grey, aromatic foliage and button-like summer flowers. Ideal for a hot spot, such as sunny banks and gravel gardens, or edging sunny borders. They can even make an attractive low, informal flowering hedge or garden divider.
Cultivation Grow in any well-drained garden soil that is poor to reasonably fertile and in full sun, but sheltered from cold winds.
Pruning To keep plants neat and compact, cut back to 5cm (2in) off ground level during mid-spring before new growth emerges. Neglected plants can be rejuvenated by cutting back hard into old wood during mid-spring

Santolina pinnata

to encourage new growth from lower down. Deadhead edging plants and hedges to keep neat all summer.
Propagation Take semi-ripe cuttings in early autumn.

Santolina chamaecyparissus var. nana
Cotton lavender

Feathery, greyish-white, aromatic leaves set off the masses of tiny, lemon-yellow button-like flowers throughout mid-summer and late summer on this dense and rounded evergreen shrub. H 30cm (12in) S 45cm (18in).
Aspect: sun
Hardiness: ❋❋ Zones: 7–8

Santolina chamaecyparissus 'Lambrook Silver'
Cotton lavender

The silvery mound of finely dissected woolly leaves that this shrub produces are the perfect foil for the tiny lemon-yellow and button-like flowers that are borne during mid-summer and late summer. H 30cm (12in) S 45cm (18in).
Aspect: sun
Hardiness: ❋❋ Zone: 9

SARCOCOCCA
Sweet box

A genus of around 15 species, including the dense-growing, evergreen shrubs featured here, grown for their neat habit and sweet vanilla-scented winter flowers. An ideal choice for a dark, shady corner where nothing else will grow. Well suited to

Santolina chamaecyparissus var. nana

Sarcococca confusa

urban gardens as it is pollution tolerant.
Cultivation Grow in a moisture-retentive, well-drained garden soil that is reasonably fertile and in dappled or deep shade.
Pruning No routine pruning is necessary. Remove any damaged growth in mid-spring.
Propagation Take hardwood cuttings in mid-autumn.

Sarcococca confusa

A dense, evergreen shrub with glossy, dark green leaves that bears clusters of sweetly scented white flowers from early winter to early spring. H 2m (6ft) S 1m (3ft).
Aspect: semi-shade to deep shade
Hardiness: ❋❋❋ Zones: 6–9

Sarcococca hookeriana var. digyna

A thicket-forming shrub with slender, pointed, dark green leaves and small creamy-white or pink-tinged flowers that are produced in clusters from early winter to early spring. H 1.5m (5ft) S 2m (6ft).
Aspect: semi-shade to deep shade
Hardiness: ❋❋❋ 6–9

Sarcococca hookeriana var. humilis (syn. S. humilis)

Compact, clump-forming evergreen shrub with slender dark green leaves and small, creamy-white or pink-tinged flowers produced in clusters from early winter to early spring. H 60cm (24in) S 100cm (36in).
Aspect: semi-shade to deep shade
Hardiness: ❋❋❋ 6–9

Skimmia japonica 'Rubella'

SKIMMIA

A small genus of just four species, including the compact evergreen shrubs featured here, grown for their fragrant flowers, neat foliage and long-lasting colourful autumn berries. They make useful border fillers in shade. Compact forms make excellent winter pots.
Cultivation Grow in a moisture-retentive, well-drained garden soil that is reasonably fertile and in dappled or deep shade. In containers, grow in any fresh general-purpose soil mix. To be sure of berries, grow both male and female forms.
Pruning No routine pruning is necessary. Remove any damaged growth in mid-spring.
Propagation Take semi-ripe cuttings in early autumn.

Skimmia japonica 'Rubella' (male form)
A compact shrub with handsome, red-margined, dark green leaves and dense clusters of deep red flower-buds in autumn that do not open until early spring to reveal fragrant white flowers. H 1.5m (5ft) S 1.5m (5ft).
Aspect: semi-shade to deep shade
Hardiness: ❁❁❁ Zones: 7–8

Skimmia japonica subsp. reevesiana (hermaphrodite form)
A large, spreading, evergreen shrub with narrow, tapered, dark green leaves and clusters of white flowers during mid-spring and late spring, followed by bright red berries. H 7m (23ft) S 1m (3ft).
Named varieties: 'Robert Fortune', dark-edged, pale green leaves, white flowers, followed by bright red berries. H 7m (23ft) S 1m (3ft).
Aspect: semi-shade to deep shade
Hardiness: ❁❁❁ Zones: 7–8

Skimmia x confusa 'Kew Green' (male form)
Dome-shaped, compact, evergreen shrub with aromatic, pointed, leaves that set off the dense clusters of sweetly scented, cream-coloured flowers produced during mid-spring and late spring. H 3m (10ft) S 1.5m (5ft).
Aspect: semi-shade to deep shade
Hardiness: ❁❁❁ Zones: 7–8

SOPHORA

A genus of about 50 species, including the evergreen shrubs featured here, grown for their clusters of bell-shaped flowers that hang from zigzag shoots covered in symmetrical leaves that are tiny, oval, dark green leaflets. Good seasonal specimens for a sunny border, or can be trained against a wall or fence.
Cultivation Grow in any well-drained garden soil in full sun. Grow against a sunny wall in colder areas.
Pruning No routine pruning is necessary. Remove any wayward or damaged growth in mid-spring.
Propagation Sow seed in early spring.

Sophora microphylla (syn. Edwardia microphylla)
Open, spreading, frost-hardy evergreen shrub that carries pendent clusters of pea-shaped yellow flowers from arching branches during mid-spring and late spring. H 8m (26ft) S 8m (26ft).
Named varieties: 'Sun King', a recent fully hardy introduction that forms a more compact, but still open, bushy shrub with drooping clusters of bell-shaped

Sophora microphylla

yellow flowers during early spring and mid-spring. H 3m (10ft) S 3m (10ft).
Aspect: sun
Hardiness: ❁❁ or ❁❁❁
Zones: 7–9

SPARTIUM
Spanish broom
A genus of just one species of deciduous shrubs grown for their long-lasting and fragrant golden summer flowers. Good border filler or back-of-the-border shrub for a sunny spot. Pollution- and salt-tolerant, they are therefore well-suited for growing in town and coastal gardens.
Cultivation Grow in any well-drained, reasonably fertile, garden soil in full sun. Grow by a sunny wall in colder areas.
Pruning Prevent it going woody at the base and encourage flowering by trimming new growth lightly directly after flowering.
Propagation Sow seed in early spring.

Spartium junceum
A slender shrub with dark green shoots that carries masses of pea-like flowers in succession from early summer to late summer, followed by dark brown seed-pods. H 3m (10ft) S 3m (10ft).
Aspect: sun
Hardiness: ❁❁ Zone: 9

SPIRAEA
A genus of about 80 species, including the easy-to-grow, deciduous, summer-flowering shrubs featured here, some of

Spartium junceum

which are grown mainly for their eye-catching foliage. A useful border filler in sun or can be grown as an informal low hedge.
Cultivation Grow in a moisture-retentive, well-drained, reasonably fertile soil in full sun.
Pruning Varieties that flower on the previous season's growth need no routine pruning. Otherwise, cut out one stem in three during early spring, starting with the oldest. Informal hedges should be trimmed after flowering. Remove all-green reverted shoots on variegated varieties as soon as they appear.
Propagation Take semi-ripe cuttings in mid-summer, or hardwood cuttings in late autumn.

Spiraea 'Arguta'
Bridal wreath
Beautiful arching sprays of tiny, saucer-shaped, white flowers dominate this dense, rounded shrub during mid-spring and late spring. H 2.5m (8ft)
S 2.5m (8ft).
Aspect: sun
Hardiness: ✾✾✾ Zones: 7–8

Spiraea japonica 'Anthony Waterer'
Emerging bronze-tinted, the sharply toothed foliage matures to

dark green with pink and cream margins. Flat heads of rose-pink flowers appear from mid-summer to late summer. Good informal hedge. H 1.5m (5ft)
S 1.5m (5ft).
Aspect: sun
Hardiness: ✾✾✾ Zones 7–8

Spiraea japonica 'Goldflame'
Bronze-red emerging foliage turns bright yellow and then ages to luminous green on this compact shrub. Dark pink flowers are borne in clusters during mid-summer and late summer. Good informal hedge. H 75cm (30in)
S 75cm (30in).
Aspect: sun
Hardiness: ✾✾✾ Zones: 7–8

Spiraea japonica 'Golden Princess'
The foliage emerges bronze-red on this clump-forming shrub before turning bright yellow then red in autumn. Purplish-pink flowers are produced in clusters during mid-summer and late summer. H 2m (6ft)
S 1.5m (5ft).
Aspect: sun
Hardiness: ✾✾✾ Zones: 7–8

Spiraea nipponica 'Snowmound' (syn. S. nipponica var. tosaensis)
The rounded, dark green leaves of

Stephandra incisa 'Crispa'

this spreading deciduous shrub make the perfect backdrop for the arching sprays of cup-shaped white flowers that are produced throughout early summer and mid-summer. H 2.5m (8ft)
S 2.5m (8ft).
Aspect: sun
Hardiness: ✾✾✾ Zones: 7–8

Spiraea prunifolia (syn. S. prunifolia 'Plena')
Finely toothed, bright green leaves that are silvery beneath, cover this deciduous shrub, which has arching stems that are wreathed in double white flowers throughout early spring and mid-spring.
H 2m (6ft) S 2m (6ft).
Aspect: sun
Hardiness: ✾✾✾ Zones: 7–8

Spiraea thunbergii
From mid-spring to early summer, arching sprays of tiny, saucer-shaped, white flowers cover this dense and bushy deciduous shrub. The pale green leaves turn yellow in autumn. H 1.5m (5ft)
S 2m (6ft).
Aspect: sun
Hardiness: ✾✾✾ Zones: 7–8

STEPHANANDRA
This is a small genus comprising just four species, including the deciduous early summer-flowering shrubs featured here. These plants make useful front-of-the-border fillers when planted in sun or

dappled shade. They can also be used for edging or ground cover.
Cultivation Grow in a moisture-retentive, well-drained garden soil that is reasonably fertile in full sun or dappled shade.
Pruning Prune out one stem in three during early spring, starting with the oldest.
Propagation Take semi-ripe cuttings in mid-summer or hardwood cuttings in late autumn.

Stephanandra incisa 'Crispa'
The deeply lobed and wavy-edged leaves cover this thicket-forming, low-growing shrub and turn orange-yellow in autumn before they fall to reveal rich brown stems. This shrub makes a good edging and ground cover plant.
H 60cm (24in) S 3m (10ft).
Aspect: sun or semi-shade
Hardiness: ✾✾✾ Zones: 7–8

Stephanandra tanakae
This is a thicket-forming, bushy shrub that has striking bright orange-brown stems that are revealed during the winter. The arching shoots are covered in toothed green leaves at other times before turning shades of yellow and orange in autumn. Bears greenish-yellow flowers throughout the summer.
H 3m (10ft) S 3m (10ft).
Aspect: sun or semi-shade
Hardiness: ✾✾✾ Zones: 7–8

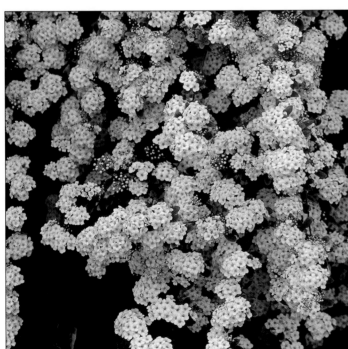
Spirea 'Arguta'

Symphoricarpos x doorenbosii 'Mother of Pearl'

SYMPHORICARPOS
Snowberry

A genus of over 15 species, including the deciduous thicket-forming shrubs featured here, grown mainly for their handsome foliage or long-lasting, marble-sized, autumn berries. Useful border fillers in sun or dappled shade. They make attractive informal low hedges.

Cultivation Grow in any reasonably fertile, well-drained soil in full sun or dappled shade.

Pruning For brightly coloured foliage displays, prune out one stem in three during early spring, starting with the oldest. Informal hedges can be trimmed every couple of months during the summer to keep neat.

Propagation Take semi-ripe cuttings in early summer or hardwood cuttings in late autumn.

Symphoricarpos x chenaultii 'Hancock'
Low-growing and spreading snowberry that has green leaves that turn orange-red in autumn. Small bell-shaped flowers are produced in late summer, followed by conspicuous dark pink berries. H 3m (10ft) S 3m (10ft).
Aspect: sun or semi-shade
Hardiness: ❀❀❀ Zones: 7–8

Symphoricarpos x doorenbosii 'Mother of Pearl'
A thicket-forming shrub with dark green leaves and arching stems that carry small, bell-shaped

flowers during mid-summer, followed by conspicuous pearl-like pink-flushed white berries from early autumn. The best fruiting variety. H 2m (6ft) S indefinite.
Aspect: sun or semi-shade
Hardiness: ❀❀❀ Zones: 7–8

Symphoricarpos orbiculatus 'Albovariegatus'
A compact, thicket-forming shrub with variegated white and green leaves on a dense and busy shrub. Few berries are produced.
H 2m (6ft) S 2m (6ft).
Aspect: sun or semi-shade
Hardiness: ❀❀❀ Zones: 7–8

SYRINGA
Lilac

A genus of about 20 species including the large, spreading deciduous shrubs featured here, grown for their highly fragrant spring flowers. They make useful seasonal specimens and can be trained into attractive multi-stemmed trees.

Cultivation Grow in a moisture-retentive, well-drained neutral to alkaline soil that is reasonably fertile and in full sun.

Pruning After flowering, cut back the fading flowering shoots to the first leaves below the flower cluster. In the dormant season thin out overcrowded branches and rejuvenate neglected shrubs by cutting the whole shrub back to within 1m (3ft) of the ground. Create a multi-stemmed tree by selecting three, four or five of the strongest stems, removing all others and cutting off side branches in successive seasons to raise the height of the canopy. All major pruning should be carried out during the dormant season (early winter to early spring).

Propagation Bud named varieties during mid-summer.

Syringa meyeri var. *spontanea* 'Palibin'
Fragrant, purple-pink flowers are produced in dense clusters throughout late spring and early summer on this slow-growing Korean lilac. Ideal for small gardens. H 2m (10ft) S 1.5m (5ft).
Aspect: sun
Hardiness: ❀❀❀ Zones: 7–8

Syringa pubescens subsp. *microphylla* 'Superba'
The oval green leaves provide a backdrop for the rose-pink fragrant flowers that are borne in dense clusters during mid-spring and late spring and intermittently thereafter until mid-autumn.
H 6m (20ft) S 6m (20ft).
Aspect: sun
Hardiness: ❀❀❀ Zones: 7–8

Syringa vulgaris 'Charles Joly'
A spreading shrub with heart-shaped, dark green leaves and dense, cone-shaped clusters of double, dark purple flowers in late spring and early summer.
H 7m (23ft) S 7m (23ft).
Aspect: sun
Hardiness: ❀❀❀ Zones: 7–8

Syringa vulgaris 'Katherine Havemeyer'
Dense, cone-shaped clusters of purple buds open during late spring and early summer to reveal strongly scented, double, lavender-purple flowers above heart-shaped leaves. H 7m (23ft) S 7m (23ft).
Aspect: sun
Hardiness: ❀❀❀ Zones: 7–8

Syringa vulgaris 'Madame Lemoine'
This elegant white lilac produces dense, cone-shaped clusters of very fragrant, double, white flowers during late spring and early summer above heart-shaped, apple-green leaves. H 7m (23ft) S 7m (23ft).
Aspect: sun
Hardiness: ❀❀❀ Zones: 7–8

Syringa protolaciniata

Syringa x josiflexa

Syringa vulgaris 'Michel Buchner'
A spreading shrub with heart-shaped, dark green leaves and large, cone-shaped clusters of fragrant, double, rose-mauve flowers with white centres during late spring and early summer.
H 7m (23ft) S 7m (23ft).
Aspect: sun
Hardiness: ❀❀❀ Zones: 7–8

TAMARIX
Tamerix

A genus of over 50 species, including the deciduous shrubs featured here, grown for their feathery, late-summer flowerheads. A good back-of-the-border shrub that makes an excellent windbreak in mild coastal gardens.

Cultivation Grow in any well-drained garden soil in full sun, but sheltered from cold winds.

Pruning To keep in shape, prune flowering stems in early spring, removing half to two-thirds of the previous year's growth.

Propagation Take hardwood cuttings in mid-autumn.

Tamarix ramosissima (syn. *T. pentandra*)
A vigorous shrub with graceful, arching, red-brown stems that carry airy, plume-like, pale pink flowers in dense clusters during late summer and early autumn.
H 5m (16ft) S 5m (16ft).
Named varieties: 'Pink Cascade',

Tamarix 'Rubra'

plumes of tiny, rich pink flowers.
H 5m (16ft) S 5m (16ft).
Aspect: sun
Hardiness: ❀❀❀ Zones: 7–8

Tamarix 'Rubra'

A vigorous shrub with graceful,
arching stems that carry airy,
plume-like, purple-pink flowers in
dense clusters during late summer
and early autumn. H 5m (16ft)
S 5m (16ft).
Aspect: sun
Hardiness: ❀❀❀ Zones: 7–8

TIBOUCHINA

A large genus of over 350 species,
including the spreading tender
evergreen shrub featured here,
grown for its exotic summer

Tibouchina semi-decandra

flowers. An attractive border filler
in warm gardens. Grow in a
container in cooler areas.
Cultivation Grow in a moisture-
retentive, well-drained garden soil
in full sun. In containers, grow in
a soil-based compost (soil mix).
Feed every month throughout the
growing season and water as
necessary. Move to a warm spot
undercover when the temperature
falls below 5°C (41°F) and water
sparingly throughout the winter.
Pruning No routine pruning is
necessary.
Propagation Take softwood
cuttings in mid-spring or semi-
ripe cuttings in mid-summer.

Tibouchina urvilleana (syn. *Pleroma macrantha. T. semidecandra*) Brazilian spider flower

A tall, spreading shrub with
velvety, dark green leaves that are
distinctively veined. Large saucer-
shaped rich purple flowers with a
satin finish are borne from mid-
summer to late autumn. H 4m
(12ft) S 5m (16ft).
Aspect: sun
Hardiness: tender Zones: 10+

VIBURNUM

A varied genus of over 150
species, including the deciduous
and evergreen shrubs featured
here, grown for their clusters of
winter or spring flowers or eye-

catching autumn berries. Most are
good border fillers, with many
coping well with a partly shady
shrub border or woodland-edge
planting scheme. The winter-
flowering deciduous varieties and
fruiting evergreen forms are
useful for adding interest during
the coldest months.
Cultivation Grow in a moisture-
retentive, well-drained garden soil
that is reasonably fertile and in
full sun or dappled shade.
Pruning Evergreen varieties require
no routine pruning. Damaged or
misplaced shoots can be removed
in late spring. If required,
deciduous varieties can be thinned
by removing one stem in three,
starting with the oldest. Prune
winter-flowering varieties during
mid-spring and summer-flowering
varieties in early summer.
Propagation Layer deciduous
shrubs in mid-spring. Take
hardwood cuttings in mid-autumn
or semi-ripe cuttings of evergreen
varieties in early autumn.

EVERGREEN VIBURNUMS
Viburnum davidii

A compact, evergreen shrub with
prominently veined, dark green
leaves that bears small flat heads
of white flowers during late
spring followed by eyecatching
metallic, turquoise-blue berries.
H 1.5m (5ft) S 1.5m (5ft).
Aspect: sun or semi-shade
Hardiness: ❀❀❀ Zones: 7–8

Viburnum x burkwoodii

Clusters of pink buds open on
this lovely viburnum during mid-

Viburnum tinus 'Eve Price'

spring and late spring to expose
deliciously fragrant white flowers
that are followed by red fruit.
H 2.5m (8ft) S 2.5m (8ft).
Aspect: sun or semi-shade
Hardiness: ❀❀❀ Zones: 7–8

Viburnum 'Eskimo'

This is a compact, semi-evergreen
viburnum that produces lovely
round clusters of pink-tinged,
cream buds that open during mid-
spring and late spring to show off
its white tubular flowers against
glossy, dark green leaves.
H 1.5m (5ft) S 1.5m (5ft).
Aspect: sun or semi-shade
Hardiness: ❀❀❀ Zones: 7–8

Viburnum rhytidophyllum

This is a spreading, evergreen
viburnum that bears flat clusters
of cream-coloured flowers
throughout late spring. They are
produced at the ends of arching
shoots of wavy-edged, dark green
leaves. Red berries follow in
autumn. H 3m (10ft)
S 4m (12ft).
Aspect: sun or semi-shade
Hardiness: ❀❀❀ Zones: 7–8

Viburnum tinus 'Eve Price'

Small flatheads of carmine-pink
buds reveal pinkish-white flowers
from early winter to mid-spring
and are followed by dark blue-
black berries. H 3m (10ft)
S 3m (10ft).
Aspect: sun or semi-shade
Hardiness: ❀❀❀ Zones: 7–8

Viburnum tinus 'French White'

This viburnum produces flat
heads of rosy-red buds open in
succession from early winter to
mid-spring to reveal white flowers
that are followed by dark blue-
black berries. H 3m (10ft)
S 3m (10ft).
Aspect: sun or semi-shade
Hardiness: ❀❀❀ Zones: 7–8

Viburnum tinus 'Gwenllian'

Masses of dark pink buds open in
succession on this shrub from
early winter to mid-spring to
reveal pink-flushed white flowers,
that are followed by a profusion
of dark, blue-black berries.
H 3m (10ft) S 3m (10ft).
Aspect: sun or semi-shade
Hardiness: ❀❀❀ Zones: 7–8

Viburnum opulus 'Roseum'

Viburnum plicatum 'Mariesii'

DECIDUOUS VIBURNUMS

Viburnum x bodnantense 'Dawn'

An upright deciduous shrub that carries dense clusters of fragrant dark pink flowers on bare stems from late autumn to early spring. H 3m (10ft) S 2m (6ft).
Aspect: sun or semi-shade
Hardiness: ❋❋❋ Zones: 7–8

Viburnum x bodnantense 'Charles Lamont'

Strongly scented, bright pink flowers are carried in dense clusters on bare stems from late autumn to early spring on this upright deciduous shrub. H 3m (10ft) S 2m (6ft).
Aspect: sun or semi-shade
Hardiness: ❋❋❋ Zones: 7–8

Viburnum x carlcephalum

Rounded clusters of pink buds open during mid-spring and late spring to reveal fragrant white flowers against heart-shaped, dark-green leaves, that turn red in autumn. H 3m (10ft) S 3m (10ft).
Aspect: sun or semi-shade
Hardiness: ❋❋❋ Zones: 7–8

Viburnum carlesii

Dense clusters of pink buds open throughout mid-spring and late spring into fragrant white or pink-flushed white flowers. The dark green leaves take on red-purple tints in autumn.
H 2m (6ft) S 2m (6ft).
Aspect: sun or semi-shade
Hardiness: ❋❋❋ Zones: 7–8

Viburnum x juddii

Pink buds in rounded clusters open during mid-spring and late spring to reveal fragrant pink-tinted white flowers. The oval, dark green leaves take on red-purple tints in autumn.
H 1.2m (4ft) S 1.5m (5ft).
Aspect: sun or semi-shade
Hardiness: ❋❋❋ Zones: 7–8

Viburnum opulus 'Roseum' (syn. V. 'Sterile') Snowball tree

Rounded, snowball-like clusters of white flowers are produced during late spring and early summer against a backdrop of dark green leaves that become purple-tinted in autumn. H 4m (12ft) S 4m (13ft).
Aspect: sun or semi-shade
Hardiness: ❋❋❋ Zones: 7–8

Viburnum plicatum 'Mariesii' Japanese snowball bush

Tiered branches carry white, lacecap-like flowers throughout late spring over toothed, prominently veined, dark-green leaves that turn red-purple in autumn. H 3m (10ft) S 4m (13ft).
Aspect: sun or semi-shade
Hardiness: ❋❋❋ Zones: 7–8

Viburnum plicatum 'Pink Beauty'

Horizontal, tiered branches of this deciduous shrub show off the white, lacecap-like flowers in late spring that age to pink. The toothed, prominently veined, dark green leaves turn red-purple in autumn. H 3m (10ft) S 4m (13ft).
Aspect: sun or semi-shade
Hardiness: ❋❋❋ Zones: 7–8

VINCA
Periwinkle

This genus of seven species includes the low-growing sub-shrubs featured here, grown for their colourful spring flowers and their weed-smothering carpet of attractive foliage. It makes excellent ground cover in sun or shade as well as a useful addition to winter containers.
Cultivation Grow in a moisture-retentive, well-drained soil that is reasonably fertile and in full sun or dappled shade. Grow in sun for better flowering displays. In containers, grow in any fresh general-purpose compost (soil mix).
Pruning No routine pruning is necessary, other than to keep it within bounds. Neglected plants can be rejuvenated by cutting all stems back to near ground level during late winter.
Propagation Lift and divide clumps as for perennials or separate and pot-up rooted layers.

Vinca major
Greater periwinkle

This is a fast-growing, sprawling, evergreen sub-shrub with large, violet-blue flowers that are

Viburnum carlesii

Vinca minor 'Aureovariegata'

Vinca major

produced in succession from mid-spring to early autumn above dark green leaves. This shrub makes excellent ground cover between deciduous trees and shrubs. H 45cm (18in) S indefinite.
Aspect: sun or semi-shade
Hardiness: ✿✿✿ Zones: 7–8

Vinca minor
Lesser periwinkle
This is a less invasive version of the periwinkle, which has evergreen, lance-shaped, dark green leaves and pale blue flowers borne from mid-spring to early autumn. Good ground cover choice for small areas or for softening the edges of raised beds and containers. H 20cm (8in) S indefinite.
Named varieties: 'Aureovariegata', variegated form with deep purple flowers. H 20cm (18in) S indefinite. 'Gertrude Jekyll', white flowers. H 20cm (8in) S indefinite.
Aspect: sun or semi-shade
Hardiness: ✿✿✿ Zones: 7–8

Vinca minor 'Illumination'
This is a recent introduction that has glossy golden, green-edged leaves on sprawling stems. Light blue flowers are carried in succession from mid-spring to early autumn. Ideal for use in containers or even for trailing over the edge of a hanging basket. H 15m (50ft) S 1m (3ft).
Aspect: sun or semi-shade
Hardiness: ✿✿✿ Zones: 7–8

WEIGELA
A genus of over 10 species, including the summer-flowering deciduous shrubs featured here. These plants can be used all around the garden filling gaps and boosting early summer displays.
Cultivation Grow in any well-drained garden soil that is reasonably fertile and in full sun or dappled shade.
Pruning To keep established shrubs flowering well, cut back one stem in three to near ground level after flowering, starting with the oldest stems.
Propagation Take semi-ripe cuttings in mid-summer or hardwood cuttings in mid-autumn.

Weigela 'Bristol Ruby'
An upright-growing shrub with dark green leaves that is covered in clusters of purple buds. These open into bell-shaped, ruby-red flowers throughout late spring and early summer. H 2.5m (8ft) S 2m (6ft).
Aspect: sun or semi-shade
Hardiness: ✿✿✿ Zones: 7–8

Weigela florida 'Foliis Purpureis'
A deciduous shrub with bronze-green leaves that carries clusters of funnel-shaped, deep pink flowers on arching stems during late spring and early summer. H 1m (3ft) S 5m (16ft).
Aspect: sun or semi-shade
Hardiness: ✿✿✿ Zones: 7–8

Weigela 'Florida Variegata'
Clusters of pale pink funnel-shaped flowers are borne on arching stems throughout late spring and early summer against a

Weigela 'Apple Blossom'

Weigela 'Candida'

backdrop of greyish-green leaves that are edged with white. H 2.5m (8ft) S 2.5m (8ft).
Aspect: sun or semi-shade
Hardiness: ✿✿✿ Zones: 7–8

YUCCA
This genus of about 40 species includes the spiky, evergreen shrubs with sword-shaped leaves featured here. Ideal focal points in a mixed border in sun or shade and provide architectural interest throughout the year.
Cultivation Grow in any well-drained, reasonably fertile soil in full sun or dappled shade. Mulch with gravel to protect the crown.
Pruning Pruning is unnecessary. Remove dead or damaged leaves in mid-spring.
Propagation Separate young offshoots during mid-spring.

Yucca filamentosa
Adam's needle
Spiky clumps of stiff, dark green, sword-shaped leaves provide year-round interest, with the bonus of towering spikes of white, bell-shaped flowers during mid-summer and late summer. H 75cm (30in) S 150cm (60in).
Aspect: sun or semi-shade
Hardiness: ✿✿✿ Zones: 7–8

Yucca flaccida 'Ivory'
Impressive clumps of dark, blue-green, sword-shaped leaves look good all year round, with tall spikes of green-tinged, creamy-white flowers produced in mid-summer and late summer. H 1.5m (5ft) S 1.5m (5ft).
Aspect: sun or semi-shade
Hardiness: ✿✿✿ Zones: 7–8

Yucca flaccida 'Golden Sword'
Clumps of spiky, yellow-striped, sword-shaped, blue-green leaves with green-tinged, creamy-white flowers appearing in mid-summer and late summer. H 55cm (22in) S 150cm (60in).
Aspect: sun or semi-shade
Hardiness: ✿✿✿ Zones: 7–8

Yucca gloriosa 'Variegata'
Spiky clumps of stiff yellow-edged, sword-shaped, dark green leaves are joined by white bell-shaped flowers on vertical spikes from late summer to early autumn. H 2m (6ft) S 2m (6ft).
Aspect: sun or semi-shade
Hardiness: ✿✿✿ Zones: 7–8

Yucca filamentosa

A directory of climbers

This section provides a highly illustrated listing of popular climbers that are available. It demonstrates very clearly just how versatile these plants can be – providing every conceivable colour of bloom, growth achievements and types of foliage. Bearing these factors in mind will enable you to create wonderful effects in any style or size of garden. Increasingly, plants are becoming known by their Latin (botanical) names, so these are given throughout, together with their English (common) names.

The hardiness zones given in the text refer only to the selected main plants featured and not to the whole genus. The height and spread given for each of the plants is an indication only. The dimensions will vary, depending on the growing conditions and the vigour of the individual plants – as well as your ability to care for them. The spread is particularly difficult to predict, as many plants go on increasing their width throughout their lives.

This magnificent climber, *Clematis montana* var. *rubens* 'Elizabeth', tumbles over a wall in full bloom to display its magnificent flowers. It is a prime example of how climbers can enhance any structure in the garden.

Actinidia kolomikta

ACTINIDIA

A genus of about 40 species, including the deciduous, twining climber featured here, which is grown for its seemingly paint-dipped foliage. Useful for adding interest to sunny walls and fences and will quickly cover trellis and arbours. Fast growing, it is an ideal choice for a quick cover-up, too, with a single plant able to smother about two standard fence panels in five years.
Cultivation Grow in any well-drained garden soil that is reasonably fertile and in full sun, but sheltered from strong winds.
Pruning No routine pruning is necessary. Thin out over-crowded stems in late winter. For a quick cover-up, train stems 20cm (8in) apart across the screen and tie in new shoots as necessary. When the screen is complete, cut back new growth to within 15cm (6in) of the established framework of stems in late winter. Neglected plants can be rejuvenated by cutting the oldest stems back to a younger side shoot lower down in late winter.
Propagation Take semi-ripe nodal cuttings in mid-summer.

Actinidia kolomikta
Kolomikta vine
A deciduous climber with dark green, heart-shaped leaves that are splashed pink and white as if the

tips had been dipped in paint. Clusters of fragrant white flowers are produced in early summer.
H 5m (16ft) S 4m (13ft).
Aspect: sun
Hardiness: ❀❀❀ Zone: Min. 7

AKEBIA
Chocolate vine
A genus of around five species, including the semi-evergreen vigorous twining climber featured here, grown for its fragrant chocolate-coloured spring flowers. Good for growing up screens and walls next to an entrance, where its fragrance can be appreciated. It is fairly fast-growing, with a single plant covering one standard fence panel in five years.

Cultivation Grow in a moisture-retentive, well-drained garden soil that is reasonably fertile and in full sun or dappled shade.
Pruning No routine pruning is necessary. Encourage dense growth and keep tidy by trimming in mid-spring. Neglected plants can be rejuvenated by cutting back the oldest stems to a younger side shoot lower down in late winter.
Propagation Take semi-ripe nodal cuttings in late summer or layer suitable stems in mid-autumn.

Akebia quinata
Pendent clusters of maroon-chocolate flowers that have a sweet and spicy fragrance are produced from early to late spring. The lobed dark green foliage becomes purple-tinged in winter. In long, warm summers, large, sausage-shaped fruit can form. H 10m (33ft) S 10m (33ft).
Aspect: sun or semi-shade
Hardiness: ❀❀❀ Zone: Min. 7

AMPELOPSIS
A genus of about 25 species, including the deciduous self-clinging climbers featured here, grown for their unusual flowers, fruit and autumn tints. They make useful and unusual climbers for south- east- and west-facing supports. If grown over a pergola or other similar open support, they can be trained to create an attractive, hanging curtain-effect of foliage.
Cultivation Grow in a moisture-retentive, well-drained garden soil

that is reasonably fertile and in full sun or dappled shade. Grow in full sun for best fruit production.
Pruning No routine pruning is necessary. Thin out over-crowded stems in late winter. For a curtain effect, cut back all new growth to within a couple of buds from the main horizontal framework overhead in late winter.
Propagation Take softwood cuttings in mid-summer.

Ampelopsis aconitifolia (syn. *Vitis aconitifolia*)
This luxuriant vine will cloak any garden structure effortlessly, creating a highly textured curtain of attractively lush foliage. This is a vigorous climber, with palmate dark green leaves, that carries insignificant green flowers during early and mid-summer, followed by showy bunches of orange-red berries. H 12m (40ft)
S 10m (33ft).
Aspect: sun or semi-shade
Hardiness: ❀❀❀ Zone: Min. 7

Ampelopsis glandulosa var. *brevipedunculata* (syn *A. brevipedunculata*)
This plant produces miniature birds' egg-like speckled fruit that change from cream to pink to clear blue as they ripen on this vigorous climber. The fruit follow insignificant green flowers produced during early and mid-summer. H 5m (16ft)
S 6m (20ft).
Aspect: sun or semi-shade
Hardiness: ❀❀❀ Zone: Min. 7

Akebia quinata

Ampelopsis brevipedunculata elegans

Aristolochia littoralis

Ampelopsis megalophylla

A vigorous twining climber with deeply cut foliage that bears insignificant green flowers during early summer, followed by unusual black fruit. H 10m (33ft) S 10m (33ft).
Aspect: sun or semi-shade
Hardiness: ❄❄❄ Zone: Min. 7

ARISTOLOCHIA
Dutchman's pipe

A very large genus of over 300 species, including the tender twining deciduous and evergreen climbers featured here, grown for their intriguing, pipe-shaped summer flowers. In warm gardens they will quickly cover supports with a cloak of handsome foliage to disguise eyesores. Elsewhere, they make an exotic choice for a frost-free conservatory.

Cultivation In the garden, grow in any well-drained garden soil that is reasonably fertile in full sun or dappled shade, but protected from cold winds. In containers, grow in a soil-based compost (soil mix). Feed every month throughout the growing season and water as necessary. Tender plants should be moved to a warm spot undercover when the temperature falls below 7°C (45°F) and watered sparingly during winter.
Pruning No routine pruning is necessary. Cut back wayward stems after flowering.
Propagation Take softwood cuttings in early spring for tender species indoors and in mid-summer for hardy species outside.

Berberidopsis corallina

Aristolochia littoralis
(syn. *A. elegans*)

A tender climber with evergreen kidney-shaped, pale green leaves. During early summer and mid-summer it bears unusual rounded purple flowers, spotted with white. H 10m (33ft) S 10m (33ft).
Aspect: sun or semi-shade
Hardiness: tender Zones: 10–12

Aristolochia macrophylla
(syn. *A. durior, A. sipho*)

A robust, twining, deciduous climber, with dark green, heart-shaped leaves, that bears unusual rounded, green flowers, spotted with yellow, purple and brown, during early summer. H 10m (33ft) S 10m (33ft).
Aspect: sun or semi-shade
Hardiness: ❄❄ Zones: Min. 7

BERBERIDOPSIS

A genus of just one species of evergreen climbers, grown for their eye-catching pendent summer flowers. Useful for adding colour to shady structures.
Cultivation Grow in a moisture-retentive, well-drained neutral to acid soil that is fertile and in dappled shade, but protected from cold winds. In colder regions, apply an insulating mulch in autumn to protect the crown.
Pruning No routine pruning is necessary. Cut back wayward stems in mid-spring.
Propagation Take semi-ripe cuttings in late summer.

Berberidopsis corallina
Coral plant

A twining climber with spiny-edged, dark green, heart-shaped leaves that are lighter beneath.

Strings of dark red flowers hang from shoot tips from early to late summer. 5m (16ft) S 6m (20ft).
Aspect: semi-shade
Hardiness: ❄❄ Zones: Min. 7

BILLARDIERA

This comprises a genus of over five species, including the evergreen climber featured here, which are grown mainly for their colourful fruit. This plant makes an unusual climber for screens and fences and will grow over many different structures, such as fences, arbours, trellis or walls.
Cultivation Grow in a moisture-retentive, well-drained neutral to acid soil that is reasonably fertile and in full sun or dappled shade, but protected from cold winds.
Pruning No routine pruning is necessary.
Propagation Take semi-ripe cuttings in late summer or layer suitable stems in mid-spring.

Billardiera longiflora
Climbing blueberry

This is a twining climber, with lance-shaped, dark green leaves, that bears pale green flowers during early and mid-summer, followed by plum-shaped, violet-purple, red, white or pink fruit. H 2.5m (8ft) S 1m (3ft). The purple colour of the fruit gives it its blueberry common name.
Aspect: sun or semi-shade
Hardiness: ❄❄ Zones: Min. 7

Billardiera longifolia

Bougainvillea

BOUGAINVILLEA

This genus of about 15 species, including the evergreen climbers featured here, is grown for their long-lasting displays of colourful petal-like bracts. All produce stiff thorny stems. It can be grown in gardens where the weather is mild and will quickly cover a large wall. Alternatively, it can be allowed to scramble over the ground. Elsewhere, grow in containers on the patio and give winter protection – they are a good choice for a large, cool conservatory that is frost-free.
Cultivation In the garden, grow in any well-drained soil that is reasonably fertile in full sun. If growing in containers, use a soil-based compost (soil mix). Feed every month throughout the growing season and water as necessary. Move to a cool but frost-free undercover spot when

the temperature falls below 3°C (37°F) and water sparingly throughout the winter.
Pruning No routine pruning is necessary, other than to keep it in within bounds.
Propagation Take softwood cuttings in early spring or semi-ripe cuttings stems in early summer.

Bougainvillea glabra
This is a vigorous evergreen climber with lustrous, dark green leaves, which bears spectacularly attractive sprays of delicate-looking white, pink and red floral bracts from early summer to mid-autumn. It is borderline half-hardy. H 6m (20ft) S 3m (10ft). Named varieties: 'Snow White', sprays of brilliant white floral bracts. H 6m (20ft) S 3m (10ft). 'Variegata' (syn. B. 'Sanderiana'), cream-edged

grey-green leaves and sprays of purple floral bracts. H 6m (20ft) S 3m (10ft).
Aspect: sun
Hardiness: ✤ (borderline)
Zone: Min. 5

Bougainvillea 'Miss Manila' (syn. B. 'Tango')
Spectacular displays of sugar-pink floral bracts are produced in sprays from early summer to mid-autumn against the rounded, lustrous green leaves on this vigorous climber. Borderline half-hardy. H 10m (33ft) S 10m (33ft).
Aspect: sun
Hardiness: ✤ (borderline)
Zone: Min. 5

Bougainvillea 'Raspberry Ice' (syn. B. 'Tropical Rainbow')
Luminescent, cerise-pink, flowering bracts shine out from early summer to mid-autumn on this vigorous-growing bougainvillea. The eye-catching cream-splashed dark green leaves provide year-round interest. Borderline half-hardy. H 10m (33ft) S 10m (33ft).
Aspect: sun
Hardiness: ✤ (borderline)
Zone: Min. 5

Bougainvillea 'Scarlett O'Hara' (syn. B. 'Hawaiian Scarlet')
This vigorous evergreen climber produces sprays of red floral bracts from early summer to

mid-autumn against lustrous dark green leaves. Borderline half-hardy. H 10m (33ft) S 10m (33ft).
Aspect: sun
Hardiness: ✤ (borderline)
Zone: Min. 5

CAMPSIS
Trumpet vine
A genus of just two species, including the vigorous deciduous climber featured here, grown for its startling, trumpet-shaped, late-summer flowers. It is an ideal choice as a scrambling plant over a sunny wall or fence, with a single plant covering about two standard fence panels in five years. The tendrils of this vigorous climber can damage old masonry, so make sure the pointing is sound before planting.
Cultivation Grow in a moisture-retentive, well-drained soil that is reasonably fertile in full sun, but sheltered from cold winds. In colder areas, grow by a sunny wall.
Pruning Keep this fast-growing climber within bounds by cutting new growth back hard to within a couple of buds from the main framework during late winter.
Propagation Take semi-ripe nodal cuttings in mid-summer or hardwood cuttings in mid-autumn.

Campsis grandiflora (syn. Bignonia grandiflora, C. chinensis, Tecoma grandiflora)
Chinese trumpet vine
Reddish-orange, funnel-shaped

Campsis radicans

flowers appear in succession from late summer to early autumn on this vigorous climber, which has dark green leaves. H 10m (33ft) S 10m (33ft).
Aspect: sun
Hardiness: ✿✿ Zone: Min. 7

Campsis radicans 'Flamenco'
Eye-catching trumpet-shaped, yellow flowers appear in succession from late summer to early autumn and stand out against the dark green leaves of this vigorous climber. H 10m (33ft) S 10m (33ft).
Aspect: sun
Hardiness: ✿✿ Zone: Min. 7

Campsis x tagliabuana 'Madame Galen'
This is a vigorous climber that bears trumpet-shaped, salmon-red flowers throughout late summer and early autumn highlighted against its dark green leaves. H 10m (33ft) S 10m (33ft).
Aspect: sun
Hardiness: ✿✿

CELASTRUS
Staff vine
A genus of about 30 species, including the vigorous deciduous climber featured here, which is

grown for its bead-like yellow berries. It provides quick cover for eyesores such as an old stump or dilapidated shed, but it also makes an attractive climber for walls and fences — one plant covers about three standard fence panels in five years. The twining stems can be constricting, so avoid planting through young trees and shrubs.
Cultivation Grow in any well-drained soil that is reasonably fertile in full sun or dappled shade.
Pruning No routine pruning is necessary. Thin out over-crowded stems in late winter.
Propagation Take semi-ripe nodal cuttings in mid-summer.

Celastrus orbiculatus (syn. C. articulatus)
Oriental bittersweet
This is a vigorous, deciduous climber with scalloped green leaves that turn yellow in autumn. Clusters of insignificant green flowers in mid-summer are followed by yellow berries that split to reveal their contrasting red seeds. H 14m (46ft) S 6m (20ft).
Aspect: sun or semi-shade
Hardiness: ✿✿✿ Zone: Min. 7

Cissus rhombifolia

CISSUS
This large genus of over 350 species includes the tender evergreen climbers featured here. They are mainly grown as house plants because of their handsome foliage. Outside in warm areas, a single plant will quickly cover several standard fence panels or can be left to scramble over the ground and up banks. Elsewhere, they are an ideal choice for a shady but warm conservatory and, as they are very pollution tolerant, they make a good choice for smoke-filled rooms, too.
Cultivation In the garden, grow in a moisture-retentive, well-drained garden soil in full sun or dappled shade. In containers, grow in a soil-based compost (soil mix). Feed every month throughout the growing season and water as necessary. Move to a warm spot undercover when the temperature falls below 5°C (41°F) and water sparingly throughout the winter.
Pruning No routine pruning is necessary. Thin out overcrowded

stems in late winter.
Propagation Take semi-ripe cuttings in mid-summer.

Cissus antarctica
Kangaroo vine
This is a woody, tendril climber with toothed, polished green, leathery leaves, which bears insignificant green flowers from early summer to late summer, followed by black fruit. H 5m (16ft) S 3m (10ft).
Aspect: sun or semi-shade
Hardiness: tender Zones: 10–12

Cissus rhombifolia (syn. Rhoicissus rhombifolia)
Grape ivy
This is a coarsely toothed, woody, tendril climber, with attractive trifoliate evergreen leaves, which bears insignificant green flowers from early summer to late summer, followed by blue-black fruit. H 3m (10ft) S 2m (6ft).
Aspect: sun or semi-shade
Hardiness: tender Zones: 10–12

Celastrus orbiculatus

Clematis alpina

Clematis 'Mrs Cholmondeley'

CLEMATIS
Old man's beard
This is a large and varied genus of over 200 species that includes the deciduous and evergreen climbers featured here, mainly grown for their spectacular flowers. Clematis makes a coverall climber that can be used on all types of structures, established trees and shrubs, as well as scrambling across the ground. Vigorous varieties are ideal for covering eyesores and will cloak up to three standard fence panels within five years. Combine different varieties to give a succession of colour throughout the year.

Cultivation Grow in a moisture-retentive, well-drained garden soil that is reasonably fertile and in full sun or dappled shade, with their roots shaded from hot sun.

Pruning Clematis can be divided into three groups: those that produce all their flowers on old wood (Pruning Group 1); those that produce blooms on both old wood and new growth (Group 2); and those that flower on new growth only (Group 3). Pruning Group 1 requires no routine pruning other than the removal of dead, damaged or diseased stems. Pruning Group 2 should be thinned to avoid congestion by pruning back unwanted stems to a pair of plump buds lower down or at their point of origin. Pruning Group 3 should have all stems cut back to the lowest pair of buds during February (late winter). For further information, *see* Pruning Clematis, page 122.

Propagation Take double-leaf bud cuttings in June (early summer).

SPRING-FLOWERING CLEMATIS
Clematis alpina
Alpine clematis
Small, bell-shaped, lavender-blue flowers with creamy-white centres are produced during mid- and late spring, followed by fluffy seed heads. Pruning Group 1.
H 3m (10ft) S 1.5m (5ft).
Aspect: semi-shade
Hardiness: ✿✿✿ Zones: 4–11

Clematis alpina 'Frances Rivis'
Nodding, bell-shaped, blue flowers are borne in profusion during mid- and late spring, followed by fluffy seed-heads. Pruning Group 1.
H 3m (10ft) S 1.5m (5ft).
Aspect: semi-shade
Hardiness: ✿✿✿ Zones: 4–11

Clematis alpina 'Frankie'
Double, nodding, bell-shaped, blue flowers are produced during mid- and late spring, followed by fluffy seed-heads. Pruning Group 1.
H 3m (10ft) S 1.5m (5ft).
Aspect: sun or semi-shade
Hardiness: ✿✿✿ Zones: 4–9

Clematis armandii 'Apple Blossom'
Almond-scented, pale pink flowers are produced during early and mid-spring against leathery evergreen leaves that are bronze-tinted when young. Pruning Group 1.
H 5m (16ft) S 3m (10ft).
Aspect: sun or semi-shade
Hardiness: ✿✿✿ Zones: 8–11

Clematis 'Early Sensation'
Masses of small, green-centred, white, bowl-shaped flowers are produced in a single flush during mid- and late spring. Pruning Group 1. H 4m (13ft) S 2m (6ft).
Aspect: sun
Hardiness: ✿✿✿ Zones: 8–11

Clematis macropetala 'Markham's Pink'
Semi-double, clear pink flowers with creamy-yellow centres are produced throughout mid- and late spring, followed by silvery seed-heads. Pruning Group 1.
H 3m (10ft) S 1.5m (5ft).
Aspect: sun or partial shade
Hardiness: ✿✿✿ Zones: 4–9

EARLY SUMMER-FLOWERING CLEMATIS
Clematis 'Barbara Jackman'
Large, pale purple flowers with a distinctive red stripe are produced during late spring and early summer and again in early autumn. Pruning Group 2.
H 3m (10ft) S 1m (3ft).
Aspect: sun or partial shade
Hardiness: ✿✿✿ Zones: 4–11

Clematis 'Bees' Jubilee'
A compact variety that bears large dark pink flowers with darker pink bars during late spring and early summer and again in early autumn. Pruning Group 2.
H 2.5m (8ft) S 1m (3ft).
Aspect: sun or partial shade (zones 4–9); partial shade (zones 10–11)
Hardiness: ✿✿✿ Zones: 4–11

Clematis 'Belle of Woking'
Large, double, silvery-mauve flowers with creamy-white centres are produced during late spring and early summer and again in early autumn. Pruning Group 2. H 2.5m (8ft) S 1m (3ft).
Aspect: partial shade
Hardiness: ✿✿✿ Zones: 4–11

Clematis 'Doctor Ruppel'
A compact variety that bears large, dark pink flowers with darker bars in succession during late spring and early summer and then again in early autumn. Pruning Group 2. H 2.5m (8ft) S 1m (3ft).
Aspect: sun or partial shade (zones 4–9); partial shade (zones 10–11)
Hardiness: ✿✿✿ Zones: 4–11

Clematis armandii 'Apple Blossom'

Clematis 'Lasurstern'

Clematis 'Duchess of Edinburgh'

Yellow-centred, double white flowers are produced in succession during late spring and early summer with a second flush occasionally produced during early autumn. Pruning Group 2. H 4m (13ft) S 2m (6ft).
Aspect: partial shade
Hardiness: ✿✿✿ Zones: 4–11

Clematis 'Fireworks'

Large purple flowers with red bars and crimped petals are borne in succession during late spring and early summer and then again in early autumn. Pruning Group 2. H 4m (13ft) S 2m (6ft).
Aspect: sun or partial shade
Hardiness: ✿✿✿ Zones: 4–11

Clematis 'Gillian Blades'

Large, mauve-flushed, white flowers that age to white with golden-yellow centres are produced in succession through late spring and early summer, with a second flush produced in early autumn. Pruning Group 2. H 2.5m (8ft) S 1m (3ft).
Aspect: sun or partial shade
Hardiness: ✿✿✿ Zones: 4–11

Clematis 'Lasurstern'

Large, cream-centred, purple-blue flowers with wavy-edged petals that fade in full sun are borne throughout late spring and early summer and again in early autumn. Pruning Group 2. H 2.5m (8ft) S 1m (3ft).
Aspect: sun or partial shade
Hardiness: ✿✿✿ Zones: 4–11

Clematis 'Miss Bateman'

Green-striped white flowers that age to white with chocolate centres are produced during late spring and early summer, with a second flush in late summer. Pruning Group 2. H 2.5m (8ft) S 1m (3ft).
Aspect: Sun or partial shade
Hardiness: ✿✿✿ Zones: 4–11

Clematis montana var. *rubens* 'Elizabeth'

Masses of fragrant, pale pink flowers with golden-yellow centres are produced during late spring and early summer, against purple-flushed, green foliage on this vigorous clematis. Pruning Group 1. H 7m (23ft) S 3m (10ft).
Aspect: sun or partial shade
Hardiness: ✿✿✿ Zones: 4–11

Clematis montana var. *rubens* 'Pink Perfection'

A vigorous variety of clematis that bears fragrant pink flowers that appear during late spring and early summer against a backdrop of purple-flushed foliage. Pruning Group 1. H 7m (23ft) S 3m (10ft).
Aspect: sun or partial shade
Hardiness: ✿✿✿ Zones: 4–11

Clematis 'Mrs Cholmondeley'

Chocolate-centred, lavender-blue flowers with darker veins appear in succession from late spring to early autumn. Pruning Group 2. H 3m (10ft) S 1m (3ft).
Aspect: sun or partial shade
Hardiness: ✿✿✿ Zones: 4–11

Clematis 'The President'

Clematis 'Multi Blue'

Large, double, pale-centred, dark blue flowers appear in late spring, early summer, late summer and early autumn. Pruning Group 2. H 4m (13ft) S 2m (6ft).
Aspect: sun or partial shade
Hardiness: ✿✿✿ Zones: 4–11

Clematis 'Nelly Moser'

One of the most commonly found clematis in gardens, chocolate-centred pink flowers with darker stripes fading in full sun appear in late spring and early summer with a second flush in early autumn. Pruning Group 2. H 4m (13ft) S 2m (6ft).
Aspect: partial shade
Hardiness: ✿✿✿ Zones: 4–11

Clematis 'The President'

Large, red-centred, purple flowers with pointed petals that are silvery underneath appear from early summer to early autumn. Foliage on 'The President' is bronze-tinted when young. Pruning Group 2. H 3m (10ft) S 1m (3ft).
Aspect: Sun or partial shade
Hardiness: ✿✿✿ Zones: 4–11

Clematis 'Vyvyan Pennell'

Double, golden-centred, mauve, violet and purple flowers appear in late spring and early summer and again in early autumn. This clematis is fully hardy. Pruning Group 2. H 3m (10ft) S 1m (3ft).
Aspect: sun or partial shade
Hardiness: ✿✿✿ Zones: 4–11

Clematis montana var. *rubens* 'Elizabeth'

Clematis 'Bill MacKenzie'

Clematis florida var. *sieboldiana*

LATE SUMMER-FLOWERING CLEMATIS

Clematis 'Alba Luxurians'
Bell-shaped, green-tipped, white flowers with purple centres are produced from mid-summer to early autumn against grey-green leaves. Wind and wilt tolerant. Pruning Group 3. H 4m (13ft) S 1.5m (5ft).
Aspect: sun or partial shade
Hardiness: ❀❀❀ Zones: 4–11

Clematis 'Betty Corning'
Nodding, bell-shaped and fragrant creamy-white flowers edged and flushed with lilac-blue, are produced in succession from mid-summer to early autumn. This variety is wind and wilt-tolerant. Pruning Group 3. H 2m (6ft) S 1m (3ft).
Aspect: sun or partial shade
Hardiness: ❀❀❀ Zones: 4–11

Clematis 'Bill MacKenzie'
Butter-yellow, bell-shaped flowers are produced in succession from mid-summer to early autumn against ferny mid-green leaves, followed by large, fluffy seed-heads. Pruning Group 3. H 7m (23ft) S 3m (10ft).
Aspect: sun or partial shade
Hardiness: ❀❀❀ Zones: 4–11

Clematis 'Comtesse de Bouchaud'
A popular variety that bears masses of large, yellow-centred, mauve-pink flowers in succession from mid-summer to early autumn. Pruning Group 3. H 3m (10ft) S 1m (3ft).
Hardiness: ❀❀❀ Zones: 4–11

Clematis 'Ernest Markham'
Large, cream-centred, purple-red flowers are produced in succession from mid-summer to mid-autumn. Pruning Group 3. H 4m (13ft) S 1m (3ft).
Aspect: sun
Hardiness: ❀❀❀ Zones: 4–11

Clematis 'Etoile Violette'
A vigorous clematis that produces masses of yellow-centred, dark purple flowers in succession from mid-summer to early autumn. Wind and wilt resistant. Pruning Group 3. H 5m (16ft) S 1.5m (5ft).
Aspect: sun or partial shade
Hardiness: ❀❀❀ Zones: 4–11

Clematis flammula
Fragrant, starry white flowers are produced *en masse* from mid-

summer to mid-autumn on this vigorous clematis, followed by shimmering seed-heads. Pruning Group 3. H 6m (20ft) S 1m (3ft).
Aspect: sun or partial shade
Hardiness: ❀❀❀ Zones: 4–9

Clematis florida var. *sieboldiana*
This is an unusual passion flower-like plant that produces creamy-white flowers with dark purple centres that appear in succession from early summer to early autumn, followed by shimmering seed-heads. Pruning Group 2. H 2.5m (8ft) S 1m (3ft).
Aspect: sun or partial shade
Hardiness: ❀❀❀ Zones: 4–11

Clematis 'General Sikorski'
Easy-to-grow clematis with large, yellow-centred, purple-blue flowers produced in succession from early summer to early autumn. Fully hardy. Pruning Group 2. H 3m (10ft) S 1m (3ft).
Aspect: sun or partial shade
Hardiness: ❀❀❀ Zones: 4–11

Clematis 'Gipsy Queen'
Red-centred, bright purple flowers are produced in succession from mid-summer to early autumn. Pruning Group 3. H 3m (10ft) S 1m (3ft).
Aspect: sun or partial shade
Hardiness: ❀❀❀ Zones: 4–11

Clematis 'Hagley Hybrid'
Cup-shaped, mauve-pink flowers with red centres that fade in the sun are produced in succession

from mid-summer to early autumn. Pruning Group 3. H 2m (6ft) S 1m (3ft).
Aspect: sun or partial shade
Hardiness: ❀❀❀ Zones: 4–11

Clematis 'Henryi'
Attractive large white flowers with chocolate centres are produced in succession from mid-summer to early autumn. Pruning Group 2. H 3m (10ft) S 1m (3ft).
Aspect: sun or partial shade
Hardiness: ❀❀❀ Zones: 4–11

Clematis 'Huldine'
Attractive and large, cup-shaped, yellow-centred, silvery-white flowers with pale lilac undersides appear from mid-summer to early autumn. Pruning Group 3. H 5m (16ft) S 2m (6ft).
Aspect: sun
Hardiness: ❀❀❀ Zones: 4–11

Clematis 'Comtesse de Bouchaud'

Clematis 'Jackmanii'

Clematis 'Marie Boisselot'

Clematis 'Rouge Cardinal'

Clematis viticella 'Purpurea Plena Elegans'

Clematis 'Jackmanii'
Large, green-centred, purple flowers are produced in succession from mid-summer to early autumn. Pruning Group 3. H 3m (10ft) S 1m (3ft). Aspect: sun or partial shade Hardiness: ❀❀❀ Zones: 4–11

Clematis 'Jackmanii Superba'
Red-flushed, dark purple flowers with cream-coloured centres are produced in succession from mid-summer to early autumn. Ideal for a north-facing site. Pruning Group 3. H 3m (10ft) S 1m (3ft). Aspect: sun or partial shade Hardiness: ❀❀❀ Zones: 4–11

Clematis 'Marie Boisselot'
Large white flowers with golden centres and overlapping petals are produced in succession from early summer to early autumn. Pruning Group 2. H 3m (10ft) S 1m (3ft). Aspect: sun or partial shade Hardiness: ❀❀❀ Zones: 4–11

Clematis 'Niobe'
Golden-centred, dark ruby-red flowers are produced in succession from mid-summer to early autumn. Pruning Group 3.

H 3m (10ft) S 1m (3ft). Aspect: sun or partial shade Hardiness: ❀❀❀ Zones: 4–11

Clematis 'Perle d'Azur'
Yellow-centred, lilac-blue flowers of medium size, that are pink-tinged at the base, are produced in succession from mid-summer to early autumn. Pruning Group 3. H 3m (10ft) S 1m (3ft). Aspect: sun or partial shade Hardiness: ❀❀❀ Zones: 4–9

Clematis 'Perle d'Azur'

Clematis 'Polish Spirit'
Red-centred and rich purple saucer-shaped flowers are produced in succession from mid-summer to early autumn on this vigorous variety. Pruning Group 3. H 5m (16ft) S 2m (6ft). Aspect: sun or partial shade Hardiness: ❀❀❀ Zones: 4–11

Clematis 'Prince Charles'
Pale mauve-blue flowers with green centres are produced in succession from mid-summer to early autumn. Pruning Group 3. H 2.5m (8ft) S 1.5m (5ft). Aspect: sun or partial shade Hardiness: ❀❀❀ Zones: 4–11

Clematis 'Princess Diana'
Clear pink, cream-centred, tulip-like flowers are produced in succession from late summer to mid-autumn. Pruning Group 3.

Clematis tangutica

H 2.5m (8ft) S 1m (3ft). Aspect: sun Hardiness: ❀❀❀ Zones: 4–11

Clematis 'Rouge Cardinal'
Rich velvet-crimson flowers appear during mid-summer to early autumn. Pruning Group 3. H 3m (10ft) S 1m (3ft). Aspect: sun or partial shade Hardiness: ❀❀❀ Zones: 4–9

WINTER-FLOWERING CLEMATIS
Clematis cirrhosa 'Jingle Bells'
From early to late winter the large, creamy-coloured, bell-shaped flowers stand out against the dark evergreen leaves. Pruning Group 1. H 3m (10ft) S 1.5m (5ft). Aspect: sun Hardiness: ❀❀❀ Zones: 7–9

Clematis cirrhosa var. balearica
Fragrant, creamy-white, bell-shaped and waxy-looking flowers blotched with maroon inside are produced from early to late winter against glossy bronze-tinted leaves. Pruning Group 1. H 3m (10ft) S 1.5m (5ft). Aspect: sun Hardiness: ❀❀❀ Zones 7–9

Clematis cirrhosa 'Wisley Cream'
Bronze-tinted leaves in winter set off the small, creamy, bell-shaped, waxy-looking flowers borne from early to late winter. Frost hardy. Pruning Group 1. H 3m (10ft) S 1.5m (5ft). Aspect: sun Hardiness: ❀❀❀ Zones 7–9

Clerodendrum thomsoniae

Clianthus puniceus 'Roseus'

CLERODENDRUM

This large genus of over 400 species includes the tender, twining, evergreen climber featured here, which is grown for its clusters of bell-shaped summer flowers. In warm gardens it can reach 3m (10ft) or more and can also be trained to make an attractive standard. Elsewhere, it makes an ideal plant for adding an exotic touch to a heated conservatory.

Cultivation In the garden, grow in any well-drained, moisture-retentive soil that is reasonably fertile. Site in full sun, but protected from wind. If grown in containers, use a soil-based compost (soil mix). Feed every month throughout the growing season and water as necessary. Move to a warm spot undercover when the temperature falls below 10°C (50°) and water sparingly throughout the winter.

Pruning No routine pruning is necessary. Cut back wayward stems, shortening shoots by about two-thirds of their length, in mid-spring.

Propagation Take softwood cuttings in mid-spring.

Clerodendrum thomsoniae
Glory bower
This is a woody-stemmed, evergreen, twining climber that during early summer to early autumn bears clusters of bi-coloured flowers made up of a white lantern-shaped calyx and a crimson star-shaped corolla, against large green leaves.

H 4m (13ft) S 2m (6ft).
Aspect: sun
Hardiness: tender Zones: 10–12

CLIANTHUS

This comprises a genus of just two species, including the evergreen climber featured here, which are grown for their unusual lobster-claw or beak-like flowers that appear in early summer. It makes an interesting choice for sunny and sheltered screens and fences or can be left unsupported to form a sprawling shrub.

Cultivation Grow in any well-drained soil that is reasonably fertile in full sun, but protected from wind. In very cold areas, grow in a cool conservatory.

Pruning No routine pruning is necessary. Cut back wayward stems and thin congested growth during early summer.

Propagation Sow seeds in early spring or take semi-ripe cuttings in early summer.

Clianthus puniceus
Lobster claw, Parrot's bill
This is a sprawling evergreen climber, with dark green leaves, which bears dramatic and unusual lobster-claw-like scarlet flowers in clusters during late spring and early summer. If not left to sprawl, it requires tying into its support. H 4m (13ft) S 2m (6ft).
Named varieties: 'Albus', white flowers. H 4m (13ft) S 2m (6ft).
Aspect: sun
Hardiness: ✿✿ Zone: Min. 6

COBAEA

This genus of about 20 species includes the evergreen tendril climber featured here, grown for its spectacular fragrant summer flowers. In warm gardens, it is a good choice for covering a sheltered sunny wall or fence. Elsewhere, grow in a container and move undercover during the winter months, or use it as a permanent addition to a large heated greenhouse or conservatory.

Cultivation In the garden, grow in any well-drained, moisture-retentive soil that is reasonably fertile in full sun, but protected from wind. In containers, grow in a soil-based compost. Feed every month throughout the growing season and water as necessary.

Move to a warm spot under cover when the temperature falls below 5°C (41°F) and water sparingly throughout the winter.

Pruning No routine pruning is necessary. Cut back wayward stems and thin congested growth during early autumn.

Propagation Sow seeds in early spring.

Cobaea scandens
Cathedral bell, cup-and-saucer plant
This is a vigorous tendril climber that bears huge, scented, bell-shaped, creamy-green flowers that age to dark purple from early summer to early autumn, against a backdrop of dark green leaves.
H 20m (70ft) S 3.5m (12ft).
Aspect: sun
Hardiness: tender Zones: 10–12

ECCREMOCARPUS
Chilean glory flower
A genus of some five species, including the vigorous evergreen climber featured here, grown for its succession of unusual and colourful summer flowers. It makes a perfect choice for a fence or screen next to a sunny patio.

Cultivation Grow in any well-drained soil that is reasonably fertile in full sun, but protected from cold wind. Plant out after the last frost in colder areas.

Pruning No routine pruning is necessary. In colder areas, treat as

Cobaea scandens

Eccremocarpus scaber

Hedera canariensis 'Gloire de Marengo'

Hedera colchica 'Dentata Variegata'

a perennial and cut frost-damaged top-growth back during mid-spring.
Propagation Sow seeds in February (late winter).

Eccremocarpus scaber
A quick-growing, evergreen, tendril climber that produces a profusion of red, pink, orange or yellow flowers in succession from early summer to mid-autumn on slender stems. It requires tying into a support to get it started. H 5m (16ft) S 5m (16ft).
Aspect: sun
Hardiness: ✿✿ Zone: Min. 7

FALLOPIA
A genus of over five species, including the very vigorous deciduous climber featured here, it is grown for its rapid speed of growth and clouds of late-summer flowers. It makes a useful plant for covering up eyesores and for quick garden makeovers. However, a word of caution is necessary with this climber: a

single plant will smother an area equivalent to about 10 standard fence panels in five years.
Cultivation Grow in a moisture-retentive, well-drained soil that is poor to reasonably fertile in full sun or dappled shade.
Pruning No routine pruning is necessary. Cut back wayward or congested stems in mid-spring.

Fallopia baldschuanica

Propagation Take semi-ripe cuttings in early summer.

Fallopia baldschuanica (syn. *Bilderdykia baldschuanica, Polygonum baldschuanicum*) Russian vine, mile-a-minute
Very fast growing and vigorous, this is a woody, deciduous climber that is covered in clouds of tiny, funnel-shaped, white flowers with pink tinges throughout late summer and early autumn.
H 12m (40ft) S 4m (13ft).
Aspect: sun or semi-shade
Hardiness: ✿✿✿ Zone: Min. 7

HEDERA
This genus of about 10 species includes many popular, self-clinging, evergreen climbers, some of which are featured here. They are grown for their easy-going nature and handsome foliage. Many of these plants are excellent on shady north-facing walls and fences, while others thrive in full sun. A single plant covers one standard fence panel in five years. Some can provide weed-smothering groundcover and a few also make year-round house plants.
Cultivation Although these plants are very tolerant of a wide range of conditions, they grow best in a moisture-retentive, well-drained neutral to alkaline soil that is reasonably fertile. Variegated ivies prefer dappled shade and shelter from cold winds; green-leaved varieties can cope with anything from full sun to deep shade.

Pruning No routine pruning is necessary. Remove frost-damaged growth and all-green reverted stems from variegated varieties in mid-spring.
Propagation Take semi-ripe nodal cuttings in early summer.

Hedera canariensis 'Gloire de Marengo'
Huge, three-lobed, silvery-green glossy leaves, edged with creamy-white, cover this vigorous evergreen climber. Use indoors or outside in sheltered, dappled shade. H 4m (13ft) S 5m (16ft).
Aspect: semi-shade
Hardiness: ✿✿ Zone: Min. 7

Hedera colchica 'Dentata Variegata'
A variegated evergreen ivy with huge, heart-shaped, cream-edged, mottled grey-green leaves. It is useful climber for brightening up semi-shade or for growing as weed-smothering groundcover.
H 5m (16ft) S 5m (16ft).
Aspect: semi-shade
Hardiness: ✿✿✿ Zone: Min. 5

Hedera colchica 'Sulphur Heart' (syn. *H. colchica* 'Paddy's Pride')
A fast-growing, self-clinging, variegated, evergreen ivy with heart-shaped green leaves splashed with creamy yellow. It is useful for brightening up semi-shade or for growing as weed-smothering groundcover. H 5m (16ft) S 5m (16ft).
Aspect: semi-shade
Hardiness: ✿✿✿ Zone: Min. 5

Hedera helix 'Goldchild'

Hedera helix 'Buttercup'

This is a sun-loving, vigorous, self-clinging, evergreen ivy with lobed bright yellow leaves that turn pale green in shade. Insignificant pale green flowers are borne in mid- to late autumn, followed by spherical black fruit. H 2m (6ft) S 2.5m (8ft).
Aspect: sun
Hardiness: ❀❀❀ Zone: Min. 7

Hedera helix 'Glacier'

Ideal for use as groundcover, this variegated evergreen climber has triangular and lobed grey-green leaves with silver and cream splashes. Pale green flowers appear in mid- to late autumn. H 2m (6ft) S 2m (6ft).
Aspect: semi-shade
Hardiness: ❀❀❀ Zone: Min. 7

Hedera helix 'Goldheart' (syn. H. helix 'Jubilaum Goldherz', H. helix 'Jubilee Goldheart', H. helix 'Oro di Bogliasco')

Vigorous once established, this fast-growing, variegated, evergreen climber has glossy, three-lobed, dark green leaves splashed with yellow. Insignificant pale green flowers are borne in mid- to late autumn. H 8m (26ft) S 5m (16ft).
Aspect: semi-shade
Hardiness: ❀❀❀ Zone: Min. 7

Hedera helix 'Green Ripple'

A vigorous evergreen climber with large, glossy, bright green leaves that are five-lobed and sharply pointed with distinctive veining. They turn copper-bronze over winter. Insignificant pale green flowers are borne in mid-autumn and late autumn. H 2m (6ft) S 2m (6ft).
Aspect: semi-shade
Hardiness: ❀❀❀ Zone: Min. 7

Hedera helix 'Ivalace' (syn. H. helix 'Mini Green')

Suitable for use indoors and outside, this adaptable ivy has glossy, five-lobed, wavy-edged, dark green leaves. Insignificant pale green flowers are borne in mid- to late autumn.
H 1m (3ft) S 1.2m (4ft).
Aspect: semi-shade
Hardiness: ❀❀❀ Zone: Min. 7

Hedera helix 'Parsley Crested' (syn. H. helix 'Cristata')

The glossy dark green and wavy-edged leaves on this vigorous, self-clinging evergreen climber are ideal for covering a wall or fence in shade. Insignificant pale green flowers are borne in mid- to late autumn. H 2m (6ft) S 1.2m (4ft).
Aspect: semi-shade to deep shade
Hardiness: ❀❀❀ Zone: Min. 7

HIBBERTIA

A genus of around 120 species, including the twining evergreen featured here, grown for their bright yellow flowers. They make useful groundcover in warm gardens, where they also look good trained over arches and pergolas. They are also tolerant of salt-laden air, and so make a good choice for mild coastal gardens. Elsewhere, grow in a container and move under cover during the cold winter months.
Cultivation In the garden, grow in any well-drained, moisture-retentive soil that is reasonably fertile in dappled shade, but protected from wind. In containers, grow in a soil-based compost (soil mix). Feed every month throughout the growing season and water as necessary. Move to a warm spot under cover when the temperature falls below 5°C (41°F) and water sparingly during the winter.
Pruning No routine pruning is necessary. Cut back wayward stems and thin congested growth during early autumn after flowering.
Propagation Sow seeds in early spring.

Hibbertia scandens (syn. H. volubilis)

This is a vigorous, twining evergreen with lustrous, leathery, green leaves that are distinctively veined and notched. The climber has red hairy stems and the leaves are also covered in paler hairs underneath. Saucer-shaped, bright yellow flowers are borne from early summer to late summer.
H 3m (10ft) S 2m (6ft).
Aspect: semi-shade
Hardiness: tender Zones: 10–12

HOYA

This genus of over 200 species includes the epiphytic climber featured here, which is grown for its waxy-looking clusters of night-scented summer flowers and handsome foliage. It is best grown in a container as this promotes flowering. It makes a good choice for a sunny conservatory, greenhouse or porch.
Cultivation Grow in a soil-based compost. Feed every month throughout the growing season and water as necessary. Move to a warm spot under cover when the temperature falls below 5°C (41°F) and water sparingly during the winter.
Pruning No routine pruning is necessary. Pinch out growing tips to promote bushy growth.
Propagation Sow seeds in early spring.

Hoya carnosa
Wax plant

A vigorous evergreen climber with leathery dark green oval leaves that climbs using clinging aerial roots. Large, dense clusters of waxy-looking star-shaped and night-scented white flowers that are pink-flushed, each with a crimson eye, are produced from late spring to early autumn.
H 6m (20ft) S 2m (6ft).
Aspect: sun
Hardiness: tender Zones: 10-12

HUMULUS
Hop

This comprises a genus of just two species, including the vigorous deciduous climber featured here, which is grown for its yellow foliage. It is ideal for growing over sturdy arches and pergolas, or for allowing it to scramble through coloured trellis.

Hibbertia scandens   *Hoya carnosa*

Humulus lupulus 'Aureus'

Cultivation Grow in any well-drained, moisture-retentive soil that is reasonably fertile in full sun or dappled shade. Choose a sunny site to achieve the best leaf coloration.
Pruning Treat this climber as a perennial in colder areas, cutting back all stems to near ground level in early spring.
Propagation Take leaf-bud cuttings in early summer.

Humulus lupulus 'Aureus'
Golden hop
This climber has striking, bright yellow, deeply lobed leaves that mature to yellow-green on twining stems. Tie these into the support in spring. Green flowering cones are produced in early autumn.
H 6m (20ft) S 6m (20ft).
Aspect: sun to semi-shade
Hardiness: ✤✤✤ Zone: Min. 7

HYDRANGEA
A genus of about 80 species, including the deciduous climber featured here, that is grown for its summer flowers and handsome foliage. They are useful for covering large north-facing walls, although they take a few years to get established.
Cultivation Grow in a moisture-retentive, well-drained and reasonably fertile soil in full sun or dappled shade. Before planting, add plenty of organic matter to the soil.
Pruning No routine pruning is necessary. Cut back wayward stems in late winter.

Propagation Take softwood basal cuttings in mid-spring or layer suitable shoots in mid-spring.

Hydrangea anomala subsp. *petiolaris* (syn. *H. petiolaris*)
Climbing hydrangea
Huge flat heads of creamy lace-cap flowers stand out against a backdrop of dark green leaves from late spring to mid-summer on this woody, deciduous climber. The leaves turn butter-yellow in autumn before falling to reveal flaking brown bark. H 1.5m (5ft) S 3m (10ft).
Aspect: sun to shade
Hardiness: ✤✤✤ Zone: Min. 7

JASMINUM
This comprises a genus of over 200 species, including the deciduous and evergreen climbers featured here, which are grown for their sweetly scented summer flowers. It is a good choice for sheltered structures near entrances, paths and patios, covering a standard fence panel in about five years. Others make excellent fragrant house plants.
Cultivation In the garden, grow in any well-drained soil that is reasonably fertile in full sun or dappled shade. Choose a sunny site for the best leaf coloration. In containers, grow in a soil-based compost (soil mix). Feed every month throughout the growing season and water as necessary.
Pruning No routine pruning is necessary. Overcrowded shoots on *Jasminum officinale* can be thinned after flowering.

Propagation Take semi-ripe basal cuttings in mid-summer.

Jasminum beesianum
Fragrant pinkish-red flowers are produced in small clusters throughout early and mid-summer against strap-shaped, dark green leaves on this twining and woody evergreen climber. This plant requires the shelter of a sunny south- or west-facing wall or fence. H 5m (16ft) S 5m (16ft).
Aspect: sun
Hardiness: ✤✤ Zone: Min. 7

Jasminum officinale
Common jasmine
A succession of fabulously fragrant white flowers cover this vigorous semi-evergreen, twining climber from early summer to early autumn. H 12m (40ft) S 3m (10ft).
Aspect: sun to semi-shade
Hardiness: ✤✤✤ Zone: Min. 7

Jasminum officinale
'Devon Cream'
A new and very compact variety of common jasmine, this woody and twining deciduous climber bears large, fragrant, creamy-white flowers from mid-summer to early autumn. Give it the shelter of a sunny south- or west-facing wall or fence. H 2m (6ft) S 1m (3ft).
Aspect: sun
Hardiness: ✤✤ Zone: Min. 7

Jasminum officinale
'Fiona Sunrise'
This is a recent introduction that has eyecatching golden foliage and a succession of fragrant white flowers from early summer to early autumn. It is a compact variety that does best in the shelter of a sunny south- or west-facing wall or fence.
H 3m (10ft) S 2m (6ft).
Aspect: sun
Hardiness: ✤✤ Zone: Min. 7

Jasminum polyanthum
This vigorous and twining evergreen climber is a very popular house plant. It produces fabulously fragrant white flowers that open from pink buds throughout mid-spring and early summer when grown outside. When grown inside, it will fill the house with scent from late autumn to mid-spring.
H 3m (10ft) S 2m (6ft).
Aspect: sun to semi-shade
Hardiness: ✤ Zone: 10+

Jasminum x stephanense
Scented pale pink flowers are produced in clusters throughout early and mid-summer on this vigorous and twining deciduous climber. Give it the shelter of a sunny south- or west-facing wall or fence. H 5m (16ft) S 5m (16ft).
Aspect: sun
Hardiness: ✤✤ Zone: Min. 7

Hydrangea anomala subsp. *petiolaris*

Jasminum officinale 'Fiona Sunrise'

LAPAGERIA

This is a genus of just one species of twining evergreen climber, grown for its exotic and colourful waxy-looking summer flowers. It is ideal for growing against a sheltered sunny wall or fence or on a post in a sheltered garden.
Cultivation In the garden, grow in a moisture-retentive, well-drained neutral to acid soil that is reasonably fertile. Site in dappled shade, but sheltered from cold winds. In containers, grow in an ericaceous compost (soil mix). Feed every month in the growing season and water as necessary.
Pruning No routine pruning is necessary. Wayward shoots can be thinned after flowering.
Propagation Sow seeds or layer suitable stems in mid-spring.

Lapageria rosea
Chilean bellflower
Exotic, elongated, bell-shaped, pink to crimson flowers are produced singly or in small clusters from leaf joints on this twining evergreen climber from mid-summer to mid-autumn. The leathery, lustrous, dark green leaves look good at other times. Borderline frost hardy. H 5m (16ft) S 3m (10ft).
Aspect: semi-shade
Hardiness: ❊❊ (borderline)
Zone: Min. 8

LONICERA
Honeysuckle
A genus of over 180 species, including the deciduous and evergreen twining climbers

Lapageria rosea

featured here, grown for their spidery, often highly fragrant, summer flowers. A coverall climber, it is ideal for east- and west-facing screens and fences or for training through established shrubs and trees. A single specimen will cover a standard fence panel in about five years.
Cultivation Grow in a moisture-retentive, well-drained soil that is reasonably fertile in full sun or dappled shade. Add plenty of organic matter to the soil before planting time.
Pruning Honeysuckles that flower on the current year's growth do not need regular pruning; those that flower on the previous season's growth should have old growth that has flowered cut back to a newer shoot produced lower down on the stem. All neglected honeysuckles can be rejuvenated by removing one in three stems, starting with the oldest.
Propagation Take leaf-bud cuttings in early summer or mid-summer, layer suitable shoots in late summer or take hardwood cuttings in mid-autumn.

Lonicera x americana
Very large, fragrant, yellow, tubular flowers that are purple-flushed are produced in succession from early summer to early autumn against a backdrop of oval dark green leaves. H 7m (23ft) S 2m (6ft).
Aspect: sun to semi-shade
Hardiness: ❊❊❊ Zone: Min. 7

Lonicera x brownii 'Dropmore Scarlet'
Long, trumpet-shaped, bright scarlet flowers are produced in succession from mid-summer to early autumn against handsome blue-green foliage, occasionally followed by red berries. H 4m (13ft) S 2m (6ft).
Aspect: sun to semi-shade
Hardiness: ❊❊❊ Zone: Min. 7

Lonicera x heckrottii 'Gold Flame'
A vigorous twining climber that bears very fragrant, orange-yellow tubular flowers that are pink-flushed in succession from early to late summer, occasionally followed by red berries.

Lonicera x brownii 'Dropmore Scarlet'

H 500cm (180in) S 50cm (20in).
Aspect: sun to semi-shade
Hardiness: ❊❊❊ Zone: Min. 7

Lonicera henryi
Scarlet trumpet honeysuckle
Reddish-purple tubular flowers, each with a yellow throat, are produced throughout early and mid-summer against lustrous, dark green leaves on this vigorous evergreen variety. H 10m (33ft) S 1m (3ft).
Aspect: sun to semi-shade
Hardiness: ❊❊❊ (borderline)
Zone: Min. 7

Lonicera japonica 'Halliana'
Fabulously fragrant, tubular, white flowers that age to yellow are borne in succession from mid-spring to late summer, appearing against handsome dark green leaves on this vigorous evergreen variety. H 10m (33ft) S 2m (6ft).
Aspect: sun to semi-shade
Hardiness: ❊❊❊ Zone: Min. 7

Lonicera japonica 'Hall's Prolific'
Tubular white and sweetly fragrant flowers that age to yellow are borne in succession from mid-spring to late summer on this free-flowering vigorous variety

that has dark green foliage. H 4m (13ft) S 3m (10ft).
Aspect: sun to semi-shade
Hardiness: ❊❊❊ Zone: Min. 7

Lonicera japonica var. repens
Very fragrant, tubular, reddish-purple flowers that age to yellow and are white-flushed are borne from mid-spring to late summer on this long-flowering and vigorous variety that has purple-tinged foliage. H 10m (33ft) S 5m (16ft).
Aspect: sun to semi-shade
Hardiness: ❊❊❊ Zone: Min. 7

Lonicera periclymenum 'Graham Thomas'

Mandevilla splendens

Lonicera periclymenum 'Belgica' Early Dutch honeysuckle

Very fragrant, tubular, reddish-purple flowers that are yellow-lipped are produced *en masse* during late spring and early summer on this twining vigorous climber. H 7m (23ft) S 1m (3ft).
Aspect: sun to semi-shade
Hardiness: ✿✿✿ Zone: Min. 7

Lonicera periclymenum 'Graham Thomas'

Large, tubular and sweetly fragrant white flowers that age to yellow are produced from mid-summer to early autumn against a backdrop of oval green leaves on this vigorous deciduous climber.
H 7m (23ft) S 1m (3ft).
Aspect: sun to semi-shade
Hardiness: ✿✿✿ Zone: Min. 7

Lonicera periclymenum 'Harlequin'

This is an unusual variegated honeysuckle that is covered in fragrant and tubular reddish-purple and yellow-lipped flowers from early summer to late summer on this twining vigorous climber. H 7m (23ft) S 1m (3ft).
Aspect: sun to semi-shade
Hardiness: ✿✿✿ Zone: Min. 7

Lonicera periclymenum 'Serotina' Late Dutch honeysuckle

Superbly fragrant and tubular creamy-white flowers that are purple-streaked are produced from mid-summer to mid-autumn on this vigorous, late-flowering, deciduous cultivar. It is a good climber to have growing in dappled shade. H 7m (23ft) S 1m (3ft).
Aspect: semi-shade
Hardiness: ✿✿✿ Zone: Min. 7

Lonicera x *tellmanniana*

Striking-looking, bright orange, tubular flowers open from red-tinged buds from late spring to mid-summer against a backdrop of large, dark green leaves. H 5m (16ft) S 2m (6ft).
Aspect: sun to semi-shade
Hardiness: ✿✿✿ Zone: Min. 7

MANDEVILLA

This genus of about 120 species includes the twining and woody climbers featured here, which are grown for their exotic summer flowers. It is an ideal patio plant in warm gardens as it responds well to being grown in pots, but it can be grown at the back of sheltered borders and used to cover trellis and fences. In cooler areas it can be grown as a houseplant and will add colour to a heated conservatory in colder areas.
Cultivation In the garden, grow in a moisture-retentive, well-drained soil that is reasonably fertile in full sun, but sheltered from cool winds. If grown in containers, grow in a soil-based compost (soil mix). Feed every month throughout the growing season and water as necessary. Move to a warm spot undercover when the temperature falls below 10°C (50°F) and water sparingly in winter.
Pruning Cut back side shoots on established plants to 3 buds of the woody framework after it has flowered.
Propagation Sow seeds in mid-spring or take softwood cuttings in late spring.

Mandevilla x *amabilis* 'Alice du Pont' (syn. *M.* x *amoena* 'Alice du Pont')

Fragrant pink, tubular flowers are produced throughout mid- to late summer against a backdrop of wavy-edged green leaves on this twining and woody climber.
H 7m (23ft) S 2m (6ft).
Aspect: sun
Hardiness: tender Zones: 10–12

Mandevilla boliviensis (syn. *Dipladenia boliviensis*)

White tubular flowers with a yellow eye are carried throughout mid- to late summer against a backdrop of glossy, narrow, green foliage on this twining, woody climber. H 4m (13ft) S 2m (6ft).
Aspect: sun
Hardiness: tender Zones: 10–12

Mandevilla splendens (syn. *Dipladenia splendens*)

Showy, rose-pink, tubular flowers are borne in succession from mid- to late summer on this twining climber, which has hairy stems and glossy green leaves.
H 5m (16ft) S 2m (6ft).
Aspect: sun
Hardiness: tender Zones: 10–12

MONSTERA

This genus of over 20 species, including the tender evergreen climber featured here, are grown for their handsomely cut, lustrous foliage. It is grown outside in tropical areas but in colder climates it makes an attractive and easy-to-please house plant.
Cultivation Grow in a fresh general-purpose compost (soil mix). Feed every month during the growing season and water as necessary. If kept outside, move to a warm spot undercover when the temperature falls below 15°C (60°F). Water sparingly in winter.
Pruning No routine pruning is necessary.
Propagation Air layer in early autumn.

Monstera deliciosa Swiss cheese plant

Large, deeply notched and sometimes perforated, glossy, dark green, leathery leaves are displayed on arching stems that splay outwards from a vigorous climbing stem supported in part by aerial roots. Mature plants may flower, producing creamy, arum-like spathes from late spring to late summer. H 10m (33ft) S 2m (6ft).
Aspect: semi-shade
Hardiness: tender Zones: 10–12

Monstera deliciosa

Parthenocissus quinquefolia

Passiflora caerulea

PARTHENOCISSUS

Comprising a genus of about ten species, including the vigorous deciduous tendril climbers featured here, they are grown for their handsome foliage and fiery autumn tints. It makes a cover-all climber that is excellent for camouflaging ugly buildings and other eyesores. A single specimen will cloak about two standard fence panels in five years.
Cultivation Grow in any well-drained soil that is reasonably fertile in full sun, dappled shade or full shade.
Pruning No routine pruning is necessary. Keep plants in check by pruning out unwanted stems in late winter.
Propagation Take semi-ripe stem cuttings in late summer; alternatively, take hardwood cuttings in late autumn.

Parthenocissus henryana (syn. *Vitis henryana*) Chinese Virginia creeper
The handsome, deeply divided dark green leaves with distinctive white and pink veins turn fiery shades in autumn. It is less vigorous than other varieties. H 10m (33ft) S 5m (16ft).
Aspect: sun, semi-shade to deep shade
Hardiness: ❃❃❃ (borderline)
Zone: Min. 7

Parthenocissus quinquefolia (syn. *Vitis quinquefolia*) Virginia creeper
The deeply divided, slightly puckered, green leaves transform in autumn as they take on brilliant shades of crimson and purple on this vigorous deciduous climber. H 15m (50ft) S 5m (16ft).
Aspect: sun, semi-shade to deep shade
Hardiness: ❃❃❃ Zone: Min. 7

Parthenocissus tricuspidata 'Robusta'
A very vigorous deciduous climber with large, dark green leaves that are deeply lobed, turning brilliant crimson and purple in autumn. H 20m (70ft) S 10m (33ft).
Aspect: sun, semi-shade to deep shade
Hardiness: ❃❃❃ Zone: Min. 7

Parthenocissus tricuspidata 'Veitchii' (syn. *Ampelopsis veitchii*)
Lustrous, deeply lobed, dark green leaves transform in autumn into a spectacular cloak of red and purple on this very vigorous variety. H 20m (70ft) S 10m (33ft).
Aspect: sun, semi-shade to deep shade
Hardiness: ❃❃❃ Zone: Min. 7

PASSIFLORA
Passion flower
This large genus of over 400 species includes the evergreen tendril climbers featured here, which are grown mainly for their distinctive and tropical-looking summer flowers. They are a very good choice for growing up a pergola, arch or open screen, as this allows the flowers and fruit to hang down attractively.
Cultivation In the garden, grow in a moisture-retentive, well-drained soil that is reasonably fertile in full sun or dappled shade, sheltered from cold winds. In containers, grow in a soil-based compost (soil mix). Feed every month in the growing season and water as necessary. Protect from severe frost in cold areas.
Pruning Thin overcrowded plants in early spring. In cold areas, treat as a perennial and cut back all stems to near ground level in mid-autumn then protect the

Parthenocissus tricuspidata

Passiflora 'Amethyst'

Rosa 'Aloha'

Rosa 'New Dawn'

Rosa 'Danse du Feu'

Rosa 'Laura Ford'

fragrant, single, creamy-white flowers during mid- and late summer, followed by bright red hips. H 10m (33ft) S 6m (20ft).

Rosa 'Gloire de Dijon'
Old glory rose
Strongly fragrant, double, creamy-yellow flowers are produced in succession from mid-summer to early autumn against lustrous, dark green leaves. H 5m (16ft) S 4m (13ft).

Rosa 'Golden Showers'
Large, double, rich-yellow flowers are produced in succession from mid-summer to early autumn on a compact climber with lustrous, dark green leaves. Ideal for small gardens. H 3m (10ft) S 2m (6ft).

Rosa 'Guinée'
Strongly fragrant, double, red-velvet flowers are produced throughout early to mid-summer against a backdrop of leathery, dark green leaves. H 5m (15ft) S 2.2m (7ft).

Rosa 'Handel'
Subtly fragrant clusters of double, pink-edged, cream flowers are produced in succession from mid-summer to early autumn against lustrous, bronze-tinted, dark green leaves. H 3m (10ft) S 2.2m (7ft).

Rosa 'Laura Ford'
(syn. R. 'Chewarvel')
Subtly fragrant, semi-double, yellow flowers are borne in

clusters from mid-summer to early autumn against lustrous, pale green leaves. H 2.2m (7ft) S 1.2m (4ft).

Rosa 'Madame Alfred Carrière'
Strongly fragrant, double, white flowers flushed with pink are produced in succession from mid-summer to early autumn. Ideal for a north-facing site. H 5m (16ft) S 3m (10ft).

Rosa 'Madame Grégoire Staechelin' (syn. R. 'Spanish Beauty')
Large, blousy, double, crimson-flushed pink flowers, which are strongly fragrant, are produced throughout early summer and mid-summer, followed by large red rosehips. H 6m (20ft) S 4m (12ft).

Rosa 'Maigold'
Clusters of fragrant, semi-double, bronze-yellow flowers on thorny stems are produced from early summer to early autumn. Shade-tolerant. H 2.5m (8ft) S 2.5m (8ft).

Rosa 'Mermaid'
Fragrant, single, primrose-yellow blooms are produced in succession from mid-summer to early autumn. Very hardy. H 6m (20ft) S 6m (20ft).

Rosa 'New Dawn'
(syn. R. 'The New Dawn')
Fragrant, double, clear pink flowers are borne in clusters from mid-summer to early autumn

against shiny mid-green leaves. Disease resistant and shade tolerant. H 3m (10ft) S 2.5m (8ft).

Rosa 'Paul's Scarlet Climber'
A vigorous climbing rose that is covered with clusters of subtly fragrant, double, bright-red flowers throughout early and mid-summer. H 3m (10ft) S 3m (10ft).

Rosa 'Schoolgirl'
Fragrant, double, coppery-apricot, almost orange, flowers are produced in succession from mid-summer to early autumn. H 3m (10ft) S 2.5m (8ft).

Rosa 'Warm Welcome'
(syn. R. 'Chewizz')
A compact and long-flowering climber that bears sprays of subtly fragrant, semi-double, orange-red flowers from mid-summer to early autumn. Disease resistant. H 2.2m (7ft) S 2.2m (7ft).

Rosa 'Zéphirine Drouhin'
Thornless rose
Double, strongly fragrant, deep pink flowers are produced from early summer to early autumn on thornless stems. This rose is ideal for growing up a north-facing wall or growing as an informal flowering hedge. H 3m (10ft) S 2m (6ft).

Rosa 'Zéphirine Drouhin'

Solanum crispum 'Glasnevin'

SOLANUM

This comprises a huge genus of over 1400 species, including the evergreen climbers featured here, that are grown for their abundant clusters of summer flowers. They are ideal for a sheltered spot where they will cover all types of garden structures. A single specimen will cover an area the size of a standard fence panel in five years.
Cultivation Grow in a moisture-retentive, well-drained neutral to slightly alkaline soil that is reasonably fertile. Grow in full sun, but protected from cold winds. In frost-prone areas, grow half-hardy solanums in containers using a soil-based compost (soil mix). Feed every month during the growing season and water as necessary. Move to a frost-free conservatory or greenhouse in winter.
Pruning Thin out established plants and cut out any frost-damaged shoots in mid-spring. Neglected climbers can be cut back hard to 15cm (6in) of ground level in mid-spring.
Propagation Take basal cuttings in early summer.

Solanum crispum 'Glasnevin' (syn. *S. C.* 'Autumnale') Chilean potato tree
A vigorous climber with dark green leaves that bears fragrant, pale purple flowers from early summer to early autumn, followed by creamy-white fruit.
H 6m (20ft) S 4m (13ft).
Aspect: sun
Hardiness: ✿✿ Zone: Min. 7

Solanum jasminoides 'Album'
Glossy, dark green leaves provide the perfect foil for the clusters of jasmine-scented flowers borne from early summer to early autumn. Each star-shaped white bloom has a yellow eye and is followed by round, purple-black berries. H 6m (20ft) S 6m (20ft).
Aspect: sun
Hardiness: ✿ Zone: Min 9

SOLLYA

A small genus of just three species, grown for its pendent flowers that appear in summer. It can be grown in a sheltered spot in mild gardens, but it will need tying into its support. It is best grown as a conservatory climber in other conditions.
Cultivation Grow in a moisture-retentive, well-drained neutral to slightly alkaline soil that is

Sollya hetrophylla

reasonably fertile in full sun, but protected from midday sun scorch and cold winds. In frost-prone areas, grow in a container using a soil-based compost (soil mix). Feed every month throughout the growing season and water as necessary. Protect in winter by moving it to a frost-free conservatory or greenhouse.
Pruning Thin established plants and cut out any frost-damaged shoots in mid-spring. Neglected climbers can be cut back hard to 15cm (6in) of ground level in mid-spring.
Propagation Take softwood cuttings in mid-spring.

Sollya heterophylla (syn. *S. fusiformis*) Bluebell creeper
From early summer to early autumn, sky blue, bell-shaped flowers hang from this twining climber, which is clothed in lance-shaped, dark green leaves, followed by edible blue berries. Borderline half hardy. H 2m (6ft) S 2m (6ft).
Aspect: sun
Hardiness: ✿ Zone: Min. 5

STEPHANOTIS

This genus of about 10 species includes the long-flowering evergreen climber featured here, grown for its fragrant clusters of waxy-looking flowers. Grow on a sunny wall in warm gardens or, in colder areas, in a heated greenhouse or conservatory.
Cultivation In the garden, grow in a moisture-retentive, well-drained

Stephanotis floribunda

garden soil in full sun but protected from midday sun scorch and cold winds. In containers, grow in a soil-based compost (soil mix). Feed every month throughout the growing season and water as necessary. Move to a warm spot undercover when below 15°C (60°F) and water sparingly in the winter.
Pruning Cut back damaged or weak stems. Lateral shoots on congested plants can be shortened to within 15cm (6in) of the main framework in late winter.
Propagation Take softwood cuttings in mid-spring.

Stephanotis floribunda (syn. *S. jasminoides*) Bridal wreath, Madagascar jasmine
Small cluster of fragrant, waxy-looking, creamy-white flowers are borne from late spring to mid-autumn on this twining evergreen climber that has glossy, leathery, dark green leaves. H 3m (10ft) S 2m (6ft).
Aspect: sun
Hardiness: tender Zones: 10–12

TRACHELOSPERMUM

This genus of about 20 species includes the woody evergreen climbers featured here, grown for their fragrant clusters of summer flowers. Grow against a sheltered, structure or through a well-established tree in a sunny spot or allow it to scramble over the soil as groundcover.
Cultivation Grow in any well-drained soil that is reasonably fertile in full sun or dappled shade that is sheltered from cold winds. In very cold areas, grow in a container using a soil-based compost (soil mix). Feed every month throughout the growing season and water as necessary. Protect against cold in winter.
Pruning No routine pruning is necessary. Wayward shoots can be removed in mid-spring.
Propagation Take semi-ripe cuttings in mid-summer.

Trachelospermum asiaticum Asian jasmine
Jasmine-scented, creamy-white, tubular flowers are produced in clusters throughout mid- and late

Trachelospermum jasminoides

summer and are set off by this twining climber's dark evergreen leaves. H 6m (20ft) S 3m (10ft). Aspect: sun or semi-shade Hardiness: ❋❋ Zone: Min. 7

Trachelospermum jasminoides
Star jasmine
Clusters of jasmine-scented, white, tubular flowers are borne in mid- and late summer on this twining evergreen climber, which has glossy, dark green leaves. H 9m (28ft) S 3m (10ft). Aspect: sun or semi-shade Hardiness: ❋❋ Zone: Min. 7

VITIS
Vine
This genus contains about 65 species, including the deciduous tendril climbers featured here, which are grown mainly for their handsome foliage. This takes on fabulously coloured autumn tints. Vitis are reliable cover-all climbers for walls and fences, but they can also be used to scramble through established trees and hedges, as well as covering the ground in a carpet of foliage. They are very fast-growing and so make an ideal choice if you are looking for a quick cover-up – a single plant will be able to smother about two standard fence panels in five years.
Cultivation Grow in any well-drained neutral to alkaline soil that is reasonably fertile, in full sun or dappled shade. Add plenty of organic matter to the soil before planting.

Pruning No routine pruning is necessary. Keep plants in check by pruning out unwanted stems in early summer.
Propagation Layer suitable shoots in late spring, take semi-ripe cuttings in mid-summer or take take hardwood cuttings in late autumn.

Vitis 'Brant'
This is a vigorous, deciduous, ornamental grape vine with serrated, lobed, apple-green leaves that turn rust-red between the main veins in autumn. Large bunches of edible blue-black grapes are also produced. H 7m (23ft) S 5m (16ft). Aspect: sun or semi-shade Hardiness: ❋❋❋ Zone: Min. 7

Vitis coignetiae
Crimson glory vine
Huge, heart-shaped and lobed, dark green leaves turn fiery shades of red in autumn, accompanied by bunches of small, blue-black, inedible grapes. H 15m (50ft) S 5m (16ft). Aspect: sun or semi-shade Hardiness: ❋❋❋ Zone: Min. 7

Vitis vinifera 'Purpurea'
This is a deciduous tendril climber with lobed, pale green young leaves that mature to claret red, becoming plum purple in autumn, accompanied by bunches of small purple inedible grapes. H 7m (22ft) S 3m (10ft). Aspect: sun or semi-shade Hardiness: ❋❋❋ Zone: Min. 7

Vitis vinifera 'Purpurea'

Wisteria sinensis

WISTERIA
A genus of about ten species, including the twining deciduous climbers featured here, wisterias are grown for their enormous pendent clusters of beautiful early summer flowers. They are ideal for growing up sun-drenched walls and sturdy structures, such as pergolas and arches, where their cascading flowers can be seen at their best.
Cultivation Grow in a moisture-retentive, well-drained soil that is reasonably fertile in full sun or dappled shade. Add plenty of organic matter to the soil before planting time.
Pruning Prune in two stages: cut back all new whippy growth to four or six leaves during late summer. Later, after leaf fall, cut these stumps back to just two or three buds of the main structural framework.
Propagation Take semi-ripe basal cuttings in late summer, or layer suitable shoots in late spring.

Wisteria floribunda
Japanese wisteria
Scented violet-blue to white pea-like flowers hang down in elegant pendent clusters during early summer, followed by felty green pods. The airy, grey-green leaves on this vigorous climber turn yellow in autumn. It is slow to get established and may take several

years to start flowering. H 9m (28ft) S 5m (16ft). Named varieties: 'Alba' (syn. W. 'Shiro-Noda'), white flowers. H 9m (28ft) S 5m (16ft). 'Macrobotry' (syn. W. 'Kyushaku', W. multijuga, W. 'Naga Noda'), mauve flowers. H 9m (28ft) S 5m (16ft). 'Royal Purple' (syn. W. 'Black Dragon', W. 'Kokuryu'), violet-purple flowers. H 9m (28ft) S 5m (16ft). Aspect: sun or semi-shade Hardiness: ❋❋❋ Zone: Min. 7

Wisteria x formosa
Fragrant violet-blue and pea-like flowers with white and yellow markings are borne in pendent clusters during late spring and early summer. H 9m (28ft) S 5m (16ft). Aspect: sun or semi-shade Hardiness: ❋❋❋ Zone: Min. 7

Wisteria sinensis (syn. W. chinensis)
Chinese wisteria
Clusters of fragrant, mauve, pea-like flowers hang down in pendent clusters during late spring and early summer, often followed by felty green pods. H 9m (28ft) S 5m (16ft). Named varieties: 'Alba', white flowers. H 9m (28ft) S 5m (16ft). Aspect: sun or semi-shade Hardiness: ❋❋❋ Zone: Min. 7

Calendar of care

Most of the essential tasks in ornamental gardens are seasonal and so have to be carried out at a certain time of the year. With many shrubs and climbers the most important job is pruning, which has to be carried out at the right stage of growth to prevent flowering production or loss in the following season. On the following pages you will find a comprehensive guide to what to prune and when.

There is also a quick-reference checklist to all the other seasonal tasks, including propagating, planting, feeding, watering, weeding and protecting, so that you can be sure to complete all necessary tasks at the right time of the year. If you are short of time, prioritize your gardening workload to make sure that the most critical tasks are carried out first.

It should be remembered that the beginning and end of the seasons varies from year to year as well as with your local climate, so the exact timing should depend on how your plants are growing at the time. For example, a spring-flowering plant in a sheltered garden in a relatively warm country can flower up to four weeks earlier than the same plant growing in a more exposed spot elsewhere.

Note: In the pruning calendars for shrubs and climbers featured on the following pages, plants featured in more than one month can be pruned at any time in this period.

The gardener's tasks continue throughout the year, making sure that each season yeilds the best show of flowers and foliage, providing a rich reward for all the work that it entails.

Seasonal jobs checklist: spring and summer

Spring is when the garden starts to come alive again. But there are also a few other tasks awaiting your attention, which are listed here.

Things to do in spring
- Check plants for winter damage
- Firm in any new plants loosened by winter frosts
- Water all new additions
- Trim winter-flowering heathers
- Plant new shrubs and climbers
- Plant evergreen and deciduous hedging
- Keep control of weeds
- Complete rose pruning
- Complete renovation of overgrown shrubs and climbers
- Check supports of all climbers
- Apply a general fertilizer to established plants
- Propagate by layering
- Sow seeds collected last summer and given cold treatment over winter
- Take leaf-bud cuttings
- Take softwood cuttings
- Separate rooted layers from parent plants and pot up or plant out
- Watch out for pests and disease
- Tie in new stems of climbers as they grow
- Prune early flowering shrubs
- Prune grey-leaved shrubs
- Prune evergreens
- Trim formal edging shrubs
- Start clipping hedges

What to prune in spring

Early spring shrubs
Artemesia
Buddleja davidii
Colutea
Convolvulus cneorum
Cotinus
Daphne (after flowering)
Forsythia (after flowering)
Fothergilla (after flowering)
Griselinia
Hamamellis (after flowering)
Hebe cupressoides
Hebe pinguifolia
Hebe rakaiensis
Hydrangea arborescens
Hydrangea paniculata
Hypericum calycinum
Lavatera
Mahonia (after flowering)
Rhus
Ribes sanguineum (after flowering)
Rosa
Skimmia (after flowering)
Spiraea japonica
symphoricarpos
Viburnum farreri (after flowering)
Viburnum opulus (after flowering)
Vinca

Early spring climbers
Cissus
Clematis (Group 3)
Cobaea
Eccremocarpus
Hedera
Humulus
Jasminum nudiflorum (after flowering)
Lonicera

Mid-spring shrubs
Abutilon megapotanum
Aucuba (fruiting)
Callicarpa
Calluna
Camellia (after flowering)
Caryopteris
Ceanothus 'Autumnal Blue'
Ceanothus 'Burkwoodii'
Ceratostigma
Cistus
Clerodendrum bungei
Corylopsis (after flowering)
Cotoneaster frigidus 'Cornubia'
Cotoneaster x *watereri*
Erica (after flowering)
Euonymus japonicus
Euphorbia pulcherrima (after flowering)
Exochorda (after flowering)
Fatsia
Forsythia (after flowering)
Hebe macrantha,
Hebe salicifolia
Hebe speciosa
Helichrysum
Hydrangea macrophylla
Hydrangea serrata
Hypericum 'Hidcote'
Kerria (after flowering)
Lavandula
Leycesteria
Ligustrum
Lonicera fragrantissima (after flowering)
Lonicera x *purpusii* (after flowering)
Olearia
Osmanthus (after flowering)
Perovskia
Phygelius

Pieris (after flowering)
Pittosporum
Potentilla
Pyracantha

Mid-spring climbers
Cissus
Passiflora
Solanum

Late spring shrubs
Abelia
Akebia quinata
Chaenomeles (after flowering)
Choisya (after flowering)
Helichrysum petiolare
Hibiscus
Ribes speciosum (after flowering)

Late-spring climbers
Berberidopsis
Cissus
Clematis (group 1, after flowering)

Prune cistus plants, including the *Cistus* x *skanbergii* shown here, after flowering.

What to prune in summer

Early summer shrubs
Berberis darwinii (after flowering)
Berberis linearifolia (after flowering)
Berberis x stenophylla (after flowering)
Cornus kousa var. *chinensis*
Cornus mas
Cornus officinalis
Cytisus x praecox (after flowering)
Deutzia (after flowering)
Helichrysum petiolare
Hippophae
Magnolia liliiflora
Magnolia x soulangeana
Magnolia stellata
Rosmarinus (after flowering)
Spiraea 'Arguta' (after flowering)
Syringa (after flowering)

Mid-summer climbers
Clematis (group 1, after flowering)

Mid-summer shrubs
Buxus
Carpenteria
Ceanothus arboreus 'Trewithen Blue'
(after flowering)
Ceanothus 'Concha' (after flowering)
Ceanothus impressus (after flowering)
Ceanothus thyrsiflorus (after flowering)
Cytisus battandieri (after flowering)
Escallonia 'Apple Blossom' (after
flowering)

Euphorbia characias (after flowering)
Euphorbia myrsinites (after flowering)
Fremontodendron (after flowering)
Helianthemum (after flowering)
Helichrysum petiolare
Kolkwitzia (after flowering)
Laurus
Lonicera nitida
Paeonia (after flowering)
Philadelphus microphyllus (after flowering)
Rhododendron luteum (after flowering)
Rubus cockburnianus (after flowering)
Sophora
Tamarix (after flowering)
Tinus (after flowering)
Viburnum plicatum (after flowering)
Weigela (after flowering)

Mid-summer climbers
Wisteria

Late summer shrubs
Buddleja alternifolia (after flowering)
Buxus Callistemon (after flowering)
Elaeagnus x ebbinge,
Elaeagnus glabra
Elaeagnus macrophylla
Elaeagnus pungens 'Maculata'
x *Fatshedera*
Genista hispanica (after flowering)
Grevillea (after flowering)
Helianthemum (after flowering)

Laurus
Nerium
Philadelphus 'Belle Etoile' (after
flowering)
Philadelphus coronarius (after flowering)
Philadelphus delavayi (after flowering)
Philadelphus 'Virginal' (after flowering)
Pyracantha
Thymus

Late summer climbers
Bilardiera (after fruiting),
Clerodendrum (after flowering)
Clianthus (after flowering)
Hydrangea (after flowering)
Jasminum polyanthum (after flowering)

Prune Clematis Group 1 plants in late spring,
like this *Clematis armandii* shown here.

Summer is when you can really enjoy the fruits of your labours and revel in the splendour of your garden. It is also a time of plant maintenance, so that you can keep your garden looking its very best and allowing your shrubs and climbers to dazzle.

Trim hedges like *Osmanthus het*. 'Tricolor' shown here. Cut out any reverted leaves on varigated types when you see them.

Things to do in summer
- Water all new additions
- Take semi-ripe cuttings
- Move out tender plants to a sheltered position outdoors
- Prune early clematis
- Prune climbers and wall shrubs after flowering
- Prune early summer-flowering shrubs after flowering
- Clear ground for autumn planting
- Spray against rose diseases
- Pot up rooted cuttings taken in the spring
- Deadhead large-flowered shrubs after flowering
- Remove suckers from roses
- Trim conifer hedges
- Train climbing and rambler roses
- Trim lavender after flowering
- Harvest lavender for drying
- Maintain control over pest and disease outbreaks
- Summer prune wisteria
- Keep weeds under control
- Cut out any reverted shoots on variegated shrubs and climbers
- Prune rambler roses after flowering

Seasonal jobs checklist: autumn and winter

Early autumn, if it is kind, can provide an Indian summer in the garden, prolonging the flowering times of your shrubs and climbers. Gradually, glorious leaf shades appear on the plants, providing a spectacular last display before dropping in mid- to late autumn.

What to do in autumn
- Take hardwood cuttings
- Pot on semi-ripe cuttings taken in summer
- Prune late-flowering shrubs
- Part-prune tall shrubs to prevent wind rock
- Plant new shrubs, climbers and hedges
- Trim vigorous hedges
- Keep weeds under control
- Tie in whippy shoots on climbers
- Collect seed and berries for propagation
- Protect borderline hardy shrubs and climbers
- Bring tender plants under cover before the first frosts
- Propagate from suitable stems by layering
- Clear away diseased leaves from roses

Autumn is the time for pruning in the garden. Vigorously growing hedges can take quite a bold cutting back at this time of year.

- Take root cuttings
- Plant deciduous shrubs and climbers
- Protect container-grown hardy shrubs and climbers, if necessary
- Take root cuttings
- Dig over vacant ground when soil conditions allow
- Move awkwardly placed shrubs and climbers or those that you wish to relocate elsewhere in the garden
- Check tree ties and stakes and replace if necessary
- Take measures to make sure nothing can be damaged on windy nights
- Plant shrubs, roses and hedging plants that are sold with bare roots

What to prune in autumn

EARLY AUTUMN
Shrubs
Abelia (after flowering)
Buxus
Lonicera nitida
Nerium

Climbers
Jasminum officinale (after flowering)
Lathyrus latifolius (after flowering)
Lonicera periclymenum
Lonicera x americana
Lonicera x brownii
Lonicera x tellmanniana
passiflora (after flowering)
Rosa (climbing, after flowering)

MID-AUTUMN
Shrubs
Santolina (after flowering)

Climbers
Parthenocissus

LATE AUTUMN
Shrubs
Amelanchier
Aucuba (non-fruiting)

Climbers
Parthenocissus

Autumn produces spectacular colour displays, as shown by Calluna vulgaris 'Wickwar Flame'.

Winter is usually a dormant time in the garden, although there is still much to do. The main aim in winter is to protect plants from the ravages of wind, frost and snowfalls. However, it is also a time for the pruning and propagation of certain shrubs and climbers.

What to do in winter

- Clear heavy falls of snow off hedges and evergreens, if necessary
- Take hardwood cuttings from roses
- Prune climbing roses
- If it's a mild winter, continue to cut the lawn, as long as it is still growing, but raise the height of the mower blades
- Prevent container-grown plants from freezing by wrapping them with bubble wrap or taking them under shelter
- Remove algae and moss patches on the patio and paving by scrubbing with a broom or blasting with a pressure washer
- Feed indoor plants occasionally
- Order seed catalogues and look on the internet to plan what you're going to grow in the spring
- Winter prune wisteria
- Carry out all winter pruning jobs
- Protect berried holly branches to preserve fruit for winter decoration
- Protect new additions with windbreak netting
- Renovate overgrown shrubs and climbers
- Prune tall-growing bush roses by about a half to help prevent wind-rock damaging roots, and shorten all the branches on standard roses for the same reason
- Plant bare-rooted rose bushes
- Water plants sparingly
- Be on the watch for any pests on overwintering plants and destroy them

What to prune in winter

EARLY WINTER
Shrubs
Amelanchier
Aucuba (non-fruiting)
Berberis thunbergii
Berberis x ottawensis
Salix caprea 'Kilmarnock'
Sambucus

Climbers
Ampelopsis
Parthenocissus
Vitis
Wisteria

MID-WINTER
Shrubs
Aucuba (non-fruiting)
Cotoneaster horizontalis
Salix caprea 'Kilmarnock'
Sambucus

Climbers
Actinidia
Ampelopsis
Bougainvillea
Campsis
Celastrus
Mandevilla
Vitis
Wisteria

LATE WINTER
Shrubs
Aucuba (non-fruiting)
Buddleja globosa
Chimonathus (after flowering)
Cornus alba
Cornus sanguinea
Cornus stolonifera
Corylus
Cotoneaster dammeri
Cotoneaster microphyllus
Euonymus europaeus
Euonymus alatus
Garrya ellipticus (after flowering)
Rosa (bush)
Sambucus

Climbers
Actinidia
Bougainvillea
Campsis
Clematis (Group 2 & Group 3)
Hedera
Humulus
Jasminum nudiflorum (after flowering)
Lonicera japonica
Lonicera henryi
Rubus

Keep the heat in the greenhouse by covering the glass panes with bubble wrap. This will help to insulate it and retain heat. Use a foil covering under the wrap on the north-facing side.

Index

Plant hardiness zones

Hardiness symbols
❋ = half-hardy (down to 0°C)
❋❋ = frost hardy (down to -5°C)
❋❋❋ = fully hardy (down to -15°C)

Zone entries
Plant entries in this book have been given zone numbers. These zones relate to their hardiness. The zonal system used (shown below) was developed by the Agricultural Research Service of the US Department of Agriculture. According to this system, there are 11 zones, based on the average annual minimum temperature in a particular geographical zone. When a range of zones is given for a plant, the smaller number indicates the northern-most zone in which a plant can survive the winter. The higher number gives the most southerly in which it will perform consistently. As with any system, this one is not hard and fast. It is simply a rough indictor, as many factors other than temperature play an important part where hardiness is concerned. These factors vary across the same state and include altitude, wind exposure, proximity to water, soil type, the presence of snow, the existence of shade, night temperature and the amount of water received by the plant. These factors can easily alter a plant's hardiness by several zones.

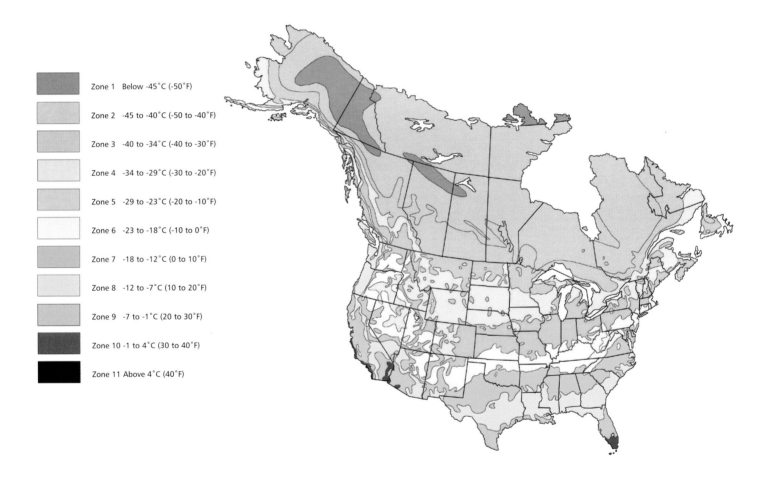

Zone 1 Below -45°C (-50°F)

Zone 2 -45 to -40°C (-50 to -40°F)

Zone 3 -40 to -34°C (-40 to -30°F)

Zone 4 -34 to -29°C (-30 to -20°F)

Zone 5 -29 to -23°C (-20 to -10°F)

Zone 6 -23 to -18°C (-10 to 0°F)

Zone 7 -18 to -12°C (0 to 10°F)

Zone 8 -12 to -7°C (10 to 20°F)

Zone 9 -7 to -1°C (20 to 30°F)

Zone 10 -1 to 4°C (30 to 40°F)

Zone 11 Above 4°C (40°F)

Acknowledgements

Unless listed below, photographs are © Anness Publishing Ltd. t = top; b = bottom; l = left; r = right; c = centre.

The publishers would like to thank Peter Anderson for his work on the original photography.

Garden World Images: 165tr, br; 168tr; 175bl; 176tr, tc; 184tr; 191tr; 194tr; 197br; 198tr; 205br; 208bl; 209br; 218bl, br; 219tr; 220tl; 227tl, tr; 234tl; bl; 235b; 236bl; 239t, b; 241tc; 244bl.

Andrew Lawson Photography: 77b; 132–3; 150-1; 164bl; 165tl; 170bl; 173tr, b; 178tl, tr; 179tl; 181tl; 184bl; 187tl; 190tr; 204b; 209bl; 244br; 246–7.